CONTRACTUAL KNOWLEDGE

Contractual Knowledge: One Hundred Years of Legal Experimentation, edited by Grégoire Mallard and Jérôme Sgard, extends the scholarship of law and globalization in two important directions. First, it provides a unique genealogy of global economic governance by explaining the transition from English law to one where global exchanges are primarily governed by international, multilateral, and finally, transnational legal orders. Second, rather than focusing exclusively on macro-political organizations, like the League of Nations or the International Monetary Fund, the book examines elements of contracts, including how and by whom they were designed and exactly who (experts, courts, arbitrators, and international organizations) interpreted, upheld, and established the legal validity of these contracts. By exploring such micro-level aspects of market exchanges, this collection unveils the contractual knowledge that led to the globalization of markets over the last century.

GRÉGOIRE MALLARD is Associate Professor in the Department of Anthropology and Sociology of Development at the Graduate Institute of International and Development Studies, Geneva.

JÉRÔME SGARD is Professor of Political Economy at Sciences Po, Paris.

CAMBRIDGE STUDIES IN LAW AND SOCIETY

Cambridge Studies in Law and Society aims to publish the best scholarly work on legal discourse and practice in its social and institutional contexts, combining theoretical insights and empirical research.

The fields that it covers are studies of law in action; the sociology of law; the anthropology of law; cultural studies of law, including the role of legal discourses in social formations; law and economics; law and politics; and studies of governance. The books consider all forms of legal discourse across societies, rather than being limited to lawyers' discourses alone.

The series editors come from a range of disciplines: academic law; socio-legal studies; sociology; and anthropology. All have been actively involved in teaching and writing about law in context.

Series editors

Chris Arup *Monash University*

Sally Engle Merry *New York University*

Susan Silbey *Massachusetts Institute of Technology*

A list of books in the series can be found at the back of this book.

CONTRACTUAL KNOWLEDGE

One Hundred Years of Legal Experimentation in Global Markets

Edited by
Grégoire Mallard and Jérôme Sgard

CAMBRIDGE
UNIVERSITY PRESS

CAMBRIDGE
UNIVERSITY PRESS

University Printing House, Cambridge CB2 8BS, United Kingdom

Cambridge University Press is part of the University of Cambridge.

It furthers the University's mission by disseminating knowledge in the pursuit of education, learning and research at the highest international levels of excellence.

www.cambridge.org
Information on this title: www.cambridge.org/9781107130913

First published 2016

A catalogue record for this publication is available from the British Library

ISBN 978-1-107-13091-3 Hardback

CONTENTS

FIGURES

TABLES

NOTES ON CONTRIBUTORS

Marco Bertilorenzi obtained his PhD in Economic History from Florence University (Italy) and in Modern and Contemporary History from Paris-Sorbonne University (France). He widely published on the history of cartels, of business-governments relationships and of foreign investments. His publications include articles published by *Histoire, Economie et Société* (2009), *Revue économique* (2013), *Business History* (2014), and *Entreprise et Histoire* (2015), chapters in edited volumes and *The International Aluminium Cartel*, published by Routledge in the International Business History Series (2015). He is currently a researcher at Centre d'histoire des techniques (Institut d'histoire moderne et contemporaine, Université Paris 1 Panthéon Sorbonne) and at Ecole des Mines de Saint-Etienne (Institut Fayol) and he is involved in a project about the history of French engineers. He also teaches business history and history of the economic though at Centre Michel Serres, heSam Université, Paris.

Susan Block-Lieb is Professor at Fordham Law School, where she holds the Cooper Family Chair in Urban Legal Studies. She specializes in personal bankruptcy, corporate reorganization and financial restructuring, secured transactions and commercial laws more generally, including international and transnational law and lawmaking in this context. She has written extensively on unification, harmonization and modernization of international private law by international organizations, on global governance by the G20, IMF, World Bank and UN, on sovereign debt restructuring and more generally on transnational legal orders. Together with Terence C. Halliday, she is author of *Global Legislators: Producing Commercial Laws for the World* (under submission), an intensive study of global lawmaking by the UN Commission on International Trade Law. She has consulted for the International Monetary Fund, served as a reporter and observer at World Bank task forces on insolvency and secured transactions law reform initiatives, and has been a delegate from the American Bar Association to UNCITRAL's Insolvency Working Group for 15 years.

Bruce G. Carruthers is the John D. MacArthur Professor of Sociology at Northwestern University and director of the Buffett Institute for Global Studies. He received his PhD from the University of Chicago, and works in the areas of comparative-historical sociology, economic sociology, and the sociology of law. His research has enjoyed financial support from the National Science Foundation, the American Bar Foundation, the Russell Sage Foundation, and the Tobin Project. He is the author or coauthor of five books, including *City of Capital: Politics and Markets in the English Financial Revolution* (Princeton University Press, 1999); and most recently *Money and Credit: A Sociological Approach* (Polity Press, 2010), as well as numerous articles. Carruthers has been a visiting fellow at the Russell Sage Foundation, the Australia National University, the Radcliffe Institute for Advanced Study, and the Wissenschaftskolleg zu Berlin, and received a John Simon Guggenheim Fellowship as well. Recently, he was the president of the Society for the Advancement of Socio-Economics, and is finishing a book on the history of credit and credit decision-making in the United States during the nineteenth and twentieth centuries.

Ariel Colonomos is Senior Research fellow at the National Center for Scientific Research (CNRS – Centre d'Etudes et de Recherches Internationales) and Research Professor at Sciences Po in Paris, where he teaches courses on international relations theory and the ethics of war. He has also taught at Columbia University where he was an affiliate at the Institute of War and Peace. His last books include *La politique des oracles Raconter le futur aujourd'hui* (Albin Michel, 2014; transl. *Selling the Future: The Perils of Global Predictions*, London, Hurst (London), New York, Oxford UP, 2016), *Le Pari de la guerre: guerre preventive, guerre juste* (Denoël, 2009; transl. *The Gamble of War: On Justifying Preventive War*,Palgrave, 2013), *La Morale dans les relations internationales: Rendre des comptes* (Odile Jacob, 2005, transl. *Moralizing International Relations: Called to Account*, 2008). He has published numerous articles in the areas of international relations, the ethics of war, political sociology.

Yves Dezalay, is Directeur de recherches at the C.N.R.S. (Centre National de la Recherche Scientifique) in Paris, where he is a senior researcher of the Centre de Sociologie Européenne (C.S.E.) a research institution founded by Pierre Bourdieu, located within the Maison des Sciences de l'Homme (M.S.H., Paris) and affiliated with the Ecole des Hautes en Sciences Sociales (E.H.E.S.S.). Since 1990, he has also been an affiliated scholar of the American Bar Foundation. For most of his professional life, his main topic of interest has been the internationalization of the legal field in relation with other professional fields of expertise. He has worked closely with Bryant Garth and together they wrote or edited six books, including *Dealing in virtue: International Commercial Arbitration and the Emergence of an International Legal Order* (University of Chicago Press, 1996), *The Internationalization of Palace Wars: Lawyers, Economists and the Contest for Latin American States* (University of Chicago Press, 2002), and *Asian Legal Revivals: Lawyers in the Shadow of Empires* (University of Chicago Press, 2010). In 2009, he was awarded the International Scholar Prize by the Law & Society Association.

Juan H. Flores Zendejas is Associate Professor at the Department of History, Economics and Society at the University of Geneva. Mr. Flores Zendejas is a recognized expert on the history of financial crises, the financing of economic development in Latin America and the role of European financial markets in the large capital inflows into the region in the late nineteenth century. He has published numerous papers on the role of financial intermediaries in the functioning of international financial markets, conflicts of interest between the major players in the financial sector, and the economic consequences of Latin American debt crises. His current research focuses on the role of multilateral organizations in the structuring of international capital flows.

Bryant G. Garth is Chancellor's Professor at the University California-Irvine School of Law, where he has been since 2012. He served as Dean of Southwestern Law School from 2005 until 2012. Before coming to Southwestern, he was Dean of the Indiana University-Bloomington School of Law (1986–90) and Director of the American Bar Foundation (1990–2004). His scholarship focuses on the legal profession, the sociology of law, and globalization. Two of his books coauthored with Yves Dezalay, *Dealing in Virtue* (1996) and

Asian Legal Revivals (2010), were given the Herbert Jacobs Award from the Law and Society Association as the best books in the field of Law and Society published that year. A third, *The Internationalization of Palace Wars* (2002), was translated and published also in French, Korean, and Spanish. He also served as coeditor of the *Journal of Legal Education* from 2011–14. He is on the Executive Coordinating Committee of the "After the J.D." project, the first longitudinal study of the legal profession, and chairs the advisory committee of the Law School Survey of Student Engagement (LSSSE).

Anna Gelpern is Professor of Law at Georgetown. She has published articles on financial integration, debt contracts, and development, and has coauthored a textbook on International Finance. She has contributed to international initiatives on financial reform and sovereign borrowing, most recently as an expert for the United Nations Conference on Trade and Development. Professor Gelpern is a nonresident senior fellow at the Peter G. Peterson Institute for International Economics.

Mitu Gulati is Professor at the Duke University School of Law. Gulati's primary research interests are in the historical evolution of sovereign debt contracts and in the mechanics of sovereign debt restructurings. Together with Robert Scott, he has coauthored *The Three and a Half Minute Transaction: Boilerplate and the Limits of Contract Design* (Chicago Series in Law and Society, 2012). His current research focus is on the pricing and restructuring of government guaranteed debt.

Terence Halliday is Research Professor at the American Bar Foundation and Co-Director of the Center on Law and Globalization. He focuses on globalization of law in markets and politics, with particular attention to global norm-making in international organizations. With Professor Bruce Carruthers, Halliday published in 2009, *Bankrupt: Global Lawmaking and Systemic Financial Crisis*, which was awarded three distinguished book prizes by the American Sociological Association. His latest books include *Transnational Legal Orders* (Cambridge University Press, 2015), edited with Gregory Shaffer, and *Global Legislators: How International Organizations make Trade Law for the World* (under submission), authored with Susan Block-Lieb. He has held visiting appointments at the University of Chicago, Oxford University, and Australian National University, and has consulted with the OECD, World Bank, Government of China, and International Monetary Fund.

Grégoire Mallard is Associate Professor in the Department of Anthropology and Sociology of Development at the Graduate Institute of International and Development Studies (Geneva). He is the author of *Fallout: Nuclear Diplomacy in an Age of Global Fracture* (University of Chicago Press, 2014) and coeditor of *Global Science and National Sovereignty: Studies in Historical Sociology of Science* (Routledge 2008). His recent publications focus on nuclear governance in Europe and the Middle East, postwar financial negotiations, and the study of harmonization as a social process. His new project focuses on the interplay between treaty-based regimes and the emerging field of financial sanctions.

Stephen C. Nelson is Assistant Professor in Political Science at Northwestern University. His main research and teaching interests lie in the subfields of International and Comparative Political Economy. His recent work explores a variety of topics, including the politics that shape the International Monetary Fund's (IMF) lending policies; the structure and governance of financial markets before and after the near-collapse of the American financial system in 2008; the political dynamics of developing and emerging market countries' decisions to open their economies to international capital flows; how organizational cultures shape the behavior of international institutions; and the American popular film industry. Professor Nelson is currently finishing a book on the International Monetary Fund; the dissertation upon which the book is based won the American Political Science Award's Helen Dwight Reid Award in 2010. An article from this project was recently published in *International Organization*.

Jérôme Sgard is Professor of Political Economy at SciencesPo, Paris. After having worked on economic reforms and crisis in emerging economies (*L'Economie de la Panique*, 2002), his research interests have focused on to the micro-level architecture of domestic and international markets: IMF conditionality, sovereign debt restructuring, private bankruptcies, the history of international commercial arbitration, early modern economic bureaucracies. Articles on these various subjects have been published as chapters in edited volumes and in journals such as: *World Economy*, the *European Review of Economic History*, the *Journal of Comparative Economics*, *Global Constitutionalism*, and the *International Review of Law and Economics*.

Gregory Shaffer is the Chancellor's Professor of Law at the University of California Irvine School of Law and the Director of the UCI Center on Globalization, Law, and Society (GLAS). His publications include six books and over eighty articles and book chapters on international trade law, global governance, and globalization's impact on domestic regulation, including *Transnational Legal Orders* (Cambridge University Press, 2015) with Terence Halliday; and Transnational Ordering and State Change (Cambridge University Press, 2013).

Giuseppe Telesca obtained his PhD in Economic History at the University of Florence (Italy). He undertook post-doctoral research in economic history as Jean Monnet Fellow at the Robert Schuman Centre for Advanced Studies, European University Institute (Italy), from 2011 to 2013. He was a Visiting Fellow at Henley Centre for Entrepreneurship, University of Reading (UK), from 2013 to 2014, and a Visiting Fellow at the Department of History and Civilisation of the European University Institute (2015). While he focuses in his research on banking, financial and monetary history, he is also interested in sport history (in particular the economic and urban impact of big sport events). He is currently collaborating with Professor Youssef Cassis (European University Institute) on a project on financial elites in historical perspectives.

Michael Waibel is Lecturer at the University of Cambridge, as well as a Fellow of the Lauterpacht Centre for International Law and of Jesus College. He holds Mag. iur. and Dr. iur. degrees from the Universität Wien, an MSc (Econ.) from the LSE and an LLM from Harvard Law School. His main research interests are public international law, international economic law with a focus on finance and the settlement of international disputes. At Cambridge he teaches international and EU law. He has also been a visiting professor at East China University of Political Science and

Law, St. Gallen and Vanderbilt. His book *Sovereign Defaults before International Courts and Tribunals* received the biannual ESIL book prize in 2012.

W. Mark C. Weidemaier is Ralph M. Stockton, Jr. Distinguished Scholar and Associate Professor of Law at the University of North Carolina at Chapel Hill. His research addresses the intersection between contracts and dispute resolution in domestic and international settings, including a focus on dispute resolution methods for financially distressed sovereigns and private creditors.

ACKNOWLEDGMENTS

The photograph on this book's cover represents the staff members of the Economic and Financial Section of the League of Nations in Geneva. With the exception of the nice little dog in the first row, these men and women were the bearers of the kind of contractual knowledge whose genesis and evolution we study in that book. For this reason, we would like to thank the United Nations Archives in Geneva, and Colin Wells, for letting us use this picture.

Every intellectual project is part of an institutional history, and this book is no exception. It is not a surprise if, among the contributors, many of us work in Paris, Geneva, but also Chicago and New York. These are some of the places where contractual knowledge, arbitration practices, and codification of international private law have been pioneered and developed for over a century. At the same time, two institutions in particular have provided great support throughout the project, and here is the time and place to express our gratitude: Northwestern University and Sciences-Po Paris, which delivered a generous grant that made possible the organization of a conference on the comparison of financial regulation in the interwar period and today. All contributors to this book attended this conference, and received ample comments on their work from other participants. For that matter, we would like to thank the following colleagues for the intellectual ideas they brought to the conference: Karen Alter, Stéphanie Balme, Eric Brousseau, Emmanuel Gaillard, Gabriel Galvez-Béhar, Ian Hurd, Claire Lemercier, Michael Loriaux, Pierre Pénet, Kim Priemel, Jakob Vogel. Additionally, some of the chapters were presented at the Society for the Advancement of Socio-Economics, which were held in July 2014 in Chicago. We would like to thank Joseph Cohen for providing us with very interesting comments.

Our gratitude goes next to our colleagues who facilitated the publication of this book: Susan Silbey and Sally Merry, Matt Gallaway and Stephen Acerra at Cambridge University Press, who so efficiently steered the process toward a successful end. Then, at last, but not least, we would like to emphasize how grateful we have felt for the enduring enthusiasm that our group of authors have demonstrated for this project throughout the process: first, when they accepted the task that was presented to them some three years ago, second, when the specialists of the contemporary period who started working on the interwar period (and vice versa) let us know of their excitement when exploring further the comparison and genealogy between the two eras. We only started with the intuition that the comparison could be very highlighting for contemporary debates about global governance, but it is their contributions that confirmed that there is much to gain from unearthing some of the key interwar debates, institutions and practices for our understanding of the governance of financial and economic affairs today. We now let the readers decide if the result was worth the while.

ABBREVIATIONS

AAA	American Arbitration Association
ASEAN	Association of South East Asian Nations
BIT	Bilateral investment treaties
CAC	Collective Action Clause
CDO	Collateralized Debt Obligation
CFTC	Commodities Futures Trading Commission
CMI	Committee Maritime International
CRA	Credit Rating Agency
ECJ	European Court of Justice
ECB	European Central Bank
ECOSOC	Economic and Social Council (UN)
EEC	European Economic Community
EMS	European Monetary System
EU	European Union
FDIC	Federal Deposit Insurance Corporation
FTA	Free Trade Agreement
GATT	General Agreement on Tariffs and Trade
ICC	International Chamber of Commerce
ICJ	International Court of Justice
ILA	International Law Association
IMF	International Monetary Fund
ISDA	International Swaps and Derivatives Association
LCA	London Court of Arbitration
LofN	League of Nations
MFN	Most Favored Nation
NBER	National Bureau of Economic Research
OECD	Organization of Economic Cooperation and Development
OTC	Over The Counter
PCIJ	Permanent Court of International Justice
RMBS	Residential Mortgage-Backed Securities
UN	United Nations

UNCITRAL	United Nations Commission on International Trade Law
UNCTAD	United Nations Conference on Trade and Development
UNESCO	United Nations Educational, Scientific and Cultural Organization
UNIDROIT	International Institute for the Unification of Private Law
WTO	World Trade Organization
WWI	World War I
WWII	World War II

CHAPTER ONE

CONTRACTUAL KNOWLEDGE: ONE HUNDRED YEARS OF LEGAL EXPERIMENTATION IN GLOBAL MARKETS

Grégoire Mallard and Jérôme Sgard

The word *contract* carries different weight in different contexts. Bankers and politicians, diplomats and economists, lawyers and judges all have complex understandings of what a *contract* is and what it means for them. In the recent sovereign debt negotiations with the Euro group and the International Monetary Fund (IMF), the newly elected radical left government of Alexis Tsipras asked their European peers to substitute for the previous "program" of structural reforms a new "contract" – a "social contract" – between the Greek government and its creditors (Quatremer 2015). The Greek leaders also inscribed their negotiation in a longer temporality than their European counterparts: arguing for a partial cancellation of the debt that Greece owed to Germany, Tsipras (2015) reminded his fellow Europeans that Germany had itself failed to compensate Greece for the costs of reconstruction after World War II (WWII) – including money directly borrowed by Germany from Greece during the war. This proposal was not at all what the European leaders expected to hear: for them, the only "contracts" in play were those of Greece's debt and related agreements with the European Union (EU) and other International Financial Institutions (IFIs) entered into as part of a stabilization program.

The episode pitted two understandings of the "contract," as well as two different temporalities, against one another: the first rests on the concept of the "general will," which Tsipras identified (following Rousseau at some distance) with the suffrage of the Greek people, and which allowed the Greek government to frame its claims in the context of a larger history that touched the core of its people's identity. The other is the juridical legitimacy of the agreed-upon legal "covenant" signed by the contracting partners a few years earlier, according to the maxim *pacta sunt servanda.*

This episode in 2015 was not an isolated incident. Over previous years, the Greek sovereign debt crisis had already become the locus where international actors tested competing conceptions of contracts, and the solidity of the boundaries defining the legitimate way to make and un-make contracts. Already in 2010 and 2011, when the EU group's efforts to restructure the Greek debt forced private banks, bondholders and government officials to join them and the IMF at the table, the evaluation of Greece's ability to honor its debt contracts was the focus of many controversies. At the time, the legitimacy and credibility of the pronouncements of the rating agencies was the object of many criticisms: the financial health of the Eurozone rested on the (private) judgment of rating agencies on the budget and social policies adopted by the sovereign Republic of Greece. Whether they displayed rating inertias, as in the case of Moody's, or whether they proceeded too clearly to downgrade Greece's rating, apparently causing an acceleration in the crisis, the rating agencies were criticized for their role.

The Greek sovereign debt crisis and the fragmented, unstable scene in which it played out illustrates in other words what Teubner (1996) calls "a global Bukovina": a metaphor he draws from the tiny northeastern province of today's Romania, which before 1914 was governed by an incredible amalgamation of allegiances and legal orders – parochial and imperial, political and communitarian, linguistic and religious. An important casualty of the crisis is that the very notion of a "contract," with its strong legal underpinning in private law, has been blurred to the point that it now encompasses ambiguous and contested principles and expectations by which third-parties outside the contracted exchange claim a stake at the table of negotiation. Professional lawyers, IMF economists and socio-legal scholars would probably tell us that we should not generalize from the Greek crisis, as a debt bond between thousands of private investors and a sovereign state belongs to a rather special class of transactions. Yet, this Greek bond is still formatted, talked about and regulated as, indeed, a contract.

The same problems that have plagued sovereign bond contracts have also affected more traditional private law contracts as well. Take the nearest equivalent to the Greek crash in a "pure" private setup, namely the collapse of Lehman Brothers. The dead body of the bank with its zillions of financial contracts piled up in its broken balance sheets immediately became the object of competing claims by many jurisdictions and authorities, some public and others private, many of them American though not all; some of them may have even come from sunny, pastoral Bukovina. Financial lawyers told the story of contracts being cut into pieces, dispatched, repackaged and then sold again into successive generations of, yes, contracts. Still today we are not so sure that the forensic experts have actually found whose solitary, individual commitment and wealth rested in these unholy remains.

In this volume we start from this point: across the world economy and over time the notion of what a contract is has proved inherently unstable and contested. The contract now implies very different understandings, expectations and social sanctions than in previous eras, not just for the parties that enter into them, but for the social order that supports and confirms market exchanges. How contracts have been framed, the understanding they have supported and the social efficacy that have come with them have always been contingent upon core political and philosophical understandings that can often be assimilated with the classic construction of sovereignty: for John Locke and Adam Smith, but also for Thomas Hobbes and Jean-Jacques Rousseau, the sovereign is the one that protects the physical integrity and the property rights of citizens (or subjects), as well as their contracts (Rousseau [1762]1971). Thus, in a context in which the very notion of sovereignty has been also debated, challenged and reframed to fit with the demands of the global economy, it comes as no surprise that the notion of the contract is open to many debates.

The ambition of this book is to trace the development over the last hundred years of the meaning of the *contract* and how it relates to the broader legal and social constructs in which international markets are embedded. In doing so, we want to extend the discussion on law and global governance to past historical periods: typically, this broad research current never ventures beyond the 1980–90 threshold that typically marks the beginning of our present-day global era.[1] In

[1] The ahistorical bias of law and globalization scholarship is in fact quite surprising, if we remember the substantial benefits drawn in other research fields from the comparison of the present Global Era with the first Global Era, that extended roughly from 1870 to 1914. Economists, for instance, have learned important lessons on growth and productivity gains by comparing these two periods, as well as on the effects of market integration, trade diversification and capital market expansion.

particular, we focus on the interwar decades that saw not only a high level of tension and overall instability, but also a considerable amount of institutional innovation and legal experimentation. The relative decline of Britain, the semi-isolation of the United States and, not least, the extraordinary experience of the League of Nations contributed to a context uniquely rich in ideological programs, policy proposals and legal experiments. Our intuition therefore is that this short and unstable period may shed more light on our theoretical debate than the more settled and more distant experience of the pre-1914 decades. Our aim however is not so much to "rediscover" or "revisit" a period that would have remained unduly ignored – which it is not –, nor is it to open up a subfield of historical inquiry and simply point out where issues of international governance arose.

For our analysis, we use a historical and micro-level (contractual) perspective to explore the shifting legal premises, assumptions and expectations that shaped how agents envisaged financial and commercial transactions across borders, then and now. We are primarily interested in an exploration of how lawyers, politicians, diplomats and investors fought with the evidence of a decline in the previous British governance and how this led them to imagine and experiment with new ways to envisage international contracting.[2] Avowedly, an underlying hypothesis at this point is that early on, perhaps on the very day when the League of Nations opened its offices and meeting rooms, early features emerged of what we now dub a "global Bukovina": experts, professions, lobbies, epistemic communities and chambers of commerce immediately laid siege to the new organization and tried to control both its agenda and its discourse – still, before World War I (WWI), Bukovina was just a distant and backward province of the old Austro-Hungarian Empire.

In order to delineate and identify analytically this complex object, we develop the concept of *contractual knowledge*. We envisage it as an analytical interface between, on one hand, a legal discourse that is typically formalistic and anchored in the worldview of international policy-makers, hence in their practice of power, and, on the other hand, the assumptions and expectations of agents that contract on international markets or advise and shape how contracting should happen. Our

[2] We shall also look backwards at the pre-1914 era, though our main aim as we center on the interwar years is to shed new light on the genealogy – economic and legal – of both the classic post-1945 multilateral decades and the current Global Era.

endeavor is to demonstrate that this perspective in general, and this concept in particular, offer a novel understanding of the governance of markets and how the legal point of view informs this governance. Contractual knowledge in other words can be understood as a range of knowledge practices associated with the negotiation and renegotiation of obligations whose origin is *contractual*, as opposed to rooted in the unilateral dimension of the transfer of resources, actual or symbolic, – such as the obligations stemming from the unilateral will of an absolute monarch (Bernardini 2007). In our definition of contractual knowledge, we thus find: (1) the legal boilerplates (Gulati and Scott 2013) and new legal provisions that have been increasingly standardized in new trade contracts, financial contracts, etc.; (2) the pricing techniques that are part of what Annelise Riles (2011) calls "collateral knowledge,"[3] which are typically used to finalize contractual exchanges, as well as all the forms of calculation or "calculative devices" (Callon and Muniesa 2005) used by international arbitration experts to determine the amount of awards in case of dispute; (3) the knowledge produced by and about the authoritative institutions in charge of legalizing market transactions, from the moment negotiations open to the moment when disputes erupt and contracting parties seek litigation or arbitration (such as public or professional regulatory agencies, or arbitration tribunals); (4) the historical narratives, philosophical justifications and political ideologies that contracting parties deploy to justify the making and un-making of contracts (here, think again about Adam Smith and the long lineage of classic political economy).

Contractual knowledge is thus a composite mix of legal and paralegal expertise, which goes beyond the sterile, scholastic opposition between "the law in the book" and "the law in action": it sums up in a pragmatic perspective the assumptions and understandings that partners share in order to make contracting possible and, in particular, in order to anticipate how the future state of the world may affect them and how they may protect themselves against possible risk. Like neoinstitutional economists, we see contracts as bundles of rights that fix prices and quantities of exchanged goods (North 1990), as well as the rules that contracting partners are supposed to respect during and after the exchange. Examples reach from a "spot" exchange for a barrel of crude oil or a sandwich, to a long-term debt or a micro-credit

[3] For instance, the knowledge that goes into the pricing of collaterals exchanged on the side of market transactions.

contract, or again to the acquisition of complex industrial equipment with a large package of long-term, after-sale services. Typically, many contracts include so-called contingent clauses that state in advance what course of action the parties should follow if commitments are broken or if a given external event occurs; alternately, they may decide ex ante whether they would go to court or ask an arbiter to decide a dispute; and at this point, significant precedents may have been issued and stored by a regulatory authority to be used as a default rule, either coercively or not. The notion of contractual knowledge thus unpacks and makes explicit the institutional and cognitive assumptions that give epistemic credence to the economists' core concept of rational expectations. What brings together our perspective and that of economists is that we assume, in our case explicitly, that participants to market exchanges share common assumptions regarding what contracts imply and how, more generally, the market works: what makes them possible ex ante (thanks to measuring and pricing devices), but also the social rules and sanctions that frame the unfolding of commitments over time, and how far their reach may extend.[4]

This concept of *contractual knowledge* is not an entirely new idea, as Emile Durkheim already emphasized in *Division of Labor* the importance of the "non-contractual elements of the contract," – for example, those tacit as well as explicit norms about the social rules and sanctions against non-compliance –, but surprisingly, the study of contractual knowledge has seldom been undertaken by social scientists.[5] Against the notion that contracts only belong to the realm of private and individualistic action, we thus insist that contracts make sense only within a *habitat*, whose constitution is part of the social and, in particular, the legal construction of society. From that specific habitat, contractual knowledge inevitably extends to, and is invested by political or constitutional meta-rules that inform more generally our view of how society is, or should be governed. In today's thoroughly integrated economy, the relationship between contracts and sovereign authorities takes utterly different forms whether they unfold at the domestic

[4] We certainly do not assume that social agents always follow principles of forward-looking, means-end, instrumental rationality; in fact we are agnostic on this point, which means that the question does not affect the present discussion. Rather, we oppose the view of contracts as simple, bilateral bonds that conjoin and seal the two parties' preferences in a social vacuum.

[5] By paying attention to the plurivocality of contractual forms of knowledge, we will thus move beyond the purely functionalist view of contracts – and more generally, of law –, which has been adopted by social scientists since at least the times of Max Weber (1978[1922]).

level, where a strong hierarchy of norms and courts rules over social exchange, or at the international level, where they take very specific and often intriguing forms (Arendt 1951; Latour 2004). Critically, the absence of a minimal degree of constitutionalization of the international legal order most often means that there is no superior text or epistemic authority that can establish basic rights, standards of fairness and shared principles of due process (Koskenniemi 1997, 2007). At best a process of constitutionalization can be observed within given subfields (Keohane, Moravcsik and Slaughter 2000; Slaughter 2000), where a body of meta-norms may gradually emerge and be accepted by most actors (Stone Sweet 1994, 1999, 2009); but in our view at least, there is no clear sign that this process will lead to a consistent, structured and binding international legal order (Teubner and Beckers 2013).

To trace the origins and evolution of contractual knowledge in global markets,[6] we have actually chosen to focus on contractual obligations that bind together sovereign entities – states, mostly represented by their diplomatic corps and finance ministries, as well as international organizations, mostly IFIs – and private interest representatives – big banks, but also multinational law firms. We focus empirically on trans-border contractual bonds, with a specific emphasis on contractual agreements involving large exchanges of assets, as in sovereign debt markets. Hence, our focus is on contracts envisaged from a rather standard economic perspective, with due regard given to the usual problems of opportunism, uncertainty and information, but we also consider the organizational practices developed within the international institutions that were put in charge of accompanying the opening of markets, codifying legal interpretations and adjudicating disputes in case of contractual breaches. Here, our book focuses on a wide range of institutions and actors; to cite just a few: the interwar Reparations Commission and different cartels, various economic offices of the League of Nations, the International Chamber of Commerce (ICC), the International

[6] Still, we do not need to go back to Roman times when tracing the notion of the contract: suffice to say, as Bruno Bernardini (2007:12) reminds us, that the two notions of contract and obligation – or *obligatio* in Roman law – are intrisincally linked, and they were first applied in order to ascribe some legal framework to trans-border exchanges, so as to create "reciprocal" and "conditional" but still "legally binding" terms for the exchange.The first definition of a contract and the "contractual obligation" it generates – or *sullagma* in Greek – comes from Labeo, a Roman jurist from the time of Augustus. For Labeo, a contract is characterized by the special type of obligation it institutes: a "reciprocal obligation" (Bernardini 2007:68), rather than a unilateral one for instance.

Monetary Fund (IMF), the World Trade Organization (WTO), the UN Conference on Trade And Development (UNCTAD), etc.

In the next section of our introduction, we describe the various narratives available about the evolution of global market governance during the last century. We underline how two narratives map onto the evolution of global governance: the evolution in the power distribution in the system of states, and the creation of an ecosystem of legal institutions and actors in charge of promoting and interpreting international private law. The transition from the First Global Era (roughly, from 1870 to 1914) to the interwar period and then the post-WWII order is often portrayed by world-system and hegemonic theorists as the demise of the British-led imperial form of governance and the emergence of a multilateral project, which was both implemented and replaced by American hegemony after 1945. The legal ambiguity and instability that marked the interwar period would then reflect the decline of an earlier order of international contracting, which, from a legal perspective, was not international, but in fact English: Britain ruled (most of) the world, and English law and English court ruled (most of) the international markets, to an extent unmatched today by American power and law. Yet, scholars of international private law have also stressed the extraordinary proliferation of transnational institutions in charge of standardizing and codifying contractual knowledge as well as litigating contractual disputes based on such evolving bodies of doctrine in this period. These developments have marked the language, hopes and forms of cooperation found among transnational networks of international law specialists and practitioners. They may actually explain why the interwar period saw the emergence of an early form of legal deformalization, or legal fragmentation (Kennedy 2006; Mallard 2014), and why in some cases the expectations and experimentations formed around contracts have stabilized and why in other cases they have drifted apart or converged.

We thus propose an analytical framework that we believe can help social scientists, anthropologists and historians capture the various factors responsible for the evolution of contractual knowledge in different periods (the Victorian era, the interwar period, the postwar era and the post-Bretton Woods era). Finally the last section of this introduction discuss how our book chapters draw from this analytical framework, and how they confirm, challenge or bring nuance to our two master narratives. The intersections and possible zones of conflict between the two master narratives are thus studied case by case, through smaller-scale descriptions of historical processes associated with contractual innovation and debates about specific forms of global governance. We address a variety of practices associated with evolving forms of contractual knowledge: (1) the evolution of writing practices in the realm of sovereign debt contracts; (2) tools and resources like the mobilization of social capital or the standardization and codification of interpretive rules by which international organizations consolidate their power over the interpretation of contracts; and (3) the market structures in the transnational field of contractual knowledge that emerged over the last century. Each contribution thus describes some aspect of the complex and often contingent evolution of micro-level practices associated with the production of contractual knowledge: how cross-border contracts were written; how domestic or international arbitration courts interpreted their meaning; how informal and tacit rules of knowledge accreditation evolved during the last hundred years. At the same time, we move from the micro-level to the more institutional and structural level, by describing the market structure of various fields in which contractual knowledge is being produced.

Our collection of case studies not only provides socio-legal scholars, institutional economists and historians with tools to understand how, over the last hundred years, legal actors and institutional entrepreneurs have shaped emerging fields of contractual exchange, hence international markets; It also provides them with an analysis of the power struggles between broad political ideologies and legal philosophies, read within the evolution of the construction and formal interpretation of contracts, but also connected to the informal values, interpretive schemes and repertoires of collective action that have been mobilized in the transnational legal fields that structure the international economy (Abbott 1988; Dezalay and Garth 1996). This focus on explicit and tacit contractual knowledge allows us to observe how public and private authorities and jurisdictions, as professional elites, have shaped global markets as they have attempted to gain jurisdiction over the making of international contracts. It provides a rich object for our analytical framework that adopts a broad definition of the law as a historically specific object of conflicts, both symbolic and material, which creates representations, supports expectations, coordinates strategies and distributes opportunities and resources that affect the outcomes of contractual exchange for a wide range of actors.

CONTRACTUAL KNOWLEDGE IN HISTORICAL PERSPECTIVE

The global governance of markets from the British to the American centuries: an externalist approach

The classical narrative that is most often used to present the history of the governance of international markets typically starts by paying respects to "hard power" before identifying shifts and cycles in the power relations between states and empires, from which it derives the history of the geo-economy of market structures (Bordo, Taylor and Williamson 2003). Hence, this narrative usually starts with a reference to the Champagne fairs and medieval Venetian trade, before moving to Genoa and Amsterdam, then to Britain and later the United States. In this narrative, intermediary periods, when no superior power ruled the world, are marked by protracted political conflicts, epistemic opacity in law and thus economic disorganization. Since Kindleberger's theory of hegemonic stability, the classic and perhaps only example of such an anomic era is the interwar period, when the United States (US) withdrew from the League of Nations and Britain's relative decline was too advanced to reestablish its pre-1914 supremacy (Kindleberger 1986). Along similar lines, "world-system" theorists (Braudel 1992; Arrighi 2010; Wallerstein 2011) thus argue that the law matters little per se; it may only reflect or formalize the balance of hard factors that structure the world society, namely military and economic power (O'Brien 2002). Law, in this view, only distributes the rewards of globalization in a way that favors the hegemon and helps it consolidate its power through economic globalization (O'Rourke and Williamson 2000; Byers 2003; Krisch 2003).

We certainly agree that the First Global Era is a paradigmatic case to illustrate this functional/strategic use of the law of international markets by the hegemon. The question is what kind of law we are talking about. Historians, whether of the legal profession or not, typically Point to the core norms of nationality, sovereignty and territoriality, which structured in a most powerful way what was then understood as international law (Kennedy 1996; Grewe 2000; Koskenniemi 2001; Mazower 2012). Yet there is little to be found under this title that actually governed commercial or financial transactions, not to mention foreign direct investments: classic textbooks from this period reflect a very limited interest in this trivial matter (Fiore 1875). Neither was it a great attraction during the pre-1914 meeting of the

Institut de Droit International or the International Law Association - the two main bodies that structured the emerging epistemic community of international lawyers (Koskenniemi 2001). While there was already before 1914 some notion that intellectual property rights had per se an international dimension (Pataille and Huguet 1855; Briggs 1906), there was no notion whatsoever that banking or antitrust regulation could be the object of a specific international legal regime (Freyer 2006). Similarly, nobody imagined that extraterritorial courts could help resolve private contractual disputes, or that firms might go forum-shopping when trying to optimize their international fiscal strategy. Even the principle that national regulators may coordinate throughmutual recognition, as is the case on a daily basis in the EU, was unheard of. What has too often been underestimated is the extent to which the legal solution to the governance of the pre-1914 global market was found outside the realm of international law. Before WWI, and still to a large extent during the 1920s, a ready substitute for an inexistent global or international law of markets was solidly established with all the necessary judicial machinery: the English law and English courts.

This moment of national hegemony was quite exceptional, and three main factors contributed to this oft-neglected, rare moment associated with Britain's imperial dominance. The first one is the British Empire's own economic *raison d'être*, which was to ease the way for trade and investment. The institutional, political and military structure of imperial control thus eschewed the need for an international or multilateral legal machinery; what started to emerge within the Empire (though after rather than before WWI) was at best an embryonic, weakly composed federal structure (Anghie 2007). The Dominions, in particular, were not commercially closed to third countries, and therefore this infrastructure served non-British interests as well.

Second is the structure of English and European imports from the rest of the world, namely commodities. Here again things were managed and regulated on English terms. The dominant role in structuring the large London-based markets was taken by so-called trade associations, which organized exchanges on a private basis, typically via standardized contracts and quality standards. They settled contractual disputes by way of arbitration and self-enforcement, that is, via the threat of market exclusion (Ellison 1886; Barker 1917; Bernstein 1992). This infrastructure was light, efficient, and entirely rule-based. It was also both local (English) and global at the same time:

these private market rules extended easily across the world, though ultimately they were anchored in English law and confirmed by English courts. Hence, the significant corollary that foreign judgments never surfaced in the deliberations of, for example, the London Corn Trade Association and its smaller sisters: although foreign trading houses operated through these London exchanges they never called upon their Belgian, French or German home courts when they ran into legal difficulties.[7]

The third factor that contributed to the Englishness of global governance was finance. At the beginning of the nineteenth century, Great Britain became a major exporter of capital, a feature that is most often associated with the development of a sovereign debt market. In essence, this market was very much governed along the same principles as commodity exchanges: private market rules, privately based dispute resolution (organized by issuing banks and the Bondholder association), and self-enforcement: a return to the primary market was closed as long as defaults had not been settled in an orderly way (Flandreau and Flores 2012; Flandreau 2013). A less visible though as important investment line was trade finance, both vis-à-vis European and non-European markets (Spalding 1926). At this point the goods and products that were sold served as collateral for English banks, shipping companies, insurers and trading houses, with the collateral being enforceable, of course, in English courts.

The very *problématique* of market governance during the First Global Era was thus founded on legal, political and microeconomic premises considerably more at odds than is usually expected in our current era. On this count, there is little symmetry in the ways the First and Second Global Eras were ordered and governed. Critically, English law was local and global at the same time; in other words, it was imperial in so far as international merchants and bankers were invited to trade out of London and under English law, as interpreted by English courts. Yet, once they had reached a certain size, they had little choice. Contrary to today, they could not go forum-shopping and trade off the relative benefits of a large set of exchanges or arbitration facilities.

[7] Before 1914, global governance was thus de facto legal, though unwillingly so – English judges had never intended their precedents to apply across the world, as a coordination device for global markets. From this development derives both the remarkably low operational costs of this global rule, as well as the absence in the collective perceptions and discourses of the very problem that was so elegantly solved.

The three reasons we have identified for this exceptionally hegemonic nineteenth century form of governance are well within the analytical framework developed by world-system or hegemony theorists: hard factors like trade, finance and military power. Naturally, these hard factors also play a role in explaining why attempts to challenge such hegemony emerged in the interwar period, why the British tried to oppose them, and why they failed. Indeed, in the interwar period, we find abundant evidence of Britain's often-antagonistic reaction to emerging forms of multilateral legal coordination. For instance, in 1919, at the same time when the League foundation was being discussed at Versailles, a group of high-level English lawyers and judges concluded their report on questions of international judicial cooperation by stating

> England has hitherto been a creditor country and, through the trade organizations of powerful importing associations, whose arbitrations are alike obligatory and respected, and also through their ability to require security for export transactions, British merchants have hitherto been comparatively rarely concerned with the question of defending legal proceedings abroad or of enforcing abroad British judgments against foreigners. Until it is apparent that this state of things has materially altered, we think that there will be but slight ground for seeking to amend the system by negotiations.
>
> (Committee on the Enforcement of Judgments and Awards 1919)

In other words, Britain had no need for any cumbersome international machinery in order to support its global trade: all the guarantees needed were provided by its (prewar) net financial position vis-à-vis the rest of the world, plus its market power over both the import and the export sides of trade. As long as hard factors like the military balance of power and the financial balance of payments were favorable to Britain, they could stay the course. This state goes a long way in explaining why Britain also opted out of The Hague Conference on International private law from 1893 till 1926.[8] More generally, from the 1860s onwards, France was the place where the most systematic effort at collecting and translating foreign codes and statutes was developed (see, for example, the *Annuaire de Législation Etrangère*). Anybody who looked at that time for a ready translation of the Swedish, Hungarian

[8] If the economic hegemon of the day had had an interest in a more integrated international legal order, these conferences would have probably taken place in London forty years earlier, and the accords would have been written in English (rather than in French).

on Spanish commercial law would have found it much more easily in Paris than in London (Sgard 2006). This effort reflects the fact that when French merchants and manufacturers did not trade through the London markets, they ultimately had to rely, in case of dispute, upon the long and costly machinery of judicial cooperation and rules of Conflicts of Law, which required in turn a thorough knowledge of the partner country's domestic legal institutions. France, in other words, just like Germany, Italy or Belgium could not grandly ignore foreign courts and foreign judgments: their second-rank position in the international economic and legal hierarchy clearly put them at a disadvantage.

The League of Nations emerged at a time when this English-based legal order was still dominant, though also under increasing pressure. What soon came out of the bureaus, meeting rooms, and conference halls in Geneva, though in a confused and piecemeal manner, was a sense that the governance of the international economy had to be founded on a new or larger institutional foundation. Economic historians or hegemony theorists typically focus, at this point, on broad, macro issues like exchange rates or German reparations, though those years have also seen a renewed legal perspective on how the international economy should be governed. The theme that we gradually see emerging is that of a move from a *de facto* international rule that (primarily) derived from the *de jure* English legal order, to a prospective *de jure* rule that would be specifically international – that is, written in international law. Unintended and silent rules were to be partially, and then more systematically substituted with voluntary rules, which would thus have to be imagined, tested, debated, bargained over, adopted and interpreted. We should not underestimate the conceptual and political step that this evolution implied. Even the very notion that there was something specifically legal and *international* (rather than just British) in the governance of global markets had to be acknowledged. In many ways, these changes reflected the relative decline of Britain and the economic ascendancy of Germany and the United States, though in Geneva neither had a strong voice. In practice, this tension would be primarily played out between Britain and France: while the former typically kept the upper hand in this forum, the later tried to imagine and defend more or less consistent rules of coordination and dispute resolution to further the project of a multilateral governance (Henig 2000; Clavin 2013; Tooze 2014).

Can we sum up the last hundred years of innovation as simply a gradual transition from a British and imperial governance, to the (failed) French-centered multipolar world of the 1920s, to the more successful US-based world of the post-WWII era? Have the changes we witnessed been purely due to a shift in the identity of the sovereign power in charge of writing and interpreting the global rules of international trade and finance? Or has there been a qualitative change in the epistemic nature of legal obligations?

World-system theorists, hegemony theorists, and to a lesser extent, Bourdieuan theorists (Dezalay and Garth 2002; Cohen and Vauchez 2007), who stand on the "externalist" side of the debate: for them, the transition in the geographical and social locus of power is one between different hegemons, which does not affect in a significant manner the quality of law and contractual knowledge. In fact, many sociologists see the meaning of a contractual obligation as being extremely malleable (Bourdieu 1987), subject to very different interpretations depending upon who has the authority to interpret it. According to this externalist view of law, to some extent one can avoid entering into the complexities of the contracts themselves – the processes of arbitration and standardization of norms and valuation techniques.

On the other side of the debate are theorists who believe that the hermeneutic or epistemic character of the law itself needs also to be taken into account (Halliday and Carruthers 2007; Mallard 2014). The assumption here is that the multilateral model of regulation, in its interwar manifestation, or in its post-1945 embodiment, introduced a qualitative innovation in the legal construction of the world order that cannot be simply subsumed in the mere horizontal translation of the locus of power, from London to Washington and New York via Paris and Geneva. In this view, the transition to the Second Global Era and its non-hierarchical, deformalized and fragmented set of transnational legal orders cannot be completely understood according to the classic hegemonic paradigm. The United States remains the most powerful nation, with the richest and most dynamic economy. But today's global governance cannot be reduced to the attempts by the US government to impose its domestic rules and courts on international investors and manufacturers, across the world, as Britain could do to a large extent. But then, which factors can account for this qualitative change in the way global governance operates?

A hundred years of legal experimentation by jurists and law practitioners: an internalist approach

There is a second entry that can help us account for the qualitative change that has characterized the shift from a hegemonic system of global governance based on the British judicial system to the later, multilateral and indeed international mode of legal regulation of markets: this narrative places emphasis on the role of jurists, lawyers, law professionals and professional experts in charge of inventing new contractual forms and creating new doctrines for their interpretation in international settings (Kennedy 1994, 2013; Koskenniemi 2001). This *internalist* account sees the creation and growth of an international law of markets over the last century as the result of a process of legal experimentation driven by law professionals.

In the juridical profession in Europe and the United States, the view that global trade should be regulated by some kind of international (private) law was a new belief that was not fully espoused before the 1920s, and even up until the 1970s. During the First Global era, when empires and Great Powers led the growth of global markets before WWI, most international law scholars did not recognize the need for new international legal instruments to accompany that expansion. The profession's faith in the capacity of "international law" to pacify relations between countries was never as high as at the turn of the twentieth century (Koskenniemi 2001), yet what was then known as "international law" was essentially international *public* law: it was about the relationships between sovereign (Western, Christian) states and their capacity to avoid conflict and to coordinate their governmental institutions (for instance, their respective legal orders), in ways that would make life easier for industrialists and bankers.

The key implication of international law being essentially public before 1914 is that international private law, addressing the rights of private individuals and firms as they cross borders, has remained thoroughly underdeveloped.[9] More precisely, it was not recognized as a self-standing body of law, or as a valuable concept for understanding the actual or optimal governance of the global economy. In practice, those individual rights only had an internal or domestic extension – such as nationality, marital status, property and inheritance, contracts and judgments. Unless they traded out of London and under English

[9] On the (non) construction of the private/public opposition in international law, see, for example, Horwitz (1982), Joel (1988) and Mills (2006).

contract law, the rights on which citizens and merchants acted and transacted beyond borders were thus defined by their own country of origin (or domicile) and by the country where they traded; that is, how countries recognized the individual rights of non-nationals and the rights that they gave them (Fiore 1875; Westlake 1880; Benton 2002). The domestic law of each country then took care of how it would recognize domestically, that is in front of its own courts, the rights of foreign nationals. Rules of "Conflict of Law" stated very precisely how each country would recognize and enforce, within its own legal and judicial order, a divorce or a bankruptcy judgment rendered by a foreign court.[10] International legal rules governing global private exchanges may have been nonexistent, but domestic rules existed in a dual regime: move under English law or accept the costs, uncertainty and delays entailed by the process of judicial cooperation.

In fact, the new brand of international public lawyers of the late nineteenth century, together with the politicians that shaped the discourse in the interwar period, never seem to have perceived a contradiction between the observation that they lived in an economically integrated world and their defense of political and legal governance that was thoroughly local, that is, national and state-controlled. For them, entrepreneurs, bankers, emigrants or tourists were steeped in national law, national identity, and national rules of economic and social interactions. In fact, they were not supposed to go global: they remained under the more or less benign protection, sponsorship and supervision of their sovereign.[11] In other words, there was no such thing as an international commercial law, or an international law of markets.

As previously said, international public law remained the dominant language for any political discussion on how to build a peaceful, liberal and progressive order; though, at the same time, the League emerged as the key forum where new market rules and contractual forms could be imagined and discussed – a hybrid of public

[10] Should it accept or ignore them entirely, without discussion? Should it ask that a domestic judge first revise and then confirm this alien judgment? Or, again, should any of these rules be conditioned by a principle of reciprocity? And so on.

[11] In the early-modern period, before 1789, and hence in an age that was not yet global in the present sense of the word, the classic literature on the Law of Nations from Grotius till Vattel had actually formalized and legitimized the possibility of recognizing individual rights beyond the jurisdiction of the sovereign, hence under the banner of natural rights (Bernardini 2007). But the international public lawyers of the late nineteenth century built their discourse and doctrine very much against this view, which they saw as romantic and, in our vocabulary, as pre-Westphalian. In other words, by the mid nineteenth century, these pre-global, transnational rights of merchants, traveling scholars and other adventurers had become totally *passé*.

and private norms and regulation involving a wide range of actors claiming legitimacy over contracting practices on behalf of specific types of expertise. Even though the League was to be the glorified servant of international public law, as soon as its office in Geneva opened, problems of a mostly micro-level nature inundated its officials and experts (Zimmern 1936; Clavin and Wessels 2005; Petersson 2013; Alessandro 2013): problems of refugees and international plagues, and closer to our field, intellectual property, cross-border bankruptcies, letters of exchange, the recognition of foreign firms and banks, competition policy, double taxation, commercial arbitration, etc. Quite significantly, the job of drafting these new texts and testing this new language of international trade was not taken over by the grand public international lawyers who staffed the new Legal Department of the League. In fact, the job was done by the economists and bankers from the Economic and Financial Section,[12] which soon started to discuss and bargain with new international actors, like the International Chamber of Commerce, the Reparations Committees, the large American investment banks, and the US rating agencies. Said differently, we can at this point observe the very first steps towards the formation and autonomization of international policy fields, where diverging interests, private or public, parochial or transnational, compete to establish the agenda, frame the discussion and shape the eventual legal texts. The fact that this experimentation did not deliver much in terms of actual market governance is not the main point: they nonetheless opened a dynamic that is still driving the evolution of global markets.

If the first experiments with an international law of markets emerged from discussion between professional bankers, private lobbyists and apprentice lawyers, working in a new and shallow transnational environment, it should not come as a surprise that their emerging contractual knowledge lacked institutional and political backing. This shortfall is the classical lament about the interwar period, voiced by international law scholars like Hans Morgenthau (1960: 277), who criticize the League of Nations for the indeterminate, vague and polysemic language

[12] In the whole book, and unless warranted, we use the generic term "Economic and Financial Section" in order to describe: (i) the Economic and Financial Section of the League, which was part of its permanent Secretariat and (ii) the Economic and Financial Committees, which were made of outside experts who were typically on short-term leave from their government or from the private sector (typically banks). Semantic confusion is also compounded by the fact that, until 1923, this structure was formally provisional.

that its most political texts used to couch the institutional basis for the enforcement of decisions. Without strong and clear institutional organization, the legal experiments in the regulation of international trade and finance could be easily dismissed, as exemplified by the outright repudiation of Germany's reparation debt in 1933. Interwar European trade and finance thus suffered from a lack of "legalization" – to borrow a concept used by many recent analysts of international regimes after Abbott and Snidal (2000: 444–5) – which resulted not only from the fact that codification preceded the establishment of institutions endowed with the legitimacy to judge specific cases and to enforce specific decisions. The weak legalization of trade and finance during the interwar years also hinged on the fact that rules were most often partial and incomplete, with no clear authority to interpret them and "plug the holes" in the legal governance of markets and insure execution. Surely, the League, and its Permanent Court of Justice, tried to fight these sources of ambiguity and lead the way toward a process of legalization, but the collapse of international markets and the decline of the League after 1933 put a halt to the effort of rationalization, codification and universalization of international private law.

This diagnosis of the interwar period was shared by lawyers and institution-builders responsible for the creation of the United Nations and Bretton Woods architecture: for them, the interwar period had not suffered from too much international law – as some German thinkers maintained, nostalgic of the Great Power game, like Carl Schmitt (2003[1950]) –, but from too little legalization of the international governance of markets (Abdelal 2010). Historians of international law and international jurists have also come to share the view that, from 1945 and at least up to the 1970s, we have seen a gradual legalization of international trade and finance, which was largely driven by the mobilization of law professionals of various countries throughout the second half of the twentieth century (Kennedy 1996; Mazower 2010, 2012). Law professionals have invested in the hallways of EU institutions, and international organizations such as the IMF and the World Trade Organization, in a manner much beyond the scale of that witnessed at the League. The result of their experimentation with contractual law has led to an increasingly legalized environment for global market exchanges (Abbott and Snidal 2000). For example, they have empowered the IMF with the new responsibility to legalize the regulation of foreign exchange rates, in order to create a predictable environment for international trade.

In a sense, the postwar generation shared Max Weber's (1978[1922]) view that trade and exchange need to be backed up by a strongly legalized set of norms and instruments (out of which contracts were only one example), as merchants and traders involved in cross-border transactions needed to clarify an unstable environment and increase predictability about the future consequences of their course of action. The success or failure of their endeavor could not depend upon the unpredictable political choices of such and such country to devalue their currency so as to boost artificially the exports of such and such nation. Global trade needed fixed and agreed upon rules, enforced by powerful international institutions. Like other legal instruments – for example, legislation, jurisprudence, academic theorizing, etc. – contracts and institutions were meant to clarify any ambiguities and inconsistencies in the world's legal system (Bourdieu 1987).

One may thus envisage the growth of an international law of markets after WWII as the outcome of a process of legal experimentation driven by law professionals whose forbears staffed the League of Nations, before moving to the various branches of the Bretton Woods and United Nations architecture (Pauly 1996; Mazower 2010). Of course, we could follow the world-system or hegemony theorists and say that without the geopolitical backing and economic power of the United States, these new U.S.-based international organizations would not have had the authority to diffuse and enforce rules worldwide. Still, the United States decided to ground its authority on a set of international and multilateral institutions rather than on its domestic judicial system and its domestic market infrastructures. This point cannot be completely accounted for with an "externalist" approach to global governance. Studying the ideas, legal imaginaries, hopes and expectations of the lawyers and politicians responsible for making these choices can provide us with a useful complement to explain both the shift in locus of power and the specific organizational choices made after WWII.

And what about now? How did these postwar experiments affect the global world we live in today? Where do the lawyers and international private law specialists now see themselves and their efforts of consolidation? Paradoxically, since at least the two oil crises of the 1970s, the common diagnosis is that the present legal system of global governance of markets suffers from too much legalization, or rather, from a too-chaotic process of norm accumulation. International law practitioners rather believe today that we have arrived at a new kind of epistemic uncertainty that results less from the "thinness" of the international legal order, as after 1919, than from the very exponential growth of bilateral treaties, regional agreements, ad hoc courts and arbitration decisions, which characterized the world economy. Hence, the dilemmas are rather those of excess "thickness," leading to obscurity.

The web of bilateral agreements, industry-based soft-laws, and international and domestic court decisions, is often perceived as producing an elusive global governance of markets, characterized altogether by fluidity, incompleteness and complexity (Shaffer and Pollack 2010). Instead of providing governments, firms and investors with ready solutions to their problem of information, knowledge, mutual commitment or dispute-resolution, the road to the best legal contractual solution typically appears long, winding and dangerous, especially for those who are ill advised or underequipped to navigate the complexity (Drezner 2009). Whereas the role of the IMF seemed clearly bound and legally defined in the immediate postwar period (as it was to serve mostly as a controller of exchange rate system), the multiplicity of superimposed and competing norm-makers, regulatory sites, dispute settlement fora which have mushroomed since the end of the Bretton Woods consensus (brought by the end of fixed exchange rates) has now stripped global governance from whatever architecture the founders of the post-WWII institutions wished to erect and have thus landed us in a legal geography quite close indeed to Teubner's global Bukovina.

According to this view, the new legal universe is primarily characterized by the fluid, overlapping, often indeterminate relations between legal and judicial orders (Nicolaidis and Shaffer 2005), which not only affects the sustainability of global trade and investments, but also contributes indirectly to the rise of global inequalities (Ruggie 2004). Think about the partial, self-standing "transnational legal orders" (Halliday and Shaffer 2015), which shape and regulate transactions in a great number of branches through industrial standards, consumer protection norms, and banking regulation: contractual knowledge in these cases is typically in the hands of discrete networks of depoliticized experts, who may or may not nominally belong to national government agencies, and who may interpret contractual obligations very differently. Commercial and investment arbitration presents similar features: this essentially decentralized institution for dispute resolution, which now extends almost to the whole universe of private international contracting (as well as to disputes between private investors and administrative authorities) leaves the parties with a very large capacity to choose between national laws, fora, and arbitrators, whose interpretive lenses on contractual provisions may widely vary.

The process of EU integration, especially its last twenty years, has accentuated the impression that deterritorialized networks of economic experts and law professional have claimed a legitimacy that once was the prerogative of a nation-state and that no clear hierarchy of norms and authorities has emerged out of this fight between national and supranational regulators. In the 1970s and 1980s, the situation was clearer: the bureaucrats in Brussels were charged with the establishment of standards, norms, codes and rules, which eventually backed-up in the post-1985 single market, a major addition to the founding European treaties (the Common Market Treaty of 1957 in particular); meanwhile, the European Court of Justice ensured the consistency of the whole legal edifice and gradually extended its reach over the national legal orders (Vauchez 2013). But with the creation of the Euro, Brussels now intervenes in highly political budgetary matters that are supposed to escape its reach, and it is no longer clear what agency national political leaders have. This widespread perception of a messy structure of governance, associated with the grey figure of the Brussels technocrat, has apparently contributed to the new appetite of voters for either far left (in Greece) or far right (in France) parties, which articulate anti-Brussels sentiments and a neotraditional construction of national sovereignty.

Against the view that global or regional institutions are solely responsible for the opaque state of affairs in finance and international trade, we also see domestic judicial institutions adding to the complexity: in particular, the United States shows its new appetite for a regulation of the world economy that would be more thoroughly anchored onto the American legal, judicial and regulatory orders, rather than on international or multilateral bodies. This trend is evidenced in the recent civil and criminal cases brought to US courts against foreign banks – European banks in general, and Swiss banks in particular – that have violated US tax laws and political embargoes set by the US government – as in the case of BNP-Paribas, which was recently ordered to pay a landmark $8.9 billion to settle a US criminal case for breaching US embargoes against Sudan and Iran.[13] Here, what is at

[13] A similar case is presented by recent sovereign debt restructurings, whose legitimacy was the object of recent US court decisions that ruled in favor of the "vulture" funds (as in the case of Argentina).

stake is the geographical validity – universal or relative – that national governments can claim for their laws over the contractual obligations of two foreign trading partners. The extra-territorial claims made by domestic courts in the United States offer another example of how the quality of the law that is used for the regulation of international markets matters. As we see, domestic courts are thus turned into instruments of a hegemonic struggle to impose one's interpretive authority across borders.

Since the interwar period, the body of international private law that one needs to master to navigate the high waters of international trade or global finance has arguably grown more opaque as it has become more diverse and fragmented – linking knowledge of complex financial instruments to the latest legal innovations and new forms of justifying the ascription of political authority to freshly erected governance bodies – and that such "opacity" (Mallard 2014) is new and surprising: no one could have predicted that the mobilization of law professionals who favored the creation and institutionalization of an international law of markets would have resulted in such a fragmented legal space at the international level. This state of affairs is indeed entirely at odds with both the relatively lean imperial governance of the British age and the thin and fragile legal construction that was painfully assembled after 1919.

To restate the same argument in the language of sociologists of science, the knowledge devices or inscription-producing instruments (Latour 1987) used by international legal practitioners and financial experts to rule over contractual exchanges have lost their ability to present the international environment in a transparent and predictable way, despite their best efforts to domesticate the environment of global exchanges. Two main processes account for this failure: the multiplication of implicit and explicit interpretations of what contracts mean; and the fragmented character of the institutional space in which contracting parties can bring their cases to be heard, which encourages forum-shopping strategies on their part (Busch 2007). If there was ever a time when the predictions drawn from the knowledge of international court judgments, codices of international law, and academic treatises could produce the impression of self-evidence, it is now a widely held conclusion that contractual instruments no longer have the property of "being not only ready-to-hand but transparent" according to "the tendency [of instruments] to disappear and become a means when we are using it" (Knorr Cetina

1997:10).[14] And to that extent, we cannot reduce contracts to yet another set of "technologies of calculability" (Callon 1998), which, like the transparent equipment described by sociologists of science when they conducted ethnographies of laboratory life (Latour and Woolgar 1979), or the algorithms that have proliferated in financial trade rooms (Lepinay 2011), would generate predictability and calculability in the globalized world of finance.[15] To take a stand on contractual practices today, one must reflect upon the historical conditions of the production of contractual instruments, their potential conflicts with contractual obligations formed by similar parties in overlapping groups, and the ways in which some degree of harmonization between dissimilar tools – rather than the simple implementation of univocal principles – can be achieved.[16]

This epistemic opacity and the subsequent need for a reflexive use of legal instruments not only raise important concerns for the efficiency of the present system of global governance (as it proves that the international regulation contracts do not always work to render the environment more predictable), but also, and more importantly, for its legitimacy. For good reason international lawyers who have crafted this master narrative of increasing legal confusion have discussed the normative consequences of such "fragmentation" of international legal rules (International Law Commission 2006; Benvenisti and Downs 2007: 596), and the resulting opaque knowledge of the law it produces. Powerful states gain an advantage from legal confusion and actively "reduce the clarity of legal obligation by introducing overlapping sets of legal rules and jurisdictions governing an issue" (Alter and Meunier 2009: 16). This state of affairs favors the rich over disenfranchised populations (Drezner 2009), as the first have the ability to choose which jurisdiction is likely to provide the more accommodating ruling with

[14] What Karin Knorr Cetina (1997:10) wrote about the status of instruments in high energy physics, for example, that "the equation of instruments with technical objects is now highly problematic, [especially] in light of today's technologies, which are simultaneously things-to-be-used and things-in-a-process-of-transformation, [which] undergo continual processes of development and stabilization," is equally true for the legal texts, contractual devices, and arbitral institutions that are granted the authority to rule over global markets.

[15] In general, with the notable exception of Annelise Riles (2011), and Pénet and Mallard (2014), scholars in the social studies of finance pay little attention to law, contracts and other legal tools as instruments of market governance.

[16] It is in that sense that we can say about international legal environment, as Clifford Geertz (1973) said about culture more generally, that, with a richer and more complex understanding of the plurivocality of legal language comes the realization that the positivist dream of achieving a transparent correspondence between norms and facts, law-in-the-books and law-in-practice, predicted behavior and actual outcomes, can never be achieved.

respect to their contractual obligations. Even when included in networks of global exchanges, aggrieved parties, especially when they come from the peripheries, often have no recourse to appeal ill founded or unjust decisions.

In this book, we keep normative discussions to a minimum and instead, question the historical validity of the processes that led to this paradoxical legalization of the international environment in which contractual obligations are read. Thus far, our two narratives have emphasized first the role of hard factors (like military and economic power), which have affected the identity of the hegemon and indirectly the kind of law that has been privileged to rule over international market exchanges; and second, the role of the beliefs, expectations and legal imaginaries that law professionals brought with them when they sought to create a rationalized system of international governance of market exchanges. With the relative exception of the immediate post-war era (corresponding to the Bretton Woods consensus), these trends resulted in a fragmented and opaque system of governance. Indeed, the present fragmentation might be due to the fact that the United States never succeeded in concentrating as much legal authority as the British had, and that international law practitioners could thus experiment and develop a uniquely large scope of contractual innovations, dispute-settlement fora or interpretative authorities. If there is some truth to this view, we present reasons why we also need to bring other actors into the play, and we explain in the next sub-section how an analysis that pays attention to both external and internal factors, analyzed at different levels, might look.

Research questions and analytical framework

In order to explain the evolution of contractual knowledge (from preparing templates and model contracts, to designing monitoring mechanisms for specific contracts, or litigating disputes in the case of denounced contractual breaches, and establishing jurisdiction for international organizations) in global markets, we have asked our contributors to consider the following questions:

- How did new contractual rules over cross-border exchanges change over time? Can we observe any standardization of contractual knowledge over time? Or at least a convergence around some expected range of legitimate actions with respect to the writing, interpretation and execution of contracts and implicit contractual rules? Did private contracting rules make it into states' public regulations and thus extend their reach to all kinds of contracting partners (private and public)? Can we see a common "episteme" emerging in each period that characterizes contractual innovation in both international private law and in public law matters?

- Who were the key actors driving the evolution of contractual knowledge: government officials, multilateral policy wonks, apolitical experts, multi-card lobbyists, private law firms, civic associations, bankers, or a new brand of business lawyers? During the last hundred years, can we observe some long-lasting structured sets of informal patterns incorporated within the *habitus* (Bourdieu 1987) of lawyers, experts and bankers who claimed jurisdiction over contractual knowledge? Have we seen some type of autonomization of the fields of high finance and private international law, which could lead us to conclude that elites in these fields have been able to reproduce their power, routines, and expectations, without suffering from external shocks?
- Historically, if contractual knowledge was initially dominated by English (private) law and international (public) law, then how did we move from there to here? Are there examples of legal or contractual practices that had emerged in the private markets of the Victorian era then moving to successor markets, even though they were founded on different bases? How did the world drift, gradually or not, willingly or unperceptively, to the present situation where international contractual knowledge has become a tangible reality even though it is far from being a well settled, well delineated transnational legal field? How can "hard" factors such as the distribution of military force and economic wealth account for the open-ended, indeterminate, and sometimes chaotic dimension of legal innovation, in this context?

Answering these questions has led our contributors to mix in their analysis some factors external to the contracts themselves with a fine-grained analysis of the evolution of key contractual clauses. Many of our chapter contributors focus on these external elements: either mechanisms outside of the legal field (changes in the military and economic power of nations, or changes in the philosophies of global governance), or mechanisms that belong to domestic legal fields (the varying quantities and types of social capital accumulated by legal and political elites, or the strength gained by legal organizations from processes of standardization and boundary-policing), so as to explain how they have affected the transition of contractual provisions from texts to practices. Other chapters pay attention to the "internal" characteristics of contracts: the valuation mechanisms adopted to fix prices, the standardized definition of the commodities, the arbitration clauses included in order to litigate disputes about noncompliance, etc. For instance, various contributors trace the evolution of historical understandings of "conditionality clauses" in sovereign debt contracts (Flores Zendejas), collective action clauses (Weidemaier, Gulati, and Gelpern), *pari passu* clauses (Nelson), and arbitration clauses (Sgard). Their study suggests that the construction and discourse of international law, and their relationship to issues of governance, seem to have a life cycle somewhat different from the cycles of hegemonic succession and long-run economic expansion, which means that the processes of commensuration and standardization of contracts that facilitate the exchange of goods on global markets need to be described in detail, as in, for instance, the more internalist accounts of the evolution of contractual law reform do (Gulati and Scott 2013).

In Figure 1.1, we provide a comprehensive representation of the different mechanisms that various theories (hegemonic, world-system, Bourdieuan, ecological and neoinstitutionalist) can illuminate. Here, we look for ways each theory can complement the others by focusing on specific factors driving change: for instance, focusing on world-historical military and economic events by hegemonic and world-systems theories, or on elite struggles in domestic fields by Bourdieuan authors.

This approach to creating a comprehensive view of the processes (both internal and external) that have affected the making and unmaking of contractual knowledge over the last century allows us to place our contributors' works in an integrated framework, which not all the authors might agree with, but, which at least, can serve as a basis of discussion for further research. Indeed, while our presentation does not assume strong relations of causality between each factor, but rather some form of "elective affinity" *à la* Weber – hence, the presence of double arrows in Figure 1.1 – it allows us to render the complexity of the interrelations between these mechanisms in a way that avoids two pitfalls: that of adhering to a master narrative that is too linear and univocal to characterize all aspects of contractual changes over the last hundred years; and that of emphasizing only contingencies, unintended

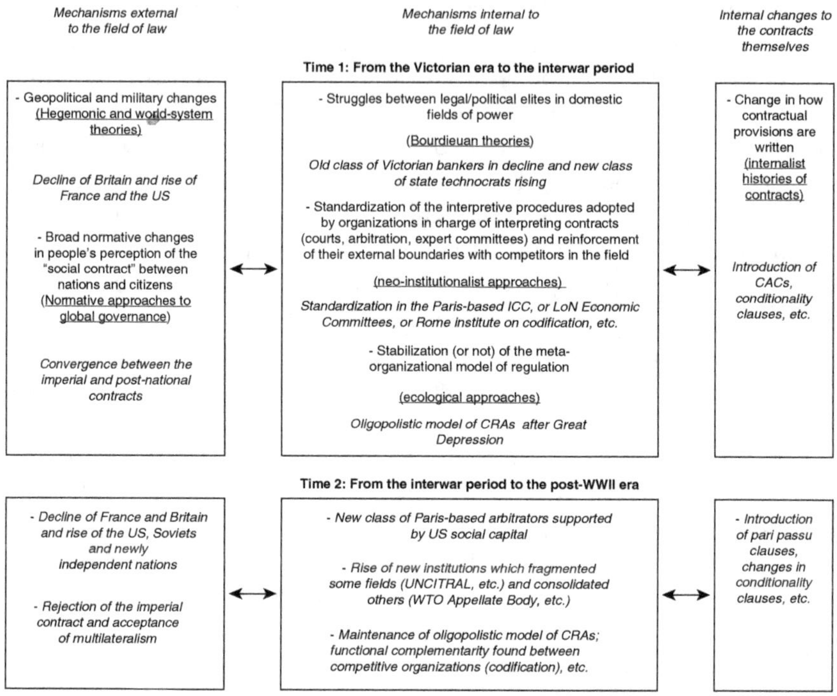

Figure 1.1 A Dynamic Approach of Recursive Cycles of Contractual Lawmaking*
* This figure is adapted from Mallard (2014:38). In this figure, we not only indicate abstract mechanisms, but we also try to list some of the historical predictions that are drawn from the book chapters regarding how each factor affected the interpretation of contracts in two historically specific periods (the interwar period, and the immediate post-WWII period). Our purpose here is illustrative rather than exhaustive.

effects, and randomness in the reinterpretations of contractual clauses in twentieth-century history. Our figure thus brings focus to how each factor confirms, adds nuance and sometimes challenges the validity of the two master narratives presented in the first section.

LEGAL EXPERIMENTATIONS IN WRITING, INTERPRETING AND STANDARDIZING CONTRACTUAL OBLIGATIONS

To help us better understand the specific historical processes that have shaped the contemporary world of contracting practices, our chapter contributors start from the assumption that innovations, experimentation and developments in contractual matters have a historical trajectory of their own, one that cannot be subsumed to the recognized macrocycles of international history, even though the latter may yield large influence. Thus, all contributors depart from a description of contracting practices to examine moments of bifurcation and of convergence with the master narratives we have sketched out in this introduction. In their respective chapters, they test the idea that dilemmas and strategies, which have surfaced in the last thirty years may originate in trends that are part of century-long processes, and which have affected various sub-fields differently, depending upon the specific issue at stake: the writing of sovereign debt contracts; the practice of arbitration in commercial disputes and the institutionalization of organizational practices; the structuration of fields around principles like competition, oligopoly or market dominance by one actor.

Writing sovereign debt contracts: textualist approaches

Our first three chapters go back in time to examine the form and content of legal clauses written in sovereign debt contracts over a hundred-year period. As far as the study of law is concerned, their perspective is largely *internalist*: they compare the writing of specific provisions and clauses found in sovereign debt contracts over the long term. In particular, they focus on contractual provisions that have protected contracting parties against the risk of contractual breach, whether the parties were private companies and individuals or public entities and even states, as in the cases under consideration.

We open our collective inquiry into contractual provisions by looking at the evolving meaning and technicalities associated with "conditionality clauses" in the sovereign debt market. The challenge of ensuring minimum guarantees that a sovereign state's future policies will not *de facto* make any debt service impossible is now often addressed via so-called conditionality arrangements: with these contractual provisions, creditors typically ask that governments commit themselves to "sound" economic policies, accept a degree of direct oversight from international financial institutions (IFIs) or other observers – thus breaking the exclusivity of the bilateral relationship between debtor and creditor – , and agree to rules that regulate how they interact and bargain with their creditors in case of default. Conditionality has thus worked as a collateral, although not a material one.

The presence of conditionality clauses in sovereign debt contracts, Juan Flores Zendejas shows, predated 1919: in fact, these clauses have roots in market-based practices from the nineteenth century, in particular, in debt contracts undersigned by major private banks (like the Rothschild) which underwrote loans contracted by national governments before 1914. These market-based practices gradually substituted themselves to the only previous option – threat of invasion against a defaulting debtor Prince.

If conditionality clauses find their origins in the nineteenth century, they obtained their first endorsement by a wide range of international investors, creditor states, and IFIs in the interwar period. Indeed, in the early 1920s, it was the Economic and Financial Section of the League that pushed for the inclusion of conditionality arrangements in multilateral stabilization programs. This experiment started with Austria in 1922 and was then extended in a number of Central and Eastern European countries. Contrary to post-WWII practices, League conditionality could also apply when the debt was issued, that is, when the country reached the primary market. By contrast, the IMF could only intervene when an already-issued debt had run into trouble and refinancing had become impossible.

The League's affinity for broad conditionality clauses is not surprising if placed in parallel with the development of what we could call "public law conditionality clauses," by which the Great Powers regulated the treatment of ethnic minorities by Central and Eastern European countries. Indeed, the leaders of the Versailles conference, which settled the 1919 peace between the Allies and Germany, imposed strong safeguards on these new states: in exchange for inter-state recognition, new states in Central Europe had to abide by Minority Treaties, which set up oversight committees in charge of monitoring adherence to minority protection rules and hearing the direct complaints of ethnic minorities. Direct, supranational oversight was thus not limited to the nascent international private law ruling over the issuance of sovereign debt, but also characterized essential developments in public international law at the time. It fitted perfectly with the imperial understanding of contracts, whereby new nations were to remain under the close control of the Great Powers, from which they derived recognition of their (limited) claim to statehood. As the French President, George Clemenceau, expressed to Poland at the signature of the Minority Treaties,

> It has for long been the established procedure of the public law of Europe that when a State is created, or when large accessions of territory are made to an established State, the joint and formal recognition of the

> Great Powers should be accompanied by the requirement that such States should, in the form of a binding International convention undertake to comply with certain principles of Government. In this regard I must recall for your consideration the fact that it is to the endeavors and sacrifices of the Powers in whose name I am addressing you that the Polish nation owes the recovery of its independence. It is by their decision that Polish sovereignty is being restored over the territories in question, and that the inhabitants of these territories are being incorporated into the Polish nation... There rests, therefore, upon these Powers an obligation, which they cannot evade, to secure in the most permanent and solemn form guarantees for certain essential rights which will afford to the inhabitants the necessary protection, whatever changes may take place in the internal constitution of the Polish State.
>
> (cited in Krasner 1999:92)

Placed in the broader context of the imperial relations that shaped public and private law in the newly created states of the interwar period, it comes as no surprise that the nation-states which broke free from imperial bonds after the 1950s rejected the concept of conditionality clauses as used in the interwar period. After WWII, conditionality clauses continued to spread to more cases, thanks to the IMF's advocacy and intermediacy, but narrowed in scope. Indeed, whereas before WWII all new states (with good or bad credit history) could a priori be subject to such third party interventions and oversight (as they obtained recognition of their statehood from the unilateral will of the imperial powers rather than from their own self-determination), after WWII only those states which had failed to reimburse their debts could have such limitations imposed on their sovereignty. From a routine practice in line with the imperial mentality of the League experts and Great Powers, conditionality became accepted only as an exception, reserved for those states that had already failed. The post-WWII evolution of conditionality clauses thus shows the changes conditionality clauses underwent to become acceptable, and in fact, quite widespread in the postwar era: through a process of narrowing and specification, the global diffusion of such contractual knowledge was harmonized with the expansion of state sovereignty as a hegemonic norm of international society, and the growing rejection of the imperial "contract" between the European Great Powers and new states.[17]

[17] Once that articulation between political and private law understandings of the notion of "contract" becomes clear, we can immediately see why the reference to a new "social contract" in relation to sovereign debt negotiations – for instance, between Greece and the Euro-Zone

World theorists may challenge the notion that imperial relations of power between superpowers and peripheries have so radically changed since the Victorian age. But they won't challenge the idea that at least, imperial ideologies have retreated from the public sphere: now, contractual obligations between the global North and South are no longer explicitly associated with the justification of Victorian imperial contracts – for example the notion that it was the White Man's burden to administer "non-civilized" populations. Broad changes in our philosophies of global governance – based on the rejection of imperialism – gradually came to be reflected in the letter of contractual provisions found in sovereign debt contracts: to survive, these provisions needed to conform to the new accepted forms of global governance. It seems that after WWII and the decolonization wars it became impossible to go back to the times of imperialism, when Britain and the other four or five European Great Powers could administer populations in contractually "leased territories" (Koskenniemi 2001:139),[18] and organize, rule and litigate disputes concerning the circulation of goods and capital across borders.

The following two chapters explore two other typical examples of new contractual clauses in sovereign debt contracts which emerged after WWI: the inclusion of contingent clauses by which lawyers tried to solve collective action problems between the many creditors of a bankrupt sovereign – for example collective action clauses (CACs) –, and clauses that prevented one creditor from being favored at the expense of others in anticipation of a default – for example *pari passu* clauses. In both cases, we can safely assume that lawyers wrote these clauses after stumbling on the same practical questions which are well-known to Weberian neo-institutionalist sociologists and economists: if commitment devices and monitoring clauses fail, and contracts have

institutions, or between Argentina and a domestic US court, or between South Korea and the IMF – is invariably filled with references to such notions as the "people's rights," or expressed as a criticism of new forms of "imperialism" and calls for new democratic forms of association at the transnational level (Badie 1999).

18 Victorian legal scholars had also purposefully tried to distance their military operations in the Middle East and Africa from the old understanding of international law as Christian law produced by the Pope and the Christian princes of the sixteenth century. Even in the Berlin Act of 1884, by which the European powers organized the administration of the Congo River basin, and which led to one of the most deadly exploitations of human life in history, international lawyers inscribed the principle that African "consent" should be sought in contractual form by European great powers so that land-appropriation procedures would be different from those of the Spanish international law scholars of the sixteenth century, who only invoked the names of God and the Pope to expropriate foreign resources (Schmitt 2003[1950]).

to be renegotiated, then the parties must choose between three main roads. First, they could rebargain on a multilateral basis between the debtor and its creditors. Second, they could look for a third party to smooth the road to a settlement. Third, and as a last resort, they could go to court and litigate. In the interwar period, it was commonly accepted that all of these actions were preferable to more dire consequences: for instance, war against a debtor state that refused to service its debt (Finnemore 2003; Mallard 2011), or imprisonment of a private debtor.

As our contributors discuss, these various contractual clauses were included through a slow process of experimentation followed by an extremely rapid and widespread adoption of the new clauses after a crisis, as if all market actors then decided to follow the same "convention," for example an arbitrary decision made by market actors to follow the same market rule in times of uncertainty, according to the definition used by Stephen Nelson. For instance, contemporary private investors as well as the IMF now see the new CACs written in sovereign debt contracts as a key innovation that helps debtors and creditors engage in "orderly debt restructuring," should future defaults occur, as CACs can mitigate the risk of negotiation being held up by minority investors. But that perceived "newness" of CACs is in fact a historical reconstruction. As Mark Weidemaier, Mitu Gulati and Anna Gelpern show, CACs have a long history going back to the interwar period when they were considered by experts and government officials at the League, but ultimately discarded, largely because the environment in which bonds were issued was too thinly legalized for them to work. When sovereign states defaulted, there was little recourse to the courts for either private or public bondholders, so what the contract said mattered little in shaping how debt restructuring was done. Indeed, the inclusion of new innovative provisions in contracts is a futile effort if no judge or arbitrator exists with the authority to read a judgment and deliver an award. Contractual provisions in themselves do not have a binding effect – they depend upon the legal environment in which the contracts will be mobilized, interpreted and discussed.

In fact, the case of the "*pari passu*" clauses, which New York-based vulture funds used to claim compensation from Argentina in a New York court, shows that the letter of contracts usually does not change to reflect evolving legal practice; rather, the uncoupling between law-in-the-books and law-in-practice often continues because the contractual provisions serve a performative function – closer to a "fiction" than to a "convention," if it is possible to separate the two. Stephen Nelson takes the specific example of *pari passu* clauses to discuss this concept of legal fiction. On paper, just like in the case of CACs, *pari passu* clauses sound right and fair, and their spread after WWII illustrated the ideals of the new era: an era in which all (creditor) states would be treated equally. In practice, no one knew what that meant, but what mattered is that they gave the impression that the problems of equity and fairness had been dealt with by contract lawyers. These clauses articulate in contractual terms the commonsense notion that in the case of restructuring, no bondholder should be privileged over others and no one should be left completely on the side. In principle, they seem to prevent corruption or malpractice, formally making it illegal for a state to reimburse a few happy bondholders before announcing a massive default (e.g. friends and families of Finance Ministers, banks controlled by the party in power, protectors/patrons in the administration of a Great Power with more influence, etc.). This articulation with common sense can explain how *pari passu* clauses became a fad among private lawyers little bothered by their practical implementation: they first appeared in sovereign debt contracts at the end of the nineteenth century and only became widespread from the 1940s to the 1970s, in parallel to the institutionalization of international arbitration.

Now that the legal environment is richer with institutions and actors in charge of interpreting and executing contractual clauses, can we say that CACs and *pari passu* clauses provide an effective recipe for "orderly debt restructuring"? More broadly, can we now deduce contractual practices from reading contractual provisions? To us, it seems that CACs do not fare much better now than in the interwar period, in a legal environment that has become opaque and fragmented. As Weidemaier, Gulati and Gelpern show, in the case of Argentina's and Greece's defaults at the beginning and end of the 2000s, the diffusion of CACs to New York-based contracts and European sovereign debt contracts has neither solved the practical problem of finding a supra-majority among creditors who will accept a "hair-cut" – as in the case of Greece –; nor that of dealing with the minority of discontents who may wish to sue the debtor country, even after an agreement is found – as in the case of Argentina, sued by "vulture funds" in New York courts for failing to treat fairly the bondholders left out of the agreement. If CAC promoters claim that CACs, at least on paper, help states avoid defaults by facilitating renegotiation among creditors, in practice, whether the international environment is unified or fragmented, the letter of contractual clauses does not drive the practice of contract renegotiation. Knowing this, we may infer that the extremely rapid diffusion of CACs after the Argentine sovereign debt crisis of 2003 – in New York-based contracts but also in European law contracts – is just a fad initiated by private law firms and lazy policymakers who would rather reassure themselves by engaging in mimetic behavior (in as far as they themselves would acknowledge the decoupling between law-in-the-books and law-in-action) that costs them little than address collectively the root problems at the heart of these banking practices.

Analytically, these chapters help us understand the need to move on from the naïve view that contractual provisions are prescriptive and descriptive – for example that they define how market behaviors should be organized and how they are organized –, to the neo-institutionalist notion (Meyer et al. 1997) that although contractual provisions may be prescriptive, they are not descriptive – as the structure of the legal environment has deep implications for how contractual provisions will be read and acted upon –, and ultimately to the view that contractual provisions are "performative" (Callon 1998) rather than prescriptive or descriptive. What interests those bankers and contract lawyers who include new contract terms – like *pari passu* – or terms that they know will not be enforced – like CACs –, is the immediate effect that they have ex ante: their performance as the contract is signed. They give the appearance that through the writing of these contractual terms, experts have recognized and solved a problem. What Annelise Riles (2010) has written about "collateral knowledge" – that collateral terms in debt contracts serve the role of a legal fiction which enables the transacting parties to act *as if* the ambiguity about what will happen in the (unknowable) future has been mapped out so that the deal can be completed –, is thus also true about the contractual knowledge found in these types of contract clauses. Rather than descriptive or prescriptive, they are "performative" in the sense that they provide market-actors with a script that enables them to act as if everything is in their control, even in the case of default – or, in the case of CACs, it enables politicians and government experts to act as if they had identified the best solution for the problem. This performative effect is present ex ante, not ex post: when states default, then, it is common that all parties reassess their interests and choose their behavior based on many other parameters than the terms of the contract.

This performative effect is context-dependent: Nelson illustrates how its effectiveness can be threatened by forum-shopping strategies specific to the fragmented mode of legal governance in which we live today. Indeed, taking the example of *pari passu* clauses, this legal fiction was for most market actors only a vague and unbinding promise to treat all creditors equally in case of default. But after the vulture funds, created by business lawyers whose market niche is the identification of loopholes in debt contracts, began to sue defaulting debtor states (like Argentina) in New York courts, the inclusion of *pari passu* clauses in debt contracts may no longer have the same performative effect. Investors might be scared that court-oriented US-based funds and New York courts will impose their interpretation of *pari passu* clauses, in violation of an implicit practical norm: that *pari passu* clauses do not open any legal action. Here, the threat of litigation in the United States has been directly responsible for a widespread feeling that the financial world no longer works according to the implicit norms held dear by a cosmopolitan elite of bankers, and that the rules of the game can be unilaterally changed by US judicial institutions, thanks to the judicial resources offered by the relocalization of the world's financial activities from London to New York. Such a shift in the location of the world's financial power generates opacity, as no one knows how US judicial authorities will reinterpret century-old contractual rules, some of which have been held dormant for much of that time, and would have remained so if not for the strategies of US law firms (as in the example of US lawyers who threatened to sue Swiss banks suspected of keeping dormant accounts from Holocaust victims as recounted by Ariel Colonomos and Grégoire Mallard). Here, it is the translation of American raw financial power into legal interpretive power that is responsible for the emergence of uncertainties and predictive discomfort, although the important time lag between the moment the United States substituted itself economically for Britain, and the moment New York courts started operating hegemonically in the same way British courts used to operate before WWI is striking. This time lag adds nuance to hegemonic or world systems theories regarding this shift in power.

Thus, while these three chapters show the importance of studying the specific terms found in contractual instruments – if only to emphasize their performative effects over their descriptive or prescriptive effects –, they also point to the necessity of including at the center of our analysis the sociological and geopolitical processes which affect the legal environment in which the interpretation of such clauses takes place.

Consolidating international organizations: mobilization of social capital and standardization processes in organizations

Now that we see both the interest and the limits of a mostly *internalist* study of contractual knowledge, which centers on the terms of contractual provisions, we turn our attention to changes found in the transnational environment of institutions which turn contracts into a set of organized practices.[19] In addition to the broad historical factors associated with a changing balance of military and economic power, our contributors emphasize the role that three mechanisms have played in affecting how contractual knowledge is turned into practice: (1) struggles between political and legal elites, which are determined in large part by the unequal distribution and circulation of social capital (as predicted by Bourdieuan theories); (2) processes by which new legal organizations have gained power (through consolidation, codification or standardization of interpretive routines and/or the active defense of hard-gained institutional niches in the broader ecology of the field of international private law); (3) processes that lead to the stabilization or destabilization of relations between organizations at the level of the field itself (relations of competition, functional differentiation, market specialization, "ententes," etc.); see Figure 1.1.

To see how these processes operate in the broad field of contractual knowledge, we have chosen to focus first on one striking success story of the last hundred years: the establishment of private arbitration as an autonomous field of knowledge and practice. Today, the relevance of arbitration is widely recognized. Any specialist of international private law will likely recommend that when contracts and renegotiation of terms fail, either because of a lack of supra-majority among bondholders, or because the situation of the debtor is too dire, the next route is typically recourse to a third party: either an official court or a private arbitration tribunal, especially if the contract includes a clause that reflects the parties' preference for arbitration. Two of our chapters

19 In order for us to better understand the economic interests, political projects and transnational values of these producers of new legal discourses, we thus need to abandon any a priori definition of what the law is: we can't exclude expert ruling from the legal realm just because it does not fit with a preestablished definition of international law conceived as public law. The law is not just an abridged, graphic description of the real world of interstate agreements and treaties (positive law).

explain how mechanisms of elite struggle, organizational standardization, niche-conquest and boundary-policing influenced tremendously in the establishment of this practice, which was not self-evident in 1919 when private actors more likely turned to courts to litigate a contractual dispute.

Today this approach to arbitration is widely practiced because, in most countries, courts are now bound to enforce both the ex ante commitment to arbitrate (as written into the contract) and the award that is eventually handed out.[20] This outcome, however, cannot be assumed from the introduction of arbitration clauses in many contracts in the 1920s. What we said in the previous section still holds true: compromissory clauses, just like CACs or *pari passu* clauses are neither prescriptive nor descriptive of the reality of financial and political relations in situations of contractual failure. In fact, in order to understand why contracts included the possibility for market actors to avoid the courts and seek arbitration after WWI, one has to look at the broader historical analysis of the conception of judiciary sovereignty. Indeed, as Jérôme Sgard shows, the acceptance of contractual arbitration clauses by states resulted from the inability to deal speedily with the surge of WWI commercial disputes in European tribunals. Before WWI, proud states like the French Third Republic had refused to break down the unitary state judiciary and admit the possibility that private actors could provide equivalent forms of justice. While England adopted statutes along these lines in the 1880s, broader changes in the way the state administered justice were needed before such contractual provisions were recognized as legal in French and American contexts.

Macro-historical processes are helpful not only to explain why arbitration clauses were finally legalized, but also to account for how arbitration clauses were implemented after their inclusion in trade and financial contracts became a routine practice. After the United States and France legalized arbitration, three cities, and three institutional regimes of arbitration, competed for monopoly over the practice of arbitration: London, where the old imperial contractual regime still operated; New York, where a new national power emerged that laid claim to world dominance on issues of trade and finance; and Paris, whose originality was to operate on an extraterritorial and completely

[20] Technically, an "arbitration clause" formalizes the decision to submit a dispute to arbiters, once it is identified that it cannot be solved bilaterally; in a "compromissory clause" it is agreed upon ex ante that the qualification of the dispute is not possible.

international basis. In the interwar period, it was unclear which model would become the "conventional" one. Each arbitration organization thus started working slowly, as in the case of Paris-based International Commercial Chamber (ICC): new institutions established facilities, published rules of procedure, formalized how they selected or identified possible arbiters, etc. But they produced very few arbitration cases. Thus, the standardization of contractual knowledge through the establishment of institutional routines proved to take longer than originally planned, as many competing options were identified and tested before one dominant form stabilized.

Sgard explains how the model favored by the Arbitration court established in 1923 by the ICC, which established the legitimacy of a largely extraterritorial model of arbitration, eventually won over the alternative ways of arbitrating cross-border disputes defended in London and New York. To understand how arbitration knowledge was institutionalized in practice, Sgard insists on the specificities of work routines in each organizational culture (London, Paris and New York). Left with little to do in the interwar period in actual matters of arbitration, European law professors and technicians working at the ICC invested their energy in codification, rationalization and textbook production, which gave a very academic tone to the ICC (Gaillard 2008). This work of rationalization led to a quasi-absolute autonomy of the ICC from external political interests – at the cost of its lack of relevance for political or financial interests in the interwar period. The lawyers and law professors working at the ICC emphasized consistency in their principles of arbitration, to the point that when asked to litigate important oil nationalization cases in the 1970s, they were positioned to translate their academic prestige into economic gain and professional credibility: their theories based on codified (although limited) cases created the legal environment that made it possible to translate open-ended arbitration clauses into specific decisions that looked fair.

The emergence of the ICC as the dominant platform for international commercial arbitration should thus be seen as an indication that transnational contracting practices do not always conform to hegemonic theories, which predict that economic and military power always translates into legal and cultural power. Here, it was the most unlikely organization that eventually imposed itself on the market of arbitration – indicating that the field of arbitration started operating with more autonomy than often assumed, and that the professionals in the shadows (from technicians in the ICC performing simple tasks to the arbitrators) successfully imposed themselves in jurisdictional conflicts over their Anglo-American competitors who had market dominance in the fields of trade and finance. The story of how arbitration moved from contractual clauses into institutionalized practice thus points to the importance of processes of autonomization and organizational boundary-policing.

The question of "autonomization" of expert knowledge and issue-specific fields has been quite central within the sociology of professions and the sociology of expertise (Bourdieu 1987; Abbott 1988; Dezalay and Garth 2002). Bourdieuan scholars add to the neo-institutionalist stories of organizational standardization and focus on the accumulation of "social capital" by early promoters of an organizational form, which, they claim, is a key element in the process by which one organizational model becomes professionalized and gains its autonomy from politics. Along these lines, to understand the delayed success of the ICC in the field of international private law, Yves Dezalay and Bryant Garth emphasize the circulation of social capital between the top elite European arbitrators working for the ICC and the American elites who represented big multinational companies and New York-based think tanks and supported the efforts of Parisian law professors. During the interwar period, even though as Sgard points out, elite European professors had little to do as the multipolar system of private arbitration that the ICC aimed to create had not yet asserted its authority over the imperial governance of international trade by British courts, the diverse actors working at the ICC were actively supported by their New York backers. Thus, post-WWII, when European law professors close to the ICC were asked to intervene in the commercial disputes that pitted European and American public and private interests against the Arab nationalized oil companies after the wave of independence wars in the 1960s, they benefited from the high social capital associated with positions of power in their academic field, and the rejection of the British-based model of arbitration, whose imperial roots disqualified it in the eyes of the Arab nations.

Two main processes were thus central to the success of the ICC and the autonomization of the field of arbitration: (1) the mobilization of social capital by ICC practitioners to secure the legitimacy of their one organizational model – the ICC – and then, of its market dominance; (2) the codification and standardization of arbitration principles and modes of evaluation, which turned the knowledge produced in a complex environment and fragmented field into the internal routines and modes of operation of one organization – the ICC. Thanks to these two processes, the ICC and its practitioners achieved in a remarkably small duration of time an extraordinary degree of professionalization and autonomization from market pressures and state politics, and gained legitimacy for the field of arbitration in the face of the state courts, although the latter operate under the authority of a pyramidal system of epistemic authority. These two processes combined also gave the impression that the world of arbitration had moved from the imperial model of governance to a multipolar model characterized by its networked form of horizontal governance organized around transnational peer panels and expert committees. We could also add a third factor that impacts the meta-organizational level of international arbitration: the high degree of market differentiation between the various organizations (ICC, ICSID, etc.), which are in charge of arbitrating various types of contracts (Pauwelyn 2015).

In many ways, this path toward autonomization and depoliticization contrasts with the development of another kind of "arbitration" over the last century: that of sovereign war-based debts – for example those debts that take the form of reparations – which, as illustrated by Germany's reaction to Tsipras' demand to reopen the German reparations file, are still heavily disputed. Here, the story of the reparations committees in the interwar period runs parallel to the story of international arbitration in the ICC, in large part because many of the same players (US bankers and philanthropists, French officials and law professors, etc.) played both games at the same time (in addition, in fact, to playing a third game centered on the regulation of trade through cartels, as Marco Bertilorenzi and Giuseppe Telesca show). The utmost failure in the field of war debt arbitration was surprising, as in the early days of the interwar period there were high hopes that the Reparations Commission set up to arbitrate the claims of each European nation regarding the public debts stemming from WWI would institute a truly international model of global governance based on expert committees, standardized evaluation techniques and peer consensus which could work in relative isolation from partisan politics, and that it would successfully settle claims by Germany, France and others on the amounts of war debts each owed. As Ariel Colonomos and Grégoire Mallard show, the Reparations Commission was in fact a fantastic laboratory where

European law professors and economists experimented with new forms of contractual knowledge. These experts, law professors, bankers and diplomats treated the amount of German reparations and the scheduling of payments as (artificial) adjustment variables that they could manipulate and restructure to avoid all-out currency wars in a context when states threatened to default on their sovereign debt if Germany failed to pay. The Reparations Commission thus anticipated some of the functions and instruments later adopted by the Bretton Woods institutions: in fact, by calculating (and recalculating) the level of reparations that Germany owed its neighbors thanks to standardized macroeconomic instruments (like standardized national accounts for each European country), and by bringing the Americans into the governance of Europe's financial and economic policies (when they were otherwise absent from many of the League Committees), the Reparations Commission sought to institute what looked like an international model of arbitration for public financial (implicit) contracts, which sought to strike a balance between the objectives of reconstruction and macroeconomic stabilization.

In this case, the attempt to institute such a multilateral model of expert governance largely failed. Members of the Reparations Commission may have benefited from the social capital of US bankers and philanthropists, but they lacked a powerful organization that – in a Latourian (1987) twist – could have swallowed the outside world and imposed its interpretive routines and arbitration procedures on sovereign debt defaults: when the French government decided to invade Germany in retaliation for a default in 1924, the Reparations Commission could only lament the decision. Unlike arbitrators involved in private dealings, the experts in the Reparations Commission failed to internalize the meaning of key instruments and concepts – like the legal notion of "collective responsibility," – which became victims of political reinterpretations expressed in the unruly and highly charged political environment of the time by nationalist parties. For Colonomos and Mallard, the massive failure of that specific form of inter-state arbitration left an important legacy, as it left the field with no strong multilateral organization in charge of arbitrating inter-state disputes in similar matters. So it is no surprise that when further disputes erupted about the failure of states and private actors to properly compensate victims – as in the case of the Holocaust era assets scandal –, lawyers (especially US lawyers) threatened to turn to domestic courts to extract new awards for the victims they claimed to represent. Although the cause was grounded on solid moral claims, the fragmentation and politicization of the field of international justice that this episode represented was disquieting. In the absence of a multilateral forum with a standardized procedure, it was New York courts that were asked to decide on an extraterritorial matter – a trend which not only signals the substitution of New York for London as the center of transnational regulation in matters of trade and finance, but also the reproduction of a quasi-imperial understanding of legal regulation on the part of the new hegemon.

These analyses show the necessity for us to separate analytically not only the textual realm of private law contracts and public law contracts (sometimes as implicit contracts, such as those recognized by warring states after the end of a conflict) from the way they are interpreted by the domestic legal fields in which they circulate, but also from the larger set of world historical events which inevitably impact the fields of law in many countries. Separating these different levels of analysis (as represented in Figure 1.1) is essential if we want to produce adequate chronologies of change in regulative fields associated with contractual practice.

This is the task undertaken by Bertilorenzi and Telesca, who ground their Bourdieuan approach to the sociology of elite struggles in financial and industrial fields in a prosopographic methodology: by focusing on the careers of emblematic bankers and industrialists in two successive generations spanning WWI, they explain the resistance to change in the already-autonomous Victorian field of financial regulation in the late 1920s. Their detailed description of the career patterns of elite bankers associated with the reformist nebula close to the ICC, the League's Economic Committee and the French legal field represented in the Reparations Commission, allows us to understand why epochal changes like WWI did not immediately affect formal and informal regulative rules in the highly cosmopolitan field of finance and finance regulation, as these world historical changes were filtered through social organization and struggles between politico-legal elites in Europe's domestic fields of power. As our authors show, it was only with Credit-Anstalt's collapse in 1931 that bankers understood that they could no longer save banks and price junk bonds through informal late-night meetings in the secluded world of London clubs, or in more formal arrangements passed by cartels: new forms of regulation and valuation techniques were badly needed, involving public authorities.[21] This time lag had important consequences: although WWI represented an epochal change for the industry and banking sector, many financiers who had been socialized in the old ways of arranging cross-border trade survived the war, and they believed that informal arrangements (through tacit contracts and honor codes) could just as well regulate the reconstruction of the European economies in the interwar era. As a result, ten years were lost in the reform of financial regulation, and it took until WWII to completely get rid of the Victorian idea that private "ententes" could work more effectively than public forms of state regulation.

Structuring fields: market dominance, differentiation and competition in complex institutional ecologies

Previous chapters show that early conditions in the process of field emergence are extremely important for the course of institutionalization and that the process of "autonomization" of contractual practices is neither incremental, nor continuous, but that it is dependent upon larger socio-political mechanisms (like the circulation of social capital, the standardization of organizational routines and the ecology of organizations competing to shape interpretive norms in the outside environment, etc.). The last three chapters focus on this last, ecological or meta-organizational dimension of the evolution of contractual practices.

Rather than situating themselves at the level of a single organization (like the ICC, the Reparations Commission, the League's Economic Committee, etc.), these chapters focus on the effects produced by the frictions and tensions between various organizations that populate the same field. In their chapter, Gregory Shaffer and Michael Waibel pay specific attention to such ecological factors in the (nongradual) process of legalization of a private and public law of markets. In particular, they pay a great deal of attention to the imbalances created when international organizations that initially pursued complementary

[21] Until then, throughout the 1920s, bankers from the Victorian era mobilized their social capital so as to force their informal rules into an organizational form which effectively worked to avoid the twin perils of inflation and uncontrolled speculation: the cartel was conceived of as an informal price-setting mechanism that was preferable to state controls of prices. In so doing, the elite of High Finance of the Victorian age succeeded in maintaining its monopoly over banking and trade regulation for a good decade after WWI, until the Great Depression really hit Europe.

mandates (like the IMF and the World Trade Organization (WTO)) later moved away from their initial sphere of activity. They show how the decoupling between the statutory objectives of one organization and the practical implementation of these goals by that organization can create imbalances not only for the organization in question, but also for other organizations that populate the same field. Their chapter presents the evolution of regulation at the meta-organizational level as an incomplete process full of uncertainties and contingent setbacks, illustrated by their comparison of how finance on the one hand and trade on the other hand evolved.

The two organizations upon which they focus are the main pillars of the post-WWII economic international order: the IMF, in charge of macro-economic stabilization through currency convertibility controls, and the WTO, which sought to accomplish similar goals through the opening of trade. These functionally differentiated regimes that were designed to evolve together unexpectedly diverged in the 1970s.[22] On the one hand, the rules of the trade regime hardened over time, in the sense that processes of autonomization and judicialization took place especially after the creation of the bi-leveled Dispute Resolution Mechanism of the WTO in the 1990s. This innovation at the level of one organization (the WTO) contributed greatly to the autonomization of international trade law, a subpart of international public law that, before 1914, was both little developed and had limited professional standing among lawyers. The autonomization of trade law translated into the routinization of adjudication rules over commercial disputes and contractual obligations, based on the delegation of interpretation to independent legal experts and quasi-judicial arbiters, whose personal allegiance typically is to the dispute-resolution process per se, or to their own professional community (Alter 2008), rather than to state parties.

On the other hand, the rules of the financial and monetary regime that had been developed by the IMF from the late 1940s onwards weakened rapidly with the gradual collapse of the Bretton Woods system in the 1970s. Since the return to (mostly) floating exchange rates and (generally) free capital movements, we have observed in many respects a process of delegalization of financial regulation, as a consequence of

[22] This comparative focus allows Shaffer and Waibel to take issue with the teleogical view of the evolution of transnational legal regimes in terms of legalization and judicialization (Abbott and Snidal 2000).

a renationalization and fragmentation of these policies. Indeed, just like during the nineteenth century, exchange rates and other instruments affecting the financial wealth of a country are now considered at least nominally as a preserve of sovereign governments – or, in Europe, of the EU institutions. As the IMF lost its jurisdiction over foreign exchange management, it moved in practice toward a twin mandate: first as a macro-economic policy advisor (under the title of "enhanced surveillance"); and second as a crisis manager. Yet, both arms of the IMF remain remarkable today for their very low level of legalization: in practice, since the 1970s, the IMF works exclusively on the basis of internal bylaws, which are at best contingent rules, or indicative signals that may suggest to third parties how it would react in certain conditions. The self-evident drawback is that its intervention in times of crisis tends to be exclusively justified on the basis of informal judgments about the trustworthiness of the debtor, or alternately, the need to control a supposed systemic risk. In this sense, the international legal framework established by the IMF has now been largely unable to produce regularity and predictability: the interpretation of what conditionality clauses – whose reformulation in specific debt contracts is described by Flores Zendejas – mean in practice (as interpreted by the IMF) has clearly moved out of the quasi-legal, contractual envelope into which the League had tried to write it. The impression of informality, the multiplication of ad hoc judgments about the relative ability of such and such nation to reimburse its debt, which are expressed by IMF officials who are not exempt of national prejudices, have increasingly shadowed the IMF's treatment of countries who seek funds outside private markets.

These trends have been prejudicial to the larger goal of regulating financial practices. As Shaffer and Waibel argue, these dual processes of judicialization in trade and delegalization in money and finance have threatened the complementarity between the two international organizations that was originally designed in Bretton Woods, thus adding another source of complexity to the current evolution of contractual knowledge.

The degree of fragmentation which has plagued IFIs since the 1970s has no equivalent in the private regulation of financial defaults: as Bruce Carruthers shows, since the Great Depression most states have delegated to three Credit Rating Agencies (CRAs) the task of valuing all kinds of bonds (including sovereign bonds) so as to avoid market failures due to credit crunches and financial panics. As in the field of private arbitration, the hegemonic reliance on the CRAs' ratings was a product of the interwar period. This practice made sense during the Great Depression, when markets were unable to compute fair prices, as the situation was one of complete uncertainty. And since the Great Depression – at least until the last Greek sovereign debt crisis –, this oligopoly has proved remarkably consistent: states and regional organizations (like the European Central Bank recently) have incorporated into their regulative frameworks an index based on the credits produced by these three CRAs – Moody's, Standard and Poor and Fitch –, so as to predict when and how they should avoid exposing themselves to systemic risk. The private production of ratings and their direct incorporation into banking regulations (regarding the limits that public regulators asked banks to respect in terms of risk) continued without addressing many of its challenges (like the fact that it often proved suboptimal, if not to say completely corrupt, as CRAs are essentially asked to rate their clients, who pay for their services), mostly because it fits with the private sector's strategy to avoid public oversight (Pénet 2014). This trend, although it has posed problems of regulative disempowerment for central banks (Pénet and Mallard 2014), shows that at the meta-organizational level, the three main units have been able to sustain a high level of complementarity, which may be the exception rather than the norm when compared to other regulative fields.

But how was the sustainability of the meta-organizational model achieved for such a long time? Bruce Carruthers shows that the CRAs never limited themselves to their predictive role (e.g. anticipating the risk of default), but that they were constantly associated in diverse activities that bolstered their market centrality: such as in the work of public regulators and contract lawyers. For instance, since the 1970s, when the new markets for derivatives and futures boomed as a result of the uncertainty over the dollar convertibility price, an international association of bankers lobbied to have CRAs' ratings incorporated into the pricing methods commonly used by banks and legal departments to evaluate the worth of collaterals in the exchange of over-the-counter (OTC) derivatives. Industry representatives produced model contracts, which addressed problems of legal uncertainty due to the cross-border type of exchange[23] by asking trading partners to post some value as

[23] Here again, because of the global nature of these new markets – which concern big international banks that trade options on the future convertibility prices between currencies –, they are characterized by a high level of uncertainty: often, one firm located in country W will bet

collateral, whose price was dependent upon the CRA's grades. The jurisdiction over the computation of that price, which is essential to the "collateral knowledge" analyzed by Annelise Riles, has since then been retained by three CRAs that already controlled the predictions upon which public authorities based their regulation of banking practices.[24] This chapter thus highlights the resistance to change when organizations are in a situation of oligopoly. It confirms that a field of practice in which a few dominant organizations agree not to seek complete monopoly but rather, to look for new jurisdictional prerogatives for the field itself – for example for themselves – can prevent change from happening despite systemic shocks (like the 2008 crisis for which CRAs have been blamed).

This story of the standardization of valuing techniques and codification of rules at the meta-organizational level is complemented by the last chapter of our book, in which Susan Block-Lieb and Terence Halliday narrate the little-known history of ex ante codification of contractual law. As they show, the codifying practices of international contract law have moved in the long twentieth century within a complex and changing ecology of international organizations, states and expert groups. Each of these groups mobilized different kinds of resources to claim jurisdictional authority over new terrains of legal work within a more or less globalized market economy. Here again, the League created the first organization (UNIDROIT) largely made up of European professors. After having remained largely dormant until the 1960s, it was awakened by the creation of alternative and competing international organizations, which pushed for contractual law reform as a result of decolonization and the rise of new oil powers – UNCTAD and UNCITRAL (Rajagopal 2003). This competition for jurisdictional hegemony (Abbott 1988) paradoxically resulted in some measure of "autonomization" of the field: UNIDROIT de facto became unsubordinated after WWII, as jurisdictional fights resulted in market segmentation among the main players. Thus, interestingly, the institutions that

on future prices of convertibility rates between currencies of countries X and Y with a financial institution located in country Z.

24 As Annelise Riles (2010) showed, the payment of a collateral is often included in contracts, especially one that involves cross-border exchange of values, as such payment mitigates the risk that the contract will not be honored in the future: the payment of a collateral is a way to agree ex ante on the price of the penalty for contractual breach, and to avoid going to court or to an arbiter in case of contractual violation.

were themselves in charge of creating some coherence in the international system (those which claimed authority over either unification or harmonization) have been increasingly competing with one another – but they were able, in a manner that is a bit different from the oligopolistic model followed by CRAs in the market of financial valuation, to agree to a seemingly long-lasting settlement based on market differentiation.

CONCLUSION

This book presents a complex picture of the evolution of the legal landscape of international governance over the long twentieth century; and in so doing it also highlights multiple processes of institutionalization and autonomization of this field that have remained remarkably unnoticed. The chapters of this book look at the many instabilities and incoherences that have existed after 1920 within and across multiple overlapping regimes-in-formation, and the failed attempts at substituting new forms of governance to Britain's weakened global rule over trade and finance. We concentrate on the innovations, experiments or attempted reforms formulated by a wide range of experts, statesmen, industrial cartels and globalized trade unions. Thus, our focus is on the strategies, perceptions and the values of individual agents (not just diplomats and statesmen) as they establish contracts, or help others to contract, across borders, in a world that has been and remains confused and unstable. We examine how social capital has circulated within and between networks of industrialists, policy experts, bankers, international public lawyers and private lobbyists, who all have had an interest in shaping the letter of the law and the boundaries of the legal field. Understanding how the law was envisaged, practiced and fought for in a wide range of international milieus, and explaining how these legal practices evolve over time, is a key ambition of all of the contributors to this volume.

Out of a split landscape, marked by the initial contrast between international public law and English private or commercial law, and their gradual convergence in the interwar period, the overall picture that emerges is one of a gradual process of autonomization and fragmentation, which in many ways complements the vision that international law scholars have of the evolution of this field of practice over the last century. But as we find, master-narratives that put emphasis on post-1970s fragmentation over the postwar consolidation are too simplistic: they miss, for instance, that in some areas the first signals of fragmentation appeared in fact very soon, during the first years of the League, while in other areas, fragmentation only dates from the early 2000s. Detailed analyses which describe and explain the successful or failed attempts to create order out of this meta-organizational mess add nuance to this vision of a fragmented and opaque world: the evolution of contractual knowledge is sometimes managed and stabilized by the creation of oligopolistic cartels (in the case of contractual valuation techniques), or market differentiation among organizations (in the cases of international arbitration and codification).

On this count, the British and American centuries seem more different than similar, though nothing supports at this point the effect of opposite political designs. What appears significant is the move from the interwar period toward a more fractured political scene, where one nation, even one as strong as the United States, can no longer single-handedly write the law of global markets; even the global liberal West could not maintain dominance once newly-independent nations entered the multilateral organization it had created. The result, after a century of legal experimentation in global markets, is a mass of treaties, bargains, extraterritorial fora, private bodies and transnational normmakers who invest resources, social capital and ingenuity in building up new institutions and new jurisdictions. At last, observing how the legal environment of contractual and institutional practices that facilitated such opening of markets evolved allows us to describe and speculate about the nature of the evolving ontology that is called international *private* law or, preferably, what we call here the law of international markets – as it also extends to public law matters as well. Beyond these sketches of an early move toward the *deformalization* of international law, which has been accentuated since 1980, lies a more substantive discussion about legal history that still has traction today: about the exact definition, consistency and impact of the international law of markets that was invented after WWI in a context still dominated by the colonial or imperial mindset, and which still haunts our political reflections about the present-day system of global governance.

References

Abbott, Andrew. 1988. *The system of professions: An essay on the division of expert labor*. Chicago, IL: University of Chicago Press.

Abbott, Kenneth W., and Duncan Snidal. 2000. "Hard Law and Soft Law in International Governance." *International Organization*. 54(3): 421–56.

Abdelal, Rawi. 2010. *Capital Rules: The Construction of Global Finance*. Cambridge, MA: Harvard University Press.

Alessandro, Michele d'. 2013. "Global Economic Governance and the Private Sector. The League of Nations's Experiment in the 1920s." In Christof Dejung and Niels P. Petersson (eds). *The Foundations of Worldwide Economic Integration. Power, Institutions, and Global Markets, 1850–1930*. Cambridge: Cambridge University Press. pp. 89–111.

Alter, Karen and Sophie Meunier. 2009. "The Politics of Regime Complexity." *Perspectives on Politics*. 7(1): 13–24.

Alter, Karen. 2008. "Agent or Trustee: International Courts in their Political Context." *European Journal of International Relations*. 14(1): 33–63.

Anghie, Antony. 2007. *Imperialism, Sovereignty and the Making of International Law*. Cambridge: Cambridge University Press.

Arendt, Hannah. 1951. *Imperialism: The Origins of Totalitarianism (2)*. New York: Harcourt.

Arrighi, Giovani. 2010. *The Long Twentieth Century: Money, Power and the Origins of Our Times*. New York: Verso.

Badie, Bertrand. 1999. "Un monde sans souveraineté." *Les Etats entre ruse et responsabilité*. Paris: Fayard.

Barker, A. 1917. *The British Corn Trade*. London: Isaac Pitman & Sons.

Benton, Lauren. 2002. *Law and Colonial Cultures: Legal Regimes in World History*. 140–1900. Cambridge: Cambridge University Press.

Benvenisti, Eyal, and George Downs. 2007. "The Empire's New Clothes: Political Economy and the Fragmentation of International Law." *The Stanford Law Review*. 60(2): 595–632.

Bernardini, Bruno. 2007. *Le principe d'obligation*. Paris: Vrin.

Bernstein, L. 1992. "Opting out of the legal system: extralegal contractual relations in the diamond industry." *Journal of Legal Studies*. 21(January):115–57.

Bordo, Michael D., Alan M. Taylor and Jeffrey G. Williamson (eds). 2003. *Globalization in Historical Perspective*. Chicago: NBER/ The University of Chicago Press.

Bourdieu, Pierre. 1987. "The Force of Law: Toward a Sociology of the Juridical Field." *Hastings Law Journal*. 38: 9–14.

Braudel, Fernand. 1992. *The Wheels of Commerce*. Berkeley: University of California Press.

Briggs, W. 1906. *The Law of International Copyright*. London: Stevens and Haynes. 850 pages.

Busch, Marc. 2007. "Overlapping Institutions, Forum Shopping, and Dispute Settlement in International Trade." *International Organization*. 61(4): 735–61.

Byers, Michael. 2003. "Introduction: the complexities of foundational change." In Michael Byers and Georg Nolte (eds). *United States Hegemony and the Foundations of International law*. Cambridge: Cambridge University Press. pp. 1–22.

Callon, Michel. 1998. "Introduction: The Embeddedness of Economic Markets in Economics." In Michael Callon (ed). *The Laws of the Markets*. Oxford: Blackwell. pp. 1–57.

Callon, Michel and Fabian Muniesa. 2005. "Peripheral Vision: Economic Markets as Calculative Collective Devices." *Organization Studies*. 26(8): 1229–50.

Clavin, Patricia. 2013. Securing the World Economy. *The Reinvention of the League of Nations, 1920–1946*. Oxford: Oxford University Press. 395 pages.

Clavin, Patricia, and Jensè-Wilhelm Wessels. 2005. "Transnationalism and the League of Nations: Understanding the Work of Its Economic and Financial Organisation." *Contemporary European History*. 14(4): 465–92.

Cohen, Antonin, and Antoine Vauchez. 2007. "Introduction: Law, Lawyers, and Transnational Politics in the Production of Europe. A Symposium." *Law and Social Inquiry*. 32(1): 75–82.

Committee on the Enforcement of Judgments and Awards. 1919. *Report to the Lord Chancellor*. London: HMSO.

Dezalay, Yves, and Bryant Garth. 1996. *Dealing in virtue: international Commercial Arbitration and the Construction of a Transnational Legal Order*. Chicago: Chicago University Press.

2002. *The Internationalization of Palace Wars: Lawyers, Economists, and the Contest to Transform Latin American States*. Chicago: University of Chicago Press.

Drezner, Daniel. 2009. "The Power and Peril of International Regime Complexity." *Perspectives on Politics*. 7(1): 65–70.

Ellison, Thomas. 1886. *The cotton trade of Great Britain*. London: Effingham Wilson. 362 pages.

Finnemore, Martha. 2003. *The Purpose of Interventions: Changing Ideas About the Use of Force*. Cornell: Cornell University Press.

Fiore, Pasquale. 1875. *Droit International privé*. Paris: Durand et Pedone-Lauriel.

Flandreau, Marc. 2013. "Sovereign states, bondholders committees, and the London Stock Exchange in the Nineteenth century (1827–68): New facts and old fictions." *Oxford Review of Economic Policy*. 29(4): 668–96.

Flandreau, Marc, and Juan Flores. 2012. "Bondholders vs Bondsellers: Investment Banks and Conditionality Lending in the London Market for Foreign Government Debt, 1815–1913." *European Review of Economic History*. 16(4): 356–83.

Foucault, Michel. 1979. *Discipline and Punish: The Birth of the Prison*. New York: Vintage.

Freyer, Tony. 2006. *Anti-trust and global capitalism*, 1930–2004. Cambridge: Cambridge University Press.

Gaillard, Emmanuel. 2008. *Aspects philosophiques du droit de l'arbitrage international*. La Haye: Martinus Nijhoff.

Geertz, Clifford. 1973. *The Interpretation of Cultures: Selected Essays*. New York: Basic Books.

Grewe, Wilhelm G. 2000. *The Epochs of International Law*. New York: de Gruyter.

Gulati, Mitu, and Robert E. Scott. 2013. *The Three and a Half Minute Transaction: Boilerplate and the Limits of Contract Design*. Chicago: University of Chicago Press.

Halliday, Terence C., and Bruce G. Carruthers. 2007. "The Recursivity of Law: Global Norm Making and National Lawmaking in the Globalization of Corporate Insolvency Regimes." *American Journal of Sociology*. 112(4): 1135–202.

Halliday, Terence C., and Gregory Shaffer. 2015. *Transnational Legal Orders*. New York: Cambridge University Press.

Henig, Ruth. 2000. "Britain, France and the League of Nations in the 1920s." In Sharp A. and Glyn Stone (eds). *Anglo-French Relations in the Twentieth Century*. London: Routledge, pp. 139–57.

Horwitz, Morton J. 1982. "The History of the Public/ Private Distinction." *University of Pennsylvania Law Review*. 130(6): 1423–8.

Institut de Droit International. 1920. *Tableau Général des Travaux* (1873–1913). New York: Oxford University Press. 366 pages.

International Law Commission. 2006. "Fragmentation of International Law: Difficulties Arising from the Diversification and Expansion of International Law." http://legal.un.org/ilc/documentation/english/a_cn4_l682.pdf

Joel, Paul R. 1988. "The Isolation of Private International Law." *Wisconsin International Law Journal*. 7: 149–78.

Kennedy, David. 1994. "The International Style of Postwar Law and Policy: John Jackson and the Field of International Economic Law." *American University International Law Review*. 10(2): 671–716.

1996. "International Law and the Nineteenth Century: History of an Illusion." *Nordic Journal of International Law*. 65: 385–420.

2013. "Law and the Political Economy of the World." *Leiden Journal of International Law*. 26: 7–48.

Kennedy, Duncan. 2006. "Three Globalizations of Law and Legal Thought: 1850–2000." In David Trubek and Alvaro Santos (eds). *The New Law and Economic Development. A Critical Appraisal*. Cambridge, Cambridge University Press. pp. 19–73.

Keohane, Robert O., Andrew Moravcsik, and Anne-Marie Slaughter. 2000. "Legalized Dispute Resolution: Interstate and Transnational." *International Organization*. 54(3): 457–88.

Kindleberger, Charles P. 1986. *The World in Depression: 1929–1939*. Berkeley: University of California Press.

Knorr Cetina, Karin. 1997. "Sociality with Objects: Social Relations in Post-social Knowledge Societies." *Theory, Culture and Society*. 14: 1–30.

Koskenniemi, Martti. 1997. "Hierarchy in International Law, A Sketch." *European Journal International Law*. 8: 566–82.

2001. *The Gentle Civilizer of Nations, The Rise and Fall of International Law* 1870–1960. Cambridge: Cambridge University Press. 567 pages.

2007. "Constitutionalism as Mindset: Reflections on Kantian Themes About International Law and Globalization." *Theoretical Inquiry into Law*. 8(1): 10–36.

Krasner, Stephen. 1999. *Sovereignty: Organized Hypocrisy*. Princeton, NJ: Princeton University Press.

Krisch, Nico. 2003. "More equal than the rest? Hierarchy, equality and US predominance in international law." In Michael Byers and Georg Nolte (eds). *United States Hegemony and the Foundations of International Law*. Cambridge: Cambridge University Press. pp. 135–75.

Latour, Bruno. 1987. *Science in Action: How to Follow Scientists and Engineers through Society*. Cambridge, MA: Harvard University Press.

2004. "Whose Cosmos, Which Cosmopolitics? Comments of the Peace Terms of Ulrich Beck." *Common Knowledge*. 10(3): 450–62.

Latour, Bruno, and Steve Woolgar. 1979. *Laboratory life: The social construction of scientific facts*. Beverly Hills, CA: Sage Publications.

Lepinay, Vincent. 2011. *Codes of Finance: Engineering Derivatives in a Global Bank*. Princeton, NJ: Princeton University Press.

Mallard, Grégoire. 2011. "The Gift Revisited: Marcel Mauss on War, Debt and the Politics of Reparations." *Sociological Theory*. 29(4): 225–47.

2014. *Fallout: Nuclear Diplomacy in an Age of Global Fracture*. Chicago: Chicago University Press.

Mazower, Mark. 2010. *No Enchanted Palace: The End of Empire and the Ideological Origins of the United Nation*. Princeton, NJ: Princeton University Press.

2012. *Governing the World, The History of an Idea*. New York: The Penguin Press.

Meyer, John, John Boli, G. Thomas, Francesco Ramirez. 1997. "World Society and the Nation State." *American Journal of Sociology*. 103(1): 144–81.

Mills, Alex. 2006. "The Private History of International Law." *International and Comparative Law Quarterly*. 55(1): 1–50.

Morgenthau, Hans J. 1960. *Politics Among Nations*. New York: Alfred A. Knopf.

Nicolaidis, Kalypso, and Gregory Shaffer. 2005. "Transnational Mutual Recognition Regimes: Governance without Global Government." *Law and Contemporary Problems*. 68(3–4): 263–318.

North, Douglass. 1990. *Institutions, Institutional Change and Economic Performance*. Cambridge: Cambridge University Press.

O' Brien, Patrick Karl. 2002. "The Pax Britannica and American Hegemony: Precedent, Antecedent or Just Another History?" In P.K. O'Brien and A. Clesse (eds). *Two Hegemonies. Britain 1846–1914 and the United States 1941–2001*. London: Ashgate. pp. 3–64.

O' Rourke, Kevin H., and Jeffrey G. Williamson. 2000. *Globalization and History, The Evolution of a Nineteenth-Century Atlantic Economy*. Cambridge, MA: MIT Press.

Pataille, J. and Alberto Huguet. 1855. *Code international de la propriété intellectuelle, artistique et littéraire*. Paris: Marescqet Dujardin. 364 pages.

Pauly, Louis. 1996. "The League of Nations and the Foreshadowing of the International Monetary Fund." *Essays in International Finance*. (201) pp. 1–47. Princeton, NJ: Princeton University.

Pauwelyn, Joost. 2015. "WTO Panelists Are From Mars, ICSID Arbitrators are From Venus." Geneva: Graduate Institute. http://papers.ssrn.com/sol3/papers.cfm?abstract_id=2549050

Pénet, Pierre. 2014. "Governing Risk in Times of Crisis: The Role of Credit Ratings in Regulatory Reasoning." Dissertation Defended at Northwestern University. Evanston, IL.

Pénet, Pierre, and Grégoire Mallard. 2014. "From Risk Models to Loan Contracts: Austerity as the Continuation of Calculation by Other Means." *Journal of Critical Globalization Studies*. 7: 4–50.

Petersson, Niels P. 2013. "Legal Institutions and the World Economy, 1900–1930." In Christof Dejung and Niels P. Petersson (eds). *The Foundations of Worldwide Economic Integration. Power, Institutions, and Global Markets, 1850–1930*. Cambridge: Cambridge University Press. pp. 21–39.

Quatremer, Jean. 2015. "Greece vs. Eurozone." *Libération*. Accessed on March 15, 2015, http://bruxelles.blogs.liberation.fr/2015/03/12/grece-vs-eurozone-histoire-secrete-dun-bras-de-fer-1/

Rajagopal, Balakrishnan. 2003. *International Law from Below: Development, Social Movements and Third World Resistance*. New York: Cambridge University Press.

Riles, Annelise. 2010. "Collateral Expertise: Legal Knowledge in the Global Financial Markets." *Current Anthropology*. 51(6): 795–818.

2011. *Collateral Knowledge: Legal Reasoning in Global Financial Markets.* Chicago: University of Chicago Press.

Rousseau, Jean-Jacques. [1762]1971. *Du contrat social: précédé du Discours sur les sciences et les arts. Presented by Roger-Gérard Schwartzenberg. Paris:* Seghers.

Ruggie, John G. 2004. "Reconstituting the Global Public Domain – Issues, Actors, and Practices." *The European Journal of International Relations.* 10: 499–531.

Schmitt, Carl. 2003[1950]. *The Nomos of the Earth in the International Law of the Jus Publicum Europeaum.* New York: Telos Press.

Shaffer, Gregory, and Mark Pollack. 2010. "Hard vs. Soft Law: Alternatives, Complements and Antagonists in International Governance." *Minnesota Law Review.* 94: 706–97.

Slaughter, Anne-Marie, 2000. "Judicial Globalization." *Virginia Journal of International Law.* 40.

Sgard, Jérôme. 2006. "Do legal origins matter? The case of bankruptcy laws in Europe 1808–1914." *European Review of Economic History.* 3: 389–419.

Spalding, William F. 1926. *The Finance of Foreign Trade.* London: Sir Isaac Pitman and sons.

Stone Sweet, Alec. 1994. "What is Supranational Constitution? An Essay in International Relations Theory." *The Review of Politics.* 56(3): 441–74.

1999. "Judicialization and the Construction of Governance." *Comparative Political Studies.* 32(2): 147–84.

2009. "Constitutionalism, Legal Pluralism, and International Regime." *Indiana Journal of Global Legal Studies.* 16(2): 621–45.

Teubner, Gunther. 1996. "Global Bukowina: Legal Pluralism in the World-Society." In Gunther Teubner (ed). *Global Law Without a State.* London: Dartsmouth.

Teubner Gunther, and Anna Beckers. 2013. "Expanding Constitutionalism." *Indiana Journal of Global Legal Studies.* 20(2): 523–50.

Tooze, Adam. 2014. *The Deluge: The Great War, America and the Remaking of Global Order* 1916–1931. London: Viking.

Tsipras, Alexis. 2015. "Discours au parlement européen." Accessed on March 20, 2015. https://entreleslignesentrelesmots.wordpress.com/2015/03/12/discours-da-tsipras-sur-les-reparations-allemandes/

Vauchez, Antoine. 2013. *L'Union par le droit: L'invention d'un programme institutionnel pour l'Europe.* Paris: Presses de Sciences Po.

Wallerstein, Immanuel. 2011. *Historical Capitalism with Capitalist Civilization.* New York: Verso.

Weber, Max. 1978[1922]. "Emergence and Creation of Legal Norms." In *Max Weber, Economy and Society*, v.2. Translated by Guenther Roth. Berkeley: University of California Press. pp. 743–68.

Westlake, John. 1880. *A Treatise on International Private Law*. London: William Maxwell & Sons. 340 pages.

Zimmern, Alfred. 1936. *The League of Nations and the Rule of Law, 1918–1935*. London: Macmillan and Co. 527 pages.

PART ONE

CONTRACTS AND SOVEREIGN DEBT OBLIGATIONS: THE EVOLUTION OF CONTRACTUAL PROVISIONS

CHAPTER TWO

FINANCIAL MARKETS, INTERNATIONAL ORGANIZATIONS AND CONDITIONAL LENDING: A LONG-TERM PERSPECTIVE

Juan H. Flores Zendejas

Contractual practices in the field of sovereign debt management have a long history. The willingness of governments in financial distress to adopt public policies or other measures agreed upon in sovereign debt contracts in exchange for new lines of credit has varied over time. The recent European debt crisis has brought the thorny debate about the infringements upon national sovereignty that are associated with "conditional lending" to the forefront. While this crisis remains unique in that its causes are related to potential loopholes in the monetary union structure, nevertheless raises relevant issues regarding the relationship between national governments, international financial institutions (IFIs), and global financial markets. Indeed, the main institutions involved in the sovereign debt crisis management, located in Brussels (European Commission), Frankfurt (European Central Bank), and Washington (the IMF), have strongly advocated that the provision of financial support be conditioned upon banking sector reforms, debt restructuring and fiscal austerity.

Although still controversial, the incorporation of "conditionality" clauses – defined as the implementation of specific policies in order to obtain financial assistance (Dreher 2009) – into sovereign debt contracts is not new. Throughout the post-World War II period, when states faced limited access to private financial markets, IFIs provided financial support through emergency loans, requiring debtor states to adopt specific economic policies and oversight structures built with the purpose of monitoring the implementation of their commitments. While this had been the case during balance of payments crises, since the

1970s, conditional lending has been primarily associated with sovereign defaults.

This paper aims to provide a historical insight into past experiences of conditional lending in sovereign debt contracts.[1] It shows that the history of conditional external lending first emerged in early nineteenth century financial markets. This practice was related to predominantly primary market access that was strongly controlled by two entities. First, an institutional authority established a set of requirements that borrowers were expected to meet to have access to liquidity. Second, financial intermediaries developed the means and capacity to exclude, de facto, a borrower that would not comply with the conditions set in the contract. The management of sovereign defaults was framed by these two actors who could condition market access to the resumption of debt service. Averting further future defaults could incite financial intermediaries to extend the condition of no-default to economic policies related with fiscal and monetary issues. Governments in creditor countries would occasionally intervene and, in certain cases, conditionality could be further enforced by coercive measures such as external fiscal control. The existing breakthroughs in the twentieth century, in particular, the emergence of multilateral organizations, legitimized and spread these practices without modifying the basic principles that were put in place in the nineteenth century.

This paper has a chronological framework and is structured as follows. In the first section, I present various cases of conditional lending in the nineteenth century. It emphasizes the processes and historical contexts that led to the inclusion of conditions in sovereign debt contracts. I further discuss the case of conditionality in the case of sovereign defaults during the 1890s, a decade that saw a wave of defaults affect the volume of capital flows from London. The main defaults of this decade were settled through final agreements which included conditions related with economic policies and in one case the imposition of an international commission of foreign control.

Section II addresses one of the major institutional innovations in terms of conditional lending, which was the League of Nations' Economic and Financial organisation. This multilateral public entity mainly dealt with the reconstruction of Central and Eastern Europe

[1] In that regard, I am grateful to archivists at ING Baring, the League of Nations Archive, the Rothschild Archives, Hambro, IMF Archives, the Bank of England Archives and JP Morgan Library and Museum – here is also the place to thank the Swiss National Science Foundation for its financial support.

countries in the 1920s. It attempted to attract external funds to these countries, as it did not have any financial assets that it could loan itself. The League therefore promoted so-called "League Loans," which were issued in coordination with underwriting banks and, when necessary, with the governments that guaranteed the loan. In doing so, the League also acted as a financial intermediary. The implementation of "stabilization programs," under a close monitoring system organized by the League, was the major condition *sine qua non* a borrowing country could maintain the League's support. Finally, the League also incorporated other non-market roles, which formalized forms of coordination between creditor countries' governments, by using a contractual practice that was pioneered in the nineteenth century. In the third section, the paper presents contrasts between these historic practices of conditional lending and those that have been developed since 1953 by the IMF. While the latter has only indirectly adopted a certification role that would allow governments to have access to external finance, it has predominantly focused on managing sovereign debt crises, particularly those that have taken place after the onset of the 1982 Mexican crisis. This paper shows that unlike the League, the IMF has switched its focus from conditional lending in primary markets to one in which it has emphasized the need for a lender of last resort when sovereign defaults constitute a real threat.

By tracing the long-term evolution of the practices of financial intermediaries, creditor governments, and IFIs associated with conditional lending, this paper helps us identify these contractual practices that have been put in place in recent decades. While enforcement mechanisms may differ in degree, IFIs today have tools that were absent in historical cases of conditional lending. This paper examines the historical role of the League of Nations in the construction of the world economy and positively assesses these attempts. Previous works have argued that the League failed because it could not halt the slide into the Great Depression and war (Pauly 2003; Schuker 2003), which were associated with a wave of defaults on the League loans in the 1930s. Similarly, the IMF has been criticized for imposing economic regimes that lead to low rates of economic growth and continued dependence on external funds. In fact, most policy evaluations of conditional lending have concentrated on the *ex post* handling of financial and economic crises by IFIs. This paper claims that focus on *ex post* effects is too narrow to give an accurate picture of the effects of contractual practices promoted by IFIs such as the League. If the IMF were judged according to the same criteria as the League, it would be considered a failure, as it has neither prevented the breakdown of the Bretton-Woods system, nor the defaults of the 1980s and the 1990s and the slide into the new Great Recession. In contrast, this paper shifts the focus on IFIs and conditional lending to the *ex-ante* role of IFIs as a facilitator in the development of financial markets. It shows the important role IFIs played in establishing the formal contractual framework of international cooperation between governments and private agents that ultimately restored international capital flows during both the 1920s and in the post-WWII period.

THE CONSTRUCTION OF CONDITIONALITY: LIGHTS AND SHADOWS OF THE LONG NINETEENTH CENTURY

Institutions, market actors and early experiences of conditionality

Conditional lending existed in the early nineteenth century and perhaps even before. During this period, the London Stock Exchange (LSE) acquired a new relevance in the sovereign debt market. The LSE held the authority to veto the listing of new securities on the exchange, thereby cutting off access to the capital market.[2] This veto would arise in cases of bonds issued by a defaulting government, where a satisfactory arrangement with bondholders had not been reached. In practice, the LSE emerged as an Arbitration Court and triggered the formation of a system that mirrored today's collective action clauses, where majority agreements among bondholders are encouraged (Flandreau 2013).[3]

This "non-default" clause was therefore a generic, institutional condition that served as a dispute solution mechanism between borrowing governments and bondholders. Nevertheless, other cases occasionally appeared in the sphere of primary capital markets that led to the inclusion of conditions in sovereign debt contracts that corresponded to the interests of certain market actors. The agents in charge of imposing such conditions on international loans were mostly underwriting banks and creditor governments.[4] The reasons for direct intervention of creditor

[2] On the listing requirements established by the LSE, see Neal and Davis (2006).

[3] While exchanges have ceased to be functional today, they nevertheless have a certain capacity to inflict reputation penalties on sovereign borrowers, acting thus as an additional enforcement device (Weidemaier and Gulati 2014).

[4] Yafeh and Sussman (2003: 25) report some cases in which the Corporation of Foreign Bondholders offered advice on economic policies and sought to impose conditions related to fiscal sustainability, though they described this experience as mostly unsuccessful.

governments (Great Britain and France, in particular) in the sovereign debt markets were diverse. Often the type of conditionality that accompanied those historical cases involved imposing foreign control on fiscal and monetary policies, along with a debt restructuring that was favorable to bondholders and without the issuance of new funds.[5] One line of historiography remains skeptical of the role of sovereign debt disputes – whether sovereign defaults or debt repudiation – as the main factor that encouraged the creditor- government activism. Certain scholars explain such activism as evoking geopolitical issues constituted by so-called "gunboat diplomacy" that was part of the colonial expansion that took place in the nineteenth century.[6] In contrast, the conditions negotiated between borrowing sovereign governments and underwriting banks were embedded in a systematic procedure of sovereign debt contracting. These conditions could be included in the debt contracts signed by borrowing governments. In most cases, the enforcement was structured through a monitoring mechanism – often through permanent agents sent by underwriting banks to borrowing countries – that coordinated the gradual release of loan funds upon compliance with the agreed-upon conditions (Liedtke 2008; Flores 2012).

One early instance of this procedure, reported by Flandreau and Flores (2012a), is a 1832 Belgian loan. During the Belgian revolution of 1830, wherein the country emancipated from the Netherlands, the Rothschild Bank succeeded in including a clause in the loan contract signed by the Belgian government that committed Belgium to respect the peace agreement signed at the London conference (an international parlay group) and abandon its claims for further territorial expansion. The enforcement mechanism was market-induced, to the extent that Rothschild was a dominant player in international finance – its market shares during the early nineteenth century were, on an average, around 60 percent[7] – could determine the terms, the amount, and the time when the funds would be available to borrowing governments.[8] Historical evidence shows that the Belgian government sought alternative

[5] The case where additional funds were envisaged is described below.

[6] Platt (1968) describes this in the case of Great Britain, and Rosenberg (1999) analyzes the case of the US Tomz (2007) looks at the case study of Argentina.

[7] Precise figures in subperiods of the nineteenth century can be found in Flandreau et al. (2010).

[8] On the other hand, Rothschild and other prestigious merchant banks in London developed a business model where reputation was essential. While the system evokes today's originate-to-distribute practice, the willingness to keep market shares and extract the consequential rents related to market power meant that these banks were interested in maintaining a positive record for the loans they issued. See Flandreau and Flores (2009, 2012b).

financial possibilities – the exit option – appealing to two minor, forced internal loans in October 1830, though these were insufficient to meet the needs of the treasury (Gille 1965).[9]

Rothschild's successful experience was, nevertheless, exceptional throughout the nineteenth century and no other serious attempt to explicitly require conditions on new loans were included until 1898.[10] Rothschild's subsequent record as default manager, which often required more proactive reactions from defaulting governments, was rather negative. When the bank attempted to provide solutions for the partial defaults of Austria and Italy – both governments had introduced a tax on coupon payments of their external loans in 1868 (Fenn 1883; Gille 1965) – Rothschild could not convince them to withdraw this new imposition. Austria's bonds were banned from the LSE after bondholders complained, and remained so until the Hungarian government, having gained autonomy from Austria, reached an agreement in 1871 that allowed it to issue a new loan. Rothschild's failure as default manager was not unique. Baring had also been very active in the cases of Mexico, Venezuela, and Argentina during the first half of the nineteenth century, but it obtained mixed results partly due to the banks' reluctance to commit new funds to these countries.[11]

The case of conditional lending by creditor governments was different in forms though not in the outcomes. The British government, for instance, granted explicit guarantees to the loans issued by sovereign governments, as in the cases of Greece (1833, 1896) and Turkey (1855), all of which led to a reduction in the costs associated with these loans. In return, borrowers were expected to provide the necessary insurances and attach pledges to the loans, and even, if necessary, to accept third party control and monitoring of public expenditure.[12] In the case of the 1833 Greek loan, even though there had been no explicit conditions originally requested, Greece's repayment difficulties and the need for further advances urged the British government (along with the other

[9] I am grateful to Stefano Ugolini for providing details on these domestic loans.

[10] This assertion should be qualified, as it is based on the revision of debt contracts from the archives of certain banks in London and Paris and from the prospectuses published in British Newspapers, such as *The Times*. It could have been that banks had attempted but failed to include conditional clauses in their underwriting contracts, though we have not made a thorough revision of debt contract drafts.

[11] See Costeloe (2003) for the case of Mexico, Dawson (1992) for Venezuela and Ferns (1992) for Argentina.

[12] See Esteves and Coskun Tuncer (2014) on a pricing analysis of the guaranteed loans by the British government during the nineteenth century.

guaranteeing governments, France and Russia), to impose new pledges and controls on public expenditure. None of these measures, however, prompted the Greek government to resume payments.[13]

A similar episode involved present-day Turkey, whose loan was jointly guaranteed by the governments of Britain and France to support the Ottoman Empire in its joint war against Russia. The original convention between the guaranteeing governments and the Ottoman Empire did not explicitly include any condition clauses, though it was stated that the loan would enable "His Imperial Majesty to prosecute with vigour the war against Russia."[14] The contract signed between the government and Rothschild, who thereafter underwrote the loan did not include any condition clauses either. This can be explained by the limited role Rothschild assumed, as the bank was merely in charge of receiving the subscriptions at the time of the public offering.[15] On the other hand, the Bank of England was responsible for administrating funds and establishing a commission that monitored the Turkish public finances. A second agreement, signed between Britain and Turkey, determined the terms and conditions of this commission, though the effectiveness of this procedure failed. The state of the Ottoman Empire's public finances, which had been meandering even before the war, never recovered and the government defaulted in 1876 (Anderson 1964).[16]

The case of sovereign defaults in the late nineteenth century

Despite the reversals suffered by merchant banks as default managers, some of these banks were obligated to assume this role, particularly when a defaulting country was willing to issue a new loan – for which banks earned underwriting fees – and was obligated to fill the requirement of no-default from the LSE. However, most of these banks were either unable or unwilling to condition the loans that they underwrote

[13] The pledges and monitoring devices were agreed upon in a convention signed between Russia, Britain, France, and Greece on September 1843. A new Greek government refused to ratify the convention (Wynne 1951). The convention is published in De Martens (1898).

[14] Bank of England Archives, 13A84/7/4, "Imperial Ottoman Guaranteed Loan 1855."

[15] Rothschild contract with Constantine Musurus Rey, as representative for the government of the Ottoman Empire. (20 August, 1855). A supplementary agreement between that government and the Bank of England determined that the Bank was the payment agent for the loan. The Rothschild Archives, file 000/401B/15.

[16] Lengthy negotiations followed the default before settlement in 1881, which resulted in a more active foreign participation in Turkey's public finances, whereby creditor governments and different bondholders groups participated. Pamuk (1987: 56) suggests that this agreement was part of a longer process of "imperialist penetration short of *de jure* colonialism." While there is an abundant literature that analyzes the link between sovereign debt and colonial expansion, this issue goes beyond the scope of this chapter and is not considered in the present analysis.

on economic policies or any other government action that would avert future defaults.[17] Even in the cases where this was attempted, the nineteenth century, for the most part, represented a history of failed enforcements of policy commitments. During the 1890s, three bailouts on behalf of foreign governments were organized solely by financial intermediaries with attached conditions on fiscal and monetary policies. The 1890 Rothschild committee bailout for Argentina was followed by the 1893 Hambro loan for Greece and some years later by the 1898 Funding loan for Brazil, organized by Rothschild (Flores 2012).[18] In all the three cases, the conditions of the loans aimed at improving the solvability position of the borrowers. However, the results of these experiences were rather disappointing, as the financial position of these governments never stabilized, leading to a lack of compliance.

Argentina's bailout in 1890 entailed a three-year moratoria and a bondholder haircut that had to be renegotiated in 1893, as the country's public finances had not sufficiently improved to continue to pay the initially agreed upon debt service (Rapoport 2006). Three conditions were laid down in a set of documents (other than the debt contract), once a bankers' commission had first prepared a report presented to the Bank of England on Argentina's economic position in general and on the government's public finances in particular. The General Bond that accompanied the funding loan enumerated the government's engagements, which were basically the banker recommendations spelled out in the report, among which: pledging the bailout loan to the revenues from import duties, which had to be collected in gold pesos, avoiding thereby the risk from further exchange rate depreciation; the reduction of the monetary supply along with the formation of a *Caja de Conversión*, which was to lead to the later adoption of the gold standard; and the compromise not to assume any new external debt engagements.

The 1893 Greek loan shared certain common elements with Argentina's bailout loan. The conditions were mostly related to

[17] The main reason behind this was the short-term nature of the relationship between banks and borrowing countries. The turnover ratio, defined as the frequency at which governments switched underwriting banks, was close to 100 percent for recurrent defaulters (Flandreau et al. 2010).

[18] In all three cases, the basic idea was to pay interest on the external loans with new bonds (funding loan bonds) equivalent to the amount due during a limited period of time (usually three years). These new bonds offered interest payments in cash. See Flandreau and Flores (2012b) on Brazil's funding loan of 1898 and Wynne (1951) and Flores (2012) for the funding loans of Argentina and Greece.

public revenues that would be utilized as a guarantee, and the creation of a "Caisse," made up of bank agents who were tasked with managing the loan. While a first agreement project between the government and Hambros Bank established a set of clauses with the details related to the *Caisse modus operandi*, the final convention excluded all of these clauses, which were instead embedded in a decree by the Greek executive.[19] After a change in government some months thereafter, this agreement was not ratified, leading to a debt default (Wynne 1951). A final solution was found in 1896, wherein a second bailout, this time organized with the support of creditor governments and the establishment of an international control commission, as we explain below. Finally, Brazil's loan, which took place two years afterwards, was a relative success in terms of compliance – the sole condition regarding economic policy was reducing the money supply in an attempt to allow the local currency to appreciate.[20] Brazil's economic conditions remained poor and the government needed a second bailout in 1914, which was again organized by the Rothschild Bank.

Throughout these examples, one common feature can be observed in the type of conditions put into place in each of the bailout loans. Whereas the conditions related to fund management and the monitoring of public revenues pledged as guarantees were essentially contractual in nature, this was not the case of the conditions that sought to reinforce the borrowers' capacity to repay the loan and, thus, relied solely on the market mechanism for compliance and enforcement. Babb and Carruthers (2008) classify these type of conditions as the narrowest form of conditionality that can be found when private lenders are the sole agents requiring the conditions. As conditions were not legally binding, exit-options were open, realistic alternatives. On the one hand, benefits from conditionality compliance were directly linked to, first, having market access and second, to lower borrowing costs, as defaults generated increased costs on future loans (Flandreau and

[19] The agreement project can be found at the Hambros Archives, Greece 1893 # 27 Ms 19103. The final convention and decree were published in Georgiadès (1893), pp. 128–134.

[20] Whether development targets were considered in conditional lending is an open issue. Accominotti et al. (2009) quotes the British administrator for Egypt (British intervention in that country followed a default by the Egyptian government in 1873) who suggests that the policies applied to that country probably had a development purpose. Jenks' (1927) history of international finance presents a subsection devoted to "Foreign loans and public policy," though he basically advocates for the benefits of free trade and free capital flows and the non-intervention of creditor governments.

Zumer 2004; Tomz 2007). On the other hand, costs could lead to a certain degree of loss of sovereignty, through the acceptance of third-party intermingling and intervening into a country's economic policies. However, extreme cases of gunboat diplomacy, which had previously been evoked as an important factor that restrained countries from defaulting (Mitchener and Weidenmier 2010), were rare events that did not constitute a norm in the functioning of sovereign debt markets (Tomz 2007; Flores 2012).

From this brief examination, we can conclude that only a handful of underwriting banks attempted to place conditions on their loans: three out of at least ninety-three banks participating in the underwriting market for foreign government loans in the nineteenth century. Given the high concentration in the market (the three banks covered 66 percent of the market between 1877 and 1895, see Flandreau et al. 2010), other banks were not in a position to impose any conditions on borrowers because their enforcement possibilities were weak. However, the dominant banks had an incentive to screen the market and avoid more risky borrowers before issuing a loan; governments would be willing to comply according to lender expectations. The main reason why conditional lending was such a rare event was precisely that the majority of defaults that took place were those issued by minor underwriters, who were unwilling to act as default managers. This meant that finally investors were obliged to find other means to defend their interests, which they did through forming bodies of bondholders, which led to the final establishment of Corporation of Foreign Bondholders and analogue bodies in other countries (Flandreau and Flores 2012b). However, even if attempts were made to impose conditions in their agreements, they were largely unsuccessful.

The final attempt to find more efficient enforcement mechanisms – in which national rivalries would also play an important role – occurred in the case of Greece in 1896. The default resolution was framed with the participation of creditor governments, underwriting banks, and bondholders associations. In 1897, after the defeat of Greece in the Greco-Turkish War, an International Control Commission was established. This was a condition accepted by the Greek government to obtain the necessary additional external funds to meet indemnity payments and to resume payments of defaulted bonds. This commission supervised both that the specific revenues assigned as security for the new loan were delivered to meet the debt service and that the government-pursued expenses did not interfere with the interests of the bondholders (Wynne 1951). The commission also made recommendations to balance the budget and to reevaluate the drachma, mainly through monetary contraction. This body would last even after WWI, where it was utilized by the League of Nations when the League agreed to provide support to Greece in the 1920s.

In his analysis on how global capital markets operated in the nineteenth century, Pauly (1998) argued that domestic British policy was largely passive, leaving the market to self-regulate itself during the late nineteenth century. While this may have been the case for the monetary regime – the gold standard – that dominated the period, it was not the case for financial markets. As we have seen, there had been a limited, yet effective amount of state intervention, which was occasionally utilized and that was to be further developed during the interwar period. Several practices were employed to justify public intervention: loan guarantees to third countries, the establishment of permanent fiscal agents, and the capacity to ban foreign government loans from financial markets (though Britain pursued a laissez-faire policy) (Fishlow 1985). States also acted as information providers through embassy network and the communications they occasionally engaged with underwriters and associations of bondholders (Ferns 1960).

The approach to enforcement mechanisms was unsurprisingly "pragmatic" and similar to the approach that the League would adopt after World War I.[21] This meant that when third parties assumed the administration of fiscal revenues, defending the interests of investors was a primary objective. The external interference in fiscal management – the recollection of specific public revenues and their use to secure the payment of external debts – was a cost that a defaulting country was required to assume both for geopolitical reasons but also, primarily, to allow it to maintain its access to financial markets. In the nineteenth century, certain underwriting banks strongly preferred to request public guarantees as a condition to issue new loans. Overall, while the absence of international courts complicated the enforcement of these guarantees, their inclusion could serve to justify the intervention of bondholders associations, the banning of new loans from the London Stock Exchange and most drastically, the intervention of creditor governments.

[21] Pauly (2003) describes the League's approach compared to the approach followed by the IMF as "interventionist." This feature was not exclusive to the League but, as I demonstrate, in line with practices already present during the nineteenth century.

CONDITIONAL LENDING DURING THE INTERWAR PERIOD: THE LEAGUE LOANS EXPERIENCE

At the end of World War I, the poor state of international credit constituted a major hurdle in the struggle for economic recovery in Europe. The institutional innovations that followed during the 1920s – similar to those of the late 1970s – were multilateral responses to immediate financial needs, even if these innovations were ad hoc measures of coordinated international support that successfully met the targets for which they were conceived. In a nutshell, the Economic and Financial Organisation of the League of Nations promoted the establishment of the economic and institutional policies that were necessary to restore the productive basis of countries in economic distress. This planning would have involved some form of external funding, which generally took the shape of an external long-term loan issued on international financial markets. In these cases, the League served as an intermediary, functioning as a monitor and fund manager, as well as coordinating the intervention of creditor governments when necessary.

Comparatively speaking, the League of Nations emerged as a more ambitious money doctor than its predecessors of the nineteenth century.[22] The conditionality that the League requested adopted two forms: adherence to the programs the League had helped set up and government acceptance of external surveillance and external fund management, including the proceeds from loans and revenues that were attached as loan guarantees. To a large extent, these conditions were related to information asymmetries that were rampant in the early interwar period, given the extremely deteriorated macroeconomic position of most European countries. While adverse selection was in principle absent,[23] the League faced an important problem of moral hazard, as countries had a stronger interest in meeting their most urgent needs rather than achieving long-term debt sustainability.[24] In order to avoid opportunistic behavior from potential borrowers, the League adopted an enforcement mechanism, through the nomination of fiscal agents that directly managed the proceeds from the loans and also a

[22] Even if I concentrated on banks as money doctors, other cases existed that worked close to financial intermediaries (Flandreau 2003).

[23] The League provided its support to countries that were unable to obtain resources from private capital markets, so that there was a self-selection process of countries obtaining the League's assistance.

[24] For instance, debt overhang may reduce the incentives of countries to comply with policy reform. See Sachs (1989); Diwan and Rodrik (1992), and Dreher (2009) for a literature review.

monitoring procedure based on the establishment of permanent missions that were in charge of obtaining all the necessary information on public expenditures, the state of the economy, and the progress of the agreed reforms.

The procedure followed by the League for issuing new loans was not different from the work that had been pursued by private bankers in London and New York in the nineteenth century. A preliminary phase was initiated via informal contacts with the borrowing government. Once an institutional demand for support was made to the League, a delegation from the Economic and Financial Organisation was sent to the country. The resulting reports were then presented and discussed at the Financial Committee, which then could draft a stabilization program that would frequently include the need for an external loan. If this was the case, these plans – captured in documents called "Protocols," which were the government promises regarding economic policies to be adopted – were distributed to the banks that were invited to participate as underwriters.

The similitudes between the League and the banks' modus operandi can be best illustrated once we analyse the process that led to the loan on behalf of Austria in 1923. Prior to the League's intervention, the Austrian government had attempted to issue a foreign loan, with Baring and Rothschild acting as underwriters. While the conclusion reached by the banks regarding mainly Austria's economic condition was not different from the one delivered afterwards by the League – particularly in regards to the possible assets that could be pledged as collateral for the new loan – banks initially refused the deal, only accepting once the League had set up a long-term plan. The League's participation added value because it provided missing elements, such as support from creditor governments and an enforcement mechanism that went beyond banks' capabilities, which ultimately allowed Austria access to foreign funds.

In short, the practice of foreign control that the League was soon to implement was no novelty in the 1920s, though it would become democratized as the countries that participated in the League were not limited to those emanating from creditor governments. This implied an enlargement of stakeholders' participation to allow for increased legitimacy, an argument raised by borrowing governments. Moreover, governments in creditor countries were already actively involved in sovereign debt markets through the imposition of capital controls used during the war. Even as these controls were gradually relaxed during the 1920s, they remained relevant as a potential voice for governments to intervene in their financial markets. In Britain, the British Foreign Office, along with the Bank of England later on, was in permanent communication with underwriting banks and could encourage or refuse any loan to foreign governments (Ziegler 1988). A similar process was taking place in the United States, in which banks were in permanent communication with the US State department (Rosenberg & Rosenberg, 1987; Chernow 1990).

League involvement in the 1923 Czechoslovakian loan

How the League came to adopt such a prominent role in the financial markets of the interwar period is not a settled issue.[25] One way to respond to this question is to identify the needs of market actors that would have required some form of public intervention that were specific to the new conditions of the interwar period. This new environment, however, could also have helped to consolidate a growing trend toward the more active intervention of creditor governments in private financial markets that had already been present since the late nineteenth century. This could be seen, for instance, by the introduction of compromissory clauses in sovereign debt contracts (on this point, see Sgard in this volume). In fact, it was a fortuitous event that would trigger a debate within the League that would lead it to increase its participation in the contracting process of sovereign lending during the 1920s. It was the League involvement in the 1923 Czechoslovakian loan that was responsible for the now-famous arbitration clause in the contract negotiated between the Czechoslovakian government and Baring. Although arbitration clauses were still rare in the sovereign debt contracts issued in London, they had been present since the mid nineteenth century (Weidenmier, 2010).

There are two major points that would determine the League's role in the market for sovereign debt. One is related with the reason for the appearance of arbitration clauses; the other is the choice of the arbitrator. According to Weidenmaier (2010), the original motive for the emergence of arbitration clauses in the United States was to involve states from creditor governments in the resolution of potential

[25] To some scholars, the League was set up as a means to defend national interests, in particular those from Britain and the United States. See for instance, Hogan (1977); Orde (1990) and Berger (2003). For a different view, mostly related with the necessities of the world economy, see Eichengreen (1989), and for a case study (Austria) see Beyersdorf (2011).

conflicts with borrowers. This would also explain the choices of arbitrators, which were mostly, though not always, US politicians. Arbitration clauses became common in many loans issued in New York on behalf of Latin American countries in the early twentieth century.

The inclusion of arbitration clauses also became a widespread practice in London during the interwar years. For Pauly (1998:52), Czechoslovakia can be described as the first country that the League assisted: the League Council acted as arbitrator in the contract signed with Baring. The need for an arbitrator surged when Baring and the Czechoslovakian government initially disagreed about the bank's request to administer customs and tariffs receipts pledged as security for the loan, a request that the government refused to concede (Pauly 1998:53). But this statement should be qualified, as the League's role was limited – loan negotiations certainly did not hinge on the inclusion of this clause. Furthermore, the League did not serve as an arbitrator. The Council of the League was invited to *nominate* the Financial Committee, or any other committee or representative, who would be empowered to make the best arrangement to protect bondholders.[26] This subtlety was considered relevant because the Council sought to avoid any involvement in actual financial activities and responsibilities. In fact, archival evidence further demonstrates that the League did not perceive itself as being in a position to settle disputes arising from debt contracts, though the Council was empowered to nominate arbitrators.[27]

The parties also disputed the amounts of the loans and the legal guarantees on the securities offered by the Czechoslovakian government. In regards to the first issue, Baring would only agree to underwrite the loan once it was clear that a major part of the loan would be issued on the New York market.[28] As for the second issue, the Czechoslovakian government agreed to provide as security for the loan the receipts from the Tobacco Monopoly and on Customs duties, though it refused to pass a law to formalize this part of the agreement. This was a condition that Baring required, as it doubted that the Prime Minister could legally

26 Letter by the Secretary General of the League of Nations to Dr. Vilem Pospisil dated the 12th September 1922. The League of Nations Archives, Box R 376, file 20068. This was essentially the resolution adopted by the League on July 21, 1922.

27 Comments to the Draft resolution of the Council by Jost Van Hamel, Director of the Legal Section of the League. 4 July 1922, The League of Nations Archives, Box R 376, file 20068.

28 Negotiating details between the Czechoslovakian government and Baring can be found in ING Baring Archives, Folder 2011882.1.

provide these securities.[29] In the end, the government agreed to vote on a law that would authorize the government to contract the loan and provide the previously agreed upon securities.

The League could not intervene in any of these disputes. The mediation role was provided by the British *chargé d'affaires* in Prague, as he was in contact with both Czechoslovakia's government and with Baring. He provided background information to the bank and gave his personal impression and advice on specific matters. On the contrary, the banks cast serious doubts about the convenience of having the League as an arbitrator and pushed for a London-based arbitrator instead.[30] The banks had been similarly displeased with the second potential candidate, the Hague Tribunal. As in the case of the League, the banks contemplated the possibility that the Tribunal would cease to exist before the loan was completely reimbursed. These fears were not unfounded regarding the Financial Section of the League. In fact, at the moment where the Council had finally accepted the arbitration clause, the Financial Section's usefulness was being called into doubt and faced the risk of definitive closure (Jacobsson, 1979:48). As we shall see, it was rather a problem related with the economic need of a country in financial distress which was determinant for the League's own future as a main actor in international financial markets.

League involvement in the 1923 Austrian loan

The proposals advanced by banks and different governments to support Austria, on the other hand, counted on the active participation of the League. Among these proposals, Austria was the only country in which the "Ter Meulen scheme"[31] could be implemented (Myers 1951:493–494; Eichengreen 1995:156–157; Schuker 2003:58–59). This program aimed to support international trade through obtaining government guarantees and other securities that would be administered by the League. Its financial committee was also actively making proposals to facilitate the reconstruction of Austria, both at a diplomatic and at a more internal, technical level. While none of these proposals were actually implemented, the degradation of the situation only emphasized the need for international cooperation. Though not providing any

[29] This is reflected by the correspondence between the bank, Czechoslovakia's government and the British chargé d'affaires in Prague. ING Baring Archives, file 201882.1.

[30] Draft proposals for the inclusion of indemnity and arbitration clauses in agreement sent by Baring to Dr. Pospisil. 21 January 1922. ING Baring Archives, file 201882.1.

[31] Named in reference to the Dutch banker who designed it.

definitive solution, bilateral short-term loans were provided by several countries. (Williams 1929). Austria's government had also been unable to obtain a long-term private loan, though a reversal of this situation was envisaged through a third-government guarantee. This was initially refused by the Allied Ministers. However, this guarantee was obtained some months later and was considered a major diplomatic success in the history of the League.

The contrast between the Czech Republic and Austrian cases is emblematic. Both states approached Baring (along with other New York banks in both cases) to request that it underwrite their new loans. In both cases, informal contacts were followed up on by the bank, which sent agents to analyze the economic situation of the country and the fiscal position of the governments. While the bank ultimately decided to underwrite the loan on behalf of the government of Czechoslovakia, it refused to do so for Austria.

In fact, the role of Baring in Austria was complementary to the League's activities in that country. The Financial Section prepared a program before the enquiry and the procedure foresaw meetings with the Chancellor and leaders from the main political parties to discuss the nature of the enquiry, and with different commissions to discuss the fiscal budget, the state of public enterprises, and that of the agriculture and the industrial sectors.[32] Each of these commissions was composed of members of the government along with representatives of other social groups, such as industrialists, trade union officials, and other non-official representatives from particular sectors. The aim of these commissions was to provide a general overview of the problems faced by each particular sector, along with proposals and policy measures to address them. The reports of each commission were to be delivered in two months, and were to be accompanied by an additional report that was to be prepared by Austria's statistical bureau and Baring's own representatives. Finally, the program foresaw that additional work was to be pursued in order to take control of the Austrian Bank of Issue and of the customs revenues. The League, then, appeared as one of the agents whose agreement was necessary, along with that of other governments and the Reparations Commission, to accept a scheme that would foresee this kind of control.[33]

[32] This enquiry was to be based on a plan advanced by Dr. Rosenberg, who was advisor to Alfred Gürtler, Austria's Finance Minister. See Marcus (2011:33).

[33] The Program was originally prepared by G.M. Young, director of the Anglo-Austrian Bank, and then distributed to the banks interested in the loan (J.P. Morgan, Schroeder, Rothschild,

The Baring case is one example that can be extrapolated to other banks in London or New York. J.P. Morgan also actively selected countries to collaborate with Latin American countries were typical examples. In the early 1920s, the bank received requests for either short- or long-term loans from Brazil, Colombia, Peru, Paraguay, and Argentina. J.P. Morgan was equally active in debt negotiations with Mexico, a country that, although it was in default, was important for the bank given its commercial and financial activities. US government representatives also served as an intermediary between the bank and the local borrowing country. As in the case of Britain, once the bank assumed a favorable position on these requests, it sent a letter to the US Secretary of State to confirm that the Department posed no objection to the operation. The replies specified that this did not imply any responsibility regarding the transaction or whether the approval should be advertised in the loan's prospectus.[34]

The economic information required was not different from the Baring case, which was related to the gold reserves at the central banks, floating and consolidated debt levels, current external and internal loans, and the state of public finances and of the current account. The correspondence with their agents and American diplomats also concerned the political situation and the evolution of major sectors of each economy. These were the kind of tasks evoked by the EFO of the League, which continued with these practices and formalized the coordination efforts with creditor governments.

League involvement in defaults caused by the Great Depression

After the eruption of the economic crisis that hit Central Europe in the early 1930s, the Economic and Financial Organisation had to deal with the problem of sovereign defaults. Before those critical years, the League was only indirectly obliged to act on behalf of the countries it supported that were in default. This was the case of Bulgaria, whose default consisted of some loans the government had issued before the war. The government had been expected to reach a permanent agreement with the bondholders before issuing a new loan, as this was an

Baring, on the 28th May 1922). ING Baring Archives file 203202, pp. 6–8. Baring also sent an additional questionnaire to be answered by Austria's government regarding the particulars of the loan requested, such as purpose of the issue, amount, securities, other debts, current account, and information regarding the efforts by the government to reduce the budget deficit.

34 Some examples on loans to Latin American countries can be found in ARC 1214 (15), Vincent P. Carrosso Papers. The Morgan Library & Museum.

implicit condition that the League required to grant its support.[35] However, the League did not directly intervene in the negotiations.

The focus of the League in regards to sovereign defaults can be described as preemptive. The design of each debt contract reflected this approach, as the League drafted a set of clauses that attempted to preemptively discourage debt service disruptions. That was the main motivation behind the existence of trustees, figures that were systematically included in all contracts, who could also act as payment agent, but whose main motivation was to defend the interest of bondholders (Borchard 1951). Trustees were in charge of managing of the proceeds of the loans and on ensuring that sufficient revenues would be provided to service the loan. In the event of default, nevertheless, the trustee could only "make it good out of the entire assigned revenues" (Tyler 1945:53), but was excluded from undertaking any other actions, such as a foreclosure, and appeals were limited to the League Council.

Nonetheless, the Council could only act as arbitrator between trustees and governments in the case of disagreements or differences in the interpretation of protocols. Moreover, an implicit fragility stemmed from the conception of the stabilization programs and the debt service requirements from the external loans. The type of intervention planned by the League corresponded to the League's overall economic policy principles, which were centered on the promotion of liberal trade, balanced budgets, the adoption of the gold standard, and the establishment of autonomous central banks (League of Nations 1930). While these objectives could be attained in a brief period of time, the time span needed to achieve a sustainable position as a borrower was far more uncertain. In most of the League's stabilization programs, the League promoted loans that had a long-term maturity (typically twenty years), as this focus was most in line with the objectives of the League (Polak 1991).[36] Comparatively speaking, this was in blatant contrast with the practice that the IMF would develop in the post-1945 period, and whose programs, along with the necessary attached funds, have

[35] This recommendation was established by the Financial Committee and expressed in a Council meeting on June 1926 (Tyler, 1945, p. 102; League of Nations Archives, Box R 434, file 52081). The "encouragement" by the League for such an agreement was also provoked by the recurrent petition for League involvement made by national bodies of bondholders and underwriters from defaulted bonds (League of Nations Archives, Box R 434, file 51919).

[36] The loans were issued in tranches, and were denominated in the currencies of each financial market. In the last loans the currency utilized were limited to British pounds and US dollars.

focused primarily on the short term (see section "Discussion: The IMF practice of conditional lending in historical perspective"). Even with a long-term focus, the Commissioner-General, who was the permanent agent responsible for carrying out the program, was expected to leave once the objectives set out in the protocols were achieved. For the first loans (Austria and Hungary), this took place after three and four years, respectively. The consequent maturity mismatch resulted from the fact that while the proceeds from the loans were utilized during the first years of the programs, often to deal with emergencies resulting from the reconstruction needs of the war or the destabilization from unexpected internal or external shocks (such as the resurgence of inflation in Central European countries in 1924), the contracted loan had to be repaid over a much longer time span. This implied that the immediate enforcement mechanism stemming from market-related incentives vanished. The indirect incentives to commit to the League's imposed conditions, which League support was contingent upon, were thus limited in several regards.[37] Once the Great Depression affected financial markets in creditor countries, the League could not offer alternative tools to impede a financial meltdown. As the enforcement mechanisms failed, defaults became the natural outcome.

In fact, in the 1930s, the majority of League loans were in default. At the onset of the crisis, a default by Austria had been adverted under exceptional circumstances. A severe banking crisis erupted in 1931 (the famous Credit Anstalt crisis) that could only be faced through public support and a short-term advance by the newly established Bank for International Settlements (Toniolo 2005). As the government position weakened with the economic crisis and debt default threatened, the League coordinated actions from the governments that had guaranteed Austria's 1923 League loan to issue a new loan in 1933 and then a second conversion loan in 1934 (Marcus 2011). The conditionality requested by the guaranteeing governments in exchange for their support was embedded in the Austrian Protocol (also known as the Protocol of Lausanne, signed on the 15 July 1932), which had to be ratified by each government afterwards.[38] The new protocol included many of the same provisions as the protocols agreed upon in 1922, including monetary and fiscal policy and the need for a permanent advisor for

[37] In the case of the IMF, the incentives to adopt recommended policies depended on previous relationships with the organization.
[38] The protocol and its annexes are published in Hudson and Bacon (1937:84).

the central bank and a General-Commissioner. Historians have further emphasized the commitment adopted by Austria to ratify one particular condition, which was already included in the first protocol of 1922, in which Austria refused to form a customs union with Germany. The non-compliance would later create a legal controversy with the Anschluss in 1938,[39] though the payments for the Austrian guaranteed loans continued to be temporarily paid by Germany under the terms of Anglo-German transfer agreement (Borchard 1951).

Nevertheless, for other defaulting countries whose loans were backed by the League, no support from third governments was available. Even the League itself, lacking its own funds, could not provide additional funds. That being said, as *The Economist* echoed in the first meeting by the League loan committee – formed in 1932 to act as a negotiating agency between bondholders and defaulters – that even if the League held no legal obligation toward bondholders, the moral responsibility was "clearly a heavy one."[40] However, the experience of the League loan committee was short and unsuccessful, as no permanent agreement could be reached before World War II.

Unsurprisingly, modern scholars have evaluated the League's focus and reaction to sovereign defaults as that of plain failure. These criticisms join other more macroeconomic arguments, such as Fior (2008), who blames the League for the poor economic performance of the countries in which it had intervened. For him, the League – as any other global institution interacting with financial markets – served to diffuse specific economic policies, related to the dominant liberal traditions of the time, and that later contributed to amplify the effects of the Great Depression. Another set of criticisms refer to the League's failure in terms of monitoring. Pauly (1997, 2003) has emphasized that the League failed to implement multilateral monitoring schemes and that this failure foreshadowed a similar failure by the IMF. Highlighting the tension between free capital markets and democratic governments' sovereignty (or freedom of action), two features that were already present during the interwar period, Pauly believes that the League's inability to develop a system of multilateral surveillance centered on international institutions, suggests that the IMF will similarly

[39] Hendrik Willem Verzijl (1968:362) has argued that Austria's government never fully ratified the protocol as the Bundesrat rejected it. One year after the loan's issuance, the League agreed to deviate part of the loan proceeds for finance public investment schemes to alleviate the unemployment problem. (Bischoff et al. 2003).

[40] *The Economist*, 24 September 1932.

fail if a recession is substantial enough that debtor nations can no longer reimburse their debts.

The literature, nonetheless, is not completely in agreement with this pessimistic vision of the League Loans. Some scholars, such as Sargent (1983) or Santaella (1993) see a relative success in the League's experience securing sovereign debt contracts. These authors cite the fact that inflation rates strongly diminished in the countries where the League intervened (Sargent 1983) or that debtor countries gained credibility when announcing economic policies promoted by the League (Santaella 1993). The League's own critiques, while recognizing the negative performance of the countries after the Great Depression, attributed the lack of expected results to external factors, such as the rise of protectionism that prevented implemented programs from obtaining better results (League of Nations, 1945). However, there was perhaps less confidence within the League regarding the appropriateness of its stabilization plans. Clavin and Wessels (2004) have shown that the League's Gold Delegation had already raised questions around the convenience of the policies it promoted in relation to the adoption of the gold standard. This self-criticism may sound familiar to contemporary scholars, as they do not strongly differ from those occasionally raised by the IMF.[41]

A general agreement can be extracted regarding the effectiveness of the League in enforcing and monitoring the programs it implemented. The debate about compliance, now recurrent in IMF programs, did not emerge in the case of the League – at least in the short-term – as countries were prevented from adopting policies other than those agreed upon in the protocols.[42] These documents, that enumerated all the conditions that the country had to fulfill to secure the League's support, do not differ strongly from the Technical Memorandum of Understanding later utilized by the IMF. While the protocols as such had no legal validity, governments were expected to ratify them in parliament and thus become national acts, along with any other measures that may have been necessary for the implementation of the stabilization programs, regarding particularly the League's permanent agents. The League's *ex post* analysis, speculated on what would have happened in the absence of any multilateral organization in the 1920s. Their view suggests that

41 On these criticisms raised in the aftermath of the Argentinean crisis of 2001 see Sgard (2005).

42 On the contrary, certain authors have criticized the character of the League as too intrusive (Pauly 1996; James 2003). For Myers (1945) this may have been a reason why many countries refrained from requesting the League's support.

the market would have intended to impose the same kind of conditions, though countries would have had more facilities to repudiate its engagements (given the lack of "safeguards" granted to the League by borrowing governments), thereby making their loans more expensive (League of Nations, 1945:59). Flores and Decorzant (2015) have further demonstrated that this assertion should be qualified. While the conditions regarding economic policies were similar for other countries that issued new loans with third-party intervention, the monitoring setting was not different from that implemented by the League. These authors show, however, that negotiating times and loan costs were higher in comparison to the League loans.

DISCUSSION: THE IMF PRACTICE OF CONDITIONAL LENDING IN HISTORICAL PERSPECTIVE

Previous literature has placed considerable attention on the continuity, contrasts, and parallels between the League's Economic and Financial Organisation and the IMF.[43] Legal, economic, and political science scholars have drawn parallels between our contemporary period and the interwar years; historians have provided detailed descriptions of the evolution of our monetary and financial regimes during the twentieth century (Santaella 1993; Sargent 1983; Eichengreen 1989; James 1996; Gulati and Weidemaier 2014).[44] Money doctors, as they became to be known, were in vogue during the 1920s as much as they were in the 1990s, when scholars debated the costs and benefits of their intervention in financially distressed countries. Disagreements in the literature cover a wide range of issues, such as economic performance, social costs of the programs implemented, positive and negative effects on financial markets, and the impact on internal political issues.

Nevertheless, while the existence of historical parallels between the League and the IMF has been emphasized in the literature, there is also a need to recognize the contrasts between these two experiences. First, the League and the IMF were conceived under far different initial conditionals. Accordingly, the objectives faced by the League and by the IMF differed in their scope, methods, and perhaps even by the willingness of member countries to succeed. If anything, near to the 1982 debt

[43] I have argued in a previous article that the literature on the League's loans coincided with the first years of the Bretton Woods institutions (Decorzant and Flores 2012).

[44] On the history of the IMF see Horsefield (1965) and Boughton (2001).

crisis, the IMF's targets approached some of those noted by the League (Pauly 1996; Bordo and James 2000; Sgard 2004), as explained below. In fact, while the League's ultimate target was reconstructing the productive basis of the countries where it intervened, the IMF initially concentrated on the balance of payments' position of borrowing countries, in order to guarantee that the payment system functioned smoothly, as had been agreed upon in the Bretton Woods meetings. With the emergence of Euromarkets in the 1960s and the increasing liberalization of international capital flows, the IMF also evolved to meet the necessities of the world's financial system. Default, debt management, and the need to have access to external funds – from both the IMF and private financial markets – appeared to become the novel targets that were to be attained in the late 1970s, a field that, to a certain extent, the League had pioneered.

Conditional lending practices, moreover, differed in origin. In the case of the League, the main enforcement mechanism was linked to the *primary* access to private financial markets. The IMF, on the other hand, would provide its own external support for a very short-term (six months for its first stand-by agreements, in the particular case of macroeconomic imbalances). From this perspective, the IMF introduced certain innovative aspects in an attempt to avoid fragilities introduced into sovereign debt contracts of the 1920s, in particular, the short-term nature of the loans made available to governments. Private financial markets were an alternative exit-option that limited IMF's conditional lending during the 1960s, a natural effect from the IMF's countercyclical nature.

Once the crises of the 1970s erupted and international liquidity eroded, the IMF provided a "certification effect" similar to the one offered by its League antecessor. In both cases, the League and the IMF tried to support the economic and financial sustainability of countries that were willing to access capital markets.[45] In both cases, these institutions based economic policy plans on the credibility of their programs, in other words, the *ex-ante* perception that countries would comply with the conditions by reducing the exit-options, providing enforcement mechanisms, and minimizing transaction costs. In both cases, the institutional innovations succeeded, to a certain extent, in attracting capital to borrowing countries. Portugal is a typical example of this,

[45] Khan and Sharma (2001) argue that the IMF needs to obtain assurances that it will be repaid and links this to the necessity of conditionality.

as the country was only able to borrow from international commercial banks once it entered into a stand-by agreement with the IMF, a condition which was requested by lenders.[46]

In the years leading up the 1982 debt crisis, however, this information provision role played by the IMF would prove to be problematic. In fact, the evolution of the IMF as crisis manager and active participant of international debt markets raised challenges that the League did not face. For instance, the IMF may face potential problems of adverse selection from the population of potential borrowers, but also moral hazard, both from borrowers and lenders. Sgard (2016) has furthermore remarked that, given its recurrent and long-term relationship with borrowing countries, the IMF has developed privileged access to soft information, although the basis of this continued information flow is confidentiality. While the IMF has sought market efficiency through the provision of hard information, Sgard identifies a trade-off between both. On the contrary, this distinction did not exist in the 1920s. The League's commitment to transparency obliged this body to make the discussions of the Council public, its resolutions and the reports of the Financial Committee's missions to borrowing countries. Nevertheless, a salient similarity in both cases is the fact that conditionality emerged as a distinctive element that was unavailable to other private intermediaries during the 1970s or to creditor governments, as it had been during the 1920s.[47]

Finally, the experience of the IMF as crisis manager and promoter of financial integration presents new problems (or issues) that surpass those experienced by the League. In the debt negotiations that followed the 1982 Mexican crisis, the IMF conditioned its own support on commercial banks continued participation in Mexico and later, also in other defaulting countries. In contrast to the League, the IMF was not an external agent or pure mediator between lender and borrowers, but could have an impact on negotiation outcomes: this was reinforced by the active intervention of creditor governments. Alvarez and Flores (2013) have, for instance, demonstrated that the availability of trade finance to countries that defaulted but adopted an IMF program did not diminish in the wake of the crisis. This was made possible by the intervention of national export credit agencies, whose support had

46 IMF Archives, EBM/78/81 and EBS/78/228.

47 Sgard (2016) evokes the failed attempts by commercial banks to condition their loans. A comparison between bilateral and multilateral support to countries in Central and Eastern Europe in the 1920s is provided in Decorzant and Flores (2015).

been firstly conditioned by the countries' entering into an IMF program. Nevertheless, subsequent actions by the IMF have been controversial in terms of their effect on private capital markets.[48]

In conclusion, an *ex post* perspective of the long evolution of international finance demonstrates that IFIs made conditional lending possible and conditionality allowed for the development of a sovereign debt market. The nineteenth century offered partial solutions to the problem of default management and prevention. The interwar period saw the first attempt to provide a more comprehensive solution through the cooperation of creditor governments and underwriting banks, while providing long-term development plans to borrowing countries. These innovations led the way for a more ambitious effort that took place in the post-World War period. The conception of the IMF followed the logic evolution of previous IFIs – the first stabilization plans in the 1950s were not radically different from the League's reconstruction loans – though adapted to a new economic and monetary regime. Furthermore, the IMF's disposal of its own resources has allowed it to act in a countercyclical manner. This feature has furthermore isolated the IMF from the market mechanism logic of the nineteenth century and interwar period and given it the capacity to act as a lender of last resort, a major advantage over the tools the League had at its disposal.

SOURCES

Bank of England Archives, London; IMF Archives, Washington; Hambro Archives, London; ING Baring Archives, London; League of Nations Archives, Geneva; The Morgan Library & Museum, New York.

References

Accominotti, Olivier, Marc Flandreau, Riad Rezzik, and Frédéric Zumer. 2010. "Black man's burden, white man's welfare: control, devolution and development in the British Empire, 1880–1914". *European Review of Economic History* 14 (01): 47–70.

Alvarez, Sebastian and Juan Flores Zendejas. 2014. "Trade finance and Latin America's lost decade: The forgotten link." *Investigaciones de Historia Económica - Economic History Research* 22 (1): 79–105.

Anderson, Olive. 1964. "II. Great Britain and the Beginnings of the Ottoman Public Debt, 1854–55." *The Historical Journal* 7: 47–63.

[48] The debate on the signaling effects of IMF interventions, see Saravia and Mody (2003).

Babb, Sarah L., et Bruce G. Carruthers. 2008. "Conditionality: Forms, Function, and History". *Annual Review of Law and Social Science* 4 (1): 13–29.

Berger, Peter. "The League of Nations and Interwar Austria: Critical Assessment of a Partnership in Economic Reconstruction." In *The Dollfuss/Schuschnigg Era in Austria: A Reassessment*, edited by Günter Bischof, Anton Pelinka, and Alexander Lassner. New Brunswick, N.J.: Transaction Publishers, 2003.

Beyersdorf, Frank. 2011. "'Credit or Chaos'? The Austrian Stabilisation Programme of 1923 and the League of Nations." In *Internationalism Reconfigured: Transnational Ideas and Movements Between the World Wars*, edited by Daniel Laqua, 135–157. I.B.Tauris.

Borchard, Edwin Montefiore. 1951. *State Insolvency and Foreign Bondholders*. New Haven: Yale Univ. Press.

Bordo, Michael D., et Harold James. 2000. The International Monetary Fund: Its Present Role in Historical Perspective. Working Paper 7724. National Bureau of Economic Research.

Boughton, James M. 2000. *The IMF and the Silent Revolution: Global Finance and Development in the 1980s (EPub)*. International Monetary Fund.

Chernow, Ron. 1990. *The house of Morgan: [an American banking dynasty and the rise of modern finance]*. London; Sydney [etc.]: Simon and Schuster.

Clavin, Patricia, and Jens-Wilhelm Wessel. "Another Golden Idol? The League of Nations' Gold Delegation and the Great Depression, 1929–1932." *International History Review* 24, no. 4 (December 2004): 765–795.

Costeloe, Michael P. 2003. *Bonds and bondholders: British investors and Mexico's foreign debt, 1824–1888*. Westport, CT: Praeger.

De Martens, Frédéric. 1898. *Recueil des traités et conventions conclus par la Russie avec les puissances étrangères-* v.12 1898. St. Pétersbourg: Impr. du Ministèredes voiesde communication ABöhnke.

Decorzant, Yann and Juan Flores. 2012. Public borrowing in harsh times: the League of Nations Loans revisited (Working Papers in Economic History No. wp12-07). Universidad Carlos III, Instituto Figuerola de Historia y Ciencias Sociales.

Diwan, Ishac, and Dani Rodrik. 1992. Debt Reduction, Adjustment Lending, and Burden Sharing. NBER Working Paper 4007. National Bureau of Economic Research, Inc.

Dreher, Axel. 2009. "IMF conditionality: theory and evidence". *Public Choice* 141 (1): 233–267.

Eichengreen, Barry J. 1995. *Golden fetters: the gold standard and the great depression, 1919–1939*. NBER series on long-term factors in economic development. New York: Oxford University Press.

Til Debt Do Us Part: The U.S. Capital Market and Foreign Lending, 1920–1955. National Bureau of Economic Research Working Paper Series No. 2394 (1989).

Esteves, Rui, et Ali Coskun Tuncer. 2014. Feeling the Blues. Moral Hazard and Debt Dilution in Eurobonds Before 1914. Working Discussion Paper 9860; Centre for Economic Policy Research.

Fenn, Charles. 1883. *Fenn's Compendium of the English and Foreign Funds, Debts and Revenues of All Nations*. London, E. Wilson.

Ferns, H. S. 1992. "The Baring Crisis Revisited". *Journal of Latin American Studies* 24 (02): 241–273.

1960. *Britain and Argentina in the nineteenth century*. Oxford: Clarendon Press.

Fishlow, Albert. 1985. "Lessons from the past: capital markets during the 19th century and the interwar period". *International Organization* 39 (03): 383–439.

Flandreau, Marc, éd. 2003. *Money doctors: the experience of international financial advising 1850–2000*. Routledge International Studies in Money and Banking 26. London [etc.]: Routledge.

2013. "Sovereign states, bondholders committees, and the London Stock Exchange in the nineteenth century (1827–68): new facts and old fictions". *Oxford Review of Economic Policy* 29 (4): 668–696.

Flandreau, Marc, et Juan H. Flores. 2009. "Bonds and Brands: Foundations of Sovereign Debt Markets, 1820–1830". *The Journal of Economic History* 69 (03): 646–684.

2012a. "The Peaceful Conspiracy: Bond Markets and International Relations During the Pax Britannica". *International Organization* 66 (02): 211–241.

2012b. "Bondholders versus Bond-Sellers? Investment Banks and Conditionality Lending in the London Market for Foreign Government Debt, 1815–1913". *European Review of Economic History* 16 (4): 356–383.

Flandreau, Marc, Juan H. Flores, Norbert Gaillard, et Sebastián Nieto-Parra. 2010. "The End of Gatekeeping: Underwriters and the Quality of Sovereign Bond Markets, 1815–2007". In Reichlin, L. et West, K., NBER International Seminar on Macroeconomics, pp. 53–92.

Flores, Juan H. 2012. "Crying on Lombard Street: fixing sovereign defaults in the 1890s". *European Review of History: Revue europeenne d'histoire* 19 (6): 979–997. doi:10.1080/13507486.2012.739 144.

Flores, Juan and Decorzant, Yann. 2015. "Going multilateral? Financial markets' access and the League of Nations Loans, 1923–1928", *Economic History Review*, forthcoming.

Georgiadès, Demetrios, et E. F. G. LAW. 1893. La Grèce Économique et Financière En 1893 ... Réponse À M. E. F. G. Law, Etc.

Gille, Bertrand. 1965. *Histoire de la maison Rothschild*. Travaux de droit, d'économie, de sociologie et de sciences politiques, No 39 No 56. Genève: Droz.

Hogan, Michael J. 1977. *Informal Entente: The Private Structure of Cooperation in Anglo-American Economic Diplomacy, 1918–1928. Chicago (Ill.): Imprint publ.*

Horsefield, John Keith. 1965. *Introduction to the Fund.* 2nd edn. IMF pamphlet series, no. [1]. Washington D.C: International Monetary Fund.

Hudson, Manley Ottmer and Ruth E. Bacon. 1937. *International legislation: A collection of the texts of multipartite international instruments of general interest, edited by Manley O. Hudson, with the collaboration of Ruth E. Bacon. Volume VI, 1932–1934.* Washington: Carnegie Endowment for International Peace.

James, Harold, "Who owns "ownership"? The IMF and policy advice", in *Money Doctors: The Experience of International Financial Advising 1850–2000*, Flandreau, Marc, ed. (London, New York, 2003), pp. 49–77.

James, Harold. 1996. *International monetary cooperation since Bretton Woods.* Washington D.C.: New York; Oxford: International Monetary Fund; Oxford University Press.

Jacobsson, Erin Elver. 1979. *A life for sound money: Per Jacobsson: his biography.* Oxford: New York: Clarendon Press; Oxford University Press.

Khan, M. S., and Sharma, S. 2001. IMF conditionality and country ownership of programs. IMF Institute, IMF.

Marcus, Nathan. "Credibility, Confidence and Capital, Austrian Reconstruction and the Collapse of Global Finance: 1921 to 1931". Florence, Unpublished PhD Dissertation, European University Institute, 2011.

Mitchener, Kris James, et Marc D. Weidenmier. 2010. "Supersanctions and sovereign debt repayment". *Journal of International Money and Finance* 29 (1): 19–36.

Neal, Larry, and Lance Davis. 2006. "The Evolution of the Structure and Performance of the London Stock Exchange in the First Global Financial Market, 1812–1914". *European Review of Economic History* 10 (03): 279–300.

Orde, Anne, *British policy and European reconstruction after the First World War*, (Cambridge, 1990).

Pamuk, Şevket. 1987. *The Ottoman empire and European capitalism, 1820–1913: trade, investment and production.* Cambridge Middle East library 12. Cambridge; London [etc.]: Cambridge Univ. Press.

Pauly, Louis W. 1998. *Who elected the bankers?: surveillance and control in the world economy.* 1. Cornell paperbacks. Cornell studies in political economy. Ithaca [etc.]: Cornell University Press.

The League of Nations and the Foreshadowing of the International Monetary Fund. Princeton N.J: International Finance Section Department of Economics Princeton University, 1996.

2003. "International Financial Institutions and National Economic Governance: Aspects of the New Adjustment Agenda in Historical

Perspective". In *International Financial History in the Twentieth Century*. Publications of the German Historical Institute.

Platt, Desmond Christopher Martin. 1968. *Finance, trade, and politics in British foreign policy: 1815–1914*. Oxford: Clarendon Press.

Polak, J.J. 1991. "The changing nature of IMF conditionality", *Essays in international finance, no. 184. International Finance Section, Dept of Economics*. Princeton, NJ: Princeton University.

Rapoport, Mario. 2006. *Historia económica, política y social de la Argentina (1880–2003)*. Buenos Aires: Ariel.

Rosenberg, Emily S. 1999. *Financial missionaries to the world: the politics and culture of dollar diplomacy, 1900–1930*. Cambridge, MA [etc.]: Harvard University Press.

Rosenberg, Emily S., and Norman L. Rosenberg. 1987. "From Colonialism to Professionalism: The Public-Private Dynamic in United States Foreign Financial Advising, 1898–1929". *The Journal of American History* 74 (1): 59–82. doi:10.2307/1908505.

Sachs, J. 1989. "Conditionality, debt relief, and the developing country debt crisis". In J. Sachs, (ed.), *Developing country debt and economic performance*, Vol. 1. Chicago: University of Chicago Press.

Santaella, Julio A. 1993. Stabilization Programs and External Enforcement: Experience from the 1920s. *Staff Papers – International Monetary Fund* 40, no. 3 (1993), pp. 584–621.

Sargent, Thomas J. 1983. "The Ends of Four Big Inflations", in Robert E. Hall, (ed.), *Inflation: Causes and Effects*. Chicago, pp. 41–97.

Schuker, Stephen, "The Competition between Central Banks, Private Financial Advisers, and Multilateral Agencies, 1919–39", in Flandreau, Marc, ed., *Money Doctors: The Experience of International Financial Advising 1850–2000* (London, New York, 2003), pp. 49–77.

Sgard, Jérôme. (Forthcoming 2016). "How the IMF Did It: Sovereign Debt Restructurings during the 1980s." *Capital Market Law Journal.*

Liedtke, Rainer, 2008. "Modern Communication: The Information Network of N.M. Rothschild & Sons in Nineteenth-Century Europe", in Feldman, Gerald D. and Peter Hertner, *Finance and Modernization: A Transnational and Transcontinental Perspective for the Nineteenth and Twentieth Centuries*. Farnham and Burlington: Ashgate.

Tomz, Michael. 2007. *Reputation and International Cooperation: Sovereign Debt Across Three Centuries*. Princeton: Princeton University Press.

Toniolo, Gianni. 2005. *Central bank cooperation at the Bank for International Settlements, 1930–1973*. Studies in macroeconomic history. Cambridge [etc.]: Cambridge University Press.

Tyler, Royall. *The League of Nations Reconstruction Schemes in the Inter-war Period*. Geneva: League of nations, 1945.

Verzijl, J. H. W. 1968. International Law in Historical Perspective. Vol. no. 4 [etc.]. Nova et Vetera Iuris Gentium. Series A, Modern International Law, No. 4, 6–9. Leyden: A. W. Sijthoff.

Weidemaier, W. Mark C. "Contracting for State Intervention: The Origins of Sovereign Debt Arbitration." *Law and Contemporary Problems* 73, no. 4 (October, 2010): 335–355.

Weidemaier, Mark; Mitu Gulati. 2014. "A People's History of Collective Action Clauses". *Virginia Journal of International Law*, 1–95.

Williams, John Fischer. 1929. *Chapters on Current International Law and the League of Nations*. London: Longmans & Co.

Wynne, William H. 1951. *State Insolvency and Foreign Bondholders: Selected Case Histories of Governmental Foreign Bond Defaults and Debt Readjustments*. Beard Books.

Ziegler, P. 1988. *The sixth great power: Barings 1762–1929*. London: Collins.

CHAPTER THREE

WHEN GOVERNMENTS WRITE CONTRACTS: POLICY AND EXPERTISE IN SOVEREIGN DEBT MARKETS

W. Mark C. Weidemaier, Mitu Gulati and Anna Gelpern

At least three times in the past two decades, national governments and institutions at the regional and international levels have tried to reform sovereign bond contracts to facilitate debt restructuring. Years and continents apart, official actors did not merely regulate private contracts – mandate terms or define acceptable contracting parameters – but actively intruded in the drafting process. In most cases, governments that would not legislate or regulate instead nudged, managed, and modeled contract drafting. They convened experts, commissioned reports, and raced to produce model clauses that could be marketed to debtors and creditors. They even tried "to lead by example," using model clauses in some of their own debt contracts. This mode of government intervention, which blurs the role of regulator and market participant, was not invented in the 1990s. The Committee for the Study of International Loan Contracts, which convened under the auspices of the League of Nations in late 1935, used similar methods to promote sovereign debt contract terms, including close cousins of the clauses at the forefront of present-day debates.

Our chapter considers this method of government intervention using majority modification clauses as a case study.[1] Majority modification is a species of what are now called "collective action clauses" (CACs) in sovereign debt contracts. CAC is an umbrella term for clauses that promote creditor coordination. Majority modification CACs enable some

[1] Portions of this chapter are adapted from Weidemaier and Gulati (2013).

creditors to vote to change the debt obligation and bind the remaining creditors to the outcome. These CACs were prominent in the work of official contract drafters in the 1930s, 1990s, 2000s, and have made two more comebacks since 2010. Indeed, CACs – defined in the broad sense as clauses designed to remedy bondholder coordination problems – have been around for nearly a century.

For decades, bonds issued under English law have allowed for supermajority modification; in many of these bonds, quorum rules reduced the threshold for modification to less than twenty per cent of outstanding debt. Until 2003, however, these clauses were largely confined to the English-law market. In particular, drafting custom in the New York market seemed to preclude majority modification: all known sovereign bonds issued under New York law required each creditor's consent to change payment terms. But beginning with a bond issue by Mexico in February 2003, new sovereign bond contracts under New York law shifted to supermajority modification. The modification provision was revised again in 2014, this time both in the English-law and New York-law markets. At the time we write this, the revision appears to be taking hold rapidly across both markets.

Market-wide contract change of this sort is exceptionally rare. A large literature is devoted to the problem of *no* change – or boilerplate stickiness – even when the contract term in question is clearly suboptimal (Kahan and Klausner 1997; Gulati and Scott 2013). Modification terms in sovereign bond contracts appeared to be an important case study. The dramatic ascendance of CACs in 2003 was a rare example in which contract drafters overcame their typical inertia. To the public officials who promoted this change, the New York market offered a lesson in market failure. Lawyers and other market participants failed to understand the importance of CACs; the official sector could play a key role as catalyst and educator. Subsequent accounts of the shift embraced this narrative (Galvis and Saad 2004; Taylor 2007; Quarles 2010), which later was employed to justify additional waves of contract reform.

A review of sovereign debt contracts, however, reveals flaws in this story. For at least a century, sovereign bonds have demonstrated frequent innovation, including the adoption of new clauses designed to facilitate coordination among bondholders. These innovations did not necessarily result in majority modification clauses of the sort promoted by government officials, but this was not because market participants were unaware of these clauses. The efforts of the League of

Nations Committee for the Study of International Loan Contracts (the League Committee) reveal an equally long pedigree for official intervention in sovereign debt contracts. Then, as now, attempts to facilitate the modification of sovereign debt contracts have rested on particular ideas about market failure and ways to overcome it. Then, as now, officials called on market and academic experts from different countries, and turned bond contracts into a technocratic reform project.

In this chapter, we explore the century-long effort to promote majority modification clauses in sovereign bonds, which raises a more fundamental question about the nature of government intervention in the sovereign debt markets. Part I focuses on the interwar years. We explore the League Committee's efforts to promote majority modification clauses, juxtaposing these efforts against contracting practices during the period. We show that parties frequently experimented with ways to address creditor coordination problems, but virtually never adopted majority modification clauses. Part II turns to more recent reform efforts. We present the common story about how majority modification clauses appeared in bonds governed by English but not New York law, and about how the official sector catalyzed the 2003 shift in New York. Part III highlights flaws in this story, revealing, once again, a surprising degree of innovation in sovereign debt contracts. We conclude by exploring the implications of our findings.

THE INTERWAR PERIOD: CACs AND THE REFORM AGENDA

In the modern era, reform efforts have focused on improving sovereign debt contracts, and majority modification clauses have emerged as a key policy tool. Contemporary narratives justify the need for official intervention by positing that market participants do not fully understand the value of these clauses. But when we look to the pre-World War II era, a different story emerges. Sovereign bonds have selectively employed majority modification clauses for nearly a century. Government-sponsored contract reform efforts have likewise considered the merits of these clauses. Indeed, the League Committee's work in the 1930s bears a striking similarity to contract reform efforts in the 1990s and 2000s. The primary difference is that, in the interwar period, other forms of CAC enjoyed more widespread acceptance.

Modification clauses entered widespread use in English-law bonds in the 1980s, but they have a much longer history.[2] The earliest example we have found is a 1922 Czech bond issue negotiated in consultation with the League of Nations (see Flores Zendejas, in this volume).[3] This was a significant issuance that involved major underwriting banks acting in consultation with governments in creditor countries (Decorzant and Flores 2012). The bonds provided that, at a meeting to consider "any proposal which may be made to them by the Czechoslovak Government…, the decision of the holders of the majority in nominal value of Bonds present at such meeting, either in person or represented by proxy, shall be binding upon all Bondholders…"[4] The clause does not limit the range of permissible topics at the meeting and plainly seems to allow a binding vote on a restructuring proposal. A similar clause featuring a two-thirds modification threshold appears in restructured Belgian debt issued in 1936. However, in our data set of 460 pre-World War II bonds, no other bonds allow for majority modification. Indeed, we do not even find this clause in subsequent Czech or Belgian bond issues.

Although majority modification clauses were rare, they were not unknown to official reformers. As the Great Depression unfolded, the idea of looking into debt contracts was apparently driven by the French delegation inside the League Committee. Much as their US and UK successors many decades later, the French did not have the political space to push the process at the time, and asked the Dutch to step in to ensure a proper mandate for the League Committee. Some Committee members had misgivings about the reasons and the need for government intervention. Again and again, Committee staff presented the problem as one of market ignorance, with official education as the solution. Sovereign debt instruments, including League-sponsored loans,

[2] Our discussion in this section draws on a data set built with the help of a number of academic colleagues. It includes approximately 2,700 sovereign bond contracts and disclosure documents drawn from a variety of sources and covering the period 1823–2012. For a fuller description of the portions of the data set relevant to this chapter, see Weidemaier and Gulati (2013:63–64).

[3] The League assisted in arranging reconstruction loans for a number of countries and cities that would otherwise have been unable to access global capital markets. These included Austria, Bulgaria, Estonia, Greece, Hungary, and the city of Danzig. For history on the League Loans, see Myers (1945); Decorzant and Flores (2012). The Czech loans were not among the League Loans but the Czech government requested that any disputes with the banks be arbitrated by the League of Nations (Decorzant and Flores 2012:20).

[4] Bond for Czechoslovak State Loan of 1922; Listing Application for the Czechoslovak State $14,000,000 Eight Percent. Bonds (January 11, 1923); Listing Application for the Czechoslovak State $9,250,000 Eight Percent. Bonds (February 3, 1925).

were running into trouble and could not be modified owing to a deadlock among bondholder representatives, or the absence of a legal relationship between creditors and their purported representatives. From the staff perspective, an obvious response was to take care of the representation problem up front, in the debt contracts.

During the interwar era, standing committees played a much larger role in negotiating a settlement following default (Eichengreen and Portes 1989; Eichengreen 1991). The Corporation of Foreign Bondholders played the dominant role in negotiating on behalf of British bondholders and, in the 1930s especially, the Foreign Bondholders Protective Council played a key role in negotiating on behalf of US bondholders.[5] Their negotiated settlements, however, did not bind dissenting bondholders, and this concerned League Committee staff. Modification clauses offered one solution.

Staff informed the Committee about prevailing market practices. A background memorandum prepared for the Committee in 1937 identified the modification clauses in the Czech and Belgian bonds but conceded that, "[i]n international loan contracts, majority clauses have so far been rare" (League Committee 1937). Although staff members had a generally receptive attitude toward majority modification, this perspective ran up against Committee members' skepticism about intruding into private contract drafting, and especially "the aversion … now felt by the Committee to contracts containing clauses as to their revision."[6]

League finance officials responded to Committee skepticism by lining up experts with historical and comparative studies to show that the reforms they proposed channeled accepted practices the world over, and should be entirely uncontroversial. This approach was particularly striking with respect to majority modification:

> The purpose of the document is to show that the possibility of modifying loan contracts by meetings of bondholders authorized to do so in the loan contracts is a well known practice in Great Britain, based on a long tradition. Documents giving details on similar situations in other countries (Canada, U.S.A., and a number of Continental countries) have already been circulated to the Committee … As you may be aware, the Committee has, at its first meeting, refused point blank to envisage or discuss the possibility of modifying contracts, and the preparation of these

[5] On the complex relationship between the State Department and the FBPC, see Adamson (2002).

[6] Memorandum from De Bordes to Lovejoy, October 1, 1937.

> documents is in the nature of a flank attack to make it take up this exceedingly important question again. If we can show that bondholders in a number of countries are used to and have accepted the principle, it will be more difficult to resist it as regards international loans.[7]

This was a case of considerable "spin." For example, Committee briefings describe US practice as favoring majority modification, though a careful reader would notice that modifying payment terms required unanimous consent.

Despite initial reluctance among the members, the Committee's final report included several options for ensuring a debt settlement "binding on all bondholders" (League Committee 1937). These options did not, however, include majority modification clauses. In fact, the Committee's report primarily focused on non-binding methods of improving bondholder coordination, such as trustees and bondholder representatives. In this respect, the Committee's report mirrored market practice. In our data set, approximately 5 percent of pre-World War II bonds included collective acceleration clauses, and nearly 24 percent provided for a trustee to represent bondholder interests (Weidemaier and Gulati 2013).

Despite official concern, the idea that effective debt adjustment *requires* the participation of all bondholders did not seem to take hold until much later. Perhaps the most notable example of this indifference involves the 1922 Czech bonds, which contained the very first modification clause. Given the economic and political upheaval of the ensuing decades, these bonds not surprisingly went into default. After World War II, the Czech government entered into wide-ranging restructuring negotiations, including with the Council of Foreign Bondholders and the Foreign Bondholders Protective Council (FBPC). The FBPC archives at Stanford University include drafts of the restructuring agreements and related correspondence. Notwithstanding the modification clause in the underlying bonds – which, recall, allowed bondholders holding a majority in nominal value of the debt, voting at a meeting or by proxy, to approve "any proposal which may be made to them by the Czechoslovak Government" in a vote "binding upon all Bondholders" – we found no indication in the archives that any of the negotiating parties ever considered calling such a meeting or otherwise attempted to bind dissenters. Every draft of the restructuring proposal envisioned

[7] Letter from De Bordes to McKinnon Wood, September 24, 1937.

that individual bondholders could assent to the plan by tendering their bonds to be stamped with notice of the restructuring.[8]

It is tempting to attribute this indifference to binding holdouts to the fact that sovereigns enjoyed absolute immunity from suit during the interwar period. Yet by the 1930s, officials already saw lawsuits as a problem. According to the League Committee, "Too many lawsuits would be a bad thing; not only would they be unpleasant for the debtors, but their Stock Exchange effects would be disastrous in the case of international loans (double quotations, speculation, arousing of false hopes or misgivings among the bondholders)" (League Committee 1937:33). To limit the threat of lawsuits, however, the League Committee turned not to majority modification but to a narrower remedy: a bondholder vote to initiate litigation. One implication of this decision in the modern context is that, even if litigation can pose a barrier to sovereign restructurings, majority modification clauses are not the only potential solution. And in fact, until the sovereign debt crises of the 1980s and 1990s, majority modification clauses were almost never discussed seriously as an important mechanism of financial market reform.

MODERN CONTRACT REFORM AND THE "DISCOVERY" OF CACs

Although the sovereign bond markets were vibrant throughout much of the nineteenth and early twentieth centuries, the Depression brought bond lending to an abrupt halt. Countries continued to issue bonds sporadically and in small amounts, but the market did not revive in earnest until the 1990s (Flandreau et al. 2009; Flandreau, Gaillard, and Panizza 2010). Contemporary narratives date the "discovery" of CACs as a policy tool to the crises that followed soon after. CACs, of course, were not new. But as CACs assumed greater policy significance, the fact that many bond contracts did not use them called out for an explanation. In the sections that follow, we explore the contract reform efforts that began in the 1990s and continue today, and we highlight flaws in how reformers accounted for the (relative) lack of CACs in the marketplace. What remains is a picture with striking parallels to the 1930s: governments working to change prevailing contract terms, acting on the stated assumption that the market was not working properly.

[8] See, for example, Terms for resumption of service proposed by Czechoslovak Govt., Czechoslovak State Loan of 1922 (First Series and Series B) (1946).

The road to CACs (the 1990s and 2000s)

The modern history of sovereign debt contract reform begins in the aftermath of Mexico's "Tequila Crisis" of 1994–1995. Political turmoil, capital flight, and a plummeting currency put pressure on Mexican bonds, especially the short-term dollar-indexed *tesobonos*. If Mexico could not refinance or repay them, there seemed to be no way to restructure them. The specter of a messy default brought back fears of another Third World Debt crisis and "lost decade," a repeat of the 1980s. US finance officials, working with counterparts in other wealthy countries and multilateral institutions, engineered a rescue package. Creditor governments cited the difficulty of bond restructuring as a justification for the politically unpopular "bailout." The logical next step was to make bond restructuring plausible. The official postmortem was prepared by a "working party" under the auspices of the Group of Ten (G-10), a gathering of finance officials dominated by representatives of central banks. It proposed two options – treaty-based bankruptcy and a set of contract clauses to promote coordination, including creditor representation, majority modification, and sharing clauses. The statutory option was rejected outright; CACs remained.

The report, euphemistically entitled "The Resolution of Sovereign Liquidity Crises," (Group of Ten 1996) was noteworthy for several reasons. It was prepared by a G-10 group chaired by a Belgian official, Jean-Jacques Rey (hence its name, the "Rey Report") – apparently chosen as a compromise between the United States, thought to favor bailouts, and Germany, thought to be hyper-averse (Gelpern and Gulati 2006). The compromise message was that to the extent crises were expected to recur, official resources to resolve them were limited, and bond restructuring could not be excluded going forward. Bondholder coordination would be useful going forward, but it did not require bankruptcy. Contract clauses would be helpful, but would not be mandated.

This was a muted warning and a cautious set of recommendations. Even so, the contract reform line was puzzling, since it targeted New York-law bonds in response to a crisis in *tesobonos*, which were Mexican-law instruments. To our knowledge, no one had bothered to investigate whether these bonds could be restructured by contract, statute, or fiat. It might have been reasonable for officials to speculate that a foreign-law bond crisis was just around the corner, or simply use the discussion of well-understood New York-law contracts as a platform to signal a broad policy change.

In any case, advocacy of CACs was not a cheap rhetorical throwaway. It relied on academic research and market soundings to determine market practice and the extent to which officials would be willing to push it (Eichengreen and Portes 1995; Kenen 1996; Group of Ten 1996). The working party recommended three sets of contract clauses, one of which was majority modification. By this time, majority modification clauses had become commonplace in London, and appeared patently unobjectionable, especially since many emerging markets investors held both New York and English law bonds. But why was the New York market so behind the curve in adopting it? The Rey Report pointed to simple ignorance, a product of market segmentation:

> The resistance to qualified majority voting clauses expressed by market participants in some countries may be attributed to a lack of familiarity with such clauses in their national context. Increased public awareness of the extent to which qualified majority voting clauses are already used in some bonds, and official support for efforts by the private sector to make greater use of such clauses, should, over time, allow market participants to become more familiar and comfortable with the clauses both in principle and in practice.
>
> (Group of Ten 1996:20–21)

And so officials set out to increase public awareness and market comfort with CACs. These efforts had barely begun when the Asian Financial Crisis struck, occasioning another round of soul-searching. Again, foreign-law bonds did not figure in the crisis, but were prominently featured in the policy response document issued by the Group of Twenty Two (G-22) wealthy and developing countries, represented by senior officials from finance ministries and central banks. The recommendation essentially carried over from the Rey Report:

> To encourage the adoption of such "collective action clauses," the Working Group recommends that their governments give consideration to: (i) engaging in educational efforts with identified constituencies in major financial centres to promote the use of collective action clauses in sovereign and quasi-sovereign bonds issued in foreign offerings; (ii) identifying sovereign and quasi sovereign issuers likely to come to their markets soon and encouraging such issuers to use the collective action clauses; and (iii) examining the use of such clauses in their own sovereign and quasi sovereign bonds issued in foreign offerings.
>
> (Group of Twenty Two 1998)

Again, education and outreach were front and center, though officials now considered both direct prodding of likely issuers and "leading by example" by including CACs in their own bonds.[9] Speeches and exhortations continued for a while, but as far as the official sector knew, the market would not budge.

CACs largely receded from public view as the crisis waned. They came back with a vengeance under a new US administration, which felt pushed into bailing out Argentina in the run-up to its 2001 default. The story of how CACs re-emerged as a policy tool is well-known and involves a contest between contract reform and a treaty-based restructuring mechanism supported by the IMF (Gelpern and Gulati 2006). Leery of "top-down" institutional solutions, US officials gravitated to contract change as a substitute. They dusted off CACs, though a slightly different set than had been proposed in the Rey Report. Majority modification, however, remained a centerpiece of the US-supported policy recommendations.

As part of an intensifying education campaign, CAC advocates at the US Treasury yet again called on the G-10, this time to produce model clauses that could be adopted by sovereign issuers. The group was chaired by Taylor's deputy Randal Quarles, a partner at the law firm of Davis Polk before his government appointment. The Quarles group commissioned draft clauses from leading law practitioners, which were issued together with the policy recommendations. This drafting effort was accompanied by relentless outreach, where Taylor and his deputies would call and cajole individual finance ministers and underwriters to use majority modification in their next bond issue. G-10 drafters also found themselves in competition with private industry groups that had finally decided to take official exhortations to heart and produce their own model CACs (Group of Ten 2002).

The decisive shift in sovereign debt contracts came, courtesy Mexico, which included majority modification in a 2003 issue of New York-law bonds (Haseler 2009). Part of the story is that Mexico's status as a

[9] This was a meaningful statement inasmuch as the group included both wealthy and developing countries.On the one hand, it is not clear to what extent the developing country members of the group were expected to follow through. On the other hand, the idea of wealthy countries leading by example was either naïve or disingenuous. Emerging markets finance officials repeatedly said in interviews that they viewed rich country contract practices as largely irrelevant to their own. They worried about the pricing effects of CACs, and expected them to diverge for the two groups of countries. Moreover, since most wealthy countries issued the bulk of their debt under their own laws, the commitment to adopt CACs in foreign-law bonds was essentially an empty promise for many members of the group, notably the United States.

market leader was crucial to the shift in New York-law bonds.[10] After Mexico, Brazil, and Uruguay issued New York bonds with CACs, the market turned on a dime. Focusing only on collective modification clauses, Figure 3.1 illustrates the shift. Before 2003, only a handful of New York-law bonds included collective modification clauses. After 2003, these clauses appeared in nearly every issuance (Weidemaier and Gulati 2013; Bradley and Gulati 2014).

Officials declared victory, and with good reason: the shift was unprecedented in the history of contract boilerplate, and could not have happened without them by all accounts. Education and outreach worked; markets saw the light and improved their contracts. CACs again receded from public view.

SOME FLAWS IN THE NARRATIVE – EPISODIC USE OF CACs

This broader narrative of official intervention overcoming market ignorance was always somewhat at odds with the facts. For one thing, most English-law bonds already had modification clauses (Bradley and Gulati 2014). Additionally, although most New York-law bonds required unanimity, researchers discovered a handful of bonds from the 1980s and 1990s with modification clauses. The ubiquity of modification clauses in the English-law market, and their occasional appearance in New York, raised the possibility that the choice of unanimity was a deliberate one.[11] For example, sovereign issuers in New York tended to have lower credit ratings (Bradley and Gulati 2014). Investors in the New York-law market might have worried more about restructuring and wanted to exercise more control in that event (Weidemaier and Gulati 2013). To be sure, investors who expect to restructure might value majority modification as a tool for making the inevitable go more smoothly.

[10] This was because many market participants worried that CACs would raise their borrowing costs. The fear had some grounding in theory: if CACs reduce the need for bailouts and facilitate "private sector involvement" in debt restructuring, private lenders might price this risk into their loans. On the other hand, CACs might also reduce the cost associated with protracted restructuring negotiations, and this might lower borrowing costs. Without a test case, it was not clear that any country would risk adding CACs to their bonds. Moreover, the test case could not be a small country on the market periphery. No one would follow the lead of such a bit player. Only a market leader could prompt a widespread change in contracts. The first mover and negative signal stories are discussed in Haseler (2009) and Eichengreen (1991).

[11] In theory, the unanimity requirement could have served multiple functions. For example, some investors may have preferred bonds that made restructuring harder, and these buyers may have dominated the New York-law market (Weidemaier and Gulati 2013).

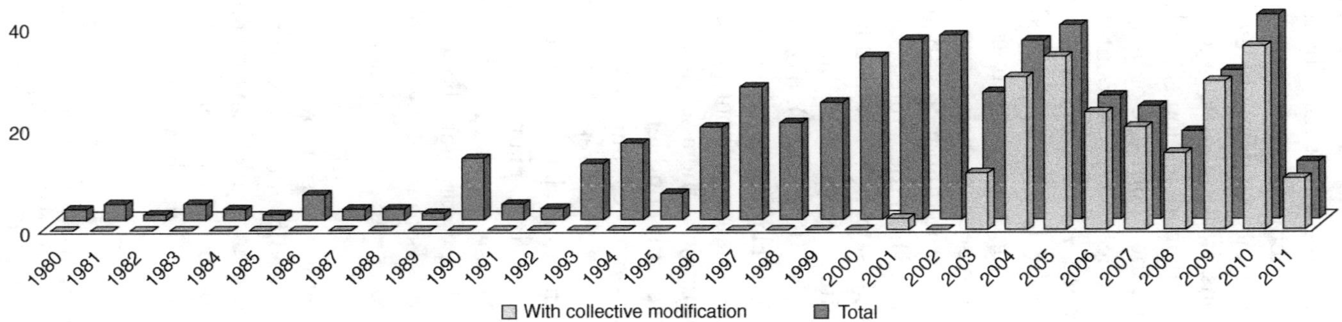

Figure 3.1 Collective modification clauses in bonds governed by NY law

Then again, they might turn to terms and techniques other than majority modification to accomplish the task (Bi, Chamon, and Zettelmeyer 2012). In sum, if market participants were aware of majority modification CACs, they might have rejected them in New York for any number of perfectly rational reasons. If this was a case of deliberate rejection, official promotion of majority modification is harder to justify.

CAC advocates adapted their narrative of market failure to accommodate these market practices. The account that emerged again emphasized lawyer ignorance. As the story goes, sovereign lending in the 1970s primarily took the form of syndicated commercial loans. Lawyers responsible for documenting sovereign bond issues in the 1980s and 1990s allegedly based the new sovereign bond documents on the closest template they could find: cross-border corporate bonds (Weidemaier and Gulati 2013). In the United States, the Trust Indenture Act of 1939 forbids the use of majority modification clauses in corporate bonds.[12] The architects of this prohibition viewed bankruptcy as the preferred alternative (Roe 1987). For sovereigns, however, bankruptcy is not an option. Had lawyers been more attentive to the need to provide for a coordinated workout process, they would have modified corporate bonds to make them suitable for sovereign borrowers. But their inexperience with bond lending meant that lawyers did little more than copy the corporate template.

This story ruled out investor preference as an explanation for the absence of majority modification clauses in the New York sovereign market. It also offered a basis for explaining the prevalence of majority modification in English-law bonds. The lawyers there, the story goes, simply copied *English*-law corporate bonds (or sovereign bonds derived from that template). Because of legal differences between the markets, the English law corporate template included CACs (Buchheit and Gulati 2002).[13]

The inadvertent copying story also provided an explanation for the occasional use of majority modification in New York. Two researchers at the Reserve Bank of Australia, Mark Gugiatti and Anthony Richards (2004:815), discovered most of the early New York CACs. The issuers were relatively obscure ones – Kazakhstan, Lebanon, Bulgaria, Egypt,

[12] 15 U.S.C. § 77ppp.

[13] The copying story drew further support from the fact that English-law CACs might, in theory, allow a restructuring to proceed with the support of only a minority of bondholders (Weidemaier and Gulati 2013). To many observers, this made them seem ill suited for the sovereign context (Group of Ten 2002).

and Qatar – and had been using majority modification clauses in their New York law bonds since the late 1990s. Another instance of pre-Mexico CACs was in the World Bank-guaranteed bond issued by the state-owned Thai power company (Liu 2004).

Gugiatti and Richards (2004:823) attributed pre-Mexico CACs in New York-law bonds to accident. They posited that the lawyers who drafted these New York-law bonds inadvertently began *with English-law forms*. According to the story, the lawyers who drafted the bonds worked in the London offices of New York firms, and they simply began with the (wrong) forms that were familiar to them. Gugiatti and Richards (2004:826) raised the question "whether the lawyers involved were cognizant of the innovative nature of the legal terms being used." Their answer, delicately phrased, was no: "[O]ur assessment is that [with one exception] the inclusion of CACs was not necessarily a deliberate decision and was perhaps even somewhat inadvertent" (Gugiatti and Richards 2004:827). For reformers, the story had clear implications, which Gugiatti and Richards (2004:827) spelled out: "[T]he marketplace has historically paid little or no attention to this particular aspect of bond contracts … [T]he inclusion of CACs has simply not been an important decision variable for borrowers or investors."[14]

Like the other copying stories, this one also supports the broader narrative of market failure. After all, if the New York-law CACs that preceded Mexico resulted from deliberate choice, this might imply that their omission elsewhere was similarly deliberate. The next section suggests, however, that inadvertent copying stories are hard to square with the contracts themselves.

Indonesia, 1983, and 1986

All of the bonds uncovered by Gugiatti and Richards (2004) were issued in the late 1990s.[15] We have uncovered modification clauses in two New York-law issues dating back to the 1980s. These bonds were issued by Indonesia in 1983 and 1986.[16]

[14] The Thai guaranteed bond was somewhat inconvenient for the story because it had been drafted by the Hong Kong office of a New York firm. The explanation given here was that this bond was somehow sui generis because it involved a co-guarantee from the International Bank for Reconstruction and Development (the World Bank).

[15] The earliest issue was in 1997.

[16] A caveat: the sales documents for these bonds do not specify the vote required to change payment terms. Instead, they refer readers to the Fiscal Agency Agreement, which we have not located. Theoretically, the Fiscal Agency Agreement could set a voting threshold of 100 percent, but we doubt this is the case. This would be an odd way to disclose that the bond's

The modification clauses found in these Indonesian bonds cannot easily be attributed to blind copying of London forms. The issues were managed out of New York. The law firms involved were White and Case for the issuer, and Sullivan and Cromwell for the underwriters. The roster of legal advisers in the prospectus includes Sullivan and Cromwell's New York office and three White and Case offices (New York, London, and Hong Kong). In theory, the bond template could have originated from White and Case offices in London or Hong Kong. However, because the underwriter's counsel typically provides the basic contract template (Gulati and Scott 2013, Chapter 2), it is more likely that the form originated in Sullivan and Cromwell's New York office. This is especially so in the Indonesian sovereign offering, because Sullivan and Cromwell was much more active in the sovereign market than White and Case at the time (Bradley et al. 2014).

Lawyers at Sullivan and Cromwell knew how to draft New York-law bonds and had plenty of forms at their disposal. It seems implausible that they would have copied the template from London, unless the issuer or the underwriter specifically requested the English law contract form or particular provisions, such as majority modification.

Lebanon, 1997

The earliest New York-law bond contracts with CACs identified by Gugiatti and Richards (2004:823) documented a 1997 bond issue by Lebanon, backed by a World Bank guarantee.[17] The US lawyers who led the work on this issue were based in New York, not London. Dewey Ballantine, headquartered in New York, represented the underwriters; Freshfields, headquartered in London, represented the issuer. Assuming standard practice, Dewey Ballantine would have provided the deal template, both because it was counsel for the underwriters and because the issuance was to be governed by New York law.

Yet even if these New York-law bonds began with English-law forms, the evidence suggests that the lawyers involved were engaged in design, not copying. Within months of its first issuance in 1997, Lebanon issued a second bond governed by New York law. Once again, Dewey Ballantine was counsel for the underwriters. This time, however, the lawyers

payment terms could *not* be modified. Moreover, it is typical for English-law bonds to refer to the underlying agency agreement for information about voting thresholds for modification. New York-law bonds typically disclose the unanimity requirement in the prospectus itself.

17 Citing July 2 Lebanon Offering Circular.

involved worked at Dewey Ballantine's London office.[18] They could have used Lebanon's English-law templates, from a bond issued only two years earlier, in 1995. They did not. Below, we reproduce the modification clause in Lebanon's 1995 English-law bonds and the modification clause in its 1997 New York-law bonds. The emphasis is ours and reveals important differences.

Lebanon, July 25, 1995 $300 million; 9.125 percent bonds due 2000 (English Law)
The Agency Agreement contains provisions for convening meetings of the Bondholders to consider matters affecting their interests, including the modification by Extraordinary Resolution of these Conditions or the provisions of the Agency Agreement. The *quorum at any meeting for passing an Extraordinary Resolution will be* one or more persons present holding or representing a *clear majority in principal amount* of the bonds for the time being outstanding, *or at any adjourned meeting one or more present whatever the principal amount* of the Bonds held or represented by him or them, *except that at any meeting the business of which includes the modification of certain of these Conditions the necessary quorum* for passing an Extraordinary Resolution will be one or more persons present holding or representing no less than *two-thirds or at any adjourned meeting not less than one-third*, of the principal amount of the Bonds for the time being outstanding. An Extraordinary Resolution passed at any meeting of the Bondholders will be binding on all Bondholders, whether or not they are present at the meeting, and on all Couponholders.

Lebanon, October 29, 1997; $400 million; 8.625 percent bonds due 2007 (New York Law)
The Fiscal Agency Agreement contains provisions for convening meetings of Bondholders to consider any matter affecting their interests, including the modification of these Conditions or the provisions of the Fiscal Agency Agreement, provided that *no modification of the Conditions or the Fiscal Agency Agreement may be had without the consent or affirmative vote (by person or proxy) of persons holding or representing no less than 75 percent in aggregate principal amount* of Bonds then represented at the relevant meeting of Bondholders which would (i) change the due date for any amount payable by the Republic under the Bonds; (ii) reduce or cancel any portion of the principal amount of Bonds or

[18] The issuer's counsel was once again Freshfields.

the amount of interest or any other amount payable under the Bonds or modify the rate of interest on the Bonds; (iii) modify the currency of payment under the Bonds; (iv) change the identity of any Person obligated under the Bonds or the release, in whole or in part, of any such Person; or (v) modify the provisions of the Conditions or the Fiscal Agency Agreement relating to the quorum required at any meeting of Bondholders or the percentage of Bondholders required to pass any resolution or otherwise modify the provisions summarized in this paragraph. A resolution duly passed in accordance with the provisions of the Fiscal Agency Agreement at any meeting of the Bondholders will be binding on all Bondholders whether or not they are present at the meeting and whether or not they vote in favor.

At a minimum, the lawyers in Lebanon's second issuance of 1997 were choosing between two models of majority modification. The 1995 clause resembles the standard English-law modification clause of the period (Bradley and Gulati 2014). It specifies diminishing quorum requirements where, at an adjourned meeting, a small minority of bondholders could potentially modify the bond's payment terms. By contrast, the New York-law bond issued in October 1997 conditions modification on a vote of holders of 75 percent of the aggregate principal amount of the debt. The elevated voting threshold makes sense in the context of Rey Report consultations (conducted just a year earlier), which suggested that US investors viewed English modification requirements as too lax (Group of Ten 1996). In response to an inquiry about their motives from one of the authors, Lebanon's lawyers explained that they had deliberately sought to create a "hybrid" clause that "anticipat[ed] the need to restructure sovereign debt" without leaving open the possibility that a minority of bondholders could approve a restructuring (as in English-law bonds).[19]

Thailand, 1998

In October 1998 the Kingdom of Thailand guaranteed a New York-law bond issued by its state-owned electricity generating authority.[20] The country was still suffering from the worst financial crisis in modern memory; its firms had lost access to the global capital markets. Meanwhile, multilateral institutions were looking for ways to stretch their

[19] Letter from Louise Roman Bernstein at Dewey & LeBoeuf to Mitu Gulati (July 17, 2008) (on file with authors).

[20] See Electricity Generating Company of Thailand, $300 million bond, issued October 13, 1998, 7 percent bond due 2008.

resources to respond to the Asian crisis. As a result, this Thai parastatal bond issue got a non-accelerable principal guarantee and a single rolling coupon guarantee from the World Bank (1999).[21] Many in the official sector knew about this bond owing to the novel guarantee structure.

The bond contracts contained a modification clause; this fact was also known to the officials promoting CACs at the time, though not before the bonds were issued. The Thai offering coincided with the release of the G-22 recommendations on CACs in sovereign and quasi-sovereign bonds in October 1998.[22] The law firms involved included the Singapore and Thailand offices of White and Case, the Hong Kong office of Cleary Gottlieb, and the Thailand office of Freshfields. There was no obvious reason why that issue documentation should have been a product of blind copying from London models, though some speculated that the World Bank guarantee made standard drafting templates inapplicable in this case. Perhaps where the creditors' surest source of repayment – the World Bank – could not be accelerated in the event of default, it behooved everyone involved to consider interim restructuring scenarios with unusual care, which led them to CACs. In sum, the Thai issue was innovative in many respects; CACs were one of them; but in all, it was *sui generis*.

Our data set, however, includes one other government-guaranteed bond that includes a modification clause, and this one is not accompanied by a multilateral guarantee. Issued less than a month after the Thai experiment, this was a New York law bond guaranteed by the Czech Republic and issued by its domestic airline, Aero Vodochody.[23] Once again, White and Case was involved, representing the underwriters out of its Prague office.[24] We have no ready explanation for why majority modification clauses appeared in these (but only these) two guaranteed New York-law bonds in 1998; one possibility is experimentation by a particular law firm – though copying from EGAT in Aero is a possible subplot.[25]

21 Because the present value of a long-term, non-accelerable guarantee is very low, and a single coupon is small, the budget cost of the guarantee to the World Bank was very small at the outset.

22 Report of the Working Group on International Financial Crises.

23 See Aero Vodochody, $200 million, issued November 10, 1998, 7.5 percent bond due 2005.

24 The issuer counsel was the Prague office of the US firm, Altheimer & Grey.

25 We also found modification provisions in issuances by one sub-sovereign in 1999: a bond issued by the Italian city of Florence under New York law. See City of Florence, Offering Circular (April 29, 1999); City of Florence, Pricing Supplement (October 19, 1999). The modification clause in this bond cannot plausibly be attributed to drafter error or copying. The Florentine

We see little evidence that these early New York-law modification clauses can be attributed to blind copying. The more plausible explanation seems to be that these were small issuers, operating on the margins and under the radar screen, for whom the standard New York-law template did not work. And so they embraced CACs. Whether other players in the New York market could do the same thing without official sector orchestration is another question. What is clear, however, is that official actors were not inclined to let evidence of market experimentation derail the market failure narrative.

CONTRACT REFORM (RE)REDUX

The success story crafted by CAC promoters implied that, by the mid 2000s, CACs were everywhere. Consequentially, CACs again receded from public view. But they came back in the unlikeliest of places: Europe. When it turned out in 2010 that Greece was insolvent and would likely need a bond restructuring, CACs quickly emerged as a prominent policy response. This time, there was little effort to articulate a need for them. Finance officials simply invoked the G-10 effort from 2002, without elaborating the collective action problem that might necessitate a similar solution.[26] Bailouts were a concern, but the notion that CACs would obviate bailouts was even more tenuous this time around. Seven years into the CAC revolution, there was little evidence that the clauses affected the level of official financing in crisis. In Europe – including Greece – most debt was also governed by domestic law, and it could be amended relatively easily by statute.[27] Much of it was held by regulated financial institutions, notoriously susceptible to moral suasion. There was simply nothing to suggest that the barriers to Greek debt restructuring were *legal* rather than political or economic. Nevertheless, a standing committee of European debt managers was charged with designing CACs for both domestic and foreign debt of EU member states. Lawyers were hired, experts were polled, and drafting began anew.

Offering Circular explicitly specifies both a unanimity provision and a non-unanimity modification provision and states that subsequent pricing supplements should be understood to use the non-unanimity provision unless a particular supplement explicitly adopts the unanimity provision. Ibid. Terms and Conditions at 79–80 (Section 15(a) "Meetings requiring majority consent," and Section 15(b) "Meetings requiring unanimous consent").

26 Statement by the Eurogroup (November 28, 2010), www.consilium.europa.eu/press/press-releases/2010/11/pdf/Statement-by-the-Eurogroup.

27 This is just what Greece did in 2012 (Zettelmeyer et al. 2013).

The European effort differed from its recent predecessors in several ways. First, CACs were mandated by treaty. Each Eurozone member state committed to adopt CACs by entering into the treaty establishing the European Stability Mechanism (a crisis response vehicle). Standardization was an express goal, since European CACs were supposed to be functionally "identical." And the clauses that emerged were designed, in the words of one lawyer involved, "for countries that did not default" (Gelpern and Gulati 2013). For example, they contained an aggregation feature and far lower voting thresholds than the now-prevalent emerging market CACs, and allowed voting by entities owned or controlled by the sovereign debtor.[28] Greece notwithstanding, Europe stood united in telling bondholders that contracts did not matter.

Ironically, it was Greece that showed the world the limits of the CAC miracle. When it finally restructured its debt in 2012, it enacted a statute to amend over 90 percent of its debt, issued under Greek law, by retrofitting a bondholder voting mechanism dramatically out of line with market practice on CACs. The statute's quorum requirement of 50 percent combined with a voting threshold of 2/3 ensured that a mere 1/3 of its creditor body could bind the rest. Although Greece's foreign-law debt contained "real" CACs – embedded in contracts in line with long-standing practice under English law – more than half of the bondholder votes attempted in this group failed to garner the majority required to amend. Holdouts under these instruments continue to be paid on schedule. Put differently, had Greece's restructuring depended on the CACs that won over the market after 2003, it might well have failed.

At exactly the same time in 2012, litigation stemming from Argentina's 2001 default was demonstrating new risks from holdout lawsuits. A federal court granted holdout creditors the right to block payments on Argentina's restructured debt, raising fresh concerns about creditor participation in future restructurings (IMF 2013). While Greece demonstrated that CACs could not block holdouts, Argentina demonstrated that holdouts were a real threat. Suddenly, the triumph of 2003 and the brand-new European initiative modeled after it looked woefully incomplete. Contract reforms that took so much time, effort, and political capital seemed partial at best, and beside the point at worst. By targeting individual clauses, with no capacity to alter the

[28] EFC Subcommittee on EU Sovereign Debt Markets, 'Supplemental Explanatory Note' (2012), http://europa.eu/efc/sub_committee/cac/cac_2012/index_en.htm.

broader contracting framework, officials seemingly missed the point. Whatever gains they secured in majority modification could be undone in other parts of the contract, or simulated elsewhere with restructuring techniques (Panizza , Sturzenegger, and Zettelmeyer 2009; Bi, Chamon, and Zettelmeyer 2012).

The officials' response? A new round of contract reform, gaining speed as we write. An informal working group convened by the US Treasury gathered market participants, officials from wealthy and emerging market countries and multilateral institutions, and academics, all with an eye toward promoting the adoption of new contract terms. The consultations resulted in a set of model clauses, published in August of 2014 by the International Capital Market Association (ICMA) (2014) and supported by a nearly contemporaneous report issued by the IMF (2014). The new clauses, modeled on the Greek "retrofit" statute used two years earlier, would permit a majority of creditors to amend their contracts in a single vote across different bond series, binding potential holdouts. Shortly after their initial publication, the ICMA clauses appeared with minor variations in several new bond issues by Mexico, Kazakhstan, and Vietnam. The rapid adoption by both major and small, infrequent issuers raised hopes that the clauses would quickly disseminate through the market. Whether this will spell the end of government-led contract reform, or encourage more, bolder efforts, is a question for another day.

CONCLUSION

For much of the life of the sovereign bond markets, officials not party to the bond contracts have tried to change their terms through research, education, and model drafting. This distinct mode of government intervention has focused, to a surprising degree, on the narrow range of contract clauses that fall under the CAC umbrella. Within this subset, official attention has narrowed even further, with modification clauses assuming key policy significance.

Of course, it is hard to fashion a coherent picture from a century of contracting practices. The snapshots we present in this paper are hardly dispositive. Even one sovereign bond issuance is the product of multiple individuals operating within different institutions having different goals and incentives. We do not pretend to offer a complete explanation of the role CACs have served in the sovereign debt markets. That said, our examination of contracts seems to depart from the standard narrative on the emergence of CACs in New York, which in turn became the predicate for the revival of CACs in the euro area, London, and New York.

First, the interest in reforming sovereign bond contracts in general, and modification clauses in particular, is hardly new. The League Committee tried mightily to improve on market standard in the 1930s. Its experts then did many of the same things that their successors did in the 1990s and 2000s – surveying market practices, searching for the origins of certain terms, and commissioning model clauses for private parties to adopt going forward. Then as now, the stated assumption among officials seemed to be that market participants needed a nudge to innovate. They would benefit from the "spade work" of government officials on their behalf, getting a valuable education in legal and economic history and comparative law, which would catalyze innovation that market participants could not manage on their own. Perhaps the major difference between government drafting efforts of the 1930s and their contemporary successors is the comprehensive focus of the former. Government drafters in the 1930s sought to take a broad view of contract reform, and as a result, came up with a relatively diffuse set of recommendations. Officials in the 1990s and 2000s have maintained a sharp focus on majority modification, even as other clauses have crept on and off the agenda, and as innovations in restructuring techniques made much of the agenda questionable if not obsolete.[29]

On the other hand, even back in the 1930s, there was evidence that private contract drafters were engaged in a fair amount of experimentation, from the rare use of collective acceleration clauses to the more frequent use of trustees (24 percent of our pre-War sample). These clauses, however, never entered widespread use. At all times, officials attributed CACs' scarcity to market failure rather than to targeted innovation and deliberate choice. To us, this tendency represents a puzzle. Historical evidence tells us that the bond markets have a greater capacity to innovate than reformers attribute to them. Market participants have long been familiar with CACs – defined in the broad sense as clauses that facilitate bondholder coordination – and have frequently adopted, adapted, and improved upon them. So why should governments assign these clauses such policy value? And why majority modification in particular?

[29] Bi et al., 'The problem that wasn't'.

Holdouts may pose a greater threat today than at any point in history. Now that lawsuits against sovereigns may do more than create hassle on the margins – indeed, now that holdouts have achieved some rather spectacular (if perhaps temporary) victories[30] – perhaps CACs have become more important as tools to limit holdout litigation.[31] If so, this does not explain the focus on *modification clauses* over other contractual methods for addressing holdout concerns. Nor does it link majority modification CACs to the other official-sector justification for them: the imperative to stop bailouts. The link between bailouts and CACs has never been tightly drawn. It is absurd to suggest that recent bailouts – of Greece in 2010, or of Mexico in 1995 – had anything to do with the absence of CACs from the relevant bonds (Gelpern and Gulati 2013). Majority modification CACs have become a talisman, invoked to imply that small contractual tokens can ward off the great problems associated with sovereign borrowing in interconnected global markets.[32]

The dominant narrative of the emergence of CACs abets this practice by suggesting that contract reform is beyond the capacity of individual market actors, but can be achieved or at least catalyzed with official involvement deep in the contractual substance. We too share the belief that bond contracts may not contain the optimal set of terms (Gulati and Scott 2013). But a more accurate historical narrative begins by acknowledging that the bond markets exhibit more innovation than is often acknowledged. Perhaps governments can play a salutary role in encouraging widespread use of contract terms; this is not the same as innovating from scratch.

We have not solved the puzzle of official involvement in sovereign bond contract drafting. However, the surprising consistency in official methods gives us pause. When governments refuse to act as regulators, but act instead as market participants, it makes for a useful thought experiment to take them at their word. Perhaps the real problem officials are trying to solve is not one of third-party private contract drafting, but rather a harder problem of governance. Time and again,

30 For example, seizing an Argentinian naval vessel, see Benson (2012), and obtaining an injunction that may require Argentina to choose between paying holdouts or defaulting on its restructured debt, see *NML Capital Ltd.* v. *Republic of Argentina*, 699 F3d 246 (2nd Cir. 2012).

31 This assumes the clause is properly drafted (Gelpern 2012).

32 As noted earlier, CACs appear to be the solution du jour. For example, we have also seen proposals to add collective action clauses to bonds issued by US municipalities. See Remarks of James E. Spiotto, Field Hearing on the State of the Municipal Securities Market (July 29, 2011), www.sec.gov/spotlight/municipalsecurities/statements072911/spiotto.pdf.

governments in some countries find themselves as guarantors of other governments' debts. Fear of contagion prods them to pay on the guarantee, despite deep misgivings about fiscal outlays and moral hazard. Private creditors then lend based on the implicit guarantee. Officials find themselves unable to solve the contagion problem, nor the policy problems in other countries that give rise to crises, and this validates private creditors' expectations of a rescue. Officials then try to limit their taxpayers' losses and control moral hazard by "bailing in" private creditors. Because governments put a premium on preserving flexibility in systemic crisis response, they refuse to structure "bail-ins" through regulation. In contrast, contract reform to facilitate bond modification makes it easier for officials to ask private creditors to share in the crisis losses. Against this background, presumptive resistance to contract reform among creditors may not be a surprise after all.

References

Adamson, Michael R. 2002. "The failure of the foreign bondholders protective council experiment, 1934–1940." 76 *Business History Review* 479.

Bi, Ran, Marcos Chamon, and Jeromin Zettelmeyer. 2012. "The problem that wasn't: coordination failures in sovereign debt restructurings." IMF Working Paper 11/265.

Bradley, Michael and Mitu Gulati. 2014. "Collective action clauses for the eurozone: an empirical analysis." 18 *Review of Finance* 2045–2102.

Buchheit Lee C. and G. Mitu Gulati. 2002. "Sovereign bonds and the collective will." 51 *Emory Law Journal* 1324–1326.

Decorzant, Yann and Juan H. Flores. 2012. "Public borrowing in harsh times: the league of nations loans revisited," Universidad Carlos III de Madrid Working Papers in Economic History, Working Paper No. 12–07.

Eichengreen, Barry and Richard Portes. 1989. "After the deluge: default, negotiation, and readjustment during the interwar years," in Barry Eichengreen and Peter H. Lindert (eds.), *The International Debt Crisis in Historical Perspective*. Cambridge: MIT Press.

Eichengreen, Barry J. and Richard Portes. 1995. *Crisis? What Crisis? Orderly Workouts for Sovereign Debtors*. Center for Economic and Policy Research.

Eichengreen, Barry. 1991. "Historical Research on International Lending and Debt." 5 (2) *Journal of Economic Perspectives* 149–169.

Flandreau, Marc, Juan Flores, Norbert Gaillard, and Sebastián Nieto-Parra. 2009. "The end of gatekeeping: underwriters and the quality of sovereign bond markets 1815–2007." NBER Working Paper No. 15128.

Flandreau, Marc, Norbert Gaillard, and Ugo Panizza. 2010. "Conflicts of interest, reputation, and the interwar debt crisis, banksters or bad luck?" HEID Working Paper.

Galvis, Sergio J. and Angel L. Saad. 2004. "Collective action clauses: recent progress and challenges ahead." 35 *Georgetown Journal of International Law* 713.

Gelpern, Anna. 2012. "Sovereign Restructuring After NML v. Argentina: CACs Don't Make Pari Passu Go Away," Credit Slips, May 3. www.creditslips.org/creditslips/2012/05/sovereign-restructuring-after-nml-v-argentina-cacs-dont-make-pari-passu-go-away.html

Gelpern, Anna and Mitu Gulati. 2006. "Public symbol in private contract: a case study." 84 *Washington University Law Review* 1656.

Gelpern Anna and Mitu Gulati. 2013. "The wonder clause." 41 *Journal of Comparative Economics* 367–385.

Group of Ten. 1996. "The Resolution of sovereign liquidity crises." www.bis.org/publ/gten03.pdf

Group of Ten. 2002. "Report of the G-10 Working Group on Contractual Clauses," www.bis.org/publ/gten08.pdf

Group of Twenty Two. 1998. "Report of the Working Group on International Financial Crises." www.bis.org/publ/othp01d.pdf

Gugiatti, Mark and Anthony Richards. 2004. "The use of collective action clauses in New York law bonds of sovereign issuers." 35 *Georgetown Journal of International Law* 815.

Gulati, Mitu and Robert E. Scott. 2013. *The Three and a Half Minute Transaction: Boilerplate and the Limits of Contract Design*. Chicago: University of Chicago Press.

Haseler, Sonke. 2009. "Collective action clauses in international sovereign bond contracts – whence the opposition." 23 *Journal of Economic Surveys* 882.

International Capital Market Association. 2014. *Standard Collective Action and Pari Passu Clauses for the Terms and Conditions of Sovereign Notes*, ICMA (August 29, 2014), www.icmagroup.org/resources/Sovereign-Debt-Information

International Monetary Fund. 2013. "Global financial stability report: transition challenges to stability." www.imf.org/ExternalPubsFTGFSR2013/02/pdf/text.pdf

International Monetary Fund. 2014. *Strengthening the Contractual Framework to Address Collective Action Problems in Sovereign Debt Restructuring*, IMF (September 2, 2014), www.imf.org/external/pp/longres.aspx?id=4911

Kahan Marcel and Michael Klausner. 1997. "Standardization and innovation in corporate contracting (or "the economics of boilerplate")." 83 *Virginia Law Review* 713.

Kenen Peter B. (ed.). 1996. *From Halifax to Lyons: What Has Been Done About Crisis Management?* Princeton: Princeton University International Economics Section.

League Committee. 1937. "Report of the League of Nations Committee for the Study of International Loan Contracts." *Legal Questions Concerning International Loans*, Note on the Literature of the Subject, Part III, Trustees and Bondholders' Representatives, November 19, 1937.

Liu, Yan. 2004. "Collective Action Clauses in International Sovereign Bonds." IMF Working Paper. www.imf.org/external/np/leg/sem/2002/cdmfl/eng/liu.pdf

Panizza, Ugo, Federico Sturzenegger, and Jeromin Zettelmeyer. 2009. "The economics and law of sovereign debt and default." 47 *Journal of Economic Literature* 651–98.

Quarles, Randal. 2010. "Herding cats: collective action clauses in sovereign debt – the genesis of the project to change market practices in 2001 through 2003." 73 *Law and Contemporary Problems* 29.

Roe, Mark J. 1987. "The voting prohibition in bond workouts." 97 *Yale Law Journal* 232.

Taylor, John B. 2007. *Global Financial Warriors: The Untold Story of International Finance in the Post-9/11 World.* New York: W. W. Norton & Company, Inc.

Weidemaier, W. Mark C., and Mitu Gulati. 2001. "A people's history of collective action clauses." 54 *Virginia Journal of International Law* 51.

Weidemaier W. Mark C., and Mitu Gulati. 2013. "How markets work: the lawyer's version." 62 *Studies in Law, Politics, and Society* 107.

World Bank. 1999. Project Finance and Guarantees, 'Thailand: EGAT Paves the Way' http://siteresources.worldbank.org/INTGUARANTEES/Resources/EGATThailand_PFG_Note.pdf

Zettelmeyer, Jeromin et al. 2013. "The Greek debt restructuring: an autopsy." *Economic Policy*. 28: 513–563.

CHAPTER FOUR

MARKET RULES: SOCIAL CONVENTIONS, LEGAL FICTIONS, AND THE ORGANIZATION OF SOVEREIGN DEBT MARKETS IN THE LONG TWENTIETH CENTURY

Stephen C. Nelson

It is puzzling that in the voluminous International Relations (IR) literatures on governance and order in world politics one finds relatively few references to social conventions.[1] After all, "it would scarcely be an exaggeration to say that almost all economic and social institutions are governed to some extent by convention" (Young 1996: 105). Some examples from a range of pricing activities illustrate the point. In the United States' property market home prices fluctuate over time; the standard deviation of Robert Shiller's real home price index in the years between 1960 and 2012 is 21.87. The commission that real estate agents take from a home sale, on the other hand, did not budge from the conventional six percent for many decades.[2] Prices of visual art in Amsterdam and New York are not determined by the intersection of demand and supply schedules; rather, artists and gallery owners follow a set of conventions, from unwillingness to lower the prices of unsold artworks to setting prices of works in an artist's oeuvre by size or type rather than anticipated demand for each piece (Velthuis 2003).

Scholars of economic sociology, by contrast, have paid considerable attention to the social and cultural embeddedness of markets. For instance, Viviana Zelizer (2011) explains how societies choose to set

[1] Andrews (1975); Young (1983); Kratochwil (1989, 1993); Koslowski and Kratochwil (1994); Hall (1997), and Daase (1999) are notable exceptions.

[2] Even in 2009, in the midst of a massive crisis in the market and after the proliferation of websites meant to reduce the power of brokers, the average commission in the United States was 5.36 percent. Susan Stellin, "You Don't Have to Pay It," *New York Times* (Online ed.), 28 January 2011. Available here: www.nytimes.com/2011/01/30/realestate/30cov.html.

limits on the things which can be priced and exchanged; despite the growing tendency to put a price on almost anything, some things (like children) remain excluded from the realm of commensurability and exchangeability (Sandel 2012; Wherry 2012). Some economic sociologists focus on the embeddedness of social relations within various forms of market coordination (Callon 1998; Beckert 2011). Philosophers and economists have also explored how communities evolve different social conventions when they face recurrent coordination dilemmas (Lewis 1969; Sugden 1989). In sum, the coordinating and stabilizing roles of social conventions shared by market actors are amply demonstrated in economic sociology (Biggart and Beamish 2003; Dobbin 2004; Beckert 2009) and in the French *économie des conventions* approach (Storper and Salais 1997; Lazega and Favreau 2002; Jagd 2007).

Markets – whether local, national, or transnational – are social institutions that are governed, at least partially, by non-codified norms and conventions. International markets are also (increasingly) spaces that are governed by law. The intertwining of law and politics at the international level has not escaped the attention of IR scholars; in 2000 the field's premier journal, *International Organization*, devoted a special issue to observing and theorizing what Finnemore and Toope (2005) call the "legal bureaucratization" of world politics. The "legalization" perspective focused on three dimensions of legal institutions: obligation, precision, and delegation (Abbott et al. 2000). Issue areas are subject to "hard law" when the legal institution governing that area features high values on all three dimensions (exemplified by the WTO's Dispute Settlement System). From the legalization perspective the most important issue is whether law in a given issue area is soft/weak or hard/strong. The actors that produce legal instruments, in this perspective, can (at least in principle) adjust the three dimensions to "produce an institution exactly suited to their specific needs" (Abbott et al. 2000: 404). Law was conceptualized as a problem-solving device, the terms of which are negotiated by instrumental, rational actors. Variation in the strength/firmness of law in different issue areas in world politics is usually explained as an outcome of the struggle between states, whose interests and material capabilities vary, to extend or restrain the force of law, and the competing demands of domestic interest groups whose interests are affected by legalization (Kahler 2000).

A very different view of law emerges from the work on derivatives markets by the economic anthropologist Annelise Riles (2010, 2011). In her ethnographic study of the writing of collateral contracts in Japan's financial derivatives market, Riles directs our attention to the way in which seemingly arcane, technical, and apolitical contractual clauses serve as "legal fictions" that enable the transacting parties to act "as if" the ambiguity about what will happen in the (unknowable) future has been mapped out so that the deal can be completed. Legal fictions do not resolve the fundamental uncertainties that parties to a financial market transaction actually face. Rather, the contractual clauses sweep uncertainty – at least for the moment – under the rug (Pénet and Mallard 2014). Market participants may not believe in or even fully understand the meaning of a "placeholder" that appears in financial market contracts (Riles 2011). The contractual clause is instead a tool, a means to produce the end (which, in Riles' case, is the swap transaction between market players backed by collateral).

The common feature of the work on social conventions and legal fictions is that both concepts are explained as responses to uncertainty. The conceptual distinction between risky and uncertain settings comes from Knight (1921) and Keynes (1921, 1937). A risky environment is one in which we have a sizeable sample of comparable past events *and* we know enough about the process by which those events were generated to be able to generate a probability distribution. With the distribution in hand we can forecast the results of our decisions with reasonable accuracy. Uncertainty, by contrast, means that we cannot forecast the future with much accuracy. We face uncertainty when, for example, a market is subject to dramatic transformations in the underlying economic structure that permanently shift the mean of the distribution of events (Meltzer 1982: 17).

Conventions allow pragmatic, intentional agents seeking steadier footing to face epistemic uncertainty. In the world of risk the assumption that agents follow consistent, rational, instrumental decision rules is plausible. But that assumption becomes untenable when parameters are too unstable to quantify the prospects for events that may or may not happen in the future (Keynes 1937; Lawson 1985: 915–16; Nelson and Katzenstein 2014). Conventions simplify uncertain situations by enabling agents to impose classification schemas on the world, thereby "delineating the set of circumstances in which it [the convention] is applicable and can serve as a guide" (Kratochwil 1984: 688; see also Kratochwil 1989: 69–72). Thus, central to my argument is the opposition between conventional judgment and rational expectations, which corresponds to the distinction between uncertain and risky environments.

For Riles, legal fictions are also responses to uncertainty that inheres in financial markets. Keynes long ago distinguished goods in product markets that are consumed "within a short interval of their being produced" from financial assets, the future market price of which cannot be forecasted with much accuracy due to the "the fact that our knowledge of the future is fluctuating, vague, and uncertain" (Keynes 1937: 213). Riles argues along similar lines: "information about past market transactions can never fully predict future market problems or opportunities. Assets have value (positive or negative) that is by definition only discoverable over time and can never be fully predicted in advance…Relationships between market participants with respect to those assets unfold in time in ways that can never be fully anticipated or ensured" (Riles 2011: 159). Legal fictions, like social conventions, serve as substitutes for axiomatically rational calculations that are only possible in markets characterized by pure risk. Legal fictions and social conventions enable pragmatic agents operating in the presence of uncertainty to overcome the paralyzing effects of "having to act in unpredictable environments" – not because social conventions and legal fictions actually transform the decision setting from uncertain to risky but because they allow agents to overlook "the profound uncertainty entailed in decisions by increasing commitment to what remain fictional expectations" (Riles 2011: 169; Beckert 2013a; Beckert 2013b).

Sovereign debt markets, like all markets for financial assets, are marked by uncertainty. Buyers of sovereign debt are making bets about the prices of financial assets that will be realized in the (sometimes distant) future. During crises the uncertainty facing market participants is pervasive; in more settled times the market functions with less uncertainty and more risk. But even in "normal" times the issuer and the buyer are engaged in an exchange that takes place in the shadow of a future state of the world that cannot be forecasted. In response to this "temporal problem of finance" market participants develop conventions and legal fictions to inform their expectations (Riles 2011).

Sovereign debt is among the largest classes of international financial assets, and it is growing in importance.[3] The chapter is organized around two puzzling, politically salient features of the market for sovereign

[3] The face value of outstanding sovereign debt rose from 11 percent of the total global value of financial assets in 1978 to 17 percent in 1990 to 19 percent in 2010 (Tomz and Wright 2013: 251).

debt. The first puzzle is the inability of governments of low- and middle-income countries to denominate the sovereign debt instruments that they place internationally in their own currencies. Eichengreen and Hausmann (1999, 2005) were the first to note the difference between the sovereign debt contracts written by the historically rich countries of North America, Western Europe, Oceania, and Japan (who can borrow in their own currencies) and everyone else; they called the condition "original sin," because "it is as if emerging markets suffer from an inherited burden, almost irrespective of the policies of their governments" (Eichengreen and Hausmann 2005: 6). I present data on the extent of original sin in so-called "developing" and "emerging" countries, examine the covariates of an indicator of original sin to see if it can be rationalized as a consequence of bad policies or weak political institutions, and ask whether it instead makes more sense to think about original sin as the product of an enduring convention followed by participants in the international sovereign debt market.

The second feature is the inclusion of the pari passu clause in sovereign debt contracts. In English "pari passu" means "in equal step." The clause is typically a single sentence occupying several lines of text, and it appears "in most cross-border credit instruments" (Buchheit and Pam 2004: 871). The conventional understanding of pari passu was that it proscribed borrowers from ranking debts, such that in a debt rescheduling event one outstanding obligation could not be paid before the others (Buccheit and Pam 2004; Gulati and Scott 2013). Unlike the practice of denominating developing and emerging countries' international debt issuances in a foreign currency, which is not a formal rule that has been written down, pari passu is a legal covenant. Even though pari passu is codified in a contract, it has a fictional quality: the precise meaning of the clause is obscure and contested, and the lawyers that include the provision in the contracts that they draft for their clients (borrowing governments) have difficulty explaining why they insert the clause in the contract and where the clause came from (Varottil 2011; Gulati and Scott 2013). The fictional element of the pari passu is that a bondholder's rights and obligations are clearly defined and enforceable. Rather than resolving uncertainty the clause introduces other ambiguities: if the sovereign borrower's legislature passes a law preventing the government from paying "holdouts" that do not participate in a debt rescheduling but the debt was issued in a different jurisdiction (in New York, for example), which legal system applies? What happens if the sovereign borrower violates the clause? What constitutes a violation of the covenant?

My chapter, like the others in the volume, foregrounds the important role in international market-based transactions played by contractual knowledge, but I approach the theme of the volume from a different angle. The two features of debt contracts I discuss in the chapter – currency denomination and the pari passu clause – are widely followed practices that have little resemblance to rational adaptation by market players. The observed inability of nearly all countries outside the subset of historically rich democracies to borrow internationally in their own currencies cannot be easily explained as a form of insurance against risks (deriving from institutional weakness or macro-economic instability) that are specific to the set of developing and emerging sovereign borrowers. The practice is more consistent with an evaluative process by which the conventional categories (rich/developed versus developing/emerging) employed by key market players (namely, the underwriters that bring the debt issuances to market and international investors who purchase sovereign debt) to sort and classify borrowers produce differences in their terms of access to the market. Likewise, the insertion of the pari passu clause in sovereign debt contracts appears to be driven by mimetic behavior among the members of the community of contract writers, most of whom did not have a clear grasp on the meaning or importance of the covenant.

Why does it matter that the decisions of members of communities – in this case, the actors involved in writing, buying, and selling sovereign debt instruments – are based in part on social conventions and legal fictions? It matters because convention-following behavior can generate outcomes that, in the words of Oran Young, "are hard to justify in terms of any reasonable standard of equity" (Young 1983: 105). Conventions are useful for coordinating agents' actions and stabilizing their expectations, and they are often reasonable ways of organizing action and making decisions. But these qualities do not imply that the conventions in use are optimal – and suboptimal rules can be widely followed and persist for a long time (Sugden 1989: 93–4; Young 1983: 96).

Conventions and contractual "placeholders" that function as rules in international financial markets are politically consequential. The inability to sell home currency-denominated debt on the international market, for example, is the wellspring from which a number of economic syndromes that trouble developing countries emerge.

Eichengreen et al. (2005b: 266) show that "the volatility of debt-servicing capacity of developing countries with original sin is nearly five times that of industrial countries that borrow abroad in their own currencies." The inability of developing countries to borrow abroad in their own currencies is a "structural defect" (Gourinchas and Obstfeld 2012) that harms their growth prospects. Original sin is related to currency mismatches on governments', firms', and individuals' balance sheets in developing countries: the different currency denomination of assets and liabilities can create a wave of bankruptcy, from the individual mortgager to the government, when the price of currency of the liability side shoots up relative to the currency on the asset side (Jeanne and Zettelmeyer 2005). Such exchange rate moves multiply the real value of external debt. The result is sometimes a triple crisis: depositors flee the banking system, the monetary authorities struggle to stabilize a sinking national currency, and, ultimately, the government has difficulty rolling over the external debt.

There is no single international organization or consistent set of formal rules to organize debt rescheduling when a government is unable to meet its obligations; rather, sovereign debt rescheduling has been handled in an ad hoc manner by a mélange of organizations and forums, including (but not limited to) commercial bankers and money managers, government officials, lawyers and judges, national and international courts, the IMF and the World Bank, the Institute for International Finance, credit rating agencies, and the Paris and London Clubs. There is wide variation in the terms of debt restructuring arrangements: creditors suffered a 75 percent loss in the Argentine restructuring concluded in 2005; when Greece reached an agreement in 2012 to reduce its external debt burden, bondholders took a 65 percent "haircut"; holders of Uruguayan bonds, by contrast, fared far better in the 2003 restructuring, taking just a 13 percent loss (Panizza et al. 2009: 673; Tomz and Wright 2013: 260). The evidence that debt restructuring after a sovereign default brings relief to the average distressed government is meager (Easterly 2002; Depetris and Kraay 2005).

The popularity of the pari passu clause was not hampered by the fact that "no one seems quite sure what the clause really means, at least in the context of a loan to a sovereign borrower" (Buchheit and Pam 2004: 875). The political consequence of the increasing usage of the clause in sovereign debt contracts over the past thirty years has been a growing shift in the balance of power away from governments toward private bondholders. Whereas prior to 1981 no sovereign bonds contained "versions of the clause that are especially favorable to holdout creditors," the toughest version of the clause now appears in 74 percent of bonds issued by developing countries (Tomz and Wright 2013: 256). The biggest beneficiaries of the conventional insertion of the pari passu clause in sovereign bonds have been the holdout creditors that refuse to participate in debt rescheduling negotiations.

What looks like a technical bit of mundane legal jargon in a contract that few (if any) bond buyers actually read is in fact a politically potent form of private governance of the market. The clause does not reduce the uncertainty that the bondholder faces; rather, it describes the exchange as a relationship involving rights and obligations of the contracting parties (see Riles 2010). Pari passu does nothing to clarify the probability of default or the price of the instrument, nor does it involve making predictions about what will actually happen in the future; rather, it generates the possibility of moving the discussion to the realm of law, and in doing so it empowers some actors and disempowers others. Like other legal fictions, the pari passu clause becomes "a kind of reality of its own . . . something that raises real world consequential problems that demand lawyers', and perhaps judges', academics', and bureaucrats' attention" (Riles 2011). The politics of the practice lie in the way in which the participants in the market struggle over the "political validity and legitimacy" of the legal fictions (Adler and Pouliot 2011: 27; Riles 2011).[4]

The two elements of the contemporary sovereign debt market discussed in this chapter do not appear to be the products of compulsory power exercised by states and private actors to rig the rules in their favor; nor do they look much like "rational, negotiated responses to the problems international actors face" (Koremenos, Lipson, and Snidal 2001: 768). "Original sin" and the *pari passu* clause each pre-date the onset of World War I by over forty years; and in both cases, the origin of the phenomenon is shrouded in mystery and the reason for its persistence is unclear.

[4] Consider this section from full page advertisements in the 30 June 2014 print editions of the *Financial Times* and *New York Times* taken out by the government of Argentina after the US Supreme Court chose not to overturn a decision by a judge in New York requiring Argentina to pay all of its bondholders, including those that did not participate in the 2005 and 2010 debt restructuring negotiations: "the fact that the prospectus transfers jurisdiction to the United States does not mean accepting court decisions that are impossible to comply with. All the more if any such decision violates the sovereign immunity principle effective in the United States as a higher-ranking institutional rule and if it interprets in a whimsical and absurd manner the pari passu principle."

SOCIAL CONVENTIONS AND THE STUDY OF INTERNATIONAL ORDERS

The two branches of the recent IR literature on sovereign debt mirror a more general division in the subfield between broadly material-rationalist and social-constructivist analytical frameworks (Katzenstein, Keohane, and Krasner 1998).

One branch emphasizes material interests, incomplete information, and political institutions. Michael Tomz (2007), for example, develops a theory to explain why sovereign debtors repay bondholders. Tomz argues that governments pay back their debts in order to preserve their reputations. He describes three types of reputations ascribed to governments by prospective investors: stalwarts, who honor the terms of debt contracts in good and bad times; fair-weathers, who repay in good times but default in bad; and lemons, who are likely to alter the terms of the debt contract in good and bad times. A country's reputation is based on its repayment history. Rational investors lack information about the government's "true" preferences with respect to its external debt load ("preferences, unlike economic statistics, exist in the hearts and minds of foreign leaders," Tomz 2007: 16); what they can observe is a borrower's behavior, which has a signaling function.

Since international bond buyers watch governments closely for signals, and rational governments know that investors use simple decision rules to screen debtors, then governments will realize that their reputations are at stake and if they care about their reputation they will honor the terms of the debt contract. Not all signals are relevant for investors; the only signal that will lead investors to update their priors is when a government acts contrary to its type (e.g., a reputed lemon fully repays during the trough of an international business cycle). The market's incentive structure "facilitates the emergence of a certain form of discipline and permits government debt to emerge" (Flandreau and Flores 2012: 215). Tomz is agnostic about whether governments care about their reputations or not, but the fact that "fair-weathers" and "lemons" pay more to borrow than reputed "stalwarts" implies that governments will not take decisions that harm their reputations lightly. In Tomz's model of the market for sovereign debt, governments and private lenders[5] are atomized, rational, and responsive to material

[5] While Tomz argues that bondholders of all kinds have "overwhelming incentives" to allocate credit based on their (rational) expectations about countries' propensities to repay, he distinguishes investment from commercial bankers, whose decisions may be shaped by other kinds of

incentives; rule-following (in the sense of honoring contractual obligations) is driven entirely by self-interest calculations; and the key contextual element of the market is incomplete information.

Others turn to the structure of domestic political institutions to explain aspects of the market for sovereign debt. Schultz and Weingast (2003) argue that since the mid 1600s every hegemonic power in the international system has had democratic institutions, and this correlation is not coincidental. In their words, "representative institutions enhance a state's borrowing power by making it easier for those with a stake in the repayment of debt to punish the sovereign in the event of default" (Schultz and Weingast 2003: 5). Democracies prevail in hegemonic competitions due to the fact that they have access to plentiful credit at comparatively cheap prices. A recent article by Beaulieu et al. (2013) similarly finds that democratic regimes benefit from better access to credit (some autocratic countries cannot even enter the international bond market) and the bonds they issue garner higher ratings from credit rating agencies.

The rationalist understanding of the market for sovereign debt follows the widely held view by IR scholars of order in world politics: forms of governance evolve in response to exogenous shocks in a given issue area that generate the need for negotiated solutions. Institutions and rules are optimal bargained solutions adopted by rational agents, differently endowed with social and material sources of power, seeking to maximize their (often material) interests (most likely to be measured by prices paid for certain goods they can obtain on markets), subject to environmental pressures and constraints. Undoubtedly this rationalist analytical lens captures a lot of what goes on in world politics. But it does not shed light on how policy issues can be the *endogenous* products of actors following social conventions; nor does it capture the "numerous cases in which subjects' expectations converge to a remarkable degree in the absence of conscious design or even explicit awareness" (Young 1983: 98).

The constructivist approach disputes the material basis of actors' interests. Martha Finnemore's (2003) work on the evolution of the norms governing the enforcement of sovereign debt is an exemplar. Finnemore traces the proscription of the practice of "gunboat

incentives (they might lend to a country in arrears as part of a "defensive" bailout package, or they might be more responsive to political incentives to extend credit to a borrower since they may derive income from activities other than lending).

enforcement" in the early twentieth century to principled arguments against the practice advanced by an emergent global epistemic legal community. Before 1907 military intervention to collect collateral pledged against an outstanding debt was common. Finnemore details how the international legal community and allies in powerful political positions, such as U.S. Secretary of State Elihu Root (a lawyer by training and the first president of the American Society for International Law), reconfigured states' and bankers' understanding of the rules of the sovereign debt market. Just a half-decade after British and German forces bombed and blockaded Venezuela after strongman Cipriano Castro repudiated the country's foreign debts, Root was able to put the end of military intervention for debt collection on the table at the Hague Peace Conference (Finnemore 2003: 33–4).

Finnemore's work is about the formulation and adoption of a norm that asserted the primacy of international law to resolve disputes between debtors and creditors (on the rise of arbitration, see Sgard as well as Dezalay and Garth in this volume). In this case states followed the norm even though it was not in their material interest to do so. The argument is consistent with a line of research in IR that explores how social norms can serve as reasons for action (Kratochwil 1984, 1989; Hurd 1999).

As I noted in the first section of the chapter, a rather small number of IR scholars have asked whether some of the patterns of behavior we observe in the international realm are consistent with convention-following. Oran Young was one exception; in his contribution to the *International Regimes* volume he argued, "it is hard to escape the conclusion that spontaneous orders are of critical importance in the international system just as they are in other realms" (Young 1983: 102). As the Bretton Woods monetary system fell apart in the early 1970s the international economist John Williamson reflected on the new "non-system" that was taking its place: "the world is to function on the basis of a set of conventions and practices that have evolved out of a mixture of custom and crisis" (Williamson John 1976: 54).

What are social conventions, and why do agents use them? In philosopher David Lewis' (1969) account, social conventions are rules adopted in order to solve recurrent coordination problems that almost every member of a community follows. Lewis' conceptualization of conventions helps us understand how, in "pure" coordination games with multiple equilibria, social conventions provide "a consistent structure of mutual expectations about the preferences, rationality and actions of agents" that facilitate stable, recurrent patterns of cooperation (David 1994: 209). But it seems too restrictive to limit the concept of conventions to include only solutions to coordination problems (Gilbert 1989). It does not make much sense to view enduring conventions in, for example, classical music or in children's bedtime stories as efficient solutions to some kind of cooperation problem (Biggart and Beamish 2003: 452–3; Marmor 2009).

Some social conventions are followed not because they are solutions to coordination dilemmas but rather because they "supply the foundations for stability . . . because they limit the debilitating effects of interactional uncertainty" (Biggart and Beamish 2003: 452). In financial markets social conventions are important because they "provide a means in the present of calculating and feigning control over a necessarily uncertain future" (Langley 2008: 481). They give agents confidence to make judgment calls when resources and prestige are at stake. In legal philosopher Andrei Marmor's (2009) conceptualization, social conventions are social rules that members of a population (more or less) follow in some circumstance(s) for a reason. For Marmor, conventions have an arbitrary quality; there may be a good reason to follow the convention in use, but there is a counterfactual scenario in which we can conceive of an alternative rule "that could have been followed instead without a significant loss in its function or purpose" (Marmor 2009: 9). Conventions are more than just observed behavioral regularities. I drink coffee every morning but that is not an instance of rule-following. Social conventions have a normative quality even if they are not norms (Young 1983: 94–5; Marmor 2009: 13). The prescriptive element of social conventions provides "a basis for judging the appropriateness of acts by self and others" (Biggart and Beamish 2003: 444).

Conventions exercise themselves at different levels. Consider four elements of the international sovereign debt markets: (1) *Actors* – government officials, staff members from international organizations, commercial bankers and money managers, lawyers, judges, and legal experts, credit rating agencies, among others; (2) *Actions* – decisions by governments to borrow internationally and to repay or not; decisions by financiers whether or not to lend and the terms (price, maturity) on which they will extend credit; decisions by lawyers about what goes into (and what's left out of) contracts; (3) *Contexts for action* – including, among many others, the density of networks connecting the actors and the degree of "regime complexity" (Alter and Meunier 2009) in which the actors are embedded; (4) *Rules for action* – formal legal obligations, requirements of membership in international organizations, causal beliefs, norms and principles, and "shared templates" that agents rely on, sometimes consciously but at other times tacitly, to classify "phenomena in order to make them manageable, and once classified, to select an appropriate program of action" (Biggart and Beamish 2003: 444, 452; see also Nelson and Katzenstein 2014).[6] Conventions enter in each of the elements; most clearly as rules that market participants follow, but also by constituting the actors that can legitimately participate in the market, shaping the kinds of actions available to participants, and forming part of the contexts in which the markets and the players operate. The arguments and evidence in this chapter suggests that we can miss important facets of the organization of international financial markets if we overlook or dismiss the role of conventions and legal fictions.

CONVENTIONS AND CATEGORIES IN INTERNATIONAL SOVEREIGN DEBT CONTRACTS: THE MYSTERY OF ORIGINAL SIN

Processes of commensuration and categorization, several prominent sociologists argue, constitute an essential part of the bedrock upon which markets rest (Espeland and Stevens 1998; Fourcade and Healy 2013; Lamont 2012). These processes are particularly important when transactions span continents; commensuration, in Espeland and Stevens' view, "makes possible precise comparisons across vast cultural and geographical distances that allow transactions fundamental to global markets" (Espeland and Stevens 1998: 325).

In the market for sovereign debt (as in all markets) the participants make use of "splitting" and "lumping" devices (in Eviatar Zerubavel's (1996) evocative terms) to organize and make their environments, rife with uncertainty, more manageable. Underwriters and money managers put countries into different categories (for example, distinguishing between "developing," "frontier," "emerging," and "developed" clusters) (Brooks, Cunha, and Mosley 2014); the lumping process makes decision making in the presence of uncertainty less paralyzing, but it comes at the cost of "abstracting and reducing information" (Espeland

6 The four elements come from Carruthers and Kim's (2011: 240–41) analysis of the organization of financial markets.

and Stevens 1998). And, as Zerubavel notes, the ways in which we slice the continuous "ocean" of reality into distinct "mental archipelagos" are based almost entirely on social conventions (Zerubavel 1996: 426–27). The conventional categories can (and do) become institutionalized, serving as rules that decision makers follow as a matter of routine (Powell and Colyvas 2008). In this section I present indirect evidence suggesting that the conventional categorization of borrowers – whether they are included with the "developed" group or not – drives the currency denomination of sovereign debt contracts.

In the canonical economic model of the sovereign debt market, all debts are denominated in real consumption (Eaton and Gersovitz 1981; Tomz and Wright 2013: 254). In the world outside the model countries issue debt denominated in national currencies. There is a remarkable concentration in the currencies in which international sovereign bonds are denominated: in the 1999–2001 period, 85 percent of bonds sold by countries that were not Eurozone members, the United States, Japan, the UK, or Switzerland were denominated in either euros, US dollars, yen, pounds sterling, or Swiss francs (Eichengreen et al. 2005a). The historically rich countries can sell debt instruments to non-residents in their own currencies and the other 180-odd countries in the world cannot. Eichengreen and Hausmann (1999, 2005) called this apparently structural feature of the sovereign debt market "original sin."

Figure 4.1 illustrates the gulf between the small group of historically rich countries and everyone else. I use a measure based on Eichengreen et al.'s (2005a) conceptualization of original sin. Their OSIN1 indicator is constructed by taking one minus the ratio of total securities issued by a country in its own currency over the total amount of currencies issued by the country in any currency:

$$\left[1 - \frac{\textit{Securities issued by country i in currency i}}{\textit{Securities issued by country i}}\right]$$

In this construction a country that has no trace of original sin would have a value of zero; for a country that enters international debt markets but is unable to raise any funds using instruments denominated in its own currency, the indicator would equal one. The indicator is imperfect as a measure of a country's financial vulnerability, but it allows us to observe the degree to which different countries differ in one aspect of their entry into the international sovereign debt market – the currency

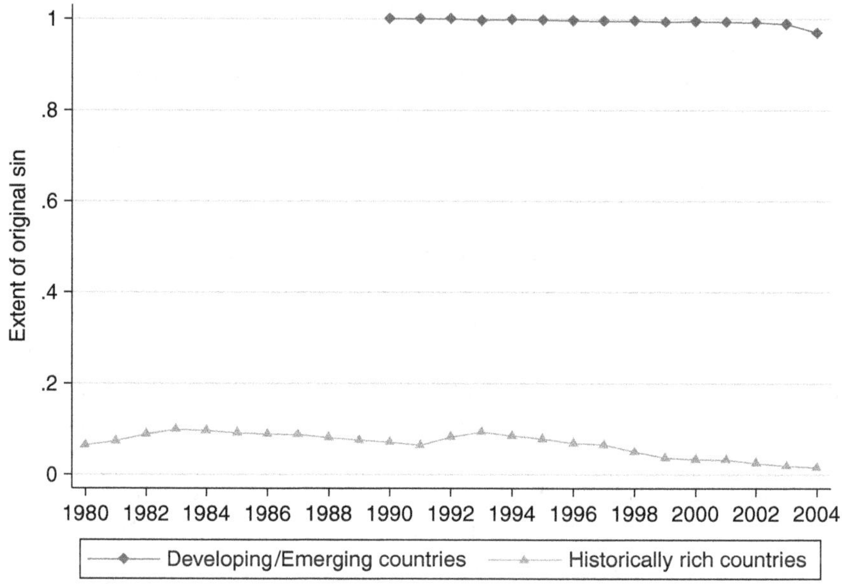

Figure 4.1 The extent of foreign currency–denominated sovereign debt

denomination of the debt contract.[7] Figure 4.1 tracks the average annual value of OSIN1 for historically rich countries after 1980 and for low- and middle-income countries between 1993 and 2004.[8]

The difference between the historically rich countries and the rest of the world is stark. Within the country groupings, however, Figure 4.1 does not give us much variation to puzzle over. The indicator of original sin barely budges over the observation window (for the low- and middle-income countries in the sample, the average value falls from one at the beginning to 0.97 at the end of the series; for the historically rich

[7] OSIN1 does not account for the possibility of hedging currency exposure in the derivatives markets. To estimate the share of debt that can be hedged, Eichengreen et al. (2005a) design the following indicator (OSIN3): $\max\left(1 - \frac{\textit{Securities issued in currency } i}{\textit{Securities issued by country } i}, 0\right)$. Hausmann and Panizza (2010) estimate that the maximum amount of foreign-denominated debt issued by developing countries that could be potentially hedged through the swap market is 18.5 percent. In other words, OSIN1 overstates developing countries' exposure to currency mismatch but the vast majority of these countries' outstanding debt is in a foreign currency and is difficult to hedge.

[8] The indicator of original sin for the developing and emerging countries comes from Obstfeld et al.'s (2010) dataset. For the historically rich countries, the indicator is drawn from Abbas et al.'s (2014) database. Their database includes thirteen historically rich countries (Australia, Belgium, Canada, France, Germany, Ireland, Italy, Japan, the Netherlands, Spain, Sweden, the UK, and the United States).

countries, the indicator of foreign currency-denominated international debt falls from 10 percent to just over 1 percent).

The inability of a large set of the world's governments to sell debt denominated in their domestic currencies to non-residents looks like a patterned regularity, but that does not mean that it is consistent with a rule arising from a social convention. Martin Wolf of the *Financial Times* has asserted: "I don't believe in original sin."[9] The structural difference between historically rich and non-rich countries may simply be a legacy of historically "strong" institutions and "good" macroeconomic policies in some countries. And not all developing and emerging countries suffer equally from the condition.[10]

Bondholders dislike currency depreciation and price inflation. Chinn and Frieden (2011: 188) explain: "one tried-and-true way countries make it easier to pay their debts is to inflate or depreciate some of them away. With just 5 percent inflation, 100bn in debts loses more than a fourth of its real value in just five years ... Many countries with foreign debts in their own currency reduce their real debt burden by allowing their currency to drop in value, so that foreigners get repaid in less-valuable currency." If all non-historically rich countries have demonstrated a propensity to follow policies that harm creditors, then there is no mystery to original sin: it is an international-level regularity produced by pathologies of macroeconomic policymaking at the domestic level.[11] Indeed, Gourinchas and Obstfeld (2012: 232) assert: "frequent recourse to inflationary finance in the past has created a tendency for financial contracts to be denominated in a stable foreign currency, such as the US dollar or euro."

The problem with this explanation is that there's rather scant evidence to support it. Eichengreen et al (2005b) explored some of the determinants countries' level of original sin in 2001. All of the usual suspects (inflation history, fiscal deficits, the rule of law, foreign economic policy openness) were statistically insignificant in their regressions. I examined the covariates of OSIN1 indicator of the extent of foreign currency borrowing using data covering a sizeable sample of

9 Wolf is quoted in Hausmann and Panizza (2010: 4).

10 The lowest observed value for OSIN1 is 0.82 (Singapore, 2004). Several other developing countries have values below 0.9 (South Africa, Thailand, and Uruguay).

11 This view is similar to structural realists' view of international regimes. In the causal pathway sketched by Krasner (1983) (prior causal factors → regimes → related behavior/outcomes) regimes do not have any independent effect. They are artifacts of deeper causal factors (the absence of a governing authority in world politics, the distribution of material power, etc.).

countries observed between 1993 and 2004.[12] I regressed the original sin indicator on measures of country size (real GDP and the natural log of population)[13], age (recorded as a count from the date of independence if after the year 1800, or 1800 if the country's date of birth preceded that year)[14], macroeconomic performance (real GDP growth and the log of consumer price inflation), political institutions (the Polity2 indicator of the level of democracy and the number of "veto players"), foreign economic openness (exports/GDP and a measure of capital account openness), and domestic financial market depth (credit/GDP). I also included an indicator for whether a country is a member of the historically rich grouping or not.[15] I estimated cross-sectional time-series models with annual observations and cross-sectional regressions in which OSIN1 and the explanatory variables are averaged for each country over time periods noted in Table 4.1 below. Table 4.1 displays the results from the regressions.

The statistical results suggest that the level of original sin is not easily explained by differences in countries' economic policies and political institutions. No covariate is statistically significant across all the specifications. Inflation, population size, real GDP, GDP growth, and domestic credit/GDP are each significant in at least one specification, but by far the most powerful covariate is the classification of countries as being either an historically-rich country or not. The results in Table 4.1 (coupled with the evidence presented in Eichengreen et al. 2005b) suggest that the causes of original sin probably do not lie in the quality of developing countries' macroeconomic policies and political institutions.

One of the most striking pieces of evidence presented by Eichengreen et al. (2005a: 24–25) is the overlap between the group of countries that had high levels of original sin in the 1990s and the group of countries that included gold clauses in the sovereign bonds that they issued in the 1850s. Flandreau and Sussman's (2005) research on the structure of bond markets in the mid-to late-1800s suggests a possible origin for the inability of most developing countries today to borrow

[12] In starting the analysis in 1993 I follow Flandreau et al.'s (2009) dating of the onset of the "modern era" of sovereign debt markets (before 1993 "emerging" and "transition" countries were not able to place much debt internationally).

[13] Size is one of the few variables that are consistently significant in Eichengreen et al.'s (2005b) models of the determinants of original sin. The variables come from the World Bank's *World Development Indicators*.

[14] Older countries have more opportunity to build reputations for creditworthiness (Tomz 2007).

[15] The "historically rich" countries in the sample are Australia, Belgium, Canada, France, Germany, Ireland, Italy, Japan, the Netherlands, Spain, Sweden, the UK, and the United States.

TABLE 4.1 Covariates of original sin

	(1)	(2)	(3)	(4)
Exports/GDP	– 0.0001	– 0.0003	0.002	0.003
	(0.0004)	(0.0002)	(0.002)	(0.002)
Real GDP	-2.06×10^{-6}	-5.67×10^{-7}	– 0.00001*	– 0.00001*
	(1.06×10^{-6})	(5.38×10^{-7})	(4.09×10^{-6})	(5.15×10^{-6})
GDP growth	0.0006	0.0001	0.023*	0.023*
	(0.0005)	(0.0003)	(0.009)	(0.011)
Polity2 score	– 0.001	– 0.0002	– 0.002	– 0.001
	(0.001)	(0.001)	(0.004)	(0.005)
Number of veto	0.003	0.0007	– 0.005	– 0.009
players	(0.002)	(0.001)	(0.016)	(0.023)
Population size	– 0.010*	– 0.002	– 0.027	– 0.022
(log)	(0.005)	(0.002)	(0.019)	(0.022)
Inflation (log)	0.002	0.005	0.067*	0.069*
	(0.004)	(0.003)	(0.024)	(0.028)
Credit/GDP	– 0.0003*	– 0.0002	0.0004	0.00002
	(0.0001)	(0.0001)	(0.0009)	(0.000)
Cap. account	– 0.001	0.001	– 0.013	– 0.019
policy index	(0.002)	(0.001)	(0.018)	(0.024)
Country age	0.00002	– 0.00007		
	(0.00009)	(0.00005)		
Historically rich	– 0.880***		– 0.648**	
country	(0.035)		(0.079)	
Countries	71	58	52	40
Total observations	624	454	52	40

Notes:
* p < .1
** p < .05
*** p < .01. Standard errors (clustered by country in the time-series cross-section models 1 and 2) are in parentheses. Estimates are from OLS regressions. Columns (1) and (2) presents results from cross-sectional time-series estimates of the covariates of original sin (annual data, 1993–2004). Column (1) includes all countries for which data are available; column (2) excludes historically-rich countries. Columns (3) and (4) report cross-sectional models. Covariates are averages over the years between 1980 and 1993. The dependent variable in (3) and (4) (original sin) is averaged over years between 1993 and 2004. Model (3) includes all countries; historically rich democracies are excluded from the model reported in column (4).

abroad in domestic currency. Based on analysis of sovereign bond issues from the 1820s to the 1890s, Flandreau and Sussman distinguish three varieties of borrowers: the countries that in their initial public offering of sovereign bonds in London or Paris included an exchange rate clause (requiring repayment in pounds, francs, gold, etc.) in the debt instrument; countries that issued a mix of bonds in domestic currency and with exchange rate clauses; and a small set of borrowers (Belgium, Britain, Germany, Netherlands, and Switzerland) that borrowed exclusively in their own currencies. According to Flandreau and Sussman, the factor that differentiated the varieties was liquidity. Bond buyers wanted to be able "to trade the long-term bond for short term assets in that currency" (Flandreau and Sussman 2005: 181). The countries that were able to borrow in the nineteenth century debt markets in their own currencies had "intense foreign exchange relations with the rest of the world...Liquidity was achieved by transforming the national currency into a key currency" (Flandreau and Sussman 2005: 183, 186). While expiation and redemption is possible, it appears to be the case that a market convention developed in the nineteenth century for reasons specific to that historical context was sustained by path dependency into the first decades of the twenty-first century.

If domestic policy and institutional weaknesses in developing countries do not explain why international sovereign bonds remain denominated in just a handful of rich countries' currencies, what, other than convention-following, might account for the existence and persistence of original sin? Perhaps the concentration of the international sovereign debt portfolio in a handful of currencies is an efficient arrangement, because the transaction costs of denominating bonds in many different national currencies are excessively high.[16] After all, Nobel Laureate Robert Mundell (1968) showed the efficiency gains of coordinating on a single currency as the world's central money.[17] The efficiency gains of concentrating transactions in one or a few "top currencies" are evident for activities such as invoicing cross-border trade and payments; for financial assets, however, the benefits of extreme

[16] Eichengreen et al. (2005b) raise this possibility.

[17] Here is McKinnon's (2010: 2) depiction: "To see this efficiency gain, consider a world of 150 countries and 150 currencies but without a central money. To preserve monetary symmetry, you would need 11,175 bilateral foreign exchange markets for trading goods and services. However, if one money – the Nth – is mutually selected to be the common intermediary currency among banks, then only 149 markets need to be actively traded."

concentration are less obvious. In fact, the concentration of international bonds in a handful of currencies contravenes the logic of portfolio diversification.[18] The data in Griffith-Jones et al. (2002) show, for example, that the chance of a very large loss in a portfolio that is only spread across advanced industrial countries is 25 percent higher than a portfolio that includes both historically-rich and developing countries.

Until recent years only a handful of international investment firms were willing to invest in so-called "exotic" local currency-denominated sovereign bonds (Panizza 2010: 99). In the 1990s Shari Spiegel, a bond trader with Lazard Frères, pioneered an investment strategy that focused on local currency debt; in her words, "the fund was operated with the goal of capturing high rates of return paid on local currency securities while reducing risk through a diversification strategy" (Dodd and Spiegel 2005: 6). While the strategy was highly successful, Spiegel's team was nearly alone in pursuing it. Since 2007, however, there has been a wave of new investment funds specializing in local currency sovereign bonds placed internationally. The conventional classification schema that prevented many so-called "emerging" countries from denominating debt in their own currencies appears to be breaking down. The onset of the Global Financial Crisis in 2008, subsequent buildup of sovereign debt burdens as governments bailed out their damaged financial systems, and the eruption of the Eurozone debt crisis in 2010 have each served as powerful shocks forcing investors and underwriters to examine the routines and understandings that were in place in the market. A particularly interesting facet of changing contractual knowledge in the area is its embedding in a new narrative that money managers have developed to explain (in the words of the Director of Emerging Market Strategies at Bank of New York Mellon) "the rise of local currency debt." Investment fund managers and market analysts are

[18] The case for portfolio diversification is clearest in the Capital Assets Pricing Model (CAPM), which is widely used to price investment risks, based on Harry Markowitz's (1952) seminal contribution to portfolio theory. In Markowitz's model, investors start with a portfolio Q, which has an expected return μ_q and a variance of σ_q (which measures how strongly the return deviates, on average, from its mean value). The variance is the key measure of risk. A portfolio that results in the highest level of return for a given level of risk or the lowest level of risk for a given expected return is deemed efficient. The functional form is typically written as $V_q = \gamma\mu_q - \sigma_q$, where V is the value of a portfolio, and γ is a weighting factor that measures how much an investor cares about the expected return. Based on this model, the CAPM was developed to help investors balance risk and reward in a portfolio. In CAPM, all non-systematic sources of risk (political events, strategies pursued by individual firms, etc.) in a market portfolio that might cause the actual return to deviate from the expected return are completely diversified by picking a portfolio that contains securities with variances that are uncorrelated (Bechtel 2009).

TABLE 4.2 Pari passu in unsecured cross-border bonds

Decade	Number of issuances	% with *pari passu* clause
1940s	20	5.0
1950s	38	63.2
1960s	64	84.4
1970s	77	87.0
1980s	121	84.3
1990s	343	95.3
2000s	691	98.7

normalizing this new contractual feature of international bonds issued by emerging countries by reconstructing their conventional categories. Emerging markets have "improved" or "graduated" from the institutional and macroeconomic syndromes that hobbled them until a sea change arrived a half-decade ago; money managers refer to "improved EM sovereign fundamentals," the "much firmer financial footing" onto which governments have put their economies, and "victories" over "political instability, social unrest, and economic turmoil... [that were] *status quo*" in these countries until recent years.[19] The symbolic reconstruction of local currency debt as safe now that a subset of countries have "emerged" from their sinful practices is, following Marion Fourcade's dissection of the BRICs categorization, "a narrative strategy that seeks to alter investment patterns in the emerging markets fund industry" (Fourcade 2013: 263–64).

LEGAL FICTIONS IN SOVEREIGN DEBT CONTRACTS: THE PARI PASSU CLAUSE

The pari passu clause first appeared in debt contracts in the 1870s and in recent decades has appeared in nearly every international sovereign debt instrument. Table 4.2 from Gulati and Scott's (2013: 122) book on

[19] The quotes in this section are drawn from reports by the financial market research firm Research Affiliates ("An Emerging Asset Class: The Case for Emerging Markets Local Currency Debt," July 2013) and Alexander Kozhemiakin, the Director of Emerging Markets Strategies at Standish Mellon ("Emerging Markets Local Currency Debt: Capitalizing on Improved Sovereign Fundamentals," August 2011).

pari passu, tracks the proportion of unsecured bond issuances containing the covenant in each decade after 1940.

The clause has the character of a legal fiction, since "almost no one knows what it means" (Gulati and Scott 2013: 3; see also Buchheit and Pam 2004; Varottil 2011). Why would a legal covenant that is difficult to interpret and in any case does not match the reality of how sovereign debt restructuring works become ubiquitous in prospectuses that detail the terms of the transaction? The suspension of market players' disbelief resembles the way in which readers readily accept elements in works of literary fiction that are clearly untrue or impossible. Searle suggests that the suspension of disbelief is made possible by a "set of extralinguistic, nonsemantic conventions ... [that] enable the speaker to use words with their literal meanings without undertaking the commitments that are normally required by those meanings" (Searle 1975: 326; quoted also in Beckert 2013a). Beckert (2013a) suggests that market players' "fictional expectations" in the presence of Knightian uncertainty are rooted in conventions just as fiction in literature is made possible by the conventions shared by authors and readers. The legal fiction of pari passu allows bondholders to pretend "as if" the problem of discriminatory action by the sovereign issuer down the road has been resolved, so that they can pass over it in order to move onto other business. As Beckert writes, "only by being overlooked does uncertainty not lead to paralysis or randomness" (2013a).

The ostensible purpose of the contractual clause is to protect bondholders when the borrower needs to restructure its debts. In a corporate bankruptcy, pari passu prevents the debtor from ranking its creditors by giving some privileged claims on liquidated assets and subordinating other bondholders (Buchheit and Pam 2004: 873–74). The significance of this kind of protective clause in a sovereign debt instrument is less obvious: to paraphrase legendary banker Walter Wriston, countries don't go into bankruptcy proceedings. Wright (2011) argues that the general aim of the pari passu clause in sovereign debt instruments has been to reduce the risk of discriminatory action by the government involved in a restructuring against some subset of the country's nonresident creditors.

Law practitioners and scholars Buchheit and Pam (2004: 912–15) identify several specific risks that might justify the use of clause in unsecured international sovereign bonds. One is the risk that the government will set aside some assets or revenue stream (such as foreign reserves) to ensure that some bondholders, with whom the government may have informally negotiated, receive full payment, while others are subordinated. Gulati and Scott's interviews with transactional lawyers indicate that this is a commonly told origin story in the profession (Gulati and Scott 2013: 112–13).

From the mid 1970s to the present, however, a different legal covenant in sovereign debt instruments – the negative pledge clause – has been interpreted as the way to address the risk of earmarking; thus Buchheit and Pam argue that "the risk of sovereign earmarking was not the only motivation for inclusion of a *pari passu* clause in sovereign credit instruments" (Buchheit and Pam 2004: 913). Gulati and Scott argue similarly: "the historic function of the clause was unrelated to concerns about earmarking, which concerns were primarily, if incompletely, addressed by a version of the negative pledge clause" (Gulati and Scott 2013: 125).

Perhaps pari passu's enduring popularity has to do with the risk of governments issuing decrees that lead to subordination of some group of creditors in favor of a different group. Before the 1970s the principle of sovereign immunity made it very difficult for creditors to pursue litigation when a government unilaterally altered or failed to observe the terms of the debt contract. Sovereigns' insulation from legal means of enforcement eroded over time "through statutory changes and through case law" (Panizza et al. 2009: 653). Yet private litigation against governments was infrequent until a sizeable secondary market for sovereign debt emerged in the late 1980s. In this environment new, more litigious specialized firms ("distressed debt funds," colloquially known as "vulture funds") set out "to buy defaulted debt at large discounts with the aim of extracting the best possible settlement" (Panizza et al. 2009: 656). Pari passu was a useful legal covenant for these firms. But it is difficult to explain the large increase in the usage of pari passu in sovereign debt instruments from the 1940s to the 1970s as a consequence of demand by litigious creditors, given that legal means for debt enforcement only became common in the 1990s.

Buchheit and Pam offer a third rationale for the use of pari passu in debt instruments: it can be a tool for protecting international investors from the risk of discriminatory treatment emanating from quirks in national legal codes. They provide evidence from the Philippines' legal system to demonstrate "the risk that sovereign debt might be involuntarily subordinated as the result of local law procedures" (Buchheit and Pam 2004: 917). For Buchheit and Pam the risk of involuntary subordination due to provisions in national legal codes is the most powerful reason for the ubiquity of pari passu.

The extensive data on sovereign bond issues collected by Gulati and Scott, however, does not fit neatly with the Buchheit and Pam story. Their data show that modifications to the pari passu boilerplate began to appear around 1980; these new variants "were an attempt to address ... sources of local law risk" (Gulati and Scott 2013: 132). The additional language added to the clause suggests that pari passu alone wasn't regarded by contract drafters as sufficiently strong to protect against the risk of involuntary subordination due to local laws. More puzzling still is the sharp decline in the modified variants of the clause over the past two decades. Gulati and Scott ask why, if lawyers' primary reason for including the pari passu clause was to protect bond buyers from local law risk, "would they have subsequently removed language that explicitly addressed those risks?" (Gulati and Scott 2013: 132–33).

Gulati and Scott do not use the term "legal fiction" or "placeholder" in their study of pari passu's enduring presence in sovereign debt contracts. Their preferred explanation – "in the great majority of firms, lawyers rely on the herd and their myths" (Gulati and Scott 2013: 6) – is, however, consistent with the claim that rule-following behavior by economic agents is a common and, indeed, necessary element of the structure of stable markets (Biggart and Beamish 2003: 455–57). Gulati and Scott briefly suggest that the herd-like behavior of debt contract drafters is rooted in uncertainty: "when subjects are asked to make decisions under conditions of uncertainty, they often look to what others are doing (social proof and conformity) or look to well-established practices (deference to authority and anchoring) before deciding on a course of action" (Gulati and Scott 2013: 42).

The endurance of the pari passu covenant is particularly surprising given the big problems that it causes. In the late 1990s a fund specializing in distressed debt, Elliott Associates L.P., sued a Peruvian bank (Banco de la Nación, the issuer) and the government of Peru (the guarantor of the debt) for repayment of bonds the fund had purchased at steep discount just before Peru wrapped up restructuring its external debt under the auspices of the Brady Bond plan spearheaded by the US Treasury department. Elliott Associates won its case in a New York court and was awarded a $57 million judgment – but winning a case against a government and collecting on the judgment are two different problems, and the former is easier to solve than the latter (Panizza et al. 2009: 657; Varottil 2011: 227–28). To ensure that it would be paid, Elliott's lawyers constructed a legal argument, built on NYU law professor Andreas Lowenfeld's interpretation of the pari passu clause in the Peruvian debt contracts as requiring *ratability* of payments, to prevent any other bondholder (including the vast majority of bondholders that participated in the Brady negotiations) from being paid if Elliott was not also paid in full (Buchheit and Pam 2004: 877–78). Instead of the conventional interpretation of the clause as meaning that a borrower could not accumulate *new* debt that would be paid before the previously-issued debt in a restructuring event, Elliott's lawyers argued that "a debtor not yet in bankruptcy that has accepted a pari passu covenant must *pay* all its equally-ranking debts equally" (Buchheit and Pam 2004: 879). In September 2000 a Belgian court ruled in favor of Elliott over Peru, and it ordered the Euroclear system through which the first Brady payments were to flow to European bondholders to freeze Peruvian payments. Caught between two horns – give up its case against the "vulture fund" or miss the Brady bond payment and fall into technical default – the Peruvian government chose to settle with Elliott for over $56 million (Panizza et al. 2009: 658). Other distressed debt funds noted the extraordinary interpretation of pari passu in Brussels and a flurry of similar lawsuits were launched.[20]

Buchheit and Pam (2004: 883–90) lay out a series of criticisms of the Belgian interpretation of the pari passu clause. The decision strengthened the position of holdout creditors and worsened coordination problems involved in organizing debt restructuring among far-flung bondholders with different preferences. The decision also conflicted with a long-standing convention in the sovereign debt market: the debt owned by "official" creditors (the IMF, World Bank, and other international financial organizations) is, by custom, senior to privately held debt. The "ratable" interpretation of the clause threw this practice into question. Legal scholar Umakanth Varottil distills the critical view of the decision: "The overwhelming number of arguments against the judgment in *Elliott* confirms that the court's interpretation cannot stand. The market should therefore be expected to react by clarifying the language in sovereign debt documentation to avoid similar results in the future" (Varottil 2011: 229).

[20] The follow-on suits are briefly described by Buchheit and Pam (2004: 880–82) and Panizza et al. (2009: 658–59).

That's not what happened. Instead, the pari passu clause was retained in post-September 2000 sovereign debt contracts without any significant alterations (Gulati and Scott 2013). The clause is at the center of the case brought by NML Capital (a subsidiary of Elliott Associates) against Argentina. The Argentine government refused to redeem NML Capital's holdings of bonds, purchased on the secondary market at bargain-basement prices, because doing so would contravene the 2005 "padlock" law that prevents the government from paying bondholders that were not party to the country's debt restructurings (Gulati and Scott 2013: 170–71). In 2011 a judge in New York ruled that the 2005 law was a violation of the pari passu clause and moved in 2012 to freeze the country's payments to its creditors, raising the specter, as Peru experienced in September 2000, of another (this time involuntary) default on its international debt. And indeed Argentina did fall into a "technical default" in July 2014 after the Supreme Court of the United States rejected the Argentine government's challenge to the New York court's decision. Argentina has been unable to make payments to any of its creditors; as a consequence, it has been locked out of the international debt market, and as the central bank's reserves dwindle the threat of a serious balance of payments crisis looms.

CONCLUSION

Agents rely on social conventions to resolve recurrent coordination dilemmas and to stabilize their expectations in the presence of epistemic uncertainty. Conventions are an element of the organization of social institutions, including international markets. Contracts in financial markets include "legal fictions" – covenants which are not strictly true but are useful "placeholders" that allow parties to a transaction to overlook the uncertainty that characterizes the market. In this chapter I asked whether two puzzling aspects of the international sovereign debt markets – the inability of governments of low- and middle-income countries to denominate the sovereign debt instruments that they sell to nonresident investors in their own currencies and the use of the pari passu clause in sovereign debt contracts – can be viewed as conventional rather than simply behavioral regularities driven by underlying causal factors such as poor economic policies and weak institutions in developing countries, transaction costs, and constrained optimization by rational actors trying to contract around various risks. The evidence in the chapter is drawn from economists' and legal scholars' research on "original sin" and the terms of sovereign debt contracts. My interpretation of the research might be incomplete or incorrect, but there seems to be sufficient evidence to swing the burden back to IR scholars that argue that explanations rooted in the material-rationalist approach can tell us everything we want to know about sovereign debt. If we do not look for social conventions and legal fictions we are apt to miss some potentially important facets of international financial orders.

Conventions are not the only important explanatory factor in the two cases discussed in the chapter. In many, if not most, domains of world politics the regularities we observe are the output of some combination of instrumental decision making by materially oriented, risk-calculating agents and rule-following by agents following logics of appropriateness (March and Olsen 1998; Fearon and Wendt 2002; Hurd 2008: 310–11). In some contexts instrumentalism dominates; in others, behavior is driven mainly or wholly by social norms and conventions. The way to figure out if explanations built from material-rationalist, social-constructivist, or eclectic elements are right is to look at the consistency of each explanation with the data. This chapter suggests that social conventions and legal fictions ought to be an important part of the analytical toolkit employed by scholars of international organization.

References

Abbas, S.M. Ali, et al. 2014. Sovereign Debt Composition in Advanced Economies: A Historical Perspective. IMF Working Paper WP/14/162 (September).

Abbott, Kenneth et al. 2000. The Concept of Legalization. *International Organization* 54, 3: 401–19.

Adler, Emanuel and Vincent Pouliot. 2011. International Practices. *International Theory* 3, 1: 1–36.

Alter, Karen J. and Sophie Meunier. 2009. The Politics of International Regime Complexity. *Perspectives on Politics* 7, 1: 13–24.

Andrews, Bruce. 1975. Social Rules and the State as a Social Actor. *World Politics* 27, 4: 521–40.

Beaulieu, Emily, Gary W. Cox, and Sebastian Saiegh. 2013. Sovereign Debt and Regime Type: Reconsidering the Democratic Advantage. *International Organization* 66 (Fall): 709–38.

Bechtel, Michael. 2009. The Political Sources of Systematic Investment Risk: Lessons from a Consensus Democracy. *The Journal of Politics* 71, 2 (April): 661–77.

Beckert, Jens. 2009. The Social Order of Markets. *Theory and Society* 38, 3: 245–69.

Beckert, Jens. 2013a. Imagined futures: Fictional expectations in the economy. *Theory and Society* 42, 3: 219–40.

Beckert, Jens. 2013b. Capitalism as a System of Expectations: Toward a Sociological Microfoundation of Political Economy. *Politics & Society* 41, 3: 323–50.

Biggart, Nicole Woolsey and Thomas D. Beamish. 2003. The Economic Sociology of Conventions: Habit, Custom, Practice, and Routine in Market Order. *Annual Review of Sociology* 29: 443–64.

Brooks, Sarah M., Raphael Cunha, and Layna Mosley. 2014. Categories, Creditworthiness, and Contagion: How Investors' Shortcuts Affect Sovereign Debt Markets. *International Studies Quarterly*. doi: 10.1111/isqu.12173.

Buchheit, Lee C. and Jeremiah S. Pam. 2004. The Pari Passu Clause in Sovereign Debt Instruments. *Emory Law Journal* 53: 869–922.

Callon, Michel. 1998. Introduction: The Embeddedness of Economic Markets in Economics. In *The Laws of the Markets*, edited by Michel Callon, pp. 1–57. New York: Oxford University Press.

Carruthers, Bruce G. and Jeong-Chul Kim. 2011. The Sociology of Finance. *Annual Review of Sociology* 37: 239–59.

Chinn, Menzie D. and Jeffry A. Frieden. 2011. *Lost Decades: The Making of America's Debt Crisis and the Long Recovery*. New York: Norton.

Daase, Christopher. 1999. Spontaneous Institutions: Peacekeeping as an International Convention. In *Imperfect Unions: Security Institutions over Time and Space*, edited by Helga Haftendorn, Robert O. Keohane, and Celeste A. Wallander, 223–58. New York: Oxford University Press.

David, Paul A. 1994. Why Are Institutions the 'Carriers of History?' Path Dependence and the Evolution of Conventions, Organizations, and Institutions. *Structural Change and Economic Dynamics* 5, 2: 205–20.

Depetris, N. Chauvin and Aart Kraay. 2005. What Has 100 Billion Dollars Worth of Debt Relief Done for Low Income Countries? Unpublished paper, the World Bank, Washington, DC.

Dobbin, Frank. 2004. The Sociological View of the Economy. In *The New Economic Sociology: A Reader*, edited by Frank Dobbin, pp. 1–46. Princeton, NJ: Princeton University Press.

Dodd, Randall and Shari Spiegel. 2005. Up from Sin: A Portfolio Approach to Financial Salvation. G24 Discussion Paper No. 24 (January).

Easterly, William. 2002. How Did Heavily Indebted Poor Countries become Heavily Indebted? Reviewing Two Decades of Debt Relief. *World Development* 30: 1677–96.

Eaton, Jonathan and Mark Gersovitz. 1981. Debt with Potential Repudiation: Theoretical and Empirical Analysis. *Review of Economic Studies* 48: 289–309.

Eichengreen, Barry and Ricardo Hausmann. 1999. Exchange Rates and Financial Fragility. In *New Challenges for Monetary Policy*, pp. 329–68. Kansas City, MO: Federal Reserve Bank of Kansas City.

Eichengreen, Barry and Ricardo Hausmann. 2005. Editors' Introduction. In *Other People's Money: Debt Denomination and Financial Instability in Emerging Market Economies*, edited by Eichengreen and Hausmann, pp. 1–12. Chicago: University of Chicago Press.

Eichengreen, Barry, Ricardo Hausmann, and Ugo Panizza. 2005a. The Pain of Original Sin. In *Other People's Money: Debt Denomination and Financial Instability in Emerging Market Economies*, edited by Eichengreen and Hausmann, pp. 13–47. Chicago: University of Chicago Press.

Eichengreen, Barry, Ricardo Hausmann, and Ugo Panizza. 2005b. The Mystery of Original Sin. In *Other People's Money: Debt Denomination and Financial Instability in Emerging Market Economies*, edited by Eichengreen and Hausmann, pp. 233–65. Chicago: University of Chicago Press.

Espeland, Wendy Nelson and Mitchell L. Stevens. 1998. Commensuration as a Social Process. *Annual Review of Sociology* 24: 313–43.

Fearon, James D. and Alexander Wendt. 2002. Rationalism v. Constructivism: A Skeptical View. In *Handbook of International Relations*, edited by Walter Carlsnaes, Thomas Risse, and Beth A. Simmons, pp. 52–72. Thousand Oaks, CA: Sage Publications.

Finnemore, Martha. 2003. *The Purpose of Intervention: Changing Beliefs about the Use of Force*. Ithaca: Cornell University Press.

Finnemore, Martha and Stephen Toope. 2005. Alternatives to 'Legalization': Richer Views of Law and Politics. *International Organization* 55, 3: 743–58.

Flandreau, Marc and Nathan Sussman. 2005. Old Sins: Exchange Clauses and European Foreign Lending in the Nineteenth Century. In *Other People's Money: Debt Denomination and Financial Instability in Emerging Market Economies*, edited by Eichengreen and Hausmann, pp. 154–89. Chicago: University of Chicago Press.

Flandreau, Marc and Juan Flores. 2012. The Peaceful Conspiracy: Bond Markets and International Relations during the Pax Britannica. *International Organization* 66 (Spring): 211–41.

Flandreau, Marc, et al. 2010. The End of Gatekeeping: Underwriters and the Quality of Sovereign Debt Markets, 1815–2007. In *NBER International Seminar on Macroeconomics, 2009*, edited by Lucrezia Reichlin and Kenneth West, pp. 53–92. Chicago: University of Chicago Press.

Fourcade, Marion. 2013. The Material and Symbolic Construction of the BRICs. *Review of International Political Economy* 20, 2: 256–67.

Fourcade, Marion and Kieran Healy. 2013. Classification situations: Life-chances in the neoliberal era. *Accounting, Organizations and Society* 38: 559–72.

Gilbert, Margaret. 1989. *On Social Facts*. Princeton, NJ: Princeton University Press.

Gourinchas, Pierre-Olivier and Maurice Obstfeld. 2012. Stories of the Twentieth Century for the Twenty-First. *American Economic Journal: Macroeconomics* 4, 1: 226–65.

Griffith-Jones, Stefany et al. 2002. Basle II and Developing Countries: Diversification and Portfolio Effects. Unpublished paper, University of Sussex and the London School of Economics and Political Science. Available here: http://eprints.lse.ac.uk/24824/1/dp437.pdf

Gulati, Mitu and Robert E. Scott. 2013. *The Three and a Half Minute Transaction: Boilerplate and the Limits of Contract Design*. Chicago: University of Chicago Press.

Hall, Rodney Bruce. 1997. Moral Authority as a Power Resource. *International Organization* 51, 4: 591–622.

Hausmann, Ricardo and Ugo Panizza. 2010. Redemption or Abstinence? Original Sin, Currency Mismatches and Counter-Cyclical Policies in the New Millennium. CID Working Paper No. 194 (February).

Hurd, Ian. 1999. Legitimacy and Authority in International Politics. *International Organization* 53, 2: 379–408.

Hurd, Ian. 2008. Constructivism. In Christian Reus-Smit and Duncan Snidal, eds. *Oxford Handbook of International Relations*: 298–316.

Jagd, Soren. 2007. Economics of Convention and New Economic Sociology: Mutual Inspiration and Dialogue. *Current Sociology* 55, 1: 75–91.

Jeanne, Olivier and Jeromin Zettelmeyer. 2005. Original Sin, Balance-Sheet Crises, and the Roles of International Lending. In *Other People's Money: Debt Denomination and Financial Instability in Emerging Market Economies*, edited by Eichengreen and Hausmann, pp. 95–121. Chicago: University of Chicago Press.

Kahler, Miles. 2000. Conclusion: the Causes and Consequences of Legalization. *International Organization* 54, 3: 661–83.

Katzenstein, P. J., Keohane, R. O., and Krasner, S. D. 1998. International organization and the study of world politics. *International Organization*: 645–85.

Keynes, John Maynard. 1921. *A Treatise on Probability*. New York: Macmillan.

Keynes, John Maynard. 1937. The General Theory of Employment. *Quarterly Journal of Economics* 51, 2: 209–23.

Knight, Frank. 1921. *Risk, Uncertainty, and Profit*. New York: Houghton Mifflin.

Koremenos, Barbara, Charles Lipson, and Duncan Snidal. 2001. The Rational Design of International Institutions. *International Organization* 55, 4: 761–99.

Koslowski, Rey and Friedrich V. Kratochwil. 1994. Understanding Change in International Politics: The Soviet Empire's Demise and the International System. *International Organization* 48, 2: 215–47.

Krasner, Stephen D. 1983. Structural Causes and Regime Consequences: Regimes as Intervening Variables. In *International Regimes*, edited by Stephen D. Krasner, pp. 1–22. Ithaca, NY: Cornell University Press.

Kratochwil, Friedrich. 1984. The Force of Prescriptions. *International Organization* 38, 4: 685–708.

Kratochwil, Friedrich. 1989. *Rules, Norms, and Decisions: On the Conditions of Practical and Legal Reasoning in International Relations and Domestic Affairs*. New York: Cambridge University Press.

Kratochwil, Friedrich. 1993. The Embarrassment of Changes: Neo-realism as the Science of Realpolitik without the Politics. *International Studies Review* 19, 1: 63–80.

Lamont, Michele. 2012. Toward a Comparative Sociology of Valuation and Evaluation. *Annual Review of Sociology* 38: 201–21.

Langley, Paul. 2008. Sub-prime Mortgage Lending: A Cultural Economy. *Economics and Society* 37, 4: 469–94.

Lawson, Tony. 1985. Uncertainty and Economic Analysis. *Economic Journal* 95 (December): 909–27.

Lazega, Emmanuel and Olivier Favereau. 2002. Introduction. In *Conventions and Structures in Economic Organization: Markets, Networks, and Hierarchies*, edited by Olivier Favereau and Emmanuel Lazega. Northampton, MA: Edward Elgar.

Lewis, David K. 1969. *Convention: A Philosophical Study*. Cambridge, MA: Harvard University Press.

March, James G. and Johan P. Olsen. 1998. The Institutional Dynamics of International Political Orders. *International Organization* 52: 943–69.

Markowitz, Harry. 1952. Portfolio Selection. *Journal of Finance* VII, 1 (March): 77–91.

Marmor, Andrei. 2009. *Social Conventions: From Language to Law*. Princeton, NJ: Princeton University Press.

McKinnon, Ronald. 2010. Rehabilitating the Unloved Dollar Standard. *Asian Pacific Economic Literature* 24, 2: 1–18.

Meltzer, Allan H. 1982. Rational Expectations, Risk, Uncertainty, and Market Reactions. In *Crises in Economic and Financial Structure*, edited by Paul Wachtel, 3–22. Lexington, MA: Lexington.

Mundell, Robert. 1968. *International Economics*. New York: Macmillan.

Nelson, Stephen C. and Peter J. Katzenstein. 2014. Uncertainty, Risk, and the Financial Crisis of 2008. *International Organization* 48, 2: 361–392.

Obstfeld, Maurice, Jay C. Shambaugh, and Alan M. Taylor. 2010. Financial Stability, the Trilemma, and International Reserves. *American Economic Journal: Macroeconomics* 2: 57–94.

Panizza, Ugo. 2010. Is Domestic Debt the Answer to Debt Crises? In *Overcoming Developing Country Debt Crises*, edited by Barry Herman, Jose Antonio Ocampo, and Shari Spiegel, pp. 91–110. New York: Oxford University Press.

Panizza, Ugo, Federico Sturzenegger, and Jeromin Zetterlmeyer. 2009. The Economics and Law of Sovereign Debt and Default. *Journal of Economic Literature* 47, 3: 651–98.

Pénet, Pierre and Grégoire Mallard. 2014. From Risk Models to Loan Models: Austerity as the Continuation of Calculation by Other Means. *Journal of Critical Globalization Studies* 7: 4–50.

Powell, Walter W. and Jeanette A. Colyvas. 2008. Microfoundations of Institutional Theory. In *The Sage Handbook of Organizational Institutionalism*, edited by Robin Greenwood, et al. Los Angeles: Sage.

Riles, Annelise. 2010. Collateral Expertise: Legal Knowledge in the Global Financial Markets. *Current Anthropology* 51, 6 (December): 795–818.

Riles, Annelise. 2011. *Collateral Knowledge: Legal Reasoning in Global Financial Markets*. University of Chicago Press.

Sandel, Michael. 2012. *What Money Can't Buy: The Moral Limits of Markets*. New York: Allen Lane.

Searle, John R. 1975. The logical status of fictional discourse. *New Literary History* 6: 319–32.

Schultz, Kenneth and Barry Weingast. 2003. The Democratic Advantage: Institutional Foundations of Financial Power in International Competition. *International Organization* 57 (Winter): 3–42.

Storper, Michael and Robert Salais. 1997. *Worlds of Production: The Action Frameworks of the Economy*. Cambridge, MA: Harvard University Press.

Sugden, Robert. 1989. Spontaneous Order. *The Journal of Economic Perspectives* 3, 4: 85–97.

Tomz, Michael. 2007. *Reputation and International Cooperation: Sovereign Debt across Three Centuries*. Princeton: Princeton University Press.

Tomz, Michael and Mark L.J. Wright. 2013. Empirical Research on Sovereign Debt and Default. *Annual Review of Economics* 5: 247–72.

Varottil, Umakanth. 2011. Sovereign Debt Documentation and the Pari Passu Clause. In *Sovereign Debt: From Safety to Default*, edited by Robert W. Kolb, pp. 227–34. Hoboken, NJ: John Wiley & Sons.

Velthuis, Olav. 2003. Symbolic Meanings of Prices: Constructing the Value of Contemporary Art in Amsterdam and New York Galleries. *Theory and Society* 32, 3: 181–215.

Wherry, Frederick F. 2012. *The Culture of Markets*. Polity Press.

Williamson, John. 1976. The Benefits and Costs of an International Monetary System. In *Reflections on Jamaica*, edited by Edward M. Bernstein. Princeton Essays in International Finance, No. 115 (April).

Wright, Mark L.J. 2011. The Pari Passu Clause in Sovereign Bond Contracts: Evolution or Intelligent Design? UCLA, September 9.

Young, Oran. 1983. Regime Dynamics: the Rise and Fall of International Regimes. In *International Regimes*, edited by Stephen D. Krasner, pp. 93–114. Ithaca, NY: Cornell University Press.

Young, H. Peyton. 1996. The Economics of Conventions. *Journal of Economic Perspectives* 10, 2: 105–22.

Zelizer, Viviana A. 2011. *Economic Lives: How Culture Shapes the Economy*. Princeton University Press.

Zerubavel, Eviatar. 1996. Lumping and Splitting: Notes on Social Classification. *Sociological Forum* 11, 3: 421–33.

PART TWO

CONSOLIDATING INTERNATIONAL ORGANIZATIONS: THE MOBILIZATION OF SOCIAL CAPITAL AND THE STANDARDIZATION OF INTERPRETIVE PROCESSES

CHAPTER FIVE

A TALE OF THREE CITIES: THE CONSTRUCTION OF INTERNATIONAL COMMERCIAL ARBITRATION

Jérôme Sgard

Contracting for profit typically asks that sophisticated institutions help merchants and entrepreneurs as they bargain, invest and serve their obligations. Prime concerns include the processing of information, payments and dispute resolution, which in principle should be provided in an altogether efficient, predictable and flexible manner. In practice however, well-tested, ready-made institutions rarely emerge spontaneously or converge naturally toward a rational solution. Experimentation in market institutions is typically long, competing rules may coexist over time and cause uncertainty, or, for instance, an institution that emerged early on and was endowed with substantial legitimacy by its patrons may eventually prove inadequate, because it was designed for the needs of a previous time. Technological change or evolving market structures can debase old institutions and those who control them.[1]

International commercial arbitration is no exception, but rather a case in point. To start with, arbitration provides an alternative to a default rule whereby, in case of trouble over the execution of a cross-border contract, the parties go to a public court and expect that cooperation between national jurisdictions will eventually solve the problem. Arbitration, which rests on private tribunals and allows for more substantive and procedural choice by the parties, is generally seen as an

[1] I owe many thanks to Claire Lemercier, from Sciences Po, with whom part of the archival research was done and who also contributed greatly to the early formulation of the propositions that are developed here.

option that is closer to market needs, more efficient, but sometimes less predictable than courts. In particular, the enforcement across borders of the awards rendered by arbiters can be a source of concern. In practice, however, both judges and arbiters are seen in great numbers in today's global markets, in many different places and fora – local, professional, national, multilateral, transnational (Keohane et al. 2000, Alter 2008, Halliday and Shaffer 2015).

Observers also tend to assume, more often than not, that arbitration is in fact a daughter of globalization: early experiments may have been observed after the first oil shock in 1973, but the real thing would have appeared only after 1990. For arbitration in investment, that is, between private investors and public authorities, the beginning of the twenty-first century would be an even more advisable starting point. This narrow time frame thus reinforces the perception that arbitration became available just when markets needed it. Rules, procedures, facilities, enforcement guarantees, intermediaries: the whole machinery would have developed more or less spontaneously to fulfill a need when globalization took off.

This naturalized and ahistorical view of arbitration is of course wrong. The institution has a long and complex history, in which there is nothing inevitable in the ways it evolved, matured and succeeded. During the heyday of the First Global Era, between 1880 and 1914, arbitration was widely practiced in the large English commodity markets that structured international trade. It was regulated and controlled by the so-called Trade Associations which followed their own rules and precedents, and selected their own arbiters – most of the time, dominant market insiders. These private legal orders rested to a large extent on sheer market power but they were also anchored in English law and English courts, a link that was highly valued by the Trade Associations, even though very few cases were actually moved to public tribunals each year.

Against this background, the interwar years were a period of innovation and experimentation that foreshadowed the present arbitration landscape, with its strong focus on advanced equipment goods, intellectual property and complex financial structures. Some of this innovative activity took place in London, at the London Court of Arbitration (LCA); but the most successful newcomers were the International Chamber of Commerce (ICC), whose Arbitration Court was established in Paris in 1923, and the American Arbitration Association (AAA), founded in New York in 1925.

The main story line here however is not one of "hegemonic succession" or, alternately, one of sclerotic, rent-seeking insiders being pushed around by new entrants. In fact, two very different models of arbitration were proposed in each of these two new cities. In New York, the export-oriented business and the American Bar Association tried early on to build a model based again on a local (American) judicial order, in which foreigners would be invited or compelled to join. Like in England, significantly, the arbitration standards did not differentiate substantially between domestic and international cases. The ICC, on the other hand, was built from the onset in a multilateral format, and on that novel basis its Court developed over several decades a model of arbitration that would be exclusively international and increasingly extraterritorial. No case would be taken to this Court in which the two parties are from the same country, and the arbiter is always chosen from a third country. The common perception of international commercial arbitration as a more recent phenomenon only reflects, in practice, the eventual emergence of the ICC model, the key features of which have now been adopted by the large majority of arbitration organizations across the world, including in New York and London.

The present contribution explores this century-long experience and tries to account for these diverse routes to modern arbitration. In so doing, it fills a gap in the literature and builds on a large trail of unexplored archives and writings. Until now, the social scientific research on arbitration has been largely influenced by the Bourdieuan approach to global legal markets developed by Dezalay and Garth (1996, 2002). They primarily envisage this story as one of constructing legitimacy and as the result of the accumulation of social and economic capital by the business lawyers who, in practice, dominate the field and draw from it important benefits, both material and symbolic. In this viewpoint, the institutional forms taken by arbitration result primarily from the competition between national legal elites that carry with them the legitimacy they have acquired at home, in their interaction with the official judiciary, big business or the legal academy.

There is little point of course in contesting that power relationships underpin institutions, or that there are diverse and conflicting national ways toward globalization. This chapter adds however two important dimensions to this overall story. First, it gives more weight to its properly legal and institutional dimensions: inventing an extraterritorial model of arbitration was in no way a foretold story, or a self-evident answer to the new problems raised by international markets from the beginning of the twentieth century. Similarly, the perimeters of commercial arbitration were never a given: arbitration on investment has now developed into a distinct regime, though this was not always the case; conversely there have been several attempts since the early twentieth century to deal with sovereign debt restructuring through arbitration, but they have all failed miserably. More generally, the long institutional genealogy of arbitration over the last hundred years has not always responded to the same social conditioning that we see at work in the mature field, since the 1970s or during the 2000s. We shall see indeed that the "grand old men" whom Dezalay and Garth identify as the dominant players in the field, especially around the ICC, have in fact taken over more or less opportunistically from a first generation of innovators – the ones who actually developed by way of experimentation the new legal technology of international arbitration, though with limited social and professional capital. Innovation and change in this case came from the margins of existing institutions and "fields," and success rested on the development of a novel approach to cross-jurisdictional problems arising from the long-term evolution of the international division of labor.

The other dimension that is added in our examination of these developments is the relationship to national States and governments, a point that both the sociological and the legal literature tend to underestimate. Indeed, in order to make international arbitration work, two complex transactions had to be made with political and judicial elites at the domestic level. First, private firms had to be allowed to opt out from official courts and to move their cases to new, more or less identified fora, with more or less precise rules and guarantees of judicial fairness. In France and in the United States, where much of our action takes place, this was only obtained during the 1920s and with substantial expense of political capital. Second, for international arbitration to work, states also had to agree among themselves on a set of coordinating rules that would ensure easy enforcement of arbitration awards across borders. This coordination was the object of three international texts adopted successively by the League of Nations (the 1923 Protocol and the 1927 Convention) and by the United Nations (UN) (the 1958 Convention). Each of them saw long negotiations which resulted in something looking more like a list of bargains and trade-offs than a coherent and transparent rule.

The rest of this chapter unfolds in three main parts. The second section focuses on the pre-1914, classic English model of arbitration and the causes of its relative decline. The third section explores how alternate models were developed in London and New York that maintained strong roots in the local (English and American) legal orders, hence as well in the respective local legal profession, its inherited structure and its distribution of social legitimacy. The fourth and last section moves to the ICC model and underlines how its success emerged from its specific (private) multilateral structure, and from a (legal) technological innovation that was developed around the ICC Court by a small group of institutional entrepreneurs with limited professional and social capital.

THE NINETEENTH CENTURY, ENGLISH MODEL OF ARBITRATION

The English trade associations

Before 1914, the key reference in matter of arbitration was the English model, which in turn was strongly rooted in the judicial history of this country.[2] Rather than taking the road of a specialized commercial jurisdiction, as in many continental European countries, the institutional architecture that emerged in the later decade of the nineteenth century was founded on the higher London courts and the vertically-integrated, private Trade Association that actually governed exchanges. Precursors included the Bradford Chamber of Commerce (for wool) and the Liverpool Cotton Association, but the London Corn Trade Association (LCTA), founded in 1878, was arguably the benchmark model that was emulated by other professions in the following years and decades.[3] The success of this model of arbitration was indeed remarkable, whether one looks at their unique international reach, low operating costs or their large recognition within the broader judicial establishment: even though Trade Associations had little use for lawyers, their practice was seen as highly professional and efficient. At least till the 1950s their experience was the foundation for the recurring discourse about the unique experience and towering position of English arbitration in

[2] See Macassey (1939) for a long-term historical perspective in international commercial arbitration with an English perspective.

[3] On Trade Associations, see Ellison (1886), Chattaway (1907), Steever (1923), Forrester (1931), Barty-King (1978). The model of Trade Associations can be compared with that developed by the New York diamonds dealers, as analyzed by Bernstein (1992) or, even more closely, with the Tokyo Tuna courts, which also keep a formal, legal relationship to the official courts (Feldman 2006).

general. A number of further structural features explain this success and also underline their contingent character.

To start with, the 1889 Arbitration Act made the (ex ante) arbitration clause entirely legal, hence enforceable: once two parties had entered into such a commitment, courts would decline to consider a dispute arising from the underlying contract and would refer it to arbiters. This enforceable commitment gave a sound basis to the practice of arbitration as a whole and allowed for controlling opportunistic strategies by the parties.

Second, the remarkably light and efficient market governance of the Trade Associations was based on standardized contracts: if they wanted to trade through English markets, merchants from across the world had to rely upon pre-printed forms that stated a number of key market rules and the successive steps in the execution of each trade. The parties then completed the contract with the specifics of their transaction (type of product, date of delivery, price, etc.). These standardized contracts were continuously adjusted to market conditions by special committees set up by the respective associations.[4] The LCTA for instance had special committees for trade of Argentinean, Black Sea or Manchurian grains. In 1896 it had a total of fifty-one standard contracts, and more than sixty in the 1920s.

Critically, all standardized contracts included a similar key clause: in case of dispute over execution, it committed the signatories to arbitration by the respective Trade Association. Hence dispute resolution took place in London, under the hands of (English) markets insiders and under English law.[5] In the rare cases where a point of law was raised by a given case, it would be submitted to one of the London high courts, which offered a guarantee of last resort regarding the legal and judicial integrity of the whole process. Commodity arbitration also came at a low cost, because it most often boiled down to issues of technical expertise – for example, the quality of grains, the degree of moisture or the consequences of a delay in delivery. Hence cases were dispatched rapidly, the parties did not need to be present, they did not

[4] See Rakoff (1983) for a discussion of standardized contracts. London Corn Trade Association (1947) for precise examples.

[5] When consulted in 1954 on the first draft of the New York Convention (proposed by the ICC), six commodities associations jointly signed a letter emphasizing that, if English law was not to be followed and English courts were to be ousted, then: "the greatest uncertainty would prevail as to what law was to be applied in determining the dispute," and the trust of the parties in arbitration would be lost. National Archives, BT 11/5348, document 14.

rely upon lawyers or counsels, and they usually executed the award immediately. In practice, the LCTA delivered several hundreds of awards each year, out of which less than five would typically be moved to a court of justice.[6]

Lastly, the success of the Trade Associations as global regulators also rested on the very structure of international trade: international commerce was centered in Britain, most often London or Liverpool. The presence of banks, trading houses, insurance services and shipping companies created a unique business environment with no parallel at the time. Hence, together with the vertical integration of the Association, a broader dimension of market power was key to the success of this form of global regulation: the enforcement of market discipline in general, as well as of awards in particular, rested by and large on the unique capacity of private regulators to threaten market exclusion or blacklisting across the global market. This state of affairs explains in large measure why appeals to the official courts to obtain enforcement of arbitration awards were quite rare. Similarly, Trade Associations had very few interactions with foreign courts and did not wish to see the extension of arbitration abroad.[7] Problems of judicial coordination with Russian, Argentine or French courts were not a defining issue of market governance.[8] On the other hand, Schwob (1928) mentions that the LCTA contracts were regularly mentioned in French court judgments.

To summarize, the English model of arbitration-based governance thus rested on three main characteristics: disputes were about points of fact rather than points of law; awards were typically self-enforced; and the overall framework presented a clear hegemonic dimension, because international merchants and businesses had no alternative to this properly English market ecology. A significant corollary is that both the arbitration law and the Trade Associations made no formal distinction between domestic and foreign cases: they were thus local and global at the same time, which is another way of saying that this architecture was imperial rather than international.

[6] Records of arbitration proceedings by the LCTA and a number of other similar organizations are kept at the Metropolitan Archives, in London.

[7] For example, when asked about a draft of the 1958 New York Convention, the British Association of Commodity Associations wrote: "In the commodity trades, we certainly do not wish to encourage foreign arbitration where, apart from the possibility of unsatisfactory arbitration procedure, there is a lack of expertise." National Archives, BT 11/5348, document 87 (1955).

[8] This point was indeed of the main policy conclusions reached by a high-level working group convened by the Lord's Chancellor in late 1918 and early 1919, at the time when all government agencies, in London as elsewhere, were busy working on the post-war international architecture. See *Report to the Lord's Chancellor on Foreign Judgments* (1919).

Early twentieth century challenges to the old English model of arbitration

Against this background, modern trade arbitration as we know it emerged from two long-term trends that originated in the last decades before World War I. First, traders from some European countries (particularly Germany, France and Belgium) became increasingly reluctant to join the London institutions that, they thought, tended to discriminate against them. By the early twentieth century, alternative market platforms, with their own arbitration facilities, were thus established in port cities like Hamburg, Bremen, Antwerp, Le Havre and Marseille.[9] These markets never reached a size comparable to that of their English competitors however: in fact, they were port terminals, not market hubs. But they strengthened the case for a reform of arbitration law in their respective countries. Louis Dreyfus, for instance, a prominent French wheat merchant with a large operation in London was behind the first parliamentary proposal in this direction in 1908. Other merchants tested the English model by refusing to abide by the awards determined in arbitration, especially in Russia before 1914; enforcement against foreign parties then began to be perceived in England as a potential source of problems.[10] After World War I, the resistance of the American business community to English institutions and practices became even more vocal. At a time when the United States was emerging as the dominant economic powerhouse, trading and manufacturing interests clearly militated for specifically US rules. This principle applied of course to arbitration, of which both the US government (for interstate disputes) and the local Chambers of Commerce had been early defenders (Koskenniemi 2007, Petersson 2013).

The second long-term trend, in addition to the emergence of new arbitration practices, reflected the evolution of trade flows themselves. As the relative share of commodities declined against that of manufacturing products and equipment goods, later followed by international services, the model of the vertically-integrated Trade Associations was exposed to increasing pressure. Rather than disputes about facts (like the quality of grains), disputes became increasingly focused on issues of after-sale services, spare parts, intellectual property rights,

[9] See, for example, Pozzi (1921) and Ishikazi (1928) for a remarkable study of the international silk market and the trade regulation of the Lyon merchants.

[10] For attempts by the LCTA to directly negotiate enforcement with the Russian government, see LMA, series CLC/B/103/MS23172 (executive committee discussions), 1907–11 and 1914–15.

agency rights, subcontracting, revenue-sharing clauses and, not least, financial contracting. And as contracts grew more complex than the typical pre-printed forms of the Trade Associations, interpreting them demanded more legal competence. Moreover, these same trends posed further potential problems for the enforcement of awards, as sheer market power, leveraged by private regulators, could not be applied as easily as in the classic English model. Lastly, the expansion of national regulatory states also made country borders more complex: as products and processes were increasingly subjected to national standards and norms, the legal and regulatory borders between national markets became more difficult to negotiate. Judges and arbiters alike increasingly had to look at the various national substantive and procedural laws that could apply to each dispute, and issues of how to "prove" foreign law (Nussbaum 1941), then how to obtain execution of judgments abroad, and how to mobilize existing bilateral treaties (Lorenzen 1935, Yntema 1935, Nussbaum 1942) came to the fore. In other words, problems of conflict of laws and comparative law, which had remained second order problems under the English regime, rapidly gained primacy.

The overall effect of these evolutions was to increase the costs of international contracting as well as the demand by merchants, manufacturers and bankers for advanced legal. Whereas in the former English model, problems of national jurisdiction were essentially circumvented, thanks to the global reliance on English legal institutions, the model of arbitration that would come to dominate in the later half of the twentieth century emerged from a long and protracted discussion with national judiciaries and lawmakers of all trading countries. At the core of this secular transition lies therefore a defining legal and political challenge: whereas markets during the First Global Era had been governed by rules that were de facto international and de jure English, they gradually began to move toward rules that were de jure international. The many problems raised by this new legal governance of markets and jurisdictional borders thus had to be identified, addressed and settled, explicitly and formally. New legal rules and practice, indeed a new contractual knowledge, had to be invented, tested, agreed upon and shared among all the parties to international markets – merchants and bankers, lawyers, trade officials, judges, international organizations. Not least, states would have to compromise on their own judicial order, hence also on a core component of what they had perceived until then as a core attribute of their own sovereignty.

In hindsight, it should be no surprise that this experimentation was long, uncertain and contested. There was in fact no precedent, no default option on which to lean. The long genealogy of international commercial arbitration over the twentieth century reflects in practice the confused perception that a novel model of international contracting had to be invented. At the turn of the twentieth century, the very broad and ideological wording that initially imbued the discourse on international arbitration reflected this epistemic indeterminacy. The fact that the very same term was applied equally to territorial disputes, sovereign debt issues and day-to-day commerce illustrates the point.

An international public court for private disputes? The Hague model

Since the French-Prussian war of 1870, and especially from the 1880s onward, interstate arbitration had been defended *in general* by European and American elites as a modern, progressive and peaceful instrument of international governance: one that would impose at last a sharp break with the old logic of power relationships and imperial dominance (David Kennedy 1996; Koskenniemi 2001 and 2005; Duncan Kennedy 2006; Mazower 2012). Before 1914 the main achievement of this broad movement toward arbitration was The Hague Peace Conferences of 1899 and 1907, the first of which saw the creation of the Permanent Court of Arbitration (PCA) (Koskenniemi 2007; Grewe 2000). Although only states met in this Court, many PCA awards issued during the following years had in fact a civil or commercial dimension, one of the best known being the dispute between private investors and Venezuela over the latter's sovereign debt[11] (Mallarmé 1906). Moreover, the statutes of The Hague Court left open the possibility of creating specialized chambers dealing with civil and commercial disputes. Some participants to the (parallel) Hague conferences on International Private Law saw here the possibility for developing an international jurisdiction that would directly support trade across national jurisdictions.[12] The second international conference on the unification of the law on bills of exchange in 1912 officially called for

[11] See Mallarmé (1906) for a discussion of the Venezuelan arbitration. Garrié (1892) discusses the potential for arbitration to offer peaceful settlement of sovereign debt disputes; also Freund (1910).

[12] Intellectual property emerged as a prominent candidate, following the 1900 Paris Treaty and a discussion at the 1904 meeting of the Institut de Droit International, in Cambridge (Wehberg 1911, Röthlisberger 1893).

such an extension.[13] The German representative even went one step further, suggesting that an international, de facto supra-national jurisdiction could later become a specific source of law that would guarantee coordination or unification across borders.[14] In the years immediately before World War I, a small group of mostly German legal scholars published a remarkable series of essays that developed further the idea that an international Supreme Court for commercial cases could eventually become the touchstone of an international regime founded on the voluntary adhesion of states to arbitration.[15]

There is little doubt that the founders of international commercial arbitration drew extensively on this broad ideological vein to legitimize and publicize their project: the powerful utopian or messianic dimension that often imbued the public discourse on arbitration found its way as well into the International Congress of Chambers of Commerce and later in the language of the American Arbitration Association. In this sense, international commercial arbitration as we know it today may well be seen as the main heir to this global trend toward arbitration that marked the decades immediately before and after World War I.

Yet, it is not so clear that private interests had the same understanding of these great and admirable statements. We find for instance at the 1912 Congress of Chambers of Commerce a strongly worded declaration in favor of arbitration in general that includes a call to extend it to commercial affairs. But the machinery of The Hague court, and the need to first obtain the support of one's own government before reaching it, were quite at odds with the bottom-up, fast-track approaches that private interests were primarily looking for. These pro-arbitration militants thus remained strongly wedded to a private sector perspective: following the classic trope, commerce was to be a force for peace and prosperity, though it had to be allowed to self-organize. In their view, private arbitration and the new coalition of "Merchants of Peace" would bring about international peace in spite of governments rather than with them.[16]

13 See Actes, I, pp. 179–81, quoted in Mutzner (1914).

14 See Conférence internationale sur le droit des lettres de change (1912).

15 See Zorn (1910), Wehberg (1911), Klein (1914) and Mutzner (1914). The German interest in this court-driven project of legal unification may be seen as a reflection of their own experience with legal and jurisdictional unification, from the time of the Zollverein till the establishment of the new imperial institutions in the 1870s.

16 Calls to reinvest the Hague Court as a venue for commercial arbitration would occasionally pop up in the later decades, as in Hurst (1925); see Sartini van den Kerckhove (1935) and Kellor

TWO NEO-IMPERIAL PROJECTS: LONDON AND NEW YORK

The London Court of Arbitration (1906)

During the same pre-1914 years, although with no documented connection to the previous debates, the first practical response to the new challenges of the twentieth century emerged in Britain in the form of the London Chamber of Arbitration. This new facility was established jointly in 1892 by the London Chamber of Commerce and the Corporation of London (municipal authority) (Musgrave 1914, Lemercier 2012). Already by 1895 however, the Chamber acknowledged disappointing results and organized a series of hearings with market insiders, lawyers, arbitrators, etc. to address obstacles (London Chamber of Arbitration, 1895). The conclusion that came out of these hearings was that the services the Chamber offered could not compete with the rapid pace, on-site practice of Trade Associations. On the other hand, if the Chamber wanted to address other classes of disputes and firms, then it had to accept conditions imposed by the attorneys – primarily their monetary demands. These conclusions largely shaped the 1906 reform of the Chamber, through which it became the London *Court* of Arbitration (LCA), and which enabled it to find a niche that anticipated modern arbitration: the legal dimension of the cases it could now handle was more substantial than those addressed by the Trade Associations, hence lawyers had a larger role; and self-enforcement by way of market power and vertical integration was much less pronounced. Also, foreigners became a key clientele of the LCA: from 1906 and up until the Great Depression a great number of Belgian, Italian, French or Swedish firms arbitrated one against the other in London; before 1914, we even see in the LCA's registers cases of German firms arbitrating between themselves (London Court of Arbitration, 1893–1953).

Yet, this early success failed to solidify, for reasons that are complex. First, the LCA lost its German clientele after World War I and, in 1927 the LCA had sealed an alliance with the Imperial Congress of Chambers of Commerce; the collapse of international markets after 1930 reinforced further the trends towards withdrawing within the British Empire. Significantly, this strategy also presented a clear domestic and sociological dimension: whatever its relative successes, and despite the

(1937) for additional calls for some kind of commercial appellate court at the international level.

fact that it had now accommodated the interests of the lawyers, the LCA remained on the margins of the judicial establishment, hence with limited legitimacy. Contrary to the older Trade Associations, the LCA was never recognized by the higher London courts and the top tier of the legal profession as a creditable, self-standing jurisdiction, and it remained dependent upon the sponsorship of the London Chamber of Commerce. For instance, in 1926 an important government committee led by Judge MacKinnon was set up at the Chancellor's Offices in order to draft a new arbitration law that would be adopted the following year. The committee first entirely ignored the LCA, then eventually invited it to the proceedings, but clearly resisted granting it full legitimacy on the subject;[17] it even asked that the LCA did not send an attorney as a representative, because, in a convoluted way, that would have made too many attorneys on the committee.[18]

Another dimension in the eventual failure of the LCA has a properly legal origin. Since the adoption of the 1889 Arbitration Act arbiters had to closely follow English law and refer to the courts any point of law that might appear unclear to them. Arbiters were thus envisaged as a substitute to judges, though only from a procedural perspective: arbitration cases moved faster and were in the hands of trade specialists, but the link to the official courts remained a very close one. From the 1920s onwards, a key point of contention at the international level, especially vis-à-vis the emerging practice of the ICC in Paris, would be the extent to which arbiters might interpret the law, diverge from it, or even follow the (substantive) law of another country. The leeway that might thus be given or refused to the parties and their arbiters became very quickly a source of tension, and later one of open conflict. Whereas at the ICC (as in today's international practice) this room for manoeuver was seen as a guarantee of adaptability and pragmatism, the English judicial establishment saw it as a license for arbitrariness and spoliation. Transparent prejudices were in play, primarily vis-à-vis the civil law tradition: moving even one step in the direction of these new, mostly continental practices was seen largely illegitimate.[19] The LCA thus

[17] "There is a body that calls itself 'The London Court of Arbitration' which is conducted under the management of the Corporation of the City of London and the London Chamber of Commerce. You might possibly think it will be usefull [*sic*] to ascertain whether the Chairman or some leading member of that body should be considered." National Archives, LCO/1200.

[18] For the correspondence between the LCA and the McKinnon committee, see especially National Archives, LCO/1200.

[19] On the long dispute around the *Amiable Compositeur*, see, for instance, Cohn (1941) and Marx (1947).

found itself in the bizarre position of being a marginal institution within the English judicial landscape, while at the same time being anchored to a model of arbitration that remained entirely rooted in local law, though also in the sociology of the English judicial profession and judiciary.

The overall result is that beyond the well-established practice of the Trade Associations, the development of modern arbitration in Britain would long remain impaired by its lack of legal flexibility as well as by the delays and costs incurred by its close relationships to the London courts. By the 1950s the LCA was essentially a prostrated institution with an almost empty docket and no capacity whatsoever to respond to the challenges raised by the new international practice that was fast developing in Paris and New York. It was only in the late 1970s that the close oversight by official English courts was abandoned and that international commercial arbitration re-emerged in London; under the new name of the London Court of International Arbitration the LCA would then be entirely reformed and re-launched (1981, 1985).

The early American experience with international arbitration

In hindsight, therefore, the emergence and expansion of international commercial arbitration in New York should have been a foretold story, one indeed of "hegemonic succession." Very soon after the industrial, financial and commercial center of the world economy started to shift westward, private American interests showed increasing resistance to English practices and began to militate for a new and more progressive model of international market governance. The imperial dimension was however quite visible: in the future, it would be up to the Americans to organize and regulate markets, for themselves as well as for the rest of the world; and this would apply to capital markets, production standards, and the extra-territorial reach of domestic courts or arbitration laws. While foreigners may have had reservations, market power would eventually compel them to opt in.

This inclination was illustrated by the parallel development of both domestic and the international arbitration practices. Arbitration had of course been well practiced since colonial times (Jones 1922; Macassey 1939); but in spite of a number of attempts at legal reforms since the 1870s (Lemercier 2012) arbitration had developed at a rather far distance from the official judiciary, without the institutional clout and the social capital that the English Trade Associations carried. Hence, rather than having to take on established institutions and develop its own niche, as did the LCA in London, arbitration in the United States was fought for as a novel, broad-based, generic model of dispute resolution that was seen as eminently suitable altogether to the very local, the national and the international markets. The first militants of arbitration in fact applied the same generic (and often utopic) discourse to all contexts and brought forward the same expected benefits: rapid-pace, competent, low-cost dispute resolution.

On the domestic side, the first point on the agenda was to obtain the legalization of the arbitration clause. This step was achieved primarily by the two founding fathers of modern American arbitration: Charles Bernheimer (1864–1944), the long-time head of the arbitration committee of the New York Chamber of Commerce, and Julius Cohen (1873–1950), the Chamber's legal counsel. They first fought for the arbitration clause within the Chamber, then at the New York State Bar Association, before lobbying successfully for a pro-arbitration New York statute that was eventually adopted in 1920; from then on, they moved to Washington and played a large role in the adoption in 1925 of a federal statute very similar to the New York one. The "big business" dimension of their project is made clear by the list of 145 initial subscribers to the Arbitration Education Fund created by Bernheimer in 1924: twenty-one were engaged in foreign trade, and forty-one were bankers, including J.P. Morgan, Arthur and Harry Sachs (from Goldman Sachs), Paul and Felix Warburg and Kuhn, Loeb and Co.[20] Symmetrically, the main opposition to the new legislation clearly came from the other side of the Main Street/ Wall Street divide, namely the rural, populist, mid-West states. A similar divide would often appear in other countries where arbitration was discussed in parliaments, though the strength of the initial support by big business is probably unique to the US, or the New York environment.

The American Arbitration Association (AAA) was created in 1925, as an alliance of both Bernheimer's foundation and a similar association supported by the New York State Bar Association (Kellor 1937). From there on, the AAA rapidly became the dominant American institution and developed its activities across the country, including at the small-town level and in matters such as industrial relationships, consumption or movie distribution. In a parallel development at least as important, arbitration in the United States moved quite rapidly from disputes over

[20] Columbia University Libraries/ Rare books & Manuscripts. Box 326, Folder 1, Section V3: Bernheimer Arbitration Education Fund, 1924–1957.

the quality of products to disputes with a more complex, legal dimension. By the 1930s, the AAA literally celebrated its capacity to take on problems of intellectual property or mergers and acquisitions, and saw as a signal of its success the fact that lawyers were taking on an increasing role, both in its arbitration tribunals and in its own structure of governance.

On the international side, the push for arbitration first targeted the Western Hemisphere: soon after the First Pan-American Financial Conference in 1915 the US Chamber of Commerce signed a cooperation agreement with the Buenos Aires Bolsa de Commercio, which then served as a template for several other accords in Latin America, including in Sao Paulo, Santiago de Chile, and Bogota (Proceedings of the First Pan American Financial Conference, 1915). What differentiates this early Pan-American model is its basis in formal agreements with sister organisations, in clear contrast with the unilateral British approach. Still, there was no ambiguity about who was in the driving seat: this network of bilateral accords was centered on the United States and the whole project clearly benefited from the active support of the US government. This foray into international arbitration did not prove however an unmitigated success, far from it: arbitration laws in the respective countries were often inconsistent and the Latin American partners did not always meet the expected standards. The choice of arbiters for instance seems to have proved occasionally weak, leading to a clear problem of trust between the parties. Apparently, the partners in this network did not share the same understanding of the endeavor, and possibly not even the same knowledge of rules for international contracting.

This experience became however a key reference after 1918, as American interests envisaged how to expand their cooperative network toward Europe: the US Chamber of Commerce was clearly the main force behind the creation of both the ICC (1920), and its respective ICC Arbitration Court (1923). Yet, a bit like in Latin America, success was not forthcoming, in spite of the strong input of American leadership, legal expertise and superior social capital. American publications that had often been quite informative in the early years about debates in Paris soon ignored them. By the late 1930s, the AAA perceived the ICC court as a foreign and rather distant organization, not as an American creature on the Old Continent.

International arbitration as an American project surfaced again after 1942 in debates over the postwar international order, and again took a clear American and imperial accent. The May 1945 issue of the *Arbitration Magazine*, edited by the AAA, states:

> The way for Americans to plan for arbitration at home is to use an appropriate arbitration clause in all their contracts, whether with other nationals in this country or with foreign traders overseas. In insisting upon security for himself in the settlement of commercial controversy, the American at the same time offers security to foreign parties to his contracts; for this security is based upon American law and established arbitration procedure, with its fine facilities and carefully preserved traditions. (*Arbitration Magazine*, 1945)

By the end of the 1940s however, this project came to an unexpected standstill. First, the link that had been celebrated during the war with British institutions went nowhere: from 1947 on, experts from the AAA began criticizing the close control of arbitration by official English courts, and particularly the costs and delays which this rule caused. Second, constraints within the US legal order also caused difficulties: following US constitutional law, arbitration is a matter that partly belongs to state legislatures, so that any legislative reform or treaty ratification necessitates considerable lobbying activity across the country. This problem became visible in the run-up till the landmark 1958 UN Conference on Arbitration: even though the AAA had been most active in lobbying the UN, it could not secure US adhesion to the ensuing Convention: ratification would have to wait until 1970.

Here is the key point from a comparative perspective: just as in the case of the LCA, a close relationship to the domestic legal order was initially seen as a source of predictability and indeed legitimacy; it was expected that the new institution would be able to lean on the existing domestic institutions and its guarantees to provide to international businesses an effective and highly commendable arbitration machinery. The result of this strategy would be an arbitration model that would be both local and international at the same time. The experience of both the LCA and the AAA shows however that this low-cost option, based on a large inflow of domestic legal know-how, social legitimacy and geopolitical power did not provide an efficient solution to the problem at stake. The invention and construction of a properly international practice based on a principle of mutual recognition between national judicial orders would come through an entirely different route, and those who traveled that route would not come from the core of national legal institutions, neither would they benefit at first from the support of core national judicial authorities as of international business.

THE CASE FOR AN INTERNATIONAL JUDICIAL ORDER

The International Chamber of Commerce and its arbitration court

When compared to the old English imperial order and to the network-based strategy developed by the Americans, the emergence in Paris of a largely extra-territorial private arbitration court was not a banal, I-told-you-so response to the new problems of market governance that emerged from the evolving international division of labor. The fact that France is a civil law country and that it was not a prime economic force in the 1920s underlines the point: no perceived or objective comparative advantage, whether legal, economic or political can explain why the new court was located in Paris in 1923. If the Americans did not want to establish the new International Chamber neither in London, nor of course in Berlin, The Hague, Brussels or Geneva could have been ready options as well.

The creation of a permanent, collective organization had been regularly discussed since the early twentieth century at the international congresses of the Chambers of Commerce: the phrase "Chambre de Commerce Internationale" had even been used as early as 1874. At the same time, these same meetings had identified cross-border arbitration as an important aim, worth lobbying for. The point was first mentioned in 1904, and a solemn declaration to this effect was adopted at the Paris Congress of June 1914, six weeks before the outbreak of war. As early as October 1919, the US Chamber of Commerce convened its counterpart organizations from four Allied countries to a meeting in Atlantic City, where the creation of the International Chamber of Commerce was decided. Its location in Paris was agreed upon at the following, June 1920 congress, and the creation of an Arbitration Court, within the premises of the ICC, was decided in 1921. It was officially inaugurated in January 1923, with the President of the Republic and the diplomatic corps in attendance.

The early developments of both the ICC and its Court were very much marked by the leadership of American private interests and by the close relationship, established in the last phase of the war, between the respective heads of French and US Departments of Commerce, Etienne Clémentel (1864–1936) and Herbert Hoover (1874–1964). They belonged more generally to the network of high officials who had experimented during the war with new methods of international coordination among Allied powers, and many of whom would later be found at the League of Nations.[21] The militants of commercial arbitration in the United States, which had just reached their first objective of a more supportive statutory framework in New York, were also very much present in those years. The leader of this group, Charles Bernheimer, kept a close eye on the Paris experiment and even applied for membership to the ICC on a personal basis. He would be a key voice in transmitting American wishes, or suggestions, to the Paris team, which in turn proved quite open to such guidance when working on the first statutes and rules of the new court. Owen Young, then Chairman of General Electric and RCA, and a blue-blood figure of the US establishment, also intervened in this process (Streat 1922, Young 1921). He would become the first President of the Court, shortly after Clémentel had become the first chairman of the ICC. Hence the AAA and the ICC Arbitration Court were both children of the same American private interests and of their project to build a new, post-British governance of international markets.

Quite soon, however, this transatlantic network of notables started to unravel. The problem was not just that Young shortly moved to the more challenging task of restructuring the German reparations debt. Nor can it be attributed to the semi-retirement of Charles Bernheimer after the creation of the AAA in 1925, or the nomination of Clémentel as Minister of Finance, in 1924. More generally, US advocates of arbitration gradually lost interest in what was happening in Paris, a point that is well reflected in the relative withdrawal of the American representatives from the day-to-day management of the Court. And indeed, from a statistical perspective at least, the success of the ICC Court in establishing itself as a well-recognized platform was at best moot. The total number of cases submitted remained small throughout the interwar period: between January 1923 and October 1925, only a hundred cases landed on its docket, mostly of limited commercial size – wedding gowns and bicycles rather than large capital equipment or machine-tools. Moreover, the interest of American firms on this new facility proved extremely limited: only eight American parties can be found in the hundred first cases, compared to forty-six French, for

[21] Arthur Salter, who would head the League Economic and Financial Organization is a prime example: he guided the negotiations leading to the two League accords on arbitration in 1923 and 1927; his alter ego during the war, Jean Monnet, would also take a prominent position at the League, between 1919 and 1923. On Clémentel, see Druelle-Korn (2004).

instance.[22] In other words, it was not enough for this fledgling court to be established in and supported by the first international private lobby, the ICC, with its powerful network of national chambers and great patrons. Even though the ICC and the Court were supported, directly or not, by powerful US groups like General Electric, or by dominant banks like J.P. Morgan, which were all thoroughly engaged in post-war European affairs, this support was not enough to trigger a substantial flow of cases by American firms. Whereas in the early 1920s the ICC Court could be seen as an American project in Europe with junior French participation, by the 1930s it was perceived as essentially a foreign institution catering to European continental needs, following mostly civil law principles. During the war, when the ICC and its Court were relocated to Stockholm (Jarvin, 2011), it almost disappeared from the radar: at that time the AAA looked toward the British and the Soviet arbitration institutions as its key partners for the post-war years.

This broad account begs the question of whether anything relevant for the future of international arbitration happened during the interwar period, in the few offices and meeting rooms where the Court worked and met. Was this an entirely futile endeavor? Like the League of Nations, did this Parisian experiment only leave to the next generation a list of all the errors that should be avoided at any cost?

The benefits of experimentation

Still, its low-key experience during the interwar years allowed the ICC Court to test, develop and adjust its rules and procedures through hundreds of cases and countless internal meetings confronting the views of its various national committees as well as those of professional lawyers, businessmen and sometimes even law professors. On that basis, the ICC Court built a novel approach to international arbitration, based on its own multilateral (private) structure, the recognition that arbitration is about dispute resolution across jurisdictional borders, and the slow development of an alternate, extraterritorial (private) jurisdiction that would slowly reduce the costs and uncertainty of these border effects. In spite of its being established in a civil law country and its initial catering to smaller continental firms, this new legal technology would not only be eventually adopted by a great number of international businesses;

[22] ICC Archives, report by Edouard Dolléans to the *Comité d'études de l'arbitrage*, 29–30 October 1925. Only four of these hundred cases led to an award being issued. In forty-five cases, the defendant could not be contacted or refused arbitration (at that time, the compromissory clause still did not exist in many countries).

it de facto structured the social and institutional space within which, from the 1950s onward, different legal traditions, national professions and arbitration facilities would compete one against the other and share the symbolic and financial profits that the success of arbitration would soon entail. Three elements stand out in the early, foundational experience of the ICC practice.

First, from the onset the ICC targeted international disputes only: as said previously, only cases opposing firms from different countries were accepted. Against the London and the New York models, this new practice of cross-border dispute resolution was thus largely insulated from domestic concerns, whether of a substantive, procedural or of a more broadly political economic dimension. This principle certainly reflected the ICC's own organizational structure: it was no forum for attempts to realign the well-established relations between French businesses and their old, largely self-governed commercial courts. Moreover, by the turn of the twentieth century, the division between domestic and international cases was already well established in French arbitration law, which the ICC had to follow. Because the judiciary had long resisted the development of a fully independent arbitration practice, a separate legal regime was gradually developed by the courts for cross-border cases only, so as not to handicap French exporters and importers (Lachau and Daguin 1958, Godron 1919, Robert 1929). During the 1930s and much more clearly after 1945, this two-track jurisprudence provided the basis for the development of a most supportive body of case law for international arbitration, that in fact would be (and still is) closely tailored to the needs of ICC practice. The close relationship between the ICC Arbitration Court, the Cour d'Appel de Paris and the Cour de Cassation is actually a key feature of this story: one may actually speak here of a long-term co-evolution of the ICC arbitration technology and French case law, though without this closeness ever affecting the internal judicial order (Refort 1939; Domke 1943; Carbonneau 1980, 1984). Extra-territoriality is rooted here, just as the imperial approach followed in England was also rooted in the respective, domestic legal order.

The second defining element in this experience follows from the first: once domestic and international cases had different legal regimes, it became less problematic in the latter case to give a much larger franchise to the parties, the arbiters and the arbitration fora altogether. This development was reflected early on in the debate over the "amiable compositeur": a traditional form of arbitration in French law that the ICC largely adopted, which gives to the arbiter substantial room to diverge from the existing substantive law and, possibly, to take argument from accepted usages or from equity principles. This distance vis-à-vis the domestic legal order, in fact a first step toward relative extra-territoriality, was of course anathema in England, where any new point of law that arose from a given case had to be submitted to a judge. Later, in the ICC Court the parties would also be allowed to choose the (procedural) arbitration law and the (substantive) contract law that fitted best their interest – again, an option that initially was entirely alien to the English and American approaches.

A third comparative advantage was the very structure of the Arbitration Court, which was organized along the multilateral principles of the ICC itself. The Court was made up of a college of legal experts chosen by the national chapters of the ICC. When a case was submitted, the Court would first choose a third country whose domestic national Chamber would select an arbiter with the required competence; he would then manage the proceedings, following the procedural rules of the ICC and with the organizational support of the Court. Once the award had been written, it was however reviewed and possibly revised by the Court as a collective body. The point was rarely to change the substance of the decision, but rather to adjust its legal form so as to maximize the chance that, if needed, enforcement would be obtained with minimal resistance (typically in the country of the party that lost the case). Early on (and still today), this gave to the ICC awards a label of judicial soundness, predictability and institutional legitimacy.

Quite soon, in the early 1920s, this multilateral, collegial expert body started to operate as a kind of clearing house or brokerage, and on that basis it developed a specific know-how which would be socially sanctioned only decades later, and whose very object was to navigate more safely and at lower costs the rough waters of contractual exchange across jurisdictional boundaries.[23] This transnational, peer-based college that was the Court thus became the place where many underlying procedural and substantive problems raised by the development of

[23] This operating mode anticipated quite neatly on what Ginsburg (2003) calls "the culture of arbitration"; see Waters (1989) for the sociology of college. The more legal economic approach developed by Gilson (1984), who envisages lawyers as "transaction costs engineers," can also be easily applied to the emerging profession of arbitration lawyers. See Clavin and Wessels (2005) on the horizontal approach to expertise work at the Economic and Financial Organization of the League, which actually fitted directly with that developed at the same time at the ICC.

international commercial arbitration were identified and where answers were debated, settled and stored. There is of course no question that the ICC Court benefited a lot, at this point, from the network of national Chambers of Commerce, both as a conduit to national sources of expertise and as a source of authority. In fact the ICC provided to its Court a kind of passport that allowed it to leverage social and institutional resources across a great number of countries, despite the fact that it had no track record and that it could not draw on the machinery of intergovernmental coordination.

Still, its success arose from what the ICC Court did with these resources as it developed its novel business line. Contrary to the English and American approaches that tried to settle cross-border disputes primarily on the basis of their own domestic law, the ICC Court addressed head-on the problems raised by the jurisdictional fragmentation of markets. And so it became in practice a kind of high-skill or *haute couture* workshop in applied international private law. A college made up of the best experts from the British Trade Associations and the LCA, or an assembly of the top lawyers from the AAA, would never have grown a similar knowledge, whatever their respective social capital and domestic legitimacy. Therefore, its institutional structure did not primarily offer to the ICC Court a conduit for transferring domestic legitimacy, if only because, in that case, the declining interests of its American patrons would have affected its development – just as when the LCA had to ally itself to the Imperial Chambers of Commerce and thus withdraw from the international market where it had thrived before 1914. The main benefit of being part of the ICC was in the close integration, on a day-by-day basis, between the "production function" of the Court, hence the specific contractual knowledge that it developed, and the multilateral structure of the ICC as a whole. It would take half-a-century before other arbitration organizations could build a similar comparative advantage.

The sociology of institutional innovation

The rapid withdrawal of its great American patrons and the low-key, collegial dimension of the ICC Court go a long way toward defining the sociological character of this remarkable experiment. The legal innovations that international businesses adopted were long and difficult to deliver, and they asked for a lot of trial and error. Until 1950 one finds little evidence that its members earned substantial social capital and wealth from their activities at the ICC. Some among them certainly shared the sense of a mission, namely to contribute to peace and international prosperity; but for them the law was an instrument rather than a calling, and they certainly did not envisage that the success of their career would be judged by how far they had progressed within the legal profession or the legal academy. Few in the first generation did teach at a University: at best they contributed some small briefs to law journals and they had no sustained relationships with the top Parisian judiciary. And, for sure, they never moved to top positions in the business sector. They were simply professionals and *bourgeois*.

Take the pre-eminent figures who actually presided over the early development of the ICC Court. Edouard Dolléans (1878–1954), its first Secretary-General, was an economics professor in the small city of Dijon before being picked up by Etienne Clémentel; yet, he left the ICC in 1936 in order to work for the Front Populaire government and, as a whole, he remains better remembered for his research on the history of the socialist movement in France. René Arnaud (1893–1981), his deputy, was an alumnus of the Ecole Normale Supérieure and clearly had rather right-wing political leanings. But he did not have a law degree either, nor did he publish any textbook or treatise on arbitration, his free time being spent on remembrances of the four years he had spent in the trenches during World War I, or on small essays on Joan of Arc or the French Revolution of 1848. Robert Marx, a German lawyer, worked after World War I with the French-German Mixt Tribunal (an offshot of the Versailles Treaty), before joining the German delegation at the ICC and becoming a fixture of the Court; he was excluded in 1936, however, probably because of his Jewish origins, but he returned to the Court after World War II, this time as its Secretary-General and later as a technical adviser.[24]

This broad pattern remains visible well after World War II. Frédéric Eisemann (1908–1986), who was Secretary-General of the Court between 1947 and 1973, hence a key actor in this story. An Alsatian Jew who had obtained his Ph.D. in Giessen, Germany in 1931, he was only loosely associated to the Paris Faculty of Law: he never became a Professor and owed his social progress exclusively to his position at the Court at the time of its rise to international preeminence. Two

[24] Archives CCI, Cour d'arbitrage, Document 24, 120th session de la Cour, 29 juillet 1936. The Court apparently tried to re-hire Marx during the war, when it was relocated in Stockholm, in order to teach the local personnel its rules and procedures (Jarvin 1992, 2011).

other influential figures from the same decades, with strong legal credentials, Charles Carabiber and Bertold Goldman (1913–1993) had immigrated from Russia and Romania, respectively. Then is the great Martin Domke (1892–1980), who became a key man in the close relationship that emerged during the 1950s between the ICC Court and the American Arbitration Association (Aksen, 1981). Also a German Jew, he left Berlin in 1933 and lived in Paris until 1940, serving not least as the personal lawyer of Bertold Brecht, Theodor Adorno and Walter Benjamin. After reaching New York in 1941 or 1942, he rapidly joined the top tier of the AAA, thanks not to his social capital but to his specific professional capital, namely his knowledge of the discipline of Conflicts of Law.

Lastly, two exceptions confirm the rule. Arthur Nussbaum (1877–1964) and René David (1906–1990), both also with a Jewish background, entered early the *cursus honorum* of the successful law Professor. The former published four volumes of a yearbook of arbitration between 1926 and 1931 (the *Internationales Jahrbuch für Schiedsgerichtswesen*) that remains, by far, the most comprehensive publication on the topic during the interwar years. He had to leave his chair at the Humboldt Universität in Berlin in 1933, and almost immediately started a second and brilliant career at Columbia in New York. René David also had a great career at the Sorbonne, as well as at Cambridge and Columbia, while acting as a top-level consultant to the League of Nations and later the UN. In 1932 he wrote a report for Unidroit (an agency of the League) on international commercial arbitration that would contribute to shaping the international debate till the early 1950s (David 1932). Here however is the significant point in these two remarkable careers: despite their initial investment and impact on the debate on arbitration, both Arthur Nussbaum and René David left this emerging field soon afterwards and moved to more mainstream topics. The former never came back to arbitration,[25] and the latter only occasionally. It seems therefore that, at least until the mid 1950s, no matter whether you were a law professor in Berlin, New York or Paris, arbitration was not seen as a promising field of investment, either professionally or intellectually.

The move toward an established "field" of international commercial arbitration, with its stable institutional set-up and its own emerging

[25] Nussbaum (1942), (Cheatham et al. 1957).

profession, happened between 1947 and 1958: that is, between the moment when the AAA abandoned its alliance with the LCA and joined force with the ICC, and, ten years later, the adoption of the New York Convention on Arbitration (Domke 1958). On the one hand, the terms of the complex transactions with national governments had been de facto reached, both at the domestic and the international levels; on the other hand, the ICC technology was increasingly adopted by multinational firms as their first port of call when trying to settle cross-border disputes. This transition came with many signals that also indicated that arbitration was rapidly becoming institutionalized, at the international level: new specialized journals were launched, structured textbooks were published, conferences followed each other at an increasing speed and, more generally, a new transnational profession of arbitration rapidly consolidated with its own career profile and internal hierarchy. This is when this new profession, the extra-territorial character of the ICC practice and their international clientele emerged as a perfect match.

In other words, the time of idealistic early entrepreneurship, carried out by professionals with diverse backgrounds and interests, was now over. The institution, its rules and its procedures had met their true experts, who would dominate the profession and the arbitration market in the decades to come. If anything, the first personality that responded to the new profile of the grand and dominant international business lawyer was Martin Domke, though only in the second part of his career (he reached New York at age forty-nine, and when the New York Convention was signed he was sixty-six); then came Piet Sanders (1912–2012), who can be counted as the second "Grand Old Man" of the newly established international field. After having played a preeminent role in the adoption of the UN 1958 Convention, which remains today the touchstone of this regime, he would act for decades altogether as counsel, arbiter, law professor, government advisor, conference convener and editor.

CONCLUSION

This chapter has argued that the emergence of the ICC Court as the dominant institution in the new field of international private arbitration first reflected the difficulties encountered by its counterparts in London and New York in addressing the new international evolutions observed from the beginning of the twentieth century. The relative decline of Britain and the move to more complex transactions, like equipment goods or intellectual property rights, gradually made clear that new methods for backing up and regulating international markets would have to be found. It would not always remain possible to rely primarily on market power and the mediation and interpretation of a dominant national jurisdiction – British or American. Judges and arbiters thus would have to fully acknowledge the strength and legitimacy of the national legal orders and their jurisdictions. And indeed, as this trend developed, the core issue in international arbitration became how to negotiate jurisdictional borders when contracting internationally.

Within this context, the success of the ICC model was first founded on the multilateral structure of the international chamber itself: the Court benefited to some extent from the aggregated legitimacy of national chambers, it relied on their network as an instrument to mobilize local knowledge and expertise, and, lastly, it easily entered into direct discussions with the new brand of multilateral organizations – the League of Nations, then the UN. The other key feature of this experience was the creation, very early on, of an in-house college of expert lawyers with diverse national backgrounds. Through their review and confirmation of awards, this body became the place where a new practice and later a new doctrine of international arbitration was progressively debated, built up, stored and continuously tested. This new legal technology emerged during the first three decades of existence of the ICC Court, on the basis of a relatively small flow of cases, themselves of mediocre economic weight. Yet, from the 1950s onwards, this approach to international dispute settlement was increasingly endorsed by multinational firms, who thrived on the gradual reopening of international markets. At the same time, the first generation of institutional entrepreneurs was replaced by the representatives of a new transnational profession, with its settled practices and organizations, recognized competence, its career paths and high rewards for those who reached the last steps of its internal hierarchy.

The overall analysis of this remarkable experiment thus starts from the recognition of long-run changes in the international division of labor and from the ensuing need to develop and adopt new legal technologies that would better support the new form of international contracting. The previous pages should have shown that this reading does not come with a deterministic, rationalist or economicist reading of the whole experiment. To the contrary, imagination, experimentation and confrontation were observed all along, from the very first attempts to design a new model of arbitration in London at the end of the nineteenth century till the eventual success of the ICC model, sixty years later. Still, one may not account for the evolution of market institutions without acknowledging the material interests of the participants to those markets. In this measured sense, this analysis is materialist.

Change in practice also came from the margins of the social and institutional game. Those who actually developed the new ICC practice had a small background in law, many of them were Jewish immigrants from Germany or Eastern Europe, and few of them were or became card-carrying members of the legal establishment – whether judicial or academic. In general, they neither moved to the business sector nor did they reinvest the know-how or social capital had acquired at the ICC in other fields. Legitimacy, just like private wealth, was acquired ex post and quite late indeed, as a consequence of successful innovations wherein multinational firms would eventually identify the possibility of benefits.

We know well indeed that, historically, insiders and dominant players in the institutions of governance are not always able to design novel rules, when conditions change. It just happens that sometimes refugees and immigrants are in a better position.

References

Aksen, Gerald. 1981. "In Memoriam: Martin Domke." *New York University Journal of International Law and Politics*. 13 (3): 419–423.

Alter, Karen. 2008. "Agents or Trustees? International Courts in their Political Context." *European Journal of International Relations*. 14 (1): 33–63.

Arbitration Magazine. 1945. "A New Kind of Competition for American Foreign Traders." 3 (5–6). pp. 3–5.

Barty-King, Hugh. 1978. *Food for Man and Beast*. London: Hutchinson Benham. 107 pages.

Bernstein, L. 1992. "Opting out of the legal system: Extralegal contractual relations in the diamond industry." *Journal of Legal Studies*. 21 (January): 115–157.

Brachet, Paul. 1928. *De l'exécution internationale des sentences arbitrales*. Paris: Librairie Arthur Rousseau. 233 pages.

Carbonneau, Thomas E. 1980. "The Elaboration of a French Court Doctrine on International Commercial Arbitration: A Study in Liberal Civilian Judicial Creativity." *Tulane Law Review*. 55 (1): 1–62.

1984. "Etude historique et comparée de l'arbitrage. Vers un droit matériel de l'arbitrage commercial international fondé sur la motivation des sentences." *Revue internationale de droit comparé*. 36 (4): 727–781.

Chattaway, C. 1907. "Arbitration in the Foreign Corn Trade in London." *The Economic Journal*. 17 (67): 428–431.

Cheatham, E., W. Friedmann, W. Gellhorn, Ph. Jessup, W. Reese and W. Schuyler. 1957. "Arthur Nussbaum: A Tribute." *Columbia Law Review*. 57 (1): 1–7.

Clavin, Patricia and Jens-Wilhelm Wessels. 2005. "Transnationalism and the League of Nations: Understanding the Work of Its Economic and Financial Organisation." *Contemporary European History*. 14 (4): 465–492.

Cohn, Ernst J. 1941. "Commercial Arbitration and the Rules of Law, a Comparative Study." *University of Toronto Law Journal*. 4 (1): 1–32.

Conférence internationale sur le droit des lettres de change. 1912. The Hague.

David, René. 1932. *Rapport sur l'arbitrage conventionnel en droit privé*. Institut International pour l'Unification du Droit Privé. Rome: l'Universale. 289 pages.

Dezalay, Yves and Bryant G. Garth. 1996. *Dealing in virtue: International commercial arbitration and the construction of a transnational legal order*. Chicago: University of Chicago Press.

2002. *The Internationalization of Palace Wars: Lawyers, Economists, and the Contest to Transform Latin American States*. Chicago: University of Chicago Press.

Domke, Martin. 1943. "Arbitral Clauses and Awards: Recent Development in French Law." *Tulane Law Review*. 17: 447–455.

Domke, Martin, ed. 1958. *International Trade Arbitration, A Road to World-Wide Cooperation*. New York: American Arbitration Association. 311 pages.

Druelle-Korn, Clotilde. 2004. "Un Laboratoire réformateur: le Département du Commerce en France et aux États-Unis de la Première Guerre mondiale aux Années Vingt." Unpublished PhD dissertation. Paris: IEP.

Ellison, Thomas. 1886. *The cotton trade of Great Britain*. London: Effingham Wilson. 362 pages.

Feldman, Eric A. 2006. "The Tuna Court: Law and Norms in the World's Premier Fish Market." *California Law Review*. 94 (2): 313–369.

Forrester, R. B. 1931. "Commodity Exchanges in England." *Annals of the American Academy of Political and Social Science*. 155 (1): 196–207.

Freund, G.S. 1910. Der Schutz der Gläubiger gegenüber auswärtigen Schuldnerstaaten, insbesondere bei auswärtigen Staatsanleihen. Berlin: J. Guttentag, 55 pages.

Garié, Jean. 1892. *L'arbitrage international en matière financière appliqué aux dettes extérieures des Etats*. Paris: Imprimerie Pochy. 32 pages.

Gilson, Ronald. 1984. "Value Creation by Business Lawyers: Legal Skills and Asset Pricing." *The Yale Law Journal*. 98 (2): 239–313.

Ginsburg, Tom. 2003. "The Culture of Arbitration." *Vanderbilt Journal of Transnational Law*. 36: 1335–1345.

Godron, Jacques. 1919. "La clause compromissoire dans les rapports internationaux devant les Tribunaux français." *Journal de Droit International*. 46: 57–62, 654–659.

Grewe, Wilhelm G. 2000. *The Epochs of International Law*. New York: de Gruyter. 780 pages. Translated from German by Michael Byers.

Halliday, Terence C. and Gregory Shaffer. 2015. *Transnational Legal Orders*. New York: Cambridge University Press. 270 pages.

Hurst, J.C.B. 1925. "Wanted! An International Court of Piedpowder." *British Year Book on International Law*. 6: 61–67.

Ishikazi, Masaichiro. 1928. *Le droit corporatif international de la vente de la soie*. Paris: Marcel Giard. 3 volumes.

Jarvin, Sigvard. 1992. *La Cour d'arbitrage de la Chambre de Commerce Internationale à Stockholm pendant la seconde guerre mondiale*. Paris. 131 pages.

2011. "La Cour d'arbitrage de la Chambre de commerce internationale pendant la Seconde Guerre mondiale." In *Liber Amicorum en l'honneur de Serge Lazareff*, pp. 331–347. Paris: A. Pedone.

Jones, Franklin Day. 1922. *Trade Association Activities and The Law*. New York: McGraw-Hill. 360 pages.

Kellor, Frances. 1937. "Idle Machinery at The Hague." *Arbitration Journal*. 37 (1–3): 217–222.

Kennedy, David. 1996. "International Law and the Nineteenth Century: History of an Illusion." *Nordic Journal of International Law*. 65: 385–420.

Kennedy, Duncan. 2006. "Three Globalizations of Law and Legal Thought: 1850–2000." In *The New Law and Economic Development. A Critical Appraisal*, David Trubek and Alvaro Santos, eds., pp. 19–73. Cambridge: Cambridge University Press.

Keohane, Robert O., Andrew Moravcsik and Anne-Marie Slaughter. 2000. "Legalized Dispute Resolution: Interstate and Transnational." *International Organization*. 54 (3): 457–488.

Klein, Peter. 1914. "Internationale Gerichtsbarkeit für das Gebiet des Weltwechselrecht." *Zeitschrift für Internationales Recht*. 24 (2): 112–122.

Koskenniemi, Martti. 2001. *The Gentle Civilizer of Nations, The Rise and Fall of International Law, 1870–1960*. Cambridge: Cambridge University Press. 568 pages.

2005. *Nationalism, Universalism, Empire: International Law in 1871 and 1919*. New York: Columbia Department of History. 46 pages.

2007. *The Ideology of International Adjudication*. The Hague. 7 September 2007. 18 pages.

Lachau, Charles and Christian Daguin. 1889. *De l'exécution des jugements étrangers d'après la jurisprudence française*. Paris: Larose et Forcel. 240 pages.

Lemercier, Claire. 2012. *Un modèle français de jugement des pairs. Les tribunaux de commerce, 1790–1880*. Habilitation thesis, Paris 8 – online at http://halshs.archives-ouvertes.fr/tel-00685544/

London Chamber of Arbitration. 1895. *Inquiry before the Joint Committee of Management of the London Chamber of Arbitration*. 3 hand-written volumes, dated 29 March, 10 May, 18 July. 223 pages. Box: CLA/040/09/002

London Corn Trade Association. 1947. *Grain Trade Lectures*. London: Broomhill's Corn Trade News.

London Court of Arbitration 1893–1953. *Register: list of disputants, addresses, names of arbitrators, dates of hearings, awards and fees*. London Metropolitan Archives. Box CLC/B/150/MS16562.

Lorenzen, Ernest G. 1935. "Commercial Arbitration. Enforcement of Foreign Awards." *The Yale Law Journal*. 45 (1): 39–68.

Macassey, Sir Lynden. 1939. "International Commercial Arbitration: Its Origin, Development and Importance." In *Transactions of the Grotius Society*, vol. 24, pp. 170–202. London: Sweet and Maxwell.

Mallarmé, André. 1906. *L'Arbitrage Vénézuélien devant la Cour de la Haye (1903–1904)*. Paris: Pedone. 79 pages.

Marx, Robert. 1947. "Amiable compositeur. Contribution to the problem of Uniform International Arbitration." *The Arbitration Journal*. 2 (3) new series: 211–217.

Mazower, Mark. 2012. *Governing the World. The History of and Idea*. New York: The Penguin Press. 467 pages.

Musgrave, Charles. 1914. *The London Chamber of Commerce from 1881 to 1914*. London: Efingham Wilson. 93 pages.

Mutzner, Paul. 1914. "Das Postulat eines internationalen Gerichtshofes für Streitigkeiten aus dem Internationalen Privatrecht." *Zeitschrift für Internationales Recht*. 24 (1–2): 78–104.

Nussbaum, Arthur. 1941. "The Problem of Proving Foreign Law." *The Yale Law Journal*. 50 (6): 1018–1044.

Nussbaum, Arthur. 1942. "Treaties of Commercial Arbitration: A Test of International Private Law Legislation." *Harvard Law Review*. 56 (2): 219–244.

Petersson, Niels P. 2013. "Legal Institutions and the World Economy, 1900–1930." In *The Foundations of Worldwide Economic Integration. Power, Institutions, and Global Markets, 1850–1930*, Dejung and Petersson, eds. pp. 21–39. Cambridge: Cambridge University Press.

Pozzi, Roberto. 1921. "La conciliation et l'arbitrage entre commerçants de pays différents." In *Chambre de commerce internationale. Premier congrès, Londres (27 juin-1er juillet 1921)*, pp. 7–21. Paris: International Chamber of Commerce.

Proceedings of the First Pan American Financial Conference. Washington: Government Printing Office, 744 pages.

Rakoff, Todd D. 1983. "Contracts of Adhesion: An Essay in Reconstruction." *Harvard Law Review*. 96 (6): 1173–1284.

1919. *Report to the Lord's Chancellor on Foreign Judgments*. London: HMSO.

Refort, Charles. 1939. *Les Difficultés soulevées par l'application de la loi du 31 Décembre 1925 sur la Clause Compromissoire*. Paris: Chez Maurice Lavergne. 99 pages.

Robert, Jean. 1929. *La clause compromissoire et l'organisation de l'arbitrage*. Paris: Recueil Sirey. 228 pages.

Röthlisberger, Ernst. 1893. *Schrifstellerische Postulate zur Revision der Berner Konvention*. C. Heymann.

Sartini van den Kerckhove, G. 1935. "Une juridiction internationale de droit privé." *Journal du Droit International*. 62 (January–February): 775–804.

Schwob, Georges. 1928. *Les contrats de la London Corn Trade Association*. Paris: Librairie Rousseau. 406 pages.

Streat, Raymond. 1922. "The future of arbitration." *Digest*. n 27 (July 22): 1–4.

Waters, Malcolm. 1989. "Collegiality, Bureaucratization, and Professionalization: A Weberian Analysis." *American Journal of Sociology*. 94 (5): 945–972.

Wehberg, Hans. 1911. *Ein Internationaler Gerichtshof für Privatklagen*. Handelspolitische Flugschriften. Cahier 7. 35 pages.

Yntema, Heseel E., 1935. "The Enforcement of Foreign Judgments in Anglo-American Law." *Michigan Law Review*. 33 (8, June): 1129–1168.

Young, Owen D. 1921. "International Commercial Arbitration." *ICC/Digest* n 3 (October): 1–4.

Zorn, Philipp. 1910. *Das Deutsche Reich und die Internationale Schiedsgerichtsbarkeit*. Bonn University, pamphlet. 47 pages.

CHAPTER SIX

CONSTRUCTING A TRANSATLANTIC MARKETPLACE OF DISPUTES ON THE SYMBOLIC FOUNDATIONS OF INTERNATIONAL JUSTICE

Yves Dezalay and Bryant G. Garth

Legal scholars and international relations specialists examining the rise of international law and international lawyers in the twentieth century – a period that generally starts after World War I and ends in the 1990s era – assert that the growth of the international law came at the expense of national sovereignty (Koskenniemi 2002), and that the trend is toward legal complexity, understood as an overlap between international (or transnational) and national modes of governance and a fragmentation of international law (Kennedy 2006; Alter 2009; Mallard 2014). From our research perspective, however, these formulations deemed to be long-term tendencies are not helpful in explaining the genesis and subsequent evolution of transnational practices of conflict management institutionalized as international commercial arbitration – the subject of this chapter. The concepts and categories produced by lawyers and allied professionals to account for and justify legal practices obfuscate rather than clarify origins and evolutions that among other things produce the legitimating categories and concepts. Sociological research must examine the individuals and groups – and the strategies they employ – who produce the concepts, categories, and institutions of a national or transnational field.

The examination of the individuals and groups in this case reveals how internal competition for ascendency within national legal fields leads to international alliances and the construction of an international legal field. The process is also fed by competition between states for international hegemony. The production of the international must be explained out of the internal battles in national legal fields for dominant positions with alliances with political and economic interests. One resultant paradox is that the close relationship of the national and international allows the mobilization of national economic and political resources that become embedded in the international, building something that through the competing interests and a judicialized process gives the appearance of neutrality. All the interests are both present and kept at a distance, through their framing in legal terms. It is very close to the process analyzed by Kantorowicz (1997) of serving power better by creating some distance to better legitimate that service. A related paradox is that what appears as international is made up out of national and international competition between lawyers and professionals deeply embedded in national legal fields and close to the state and to dominant economic interests.

In order to understand the evolution of the lex mercatoria and international commercial arbitration in the twentieth century, we therefore need to analyze how such an expansion was deeply rooted in national and transnational battles for the acquisition of power in domestic fields, both in the dominant societies and in the dominated societies which are both the terrain of imperial competition and sites for the production of the disputes sought to be managed legally – from oil nationalizations to modern investment disputes. In this paper, we focus in particular on the transatlantic network through which a field of international commercial arbitration emerged and grew around the International Chamber of Commerce (ICC) in Paris. In this site, the self-proclaimed "merchants of peace" (Ridgeway 1959) perfected the principles and set of practices associated with the handling of international commercial arbitration. Our thesis is that the main reason for the enduring success and legitimacy of the ICC and international commercial arbitration relates to the type of alliances that European professors built with American lawyers who had built strong connections both within the US state and with major commercial interests.

To demonstrate our thesis, the article first presents in broad terms the strategies of internationalization (including the import and export of norms and institutions) that elite corporate lawyers sought in order to build their position through the accumulation of international legal capital built in alliance with European law professors (Coates 2010). These strategies of internationalization played a decisive role in building international justice as a hybrid system between common and civil law around a core of legal scholars/diplomats including learned QCs and continental law professors. Second, this paper examines how the ICC's Court of International Commercial Arbitration was established in the shadow of the Permanent Court of International Justice by borrowing its public visibility and the academic legitimacy of international law. We show that the European professors who benefitted from the establishment of the Permanent Court and related institutions in The Hague were initially relatively peripheral to the ICC, because the ICC itself was relatively marginal in the interwar period. Yet a few of them extended their academic interest to issues of private law and international disputes. Third, when European law professors were given the opportunity to intervene in commercial disputes involving oil companies, after the tide of nationalistic fights over the appropriation of profits of the oil industry, they could use the value of the symbolic foundations of international justice, as well as their early academic investment, reinvigorated through a small diaspora of continental law professors with links to both the ICC and the American Arbitration Association, such as Domke. Serving as arbitrators and scholars, they could apply and codify their doctrines and gain the recognition of international commercial arbitration as quasi-autonomous from economic and political interests. In the conclusion, we show the distinctiveness of this trajectory of relative autonomization in international economic law, by comparing the twentieth century evolution of lex mercatoria with that of human rights law and justice. This comparison, which is both synchronic and diachronic, serves to highlight the conditions that made possible the enduring role and gradual expansion of the market of international commercial arbitration as compared to the uneven and halting path of the international human rights field of practices – in spite of its judicialization and institutionalization around courts.

REMAKING CORPORATE HIRED GUNS INTO 'MERCHANTS OF PEACE'

National origins of an international field

The battles that take place within national legal fields provide the key to understanding the stakes involved in the construction and then institutionalization of international spaces or fields (Dezalay and Garth 2002). They reveal the tactical alliances that are put into play during periods of the geneses of the international – alliances evident at the level of national fields of state power as well as at the international level between fractions of national elites whose interests converge or whose resources are complementary.

This approach highlights the complementary forms of symbolic capital: academic, political and philanthropic that provided International Justice with its initial accumulation of expertise, mixing of diplomatic skills and the professional legitimacy of the key national legal fields. The alliance had on one side Europe, with continental professors seeking to promote new learned disciplines marginalized within the doctrinal hierarchies that dominated their diplomatic milieu (Sacriste and Vauchez 2007; Sacriste 2011); and on the other side of the Atlantic, a small elite of Wall Street lawyers seeking to enhance their legitimacy as colonial proconsuls newly promoted as lawyer-statesmen (Dezalay and Garth 2010). They invested the resources of their long-standing patrons, the "robber barons," whom they had converted into philanthropists/statesmen, investing in learned European law idealized as an instrument of universal peace.

The agents engaged in the creation, institutionalization and routinization of new legal practices and institutions during the interwar period had in common the accumulation of multiple expertises and resources – national and cosmopolitan; jurists/diplomats and lawyer/entrepreneurs (Koskenniemi 2001). This alliance emerged in part because of these multiple roles occupied by each side – professors who served also as diplomats and practitioners with both learned and cosmopolitan resources and interests.

They also had in common – even if in varying degrees – the ability to mix their learned expertise with practice in politics, diplomacy, or business affairs. These combinations made them well-suited to take part in conflicts, negotiations, or mediations that involved the overlap between different systems of national or transnational rules – a legal complexity of which they often were the principal architects (cf. Gordon 1984; Sklar 1988 and generally Kantorowicz 1997). The founding fathers of international law were a loose community of learned practitioners and professors who played multiple roles in order to serve the increased competition between imperial societies, yet also seeking to limit its risks by building legal channels toward the peaceful resolution of conflicts. These masters of legal rhetoric, either before or after World War I, were at ease with a discourse characterized by oppositions – making their skills as mediators and negotiators more valuable – between, for example, ideals such as international peacemaking and realist claims for national sovereignty or even imperialism.[1]

Furthermore, these leaders on both sides were also directly engaged in the use of legal learning for progressive reform, whether as professors (cf. Sacriste and Vauchez 2007; Coates 2010) or as lawyers/statesmen mobilizing the resources of financiers reconverted into philanthropists (exemplified by Elihu Root as a lawyer, Andrew Carnegie and John D. Rockefeller as sources of philanthropy). The new international legal practices appeared first as spaces of learned investment and academic debates that constructed an idealized representation of these – still quasi-virtual – institutions – in order to show what they could or should produce. Far from being born fully formed, this slow and uncertain emergence of a field of international justice is a complex process that can be understood by analyzing the internal battles which these new legal elites fought within national legal fields – and also by ricochet the competition between national legal models played out in the new transnational spaces.

This analysis requires taking into account hierarchical structures and related political alliances that are the product of very different national histories. The differentiation between the legal models is not limited, furthermore, to the classic divide between common law and civil law, analyzed by Weber as the differentiation between professorenrecht and practitioners' law. The international competition between different national models of legal hierarchies and division of labor relates also to antagonistic strategies of "clerks" of law in fields of state power. As Harold Berman noted, the two classic political strategies are, on one side, royal officers and professors who put their competencies in the service of religious or royal bureaucracies (Berman 1983; 2003; see also Martines 1968; Brundage 2008), and, on the other, learned gentlemen who mobilize their common law expertise in order to control royal power on behalf of the gentry and the rising merchant class.

The continental model of jurists of the state was constituted by the Gregorian reforms (Brundage 2008) and the growth of royal bureaucracies (exemplified by France, Spain), then reconverted as reformist strategies with protestant princes (Berman 2003), before settling with the politics of modernist states such as that of Bismarck (Rueschemeyer

[1] On the support brought by the founding fathers of international law – Sir Travers Twiss, Tobias Asser, Ernest Nys and even Gustave Rolin Jaequemyns for the "civilizing" mission of King Leopold in the Congo, see Mazover (2012: 73).

1997) and imitators such as Meiji Japan (Miyazawa and Otsuka 2002). Meiji Japan self-consciously imported the Bismarckian model to both persuade European powers that they were properly modern and ensure that law would serve the interests of the state (Bourdieu 2012; Dezalay and Garth 2013).

On the other side, the practitioners of the common law imposed themselves during the long English revolution around a professional and political strategy that was just the opposite of this continental model, yet was also later extended overseas through colonization by merchant enterprises. The expanding social and professional elite of barristers put their legal and parliamentary expertise in the service of the gentry and merchant classes – from which they largely came – in order to limit the absolutist pretensions of a royal power that was already weakened by civil wars and religious conflicts. This model was also exported to the British colonies, including the United States, where it began to break down during the Jacksonian period with the attack on the old colonial legal elites.

Partly as a result, this divide has become blurred. The new hegemonic society, the United States, reinvented itself late in the nineteenth century with a de facto hybrid out of two different modes. Law professors and law schools in the United States played a large role – borrowed from the civil law – whereas the rise of the barristers led to the dismantling of law faculties for more than three centuries. The difference between the legal fields of the continental professors and the US practitioners was therefore somewhat more ambiguous than a simple Weberian opposition between practitioners' law and professorenrecht.

In sum, the general competition – which does not preclude convergence – between the two models, differentiated by the hierarchy of professional positions and by the strategies of alliance of the notables of law within national fields of power, provides the context through which transnational spaces emerged out of the nineteenth century, during which European imperial powers (the British, the French and the Germans especially) not only fought over the military control of overseas territories, but also over the control of the definition of international legal practices.

The exacerbation of imperial competition in the early twentieth century

The confrontation between the hegemonic attempts to control international law by common law and civil law practitioners coming from

Europe was complicated by the rising role played by American lawyers. Indeed, since the American corporate lawyers controlled considerable resources – philanthropic, political and commercial – they could deploy those resources to promote alternative conceptions of law and international justice. Those conceptions conformed to their own interests and those of the large corporations that were their clients and patrons. Yet the professional and state strategy of these US practitioners led paradoxically to a position close to the continental model – and more concretely to investing in the production of learned law in the service of reformist or modernizing politics.

These practitioners and professors from elite law schools, although they belonged to the world of the common law, were also involved deeply in reform, which aimed at importing some aspects of continental civil law traditions and incorporating them within common law practices. Their objective was to reconstruct the legitimacy of the bar after the professional, political and economic upheavals that characterized US history in the nineteenth century. Corporate law firms had emerged to serve the bourgeoning national companies, but both the role of lawyers and the tremendous social inequalities associated with their clients were highly controversial. In this context more investment in social reform and in the law was a strategy to ameliorate and legitimate the emerging social order.

The emergence of the elite Ivy League law schools at that time was part of that strategy. That emergence, however, did not mean that professors in the United States achieved preeminence over judges – still holding a monopoly on the production of legal jurisprudence. It was much later, with the New Deal (Shamir 1995), that this hierarchy and division of labor between professors and judges in the legal field began to shift, at least marginally. Nevertheless, a partial recomposition occurred that was the result of the systematic importation of scientific approaches to law coming from continental Europe, financed and managed by the great philanthropic foundations under the guidance of lawyer-statesmen such as Elihu Root for the Carnegie Foundation and Richard Fosdick for the Rockfeller Foundation (Rietzler 2011). Their objective was to import at least partially the learned innovations produced in Germany and France by young generations of professors who were building new legal disciplines – for example , administrative law, public law – and new approaches to law that borrowed from the social sciences in order to educate and legitimate cadres of modernizing bureaucracies.

Even though the US practitioners moved closer to the strategies of the jurists of the state in the continental model, this reconversion was inscribed in their own professional and political trajectory – providing them with the supplementary legitimacy and prestige embedded in imported academic law presented as universal. After being enriched through service to "robber barons," like John D. Rockefeller, whose fortune derived from the concentration and standardization of oil manufacturing processes, a fraction of the elite of the New York Bar became strongly invested in the politics of US colonialism and the expansion of global trade in the service of US industrial interests. But at the same time, it sought to take advantage of its new economic wealth to regain its cultural prestige and professional legitimacy by investing both in reformists politics as enlightened and cosmopolitan statesmen reformists as well as in institutions for the reproduction of legal elites through the acquisition of systematic knowledge transmitted by law professors who could contribute also to the rationalization of legal knowledge and the moralization of legal practices. Both strategies were also helpful to disqualify the rising tide of émigré lawyers moving into populist and clientelists politics after a cheap training in night law schools.

To be sure, as with respect to all symbolic transfers (Bourdieu 2002), this importation remained very partial. Even if investing in learned production, the Wall Street practitioners made sure that they maintained control over the production of law, partly through the private status of the law schools and the ties that professors entertained with the corporate law firms. Indeed, it took a long time for these US professors to acquire the authority of stating the law, which characterizes the professorenrecht. At the same time, while investing in reformist state politics, they kept their control by relying on and supporting the private institutions that they controlled – the private foundations and the think tanks. They could avoid, thanks to the US spoils system, any competing reformist strategy through the autonomization of the state bureaucracies. The result was that they were able to preserve the profits stemming from their preeminent positions in the world of business, while at the same time making temporary incursions in the world of state power, whether as a career strategy or a response to periods of crisis or war.

Historical and political circumstances combined with professional dynamics to explain the relative success of these strategies of internationalization, but also their limits, as seen from the point of view of the Europeans whose work was introduced in the US market. The successes included the creation of the Permanent Court (see also Vauchez 2014) and the construction of a merchant edifice toward world peace – the Peace Palace in The Hague funded by Carnegie. The limits, however, were especially evident with respect to the genesis of international law and justice. Only the US partners had the power to mobilize the substantial political and economic resources required for the success of such a venture, and the continental professors found themselves in an awkward position since US law practitioners imported their work in the US mainly for domestic purposes, to help provide legitimacy to the free trade ambitions of their clients along with legitimacy and stature to themselves.

But the US generally pursued politics of withdrawal from international alliances after World War I. The European professors were unable to rely on their own resources – consisting mainly of a still marginal academic capital and a dominated position within diplomatic arenas. The European professors as a result privileged a cautious strategy that essentially cantonized the institutions of The Hague, which they had developed with the support of both American and Russian sponsors before 1914, in the role of a small, learned and cosmopolitan circle sustained by the support – at least financially and symbolically – of their US sponsors (Koskenniemi 2001). Thus, claiming that a transnational (transatlantic in this case) advocacy network (Keck and Sikkink 1998) or a transatlantic epistemic community (Haas and Adler 1992) emerged from World War I would be a mistake, as it would hide huge disparities of power and status between the US and European law practitioners involved in the interwar discussion about global trade (and other) issues.

The strategy of withdrawal into an ivory tower followed by European professors was also determined by the lack of opportunities for these European merchants of peace to act on the diplomatic or legal scene. These professors occupied dominated positions both in academic and diplomatic fields, as compared to the dominant positions of the gentlemen lawyers. The worsening of the political and financial crisis in Europe throughout the 1920s (with the problems of hyper-inflation left by the overhang of war debts and reparations as well as the rise of Bolsheviks in Russia) accentuated the weakness – even impotence – of international forums for the handling of interstate conflicts. This very weak position was reinforced by an elitist and Malthusian strategy that limited access to European positions in international law to a small group of professor diplomats, expanded to include only a few learned practitioners who occupied diverse roles – which could be accumulated – including judge, lawyer, or producer of doctrine (cf. Sacriste and Vauchez 2007). This peer group was able in this manner to accumulate the profits – which were essentially symbolic – of a small market while avoiding dissent, criticism and even over investment that might damage the weak credibility of their offerings and underline the impotence of what they were promoting in the face of growing political disorder. The result was the Permanent Court as a kind of virtual forum, barely visible outside of a few of the initiated who were making every effort to believe – and create the belief – that one day they would be able to contribute to the objectives of international peace as called for by the idealistic pronouncements of their founding fathers.

THE TRANSATLANTIC PROMOTION OF INTERNATIONAL COMMERCIAL ARBITRATION IN THE SHADOW OF INTERNATIONAL JUSTICE

With respect to international commercial arbitration, the genesis – and more precisely the rebirth and re-legitimation – varied in significant ways from the path of the institutions of The Hague. There were aspects of the same logic, however, and resultant similarities. Here, too, in particular, there was a similar transatlantic strategy between lawyers and entrepreneurs on the US side building and borrowing European legal knowledge, with the results occurring above all in the different national legal fields. European law professors were not at the forefront, but there were pronounced links to the learned European law. As an example, one of the lectures given in The Hague Academy of International Law in 1928, by Simon Rundstein, a member of the Committee of Experts of the League of Nations, was on "L'arbitrage international en matière privée" (Rundstein 1928). Furthermore, as noted by Martin Domke in a 1957 retrospective, notable international scholar Arthur Nussbaum, originally on the faculty of law in Berlin, was an enthusiast of international commercial arbitration as far back as 1912 (Domke 1957). In 1918, he produced a draft arbitration law for Germany that was enacted into law. Later, in the 1920s, he produced *International Yearbooks on Civil and Commercial Arbitration*. The first yearbook was published in German in 1926 and translated into English by the American Arbitration Association. Nussbaum moved to Columbia in 1934, part of an exodus from Germany and Eastern Europe (including Louis Sohn and many others who wrote about arbitration) that helped to cement the transatlantic alliance. Another lecture at The Hague, this time in 1935, was by Count Giorgio Balladore Pallieri, then a young professor who later in his career chaired the European Court of Human rights, on private arbitration in international relations (Pallieri 1935).

The international space for commercial arbitration in the 1920s also provided important symbolic manifestations – and again a cosmopolitan club that provided legitimacy and expanded the opportunities for US lawyers and provided a potential new market for legal scholars. That market was possible in part because a number of international law scholars advised not only states but also large state-connected companies, such as the oil companies, in their dealings with other states. The commercial arbitration arena maintained a relative porosity and openness that facilitated discrete alliances between the academic and business worlds – which also ultimately permitted professors to profit from their learning and their reputational capital.

The starting point for the (re)launch of international commercial arbitration was again a rapprochement between converging commercial and professional interests, on both sides of the Atlantic. The key promoters in these developments were business leaders – and among them the Americans in particular – looking to mobilize their international capital to thwart the submission of merchant disputes – which in the past had often been kept or sought to be kept at the margin of the legal field – to judicial authorities (cf. the romance of the lex mercatoria). These recurring merchant efforts had historical highs and lows. At certain times the merchants, or more precisely, their professional organizations and the relatively low prestige legal practitioners who often were their representatives, succeeded in enlarging and gaining recognition for para-judicial practices such as arbitration; and in other periods the reverse occurred and the judicial hierarchy reaffirmed its monopoly – and therefore that of the mainstream bar – on the market for business disputes.

The late nineteenth century was a period of the restoration of the monopoly of the "true" legal practitioners – both in the European countries and in the United States. This turn to the judicial order was perceived as even worse by business since the risks endemic to colonial and postcolonial history had favored the growth of arbitration handled by Chambers of Commerce and Industry benefiting from at least tacit recognition by the judicial orders. It is in this context that the leaders of the U.S. Chambers of Commerce, and especially the Chamber of

Commerce of New York, sought to promote the creation in Paris of an International Chamber of Commerce in order to relaunch their campaign in favor of the statutory recognition of arbitration in the United States. They sought to draw on the prestige and visibility of projects seeking to promote international arbitration as a means for handling interstate conflicts. Riding on this wave, they contended that this merchant justice would contribute to international peace in the same manner as the Permanent Court of Arbitration. They called themselves "Merchants of Peace" (Ridgeway 1959). They were strongly behind the establishment of the International Chamber of Commerce in 1920 in Paris (Ridgeway 1959) with its aspirations to promote international commercial arbitration, even though in fact the main strategy was to use the international credibility to build domestic arbitration within the United States (Szalai 2013).

In this counter-offensive, they were able to obtain the public support of the elite of the corporate lawyer-statesmen. Elihu Root even co-signed a small brochure on the merits of commercial arbitration with a relatively small textile businessman, Charles Leopold Bernheim, then the leader of the U.S. Chamber of Commerce in New York. Charles Evans Hughes, another elite corporate lawyer-statesman, signed on to the project. Owen D. Young, a business leader for General Electric, facilitated relations with the networks of the League of Nations. This counter-offensive rapidly produced effects in national spaces. The Federal Arbitration Act of 1925, which quickly followed the Geneva Protocol of 1923, was able to "reverse decades of judicial mistrust of arbitration (...and the rising hostility to arbitration from the second half of the nineteenth century, in spite of a long colonial tradition going back to the Dutch (...) refusal to enforce arbitration awards" (p. 23). The Federal Arbitration Act allowed the enforcement of arbitration clauses in contracts that applied to disputes that emerged out of the contract.

There was a similar process in France and in most of continental Europe where judges had been willing to enforce arbitration clauses only if entered into after the emergence of a commercial dispute and naming the arbitrators on which the parties agreed.[2] Even when the restrictive conditions for arbitration were met, state courts still took the position that the courts could be invoked if one of the parties chose

[2] Stever (1923) mentions that arbitration clauses were illegal in France unless specifying the names of the arbitrators and the reasons for recourse to arbitration.

to do so. These restrictions led to the focus on international accords as a potential solution. After the recognition in 1921 of the "enforcement of foreign arbitration awards," the protocol of 1923 recognized the validity of arbitration clauses "for future disputes." "French Judicial hostility to arbitration was moderated by French Courts and Legislator, first in international cases[3] and later in domestic cases" (id. p. 19).

In Great Britain, the situation was slightly different (see Sgard in this volume), but there was also the same judicial hostility to arbitration characteristic of the era: "From Coke, the soil of England never proved kindly to arbitration" (Gordon 1925). The American commentators noted also that arbitration remained under the control of the elite practitioners, high judges, and QCs, who had imposed the rule that any commercial dispute, even if involving two foreign parties, automatically was governed by the common law. This imposition notably was also a tool and a product of the imperial hegemony of Britain – forcing disputes with foreigners into British legal terrain. Thus, it makes sense that the US entrepreneurs and lawyers would want to create something outside of British imperial reach. It is also relevant that, except for routine disputes and those where the stakes were low, the parties had to resort to the very expensive services of a small number of barristers' chambers who monopolized the most lucrative commercial conflicts.

From this point of view, the signature of Great Britain to the Geneva protocol did nothing to change the situation of a market closed to the American entrepreneurs and even more their lawyers – and part of the imperial fabric of the British empire. The French, by contrast, never had far reaching and centralized judicial institutions such as the Privy Council serving to legalize a trading empire – in part because of the reluctance of the French legal elite to become involved in trade and business. Trade disputes in the colonies were outside of the jurisdiction of the French Cour de Cassation. On the contrary, as shown below, the disdain shown by the elite of the Parisian bar with respect to business (Boigeol and Dezalay 1997) helped make Paris open to foreign lawyers who were able to expand a kind of free harbor – where they could develop what we have called "off-shore litigation" on the basis of a heterogeneous alliance and a division of labor between the large law firms and a small group of continental professors and high court judges (Dezalay and Garth 1996).

[3] Gordon (1925) refers to a decision of the Tribunal de la Seine de 1922 which, even in the absence of an international treaty, allows the execution of an arbitration decision refusing to review the merits.

The entrepreneurs of the Chamber of Commerce of New York – and their advisers – lacked the learned resources to permit them to gain recognition of the legitimacy of arbitration. They could not mobilize the combination of learned and political investment that was available for interstate arbitration. The lawyer-statesmen who ostensibly supported them did not commit more than formal support since the field of commercial arbitral practice was not highly valued nor useful to their ambitions as men of the state. Still, the success, even if limited, of the internationalization strategy of the jurist-diplomats gained the interest of their private law colleagues on the continent. This interest was not based on economic motivations, since the market of international commercial arbitration was very much in its infancy with an uncertain future except for the relatively small impacts of this international recognition in domestic settings. Nevertheless, in the same way as their colleagues from public law, they sought to gain advantages from the opening of international spaces of exchange and circulation among the leaders of the business world, which was accompanied by a demand for rationalization, legitimation and thus of learned investments, in order to valorize disciplines still in their infancy and still considered relatively marginal in the European faculties of law (Sacriste 2011).

The specific genesis of commercial arbitration therefore was in the shadow of the institutions of The Hague. It therefore was a quasi-virtual institution with symbolic capital related to international law and justice but serving mainly domestic objectives. Yet there already was some learned investment in international commercial arbitration as evidenced by a number of lecures in The Hague.

THE RISING IMPORTANCE OF INTERNATIONAL COMMERCIAL ARBITRATION AFTER WORLD WAR II

Our task, as noted at the beginning of this article, is to focus on two periods that offer parallels in the history of the development of the transnational. As noted above, rather than examining the role of national sovereignty or the growth of legal complexity, our analysis looks at the relationship between national legal strategies and the development of an international legal field as a key to understanding what the international is made up of, and how it relates both to national and international hegemonic battles. Prior to the Great Depression and World War II, as we have seen, we saw variations on an alliance between, on one side, US legal practitioners identified with Wall Street Law firms, multinational corporations and banks, and philanthropic foundations, later termed the Foreign Policy Establishment (Dezalay and Garth 2010) in the United States, and on the other side an emerging but still relatively marginal group of professors of law, many with some diplomatic ties as well, on the European continent. The practically virtual institutions that they supported on the international law and justice side of international arbitration and the commercial side of international arbitration stayed in place but hardly thrived – especially after the 1930s.[4] They gained energy after World War II, in part through the funding of the Ford Foundation as part of a Cold War strategy (Scott-Smith 2007).

The renewal and expansion of international commercial arbitration is closely linked to crises associated with decolonization and the battles for the control of oil production in the period after World War II (Dezalay and Garth 1996). The oil companies known as the seven sisters – which included, among others, the Standard Oil Company created by John D. Rockefeller, British Petroleum, Texaco and Royal Dutch Shell – had supported the movement toward expansion of global trade and investment, but there were important challenges to their power and their investments (for instance, when the US and British powers made a coup to restore the Shah in Iran after Mossadegh's 1951 decision to appropriate 51percent of the shares of the Anglo-Iranian oil company).[5] Oil nationalizations were symptomatic of the rise of nationalism and the erosion of the paternalistic relationship between the Seven Sister oil companies and national leaders. The tensions led first to the nationalization of the Suez Canal (the main conduit for Middle East oil) in 1956, which was followed by the creation of OPEC, a cartel of oil producers modeled on the way that Texas controlled the supply and price of oil. OPEC remained dormant for ten years, but it suddenly woke up in 1973, when it was able to increase the price of oil dramatically – this decision followed Nixon's decision to let the US dollar float (and decline, which automatically led to the decline of the price of the oil barrel) and Nixon's military support of Israel in the 1973 war.

4 With respect to the Permanent Court of Arbitration, "All told, during the first seventy years of the PCA's existence, only twenty-five arbitrations were submitted to PCA tribunals, for a filing rate of 0.3 cases per year; even fewer nonbinding PCA conciliations or inquiries were conducted" (Born 2012: 798). The ICC caseload was relatively light until the 1980s as well. There were 3,000 requests for arbitration between 1923 and 1976 and then 7,000 more between 1976 and 1998 (Craig, Park and Paulson 2000: 2).

5 Mossadegh's rise to power had followed from a massive strike by workers of the oil business in Iran.

After 1973, the stakes over the control over oil profits therefore rose dramatically. But histories of the oil industry typically do not even mention law or lawyers (e.g., Yergin 1993). Oil companies whose positions were threatened lined up the support of their home countries, and both invested substantial resources into rebuilding their prior lucrative positions. For most analysts, law was not at the core of the response to the crises. Managers and lawyers of the oil industry used diplomacy, the threat of gun boats and personal relationships to respond to the nationalizations and other attacks on their position, and for the most part they were successful in maintaining their role in the production and distribution of petroleum resources.

If we pay closer attention to the role of law and lawyers in the reorganization of the oil industry that followed from the first shock of 1973, however, we realize that lawyer-entrepreneurs took advantage of the situation. The long-standing concession agreements entered into between the oil companies and the oil producing states – most of which dated from the times of the League of Nations and its mandates – contained arbitration clauses that could be invoked. The clauses were inserted in the interwar period because of the perceived legitimacy of state-state arbitration and the role of international law experts who consulted with the large oil companies. The 1933 oil concession agreement creating the Anglo-Iranian Oil Company, for example, was drafted by Vladimar Idelson, a Russian lawyer who emigrated to England after the Russian Revolution and became a King's Counsel and international law expert (Lauterpacht 2012). He and Hersch Lauterpacht were the legal advisors to the oil company after Iran nationalized oil in 1951 and they sought to invoke the arbitration clause at that time (id.). The arbitration clause had given appointment powers to the President of the Permanent Court of International Justice. An Iranian lawyer posited that these arbitrations involved a kind of law that in theory stood between public international law and national law (Farmanfarma 1955). Other scholars in the 1950s, also in lectures at The Hague, examined related issues. F. Munch, a German professor of international law who began as a bank apprentice, studied abroad with a Carnegie fellowship, and served as a German delegate to the Law of the Sea negotiations in 1958, wrote, for example, on the effect of foreign nationalizations (Munch 1959). The Rt. Honorable Lord Shawcross, a barrister who served as chief prosecutor for the British at Nuremburg, was a Labour Member of Parliament, the British head of the International Committee of Jurists, and at the time of his lecture a lawyer for Royal Dutch Shell, delivered his lecture on the problems of foreign investment in international law (Shawcross 1961). These well-connected and scholarly individuals were definitely setting the stage for the use of arbitration to handle the disputes emerging through decolonization and a new relationship and set of potential North-South conflicts.

There were connections to the ICC as well among these learned and multifaceted individuals. Charles Carabiber, who lectured on the evolution of international commercial arbitration in 1950, was originally from Istanbul, studied there and in Paris, became a professor in Paris and an advocate at the Cour d'Appel, was adviser to the Iranian government, and was also the President of the Court of Arbitration of the ICC. When the ICC took the lead in seeking to advance international commercial arbitration with a convention on the enforcement of awards, which became the New York Convention of 1958, academics also were strongly present in the negotiations – including Pieter Sanders, a lawyer, diplomat, professor and art collector from Rotterdam; Mario Matteucci, the director of the League of Nations Institute for the Unification of Private Law in Rome and a prestigious academic "of highest international standing," Benjamin Wortley, a Professor of Commercial Law in Manchester, England; Conseiller d'Etat Georges Holleaux, "a French academic in the best sense of the word, the very picture of the elegant Senior French Legal Officer, who was joined by Rene Arnaud, a true product of one of the French elite schools, a practitioner economist, and the cofounder of the ICC in 1918"; and others including Martin Domke of the American Arbitration Association (Glossner 1999). Domke was the major promoter of international commercial arbitration within the AAA until his retirement in 1967. He was a German-trained lawyer who went to the United States in 1943 and began a long career with the American Arbitration Association as Vice President (Sanders 1967). Domke wrote much on domestic US arbitration, but he also sought to build up the prestige of AAA arbitration by linking arbitration to international law professors and international commercial arbitration associated with the ICC. The U.S. arbitration movement, with close ties to the business community, built a strong alliance with European law professors to promote international commercial arbitration. The success of the New York Convention in 1958, which considerably enhanced the enforceability of international commercial arbitration, was a product of this alliance.

In the 1970s, according to our interviewees (1996), the oil companies chose to invoke the arbitration clauses as one additional option to fight the battle over the appropriation of economic profits with oil producing states, but arbitration was very much a side show. Thus, they paid very little attention to the processes of arbitration, since they believed that the key to their claims remained in the hands of diplomatic and commercial negotiators.

The ties of the ICC group to the oil industry, as best one can tell, were not then very strong outside of a relatively few international law professors who consulted with the oil companies, but these individuals were brought into the arbitrations and provided with what to them amounted to essentially unlimited resources. By the 1960s, as noted above, drawing in fact on the oil concession agreements existing from the 1930s, they already had produced a body of legal scholarship that could provide some of the raw material necessary to equip the field. In addition to the connections mentioned above, including Carabiber's relationship to Iran, other clear ties included Goldman (referring to oil arbitrations), Lalive (a secretary in oil arbitrations) and El-Kosheri (who represented Kuwait)). This group included professors from the north and their students from the south, such as El-Kosheri, who were also ready to see the virtues of arbitrations that would involve their mentors and likely also themselves (Dezalay and Garth 1996: 86–87). By 1972, Werner Goldschmidt, an international professor who picked up his career in Argentina after fleeing Germany, demonstrated the scholarly legalization of the field when he lectured at The Hague on international arbitration in such categories as "trialistic ontology" and "dikelogical juristic" (Goldschmidt 1972).

Partly because it was a sideshow, the arbitration lawyers on both sides were able to treat the legal disputes as epic legal battles involving grand legal principles. Lawyers in the nationalization cases developed highly formal legal arguments while the actual resolutions of the disputes proceeded by other means. The result was a series of closely reasoned arbitral opinions that have long been the staple of international law courses. They had virtually no practical impact at the time, but here as elsewhere that lack of practical impact allowed the field to develop initially. Legal capital accumulated through the initial investments, and then later, through the outpouring of scholarship promoting, rationalizing and elaborating the jurisprudence of the arbitration cases – and indeed making the cases central to casebooks. Those with key positions in the cases gained stature and credibility, and the combination of factors jumpstarted this transnational legal field and put it into a perfect position to take advantage of the disputes that then emerged in the

1970s and 1980s as petrodollars and Eurodollars were invested in major infrastructure projects leading to major arbitrations.

The oil crises, in short, provided the initial funding and credibility to a group of self-proclaimed amateurs and hobbyists who then became the backbone of what became the international commercial arbitration industry in the 1980s. They enhanced the credibility of European law and the European law professors linked to the ICC. But, as we shall see, this convergence tied to complementarity was then concretized into a division of labor between the "grand old men" – mainly the European law professors – and what could be called the "grand law firms" – which we have shown was a key to the success of this mode of handling commercial disputes. It is also this alliance between professionals that occupy opposing positions – as much through the very different legal traditions in which their careers are inscribed as the specific positions that they occupy in their national fields as producers of legal learning on one side and business lawyers on the other – that paradoxically explains the success of this hybrid form of international justice. Indeed, one can ask if the opportunism of this heterogeneous alliance is not at the base of its credibility among very different audiences – nationally and professionally. For this division of labor led to the putting in place of a pragmatic assemblage that could accommodate both legal learning and results that were strongly related to legal and political histories. This makeshift structure is also the condition of its international recognition.

PETRO-DOLLARS AND THE ROUTINIZATION OF INTERNATIONAL COMMERCIAL ARBITRATION

The legitimacy of international commercial arbitration – like other legal fields, such as human rights law – remained relatively weak at the initial stages, when it involved some combination of idealistic European international scholarship relatively marginal to national fields of economic and political power and US political and economic capital. But it emerged in a strong position in the 1980s after a period of crisis-generated investment in the 1970s. The relative success in institutionalization with respect to arbitration, coupled with the passage of time, brought a degree of routinization. The institutions such as the ICC became naturalized and decontextualized such that the particular crises and political and economic configurations that produced them initially become obscured. Instead of appearing as the product of particular strategies and configurations of interests, such as those at play in the Cold War or the oil crisis, the semi-autonomous field and its institutions appeared much more neutral and universal. The field of international commercial arbitration in the 1960s and 1970s worked out a set of rules to enforce oil concessions against sovereign states. As noted above, the rules had little impact at the time they were developed. But when arbitration took off in the 1980s, the so-called *lex mercatoria* developed by Continental arbitrators provided a legally principled manner to treat multinational agreements with sovereign states in the Middle East and Africa as if they were private contracts. The circumstances of the genesis were by then mostly obscured. Legal doctrines, furthermore, are taught as such in the law schools, sustained and further formalized through legal scholarship, used to resolve disputes, and in general legitimated and taken for granted – treated as simply the law. As a result, the fields developed some distance from the specific interests evident at the inception and embedded in the structures of the field.

Within the arbitration world, most of the brokers came from a more informal network of arbitrators concentrated in Europe but covering much of the globe – constituting what is often called the arbitration mafia. They served alternatively as lawyers and arbitrators in high stakes transnational disputes. The relatively informal and small community at the core could take advantage of many others who profited from investment in the field. Corporate law firms, as noted, developed arbitration expertise that enhanced their stake in the field. The knowledge and essentials of arbitration practice could be taken off the shelf and applied to a wide range of business disputes. The practice gained legitimacy and developed some autonomy such that it could be transported to new places and types of disputes. It became simply "off-shore litigation" even if the courts were private and not public. Indeed, one of the leading arbitrators in the field in the generation that followed the pioneers even explained the evolution as a matter of Weber's "routinization of charisma" (Dezalay and Garth 1996). Repeat players came to dominate the terrain. Indeed, the routinizers became the "stars" of the next generation of arbitrators. These characteristics allowed the field to grow and prosper in new terrains along with economic and corporate law more generally.

The field of arbitration evolved through the gradual extension of the field into new markets in terms of types of disputes and geographical reach. International commercial arbitration facilitated the relatively easy conversion of various forms of capital into arbitration, making for a relatively smooth expansion from North-South disputes to transnational contracts generally, and to new markets, such as Latin America, that had once been hostile to international arbitration. Each expansion brought new capital and subtle adjustments in the doctrine and approaches – while at the same time reinforcing the value of the core of the field. In particular, high barriers to entry to become an arbitrator allowed the gradual co-optation of national legal notables who could provide the credibility to gain the support of the national court systems. The local notables in turn invested in the legal capital connected to international commercial arbitration as a condition of entry, again reinforcing the core while extending the field to new terrains.

This relatively strong entrenchment of international commercial arbitration came not through any single transnational institutional structure but rather through a multiplicity of forums following the same business model. It is a strength that comes from weak links, with a highly flexible set of institutions which structure an internationalized market of legal expertise, and a very flexible use of concepts and doctrines.[6] That market allows national legal notables to accumulate or diversify their own portfolios by exchanging their respective forms of national capital. The local impact is therefore relatively limited. There is a spill-over into national settings, but it is segmented in the way that there used to be colonial courts in Shanghai or Cairo. It is a western justice – off-shore "litigociation" handled by corporate law firms – with a few local characteristics.

In sum, the alliances that we saw in the 1920s continued and thrived in the post-World War II period, leading to important transnational developments in international justice and in private arbitral justice. And, indeed, the transnational circulation of agents and resources that was exemplified by the moves of Lauterpacht and Lalive, moving between The Hague and international arbitration, continues. International legal practices are continuously used as spaces of strategic exchange and coalition between specific fractions of different national fields. But it is essential to go beyond issues of national sovereignty or

[6] The international circulation of ideas and approaches involves the movement of texts without the contexts that give them their meaning (Bourdieu 2002). When a particular legal technology moves from one setting to another, how it becomes translated – or mistranslated – depends on the structures of power and the positions of the translators who deploy the technology. Similar mistranslations, we hypothesize, also occur when there is movement from the national to a transnational level and even from one symbolic field – for example, human rights or arbitration – to another.

legal complexity – terms that are used as part of the strategies of the actors making these moves – to explore the national positions, strategies and processes that make up the transnational.

CONCLUSION

In this last section, we would like to emphasize that not all transnational legal initiatives can develop their own momentum as has been the case for international commercial arbitration. In fact, this success is almost a paradox since it implies the combination of contradictory conditions for the latter to occur: a decentralized demand for the handling of international commercial disputes that provides economic resources for both the initial accumulation of a capital of legal technologies and then later the growth of a sustainable professional market; and at the same time it implies a close informal network of key producers, such as the "arbitration mafia," which embodies a kind of legitimate collective authority and functions as gate-keepers over this new and decentralized field of pratice, making sure that newcomers are not going to risk damaging the reputation and credibility accumulated through a long history of scholarly investments. This loose collective hierarchy of professionals needs to be flexible in order to adjust to a shifting market of disputes, both in terms of territory and issues, for example Latin America geographically and the vastly expanded market for investor-state disputes.

When these conditions are not met, one can hypothesize that it will be unlikely that transnational legal mobilizations will coalesce in the production of a transnational legal field of practices with its own sustaining momentum. Even if new institutions such as new bodies of rules or international courts emerge out of these initial accumulation, these institutions can remain quasi-virtual if not short-lived. To make that point, we would like to use the remainder of this concluding section to briefly compare the evolution of the lex mercatoria with that of human rights law.

International human rights law represents an apt comparison since it and international arbitration emerged out of similar initial conditions: as with respect to international commercial arbitration, the movement that led to the Universal Declaration of Human Rights and subsequent human rights instruments adopted after World War II drew on the cultural capital brought by European international law professors such as

Hersch Lauterpacht (2012), and on the moral and financial support of the Wall Street elite, their corporate clients and the related philanthropic foundations (Dezalay and Garth 2006). As in the case of commercial arbitration, the elite Wall Street lawyers behind the US Cold War once again elected to invest in European international law professors, whose institutions, like the International Commission of Jurists (ICJ) – itself at one point funded by the Wall Street corporate lawyers then running the CIA in the Cold War – and the European Court of Human Rights produced learning and legitimacy for the field.[7] Amnesty International, founded in 1961 as an English outgrowth of the ICJ seeking to gain more of a distance from the partisanship of the Cold War, contributed as well. As with respect to international commercial arbitration, the mix of idealistic scholars and activists (including a diaspora in the United States fleeing Nazi Germany) and powerful resources from the United States linked to the corporate law firms – the Ford Foundation in particular, was a key to success. Again, the early period of symbolic construction was followed by a boom in the 1980s.[8]

As with respect to arbitration and the oil crisis, the dramatic recent evolutions within the field of international human rights stemmed from crises – in this case revolving around the politics of the Cold War, and the decision by the Nixon administration to support the coup that brought Pinochet to power in Chile in 1973. Even though advocates of human rights had almost no effect on the policies followed by the Democrat administrations of Kennedy and Johnson (who supported autocrats in South Vietnam and elsewhere), the rise of campus contestations had split the US Democrat establishment, which controlled the elite universities, the major philanthropic foundations, a good portion of the Congress, and much of the establishment media which had been their sources of power dating from before the 1920s.[9] Academic idealists who had been promoting the Universal Declaration of Human Rights, and who had made some connections with Amnesty International and

[7] There were connections between the two worlds of human rights law and arbitration: those who served in the ICJ included Jean Flavien Lalive, an eminent Swiss jurist (and brother of Pierre Lalive, a leading international arbitrator from the period of the 1960s) who had held leading positions in the International Red Cross, the United Nations and the Court of Justice at the Hague.

[8] It is instructive that histories of the Cold War do not see human rights activists as having influence worth even citing (e.g., Gaddis 2006).

[9] The leaders of the Foreign Policy Establishment had in fact been quite skeptical of claims that international human rights law could really be law.

the International Commission of Jurists, were essential in the strategy of the Congressional doves (and their young staffs).[10] They mobilized the neutral principles of the international law scholars, including the Europeans and the European diaspora,[11] and the existing organizations including Amnesty and the ICJ, in a series of Congressional hearings that resemble a who's who of international law and human rights at the time. International human rights law was still relatively marginal in the United States – the domain of a few immigrant-scholars with personal histories and connections that made them especially interested in the field.[12] The linking of these academic idealists, the relatively few existing human rights organizations[13] and the doves in Congress were sufficiently successful to persuade Jimmy Carter to make human rights rhetoric an essential part of his political campaign and subsequently his foreign policy. Thus, by the mid 1970s, the strategies and accomplishments of both international arbitration and human rights lawyers greatly resembled one another, although they were not exactly driven by the same dynamics. In the 1980s and 1990s the field of international human rights law thrived as a key element of international relations.

But in contrast to international commercial arbitration, the field of human rights did not really follow a specifically legal evolution that would have led to its quasi-routinization. The initial mix was an unstable alliance of political activists, philanthropic foundations, media entrepreneurs and academic idealists linked to particular political circumstances. The political issues connected to human rights were often front page news, and the institutions created to handle them, such

10 Largely due to the efforts of the existing organizations, especially the International League for the Rights of Man and the ICJ, the UN Commission on Human Rights had also passed the International Covenant on Economic, Social, and Cultural Rights and the International Covenant on Civil and Political Rights in 1966. These instruments went into effect in the mid 1970s (Korey 1998: 72). Frank Newman, while not traditionally an international law scholar, was a key figure in linking the academics and the Democratic doves. Newman had been the dean at the Law School of the University of California at Berkeley prior to taking a sabbatical in Geneva – ostensibly to explore the administrative law of the U.N. He became connected to the ICJ and contributed to their activities against the Greek colonels brought before the Council of Europe.

11 The European activity drew in large part on the institutions created after the war, especially the Council of Europe and the European Convention on Human Rights, in order to build U.S.-style legal protections against practices associated with Fascism.

12 The first casebook on international human rights, for example, was published in 1973 by Louis Sohn and Thomas Buergenthal, both of whom came to the United States as refugees from the Nazis.

13 Including also the International League for the Rights of Man and the Washington Office on Latin America (WOLA), which had ties to the National Council of Churches and to the movements of Solidarity with Chile and Argentina (Korey 1998: 186).

as Truth and Reconciliation Commissions and International Criminal Tribunals, were not easily separated from the political contexts that produced them. Those who constructed them tended to be lawyer-diplomats who continued to use them as part of diplomacy. Questions of who would be prosecuted for what crimes in particular, for example, were closely connected to substantial issues of realpolitik. The legal decisions to prosecute autocrats were ripe with contested politics within the human rights community about whom to prosecute, where and for what: these debates continued long after the Pinochet case which opened up the potential for so-called universal jurisdiction (Seroussi 2012. The public visibility translated into a relatively few cases, and the institutions created remained fragile and lacking in legitimacy.

In contrast to international commercial arbitration, in addition, political actors could force quick changes in the terms of engagement in the field of human rights. A relatively early example was the apparent decision of the Pinochet government and the generals in Argentina to use the brutal tactic of disappearances – instead of explicitly taking political prisoners – to avoid the spotlight that Amnesty International brought to prisoners of conscience. A more recent example of such a phenomenon – mass executions to avoid witnesses that might sustain a court prosecution – took place in the Sri Lankan purge of the Tamil rebels (Anderson 2011: 41). The shifting context from the Cold War and decolonization to ethnic genocides and civil wars made it hard to develop repeat players. In more recent times, the agenda of human rights NGOs has also shifted dramatically according to domestic political concerns such as the War on Terror. There is a new generation, in fact, exemplified by International Alert, that focuses on conflict resolution and peacekeeping (S. Dezalay 2012; Lefranc 2012). In the new post-September 11 era, it is therefore not a matter of extending a coherent set of principles gradually to new arenas and places. Rather, in human rights, the field jumps around in relation to highly visible politics. There is a strong contrast, in short, between the high symbolic value of human rights principles and doctrines and the very limited autonomy of the legal practices associated with this sphere, which are politicized, segmented and discontinuous. The flexibility and protective gate-keeping role associated with the so-called mafia of arbitration, coupled with a strong professional market sustaining that role, contrasts with the instability of the field of human rights and the lack of a consistent professional market to sustain it.

The only real continuity in human rights doctrines, as opposed to international commercial arbitration, has been in the academic elaboration of legal principles, but even if legal debates and legal doctrines of human rights reoccur often in the field, in practice they are reinvented and reconfigured in relatively short time intervals for battle in new political contexts. Perhaps the only exception to that rule has been the institutionalization of the human rights doctrine in Europe (Madsen 2005), which the French and British governments initially endorsed because they believed it would remain largely irrelevant,[14] but which gradually led to the development of a coherent legal doctrine that was enforced by the European Court on Human Rights (ECHR). Still, it is an exception rather than the norm, and the proliferation of countries ostensibly governed by the European human rights regime has made the European Court and Convention weaker.

To be sure, there are similarities in the geneses of the field of international human rights and that of international commercial arbitration, with both building on the same transatlantic alliance of elite corporate lawyers in the United States and European legal academics. Both were built on the symbolic foundations of international justice that began prior to World War I. But of the two fields, international commercial arbitration developed a strong sustaining momentum that has allowed it to grow and adjust to new markets and new kinds of disputes relatively smoothly while protecting the core structure and hierarchies of the field.

Bibliography

Adler, E. and P.M. Haas (1992), "Conclusion: Epistemic Communities, World Order and the Creation of a reflective research program." *International Organisation* 46 (1): 367–390.

Alter, Karen and Sophie Meunier 2009 (March), "The Politics of Regime Complexity." *Perspectives on Politics* 7 (1): 13–24.

Anderson, Jon Lee (2011), "Death of a Tiger," *The New Yorker*, January 17. p. 41.

Balladore, Pallieri and Comte Giorgio (1935), "L'arbitrage privé dans les rapports internationaux." *Recueil des Cours* 51: 287–404.

[14] They were on the human rights side in the Cold War as representatives of the anti-Communist West. They also were careful to make sure that their relationships with colonies were not included in the treaties that created these institutions. But the initial Cold War orientation shifted, and the evolving European human rights regime took aim at the repressive means by which European countries policed their colonies – especially the French.

Berman, Harold J. (1983), *Law and Revolution: The Formation of the Western Legal Tradition*. Cambridge: Harvard University Press.

Berman, Harold J. (2003), *Law and Revolution II: The Impact of the Protestant Reformations on the Western Legal Tradition*. Cambridge: Belknap Press of Harvard University Press.

Bohmer, Martin (2013), *Imagining the State: The Politics of Legal Education in Argentina, USA and Chile*. Yale Law School SJD Dissertation.

Born, Gary (2012), "A New Generation Of International Adjudication." *Duke LJ* 61: 775.

Bourdieu, Pierre (2002), "Les conditions sociales de la circulation internationale des idées." *Actes de la recherche en sciences sociales* 145: 3–8.

Bourdieu, Pierre (2012), *Sur l'État: Cours au Collège de France (1989–1992)*. Paris: Seuil.

Brundage, James (2008), *The Medieval Origins of the Legal Profession*. Chicago: University of Chicago Press.

Carabiber, C. (1950), "L'évolution de l'arbitrage commercial international." *Recueil des Cours* 99: 119–232.

Coates, Benjamin (2010), "Transatlantic Advocates: American International Law and U.S. Foreign Relations, 1989–1919" (PhD Dissertation, Columbia University Department of History).

Craig, W. Lawrence, William W. Park and Jan Paulson (2000), *International Chamber of Commerce Arbitration*, 3rd edn., Oceana.

Dezalay, Sara (2012), "Lawyering War or Talking Peace: On Militant Usages of the Law in the Resolution of Internal Armed Conflicts: A Case Study of International Alert," in Yves Dezalay and Bryant G. Garth, eds., *Lawyers and the Construction of Transnational Justice*. New York: Routledge.

Dezalay, Yves and Anne Boigeol (1997), "De l'agent d'affaires au barreau: les conseils juridiques et la construction d'un espace professionnel." *Geneses* 27: 49–68.

Dezalay, Yves and Bryant G. Garth (1996), *Dealing in Virtue: International Commercial Arbitration and the Construction of a Transnational Legal Order*. Chicago: University of Chicago Press.

Dezalay, Yves and G. Garth (2002), *The Internationalization of Palace Wars: Lawyers, Economists, and the Contest to Transform Latin American States*. Chicago: University of Chicago Press.

Dezalay, Yves and Bryant G. Garth (2006), "From the Cold War to Kosovo: The Rise and Renewal of International Human Rights Law as a Socio-Legal Field." *Annual Review of Law and Social Science*: 231–255.

Dezalay, Yves and Bryant G. Garth (2010), *Asian Legal Revivals: Lawyers in the Shadow of Empire*. Chicago: University of Chicago Press.

Dezalay, Yves and Bryant G. Garth (2013), "Lost in Translation: On the Failed Encounter Between Bourdieu and Law and Society Scholarship and Their Respective Blindnesses," in Grainne de Burca, Claire Kilpatrick, Joanne

Scott, eds., *Critical Perspectives on Global Governance: Liber Americorum for Dave Trubek*. London: Hart.

Dezalay, Yves and Bryant G. Garth (2014), "Lawyers and Transformations of the Fields of State Power: Osmosis, Hysteresis, and Aggiornamento," in Mikael Madsen, ed., *Law in the Formation of Modern Europe*. Cambridge: Cambridge University Press.

Domke, Martin (1957), "Arthur Nussbaum: The Pioneer of International Commercial Arbitration." *Colum. L. Rev.* 57: 8.

El-Kosheri, A. S. (1975), "Le régime juridique créé par les accords de participation dans le domaine pétrolier." *Recueil des Cours* 147: 219–393.

Farmanfarma, Abolbashar (1955), "The Oil Agreement Between Iran And The International Oil Consortium: The Law Controlling." *Tex. L. Rev.* 34: 259.

Gaddis, John Lewis (2006), *The Cold War: A New History*. London: Penguin.

Glossner, Ottarndt (1999), "From New York (1958) to Geneva (1961) – A Veteran's Diary," in *The New York Convention: Experience and Future*. New York, United Nations.

Goldman, B. (1963), "Les conflits de lois dans l'arbitrage international de droit privé." *Recueil des Cours* 109: 347–486.

Goldschmidt, W. (1972), "Transactions between States and Public Firms and Foreign Private Firms (A Methodological Study)." *Recueil des Cours* 136: 203–330.

Gordon, Robert W. (1984), "The Ideal and the Actual in the Law: Fantasies and Practices of New York City Lawyers, 1870–1910," in Gerald W. Gawalt, ed., *The New High Priests: Lawyers in Post-Civil War America*, pp. 51–74. Westport: Greenwood Press.

Gordon, William (1925), "International Aspects of State Arbitration." *American Bar Association Journal* 717–718.

Kantorowicz, Ernst (1997), *The King's Two Bodies: A Study in Medieval Political Theology*. Princeton: Princeton University Press.

Keck, Margaret and Kathryn Sikkink (1998), *Activists Beyond Borders*. Ithaca: Cornell University Press.

Kennedy, David (2006), "One, Two, Three, Many Legal Orders: Legal Pluralism and the Cosmopolitan Dream." Speech delivered at the International Law Association. www.law.harvard.edu/faculty/dkennedy/speeches/LegalOrders.pdf.

Korey, David (1998), *NGOs and the Universal Declaration of Human Rights: A "Curious Grapevine."* New York: St. Martin's.

Koskenniemi, Martti (2001), *The Gentle Civilizeer of Nations: The Rise and Fall of International Law 1870–1960*. Cambridge: Cambridge University Press.

Koskenniemi, Martti (2002), "Fragmentation of International Law: Postmodern Anxieties." *Leiden Journal of International Law* 15: 552–579.

Lalive, P. A. (1967), "Problèmes relatifs à l'arbitrage international commercial." *Recueil des Cours* 120: 569–714.

Lauterpacht, Eliju (2012), *The Life of Hersch Lauterpacht*. Cambridge: Cambridge University Press.

Lefranc, Sandrine (2012), "From Peace-Building in War-Torn Countries to Justice in the Global North," in Yves Dezalay and Bryant G. Garth, eds., *Lawyers and the Construction of Transnational Justice*. New York: Routledge.

Lorenzen, Ernest G. (1933–34), "Commercial Arbitration-International and Interstate Aspects." *Yale L.J.* 43: 716.

Madsen, Mikael (2005), "France, the UK, and the 'Boomerang' of the Internationalization of Human Rights (1945–2000)," in S. Halliday and P. Schmidt, eds., *Human Rights Brought Home: Socio-Legal Perspectives on Human Rights in the National Context*. Oxford: Hart.

Mallard, Grégoire (2014), *Fallout: Nuclear Diplomacy in an Age of Global Fracture*. Chicago: University of Chicago Press.

Martines, Lauro (1968), *Lawyers and Statecraft in Renaissance Florence*. Princeton: Princeton University Press.

Mazover, Mark (2012), *Governing the World: The History of an Idea*. Penguin.

Miyazawa, Setsuo and Hiroshi Otsuka (2002), Legal Education and the Reproduction of Hierarchy in Japan, in Yves Dezalay and Bryant G. Garth, eds., *Global Prescriptions: The Production, Exportation, and Importtion of a New Legal Orthodoxy*. Ann Arbor: University of Michigan Press.

Münch, F. (1959), "Les effets d'une nationalisation à l'étranger." *Recueil des Cours* 98: 411–504.

Pallieri, Giorgio Balladore (1935), "L'arbitrage privé dans les rapports internationaux." *Recueil des Cours* 51: 287–403.

Ridgeway, George L. (1959), *Merchants of Peace*. Boston: Little Brown.

Rietzler, Katharina (2011), "Experts for Peace: Structures and Motivations of Philanthropic Internationalism in the United States and Europe," in Daniel Laqua, ed., *Internationalism Reconfigured: Transnational Ideas and Movements between the World Wars*. London: I.B. Tauris, pp. 45–65.

Roth, Guenther, ed. (1978), *Max Weber on Economy and Society* Vol. II. Berkeley: University of California Press.

Rueschemeyer, Dietrich (1997), "State, Capitalism, and the Organization of Legal Counsel: Examining an Extreme Case – the Prussian Bar, 1700–1914," in Terence C. Halliday and Lucien Karpik, eds., *Lawyers and the Rise of Western Political Liberalism: Europe and North America from the Eighteenth to Twentieth Centuries*, pp. 207–228. Oxford: Oxford University Press.

Rundstein, S. (1928), "L'arbitrage international en matière privée." *Recueil des Cours* 23: 327–462.

Sacriste, Guillaume (2011), *La République des constitutionnalistes. Professeurs de droit et légitimation de l'État en France (1870–1914)*. Paris: Sciences-Po.

Sacriste, Guillaume and Antoine Vauchez (2007), "The Force of International Law: Lawyers' Diplomacy on the International Scene in the 1920s." *Law and Social Inquiry* 32: 83.

Sanders, Pieter ed. (1967), *International Arbitration: Liber Amicorum for Martin Domke*. Nijhoff.

Scott-Smith, Giles (2007), "Attempting to Secure an 'Orderly Evolution': American Foundations, the Hague Academy of International Law, and the Third World." *Journal of American Studies* 41: 507–532.

Seroussi, Julien (2012), "The Cause of Universal Jurisdiction: The Rise and Fall of an International Mobilization," in Yves Dezalay and Bryant G. Garth, eds., *Lawyers and the Construction of Transnational Justice*. New York: Routledge.

Shamir, Ronen (1995), *Managing Legal Uncertainty*. Durham: Duke University Press.

Shawcross, Lord H. W. (1961), "The Problems of Foreign Investment in International Law." *Recueil des Cours* 102: 335–364.

Sklar, M.J. (1988), *The Corporate Reconstruction of American Capitalism: The Market, the Law, and Politics*. Cambridge: Cambridge University Press.

Sohn, L. B. (1963), "The Function of International Arbitration Today." *Recueil des Cours* 108: 1–114.

Stever, Miller D. (1923), "Arbitration of Disputes Between Exporters and Importers and Its Relationship to International Good Will." *Annals of the American Academy of Political and Social Science* 108: 90–98.

Szalai, Imre (2013), *Outsourcing Justice: The Rise of Modern Arbitration Laws in America*. Carolina Academic Press.

Vauchez, Antoine (2014), "The International Way of Expertise. The First World Court and the Genesis of Transnational Expert Fields," EUI Working Paper, Robert Schuman Centre for Advanced Studies, 2014–2080.

Yergin, Daniel (1993), *The Prize: The Epic Quest for Oil, Money, and Power*. New York: The Free Press.

CHAPTER SEVEN

THE *DUTY TO REPAIR* IN PRACTICE: THE HUNDRED YEARS HISTORY OF A LEGAL CONCEPT

Ariel Colonomos and Grégoire Mallard

International norms – both social and legal – are usually the by-product of historical ruptures during which new generations of norms entrepreneurs benefit from windows of opportunities to force global structural changes. For instance, it is widely noticed that the two world wars in the twentieth century have led to massive global normative changes in financial regulation. One can only cite the sudden rise of states' recognition of a duty to provide for the social security of their citizens – a move that is often associated with the rise of Keynesianism (Hall 1989) – or a *duty to repair* war-led destructions. Most often, in the last century, the addition of new duties on the side of states has been framed in the language of hard-gained rights by citizens who suffered catastrophic destruction from the Great War to the end of the Cold War. By focusing on the emergence and evolution of such a new norm as the state's *duty to repair*, we wish to trace the origins of major shifts in international norms and citizens' rights throughout the twentieth century.

Still along with the focus adopted by the other contributors to this volume we want to move our historical focus from the level of norms as ideas to the level of norms as instruments. We therefore wish to focus on the contractual instruments invented, negotiated and generated in practice by the states and transnational actors, which worked to establish the general recognition of a *duty to repair* in the last hundred years. Indeed, as in the case of other international and transnational negotiations developed between state actors, private companies and groupings of citizens, the concept of a duty to repair found its practical expression in a form of contractual knowledge, for example, a negotiated convention which defines a set of rules that fixes not only the price and temporality necessary for the full payment of an amount commensurate with the tort suffered by the aggrieved parties, but also, a mechanism for litigation of potential disputes about the extent of each party's rights and duties in case of contractual default.

By focusing on the varied set of practical instruments that were invented to turn this new normative ideal – for example, the duty to repair – into practice, we move away from two conventional literatures: the first one, in financial history, which ignores the question of reparations; and the second one, in political history, which treats the question of reparations as a pure element of state politics. Indeed, it is remarkable that financial historians have largely focused on the creation of multilateral trade and financial institutions in the twentieth century, such as those that ensured the expansion of free trade and the preservation of the gold standard in the interwar period, or those Bretton Woods institutions after World War II (Flandreau, Holtfrerich and James 2003), but that they have overlooked the normative, legal and practical implications associated with the implementation of the state's recognition of a duty to repair. In fact, the way financial historians relegated the reparations issue to the dustbin of financial history has been comforted by a common assumption found among socio-political historians, for whom reparations belong to the realm of alliance politics (Maier 2003) and that of the legalization of warfare practices. Reparations are also more than processes of identity-formation as it has been very well documented by historians (Torpey 2006:43).[1] For most reparations scholars, the practical implementation of a duty to repair has had little influence on the way the globalization of finance has been managed throughout the century – and vice versa. The underlying assumption behind such a division of labor between financial historians, political historians and reparations scholars is that postwar reparation treaties and agreements offer compensation to very specific classes of populations who have suffered extraordinary harm, rather than they participate in the construction of new instruments of macro-economic governance whose rules concern everyone.

Our chapter seeks to challenge this division of labor, as well as the vision of the duty to repair that it carries with it. We argue that states,

[1] In the sense that, through reparations, nations seek to restore a sense of pride after great trauma (Torpey 2006).

experts and opinion leaders have put forward specific conceptions of such a duty to repair that were deeply embedded in the transformations of financial capitalism both at the institutional and intellectual level. First, we illustrate this intricate articulation with the case of the reparations that were imposed upon Germany after the Great War: as we will show, the multilateral institutions created to implement and renegotiate the sovereign debt transfers between Germany and its former enemies played an essential role alongside the stabilization plans proposed by interwar experts (economists, lawyers, socio-legal scholars as well as politicians) in order to help European economies move from protectionism to a globalized open economy. Second, we show that, in the case of the Swiss restitutions debate in the wider context of reparations politics that started after the end of the Cold War, the global integration of banking practices played an essential role in explaining the process of renegotiation and the success of restitutions claimants. Although both cases exemplify very different logics of reparations settlements, they both illustrate the deep association between financial logics of (reparations) debt swaps and the globalization of financial activities.

Even if attentive to such broad processes, our chapter also pays attention to the historical specificity of each case, and the particular philosophical understanding of key legal notions like that of "collective responsibility," which justified the payment of reparations; the historically specific association between the financial mechanisms and instruments set up to transfer reparations money; and the broader institutional context of regulation of financial flows.[2] Indeed, when we look closer at various reparations as well as restitutions contracts – the two being sometimes hard to disentangle –[3] we realize that these have been articulated around very different notions and understandings of responsibility: whether direct or indirect, or associated with guilt or not, the notion of "collective responsibility" has garnered very different meanings, and the articulation between morality and legality in reparations agreements has changed quite a lot over the twentieth century.

Thus, in addition to orienting the historiographical debate about reparations toward a more transnational understanding of history, as well as toward a deeper attention to the articulation of reparations

[2] On collective responsibility, see notably Feinberg (1968); French (1974) and May (1992). In the context of reparations for historical injustice, see Colonomos (2008:159–186).

[3] Indeed, the money that Swiss banks were asked to restitute and that were deposited by their clients who perished in the Holocaust, a financial agreement was reached on the basis of a lump sum to be distributed among the beneficiaries of these accounts.

claims with the evolution of financial capitalism, we also show that reparations debates offer particular good sites of investigation for historical sociologists who have an interest in exploring the moral claims made about financial practices.[4] Indeed, reparations debates deploy very different concepts of morality and legality associated with justifications for the payment of reparations – and very different understandings of torts, like individual guilt, individual and collective responsibility – and they also greatly vary with regard to the associations that participants to these debates draw between legal principles and financial instruments – in particular, which types of sanctions shall be applied in case of contractual defaults.

We hereby describe which legal and moral versions of a duty to repair we find in various reparations contracts, and whether we can say that such socially constructed conceptions of morality distinguished reparations settlements from other types of financial settlements in each of the two eras under investigation: post-WWI negotiations and the 1990s Holocaust Era Assets scandal. We show that in post-WWI reparations, the notion of collective responsibility was defined in contradistinction to the notion of guilt, especially in the legal doctrines of French "solidarist" politicians, diplomats and legal experts who invented, negotiated and re-deployed new financial instruments of national accounting which were used to assess the amount of public debt that Germany owed to the Allies. Their actuarial conception of responsibility associated reparations with a collective mechanism of insurance against the future risk of war, and the manifestation of a collective responsibility toward the victims of a war. But more broadly, this mechanism of sovereign debt swap participated in the creation of a host of other instruments of macro-economic governance that later came to be institutionalized into national and international financial institutions – such as national account systems, arbitration commissions, etc. In contrast, the restitutions claimants in the case of the Holocaust Era Assets tightly associated notions of collective responsibility and collective guilt, which they deployed in public relations campaigns aimed at labeling and shaming categories of profiteers on the world scene. These claims contributed greatly to a reflection on corporate responsibility in the context of a debate on the transnational regulation of multinationals' behavior in wartime as well as peacetime, whose terms grafted themselves later on further debates about tax evaders, sanctions-busters and

[4] On this very extensive literature, see Abend 2014.

other profiteers who face the risk of court action in the form of criminal prosecution.

Hence, both cases show that even though the intellectual history of the *duty to repair* may be read in continuous terms – from the Great War to the Second World War to the Holocaust Assets Scandals – when seen from purely normative and intellectual perspectives, the practical implementation of the duty to repair has had each time a very specific history, which had more to do with the contemporary development of instruments of financial governance in each period than with prior experimentation in the field of reparations.

THE REPARATIONS SETTLEMENT AFTER THE GREAT WAR: A LABORATORY FOR MACRO-ECONOMIC GLOBAL GOVERNANCE

The duty to repair and the concept of collective responsibility in legal thought

Since the early days of the Versailles Treaty, by which the Allies made peace with Germany in 1919, the extent of the responsibility of Germany in the destruction of the war on non-German soil has been hotly debated, both by contemporaries and by political historians. At the time it was discussed, many German legal scholars and politicians indicted the treaty as they claimed that it explicitly assumed Germany's (collective) responsibility in the destructions (and the individual guilt of its leaders) – a claim that they adamantly rejected. They talked of the "war guilt clause," (by which they referred to the "responsibility" clause, or article 231) unilaterally imposed on Germany (Schmitt 2003[1950]: 266) in which they saw a bounty that the Allies unfairly asked from the defeated nation.[5] In particular, they hated that the Treaty should establish a Commission of Reparations, to determine the extent to which Germany could "make complete reparation for all such loss and damage done to the civilian population of the Allied and Associated Powers and to their property during the period of the belligerency"[6] (Article 232), and that the Allies based their financial claim on "the responsibility of Germany and her allies for causing all the loss and damage to which the Allied and Associated Governments

[5] For instance, France had to pay such an indemnity to fund German colonial adventures after France lost the 1870 war to Germany.

[6] And in general all damage as defined in Annex I of the Versailles Treaty.

and their nationals have been subjected as a consequence of the war imposed upon them by the aggression of Germany and her allies" (Article 231). Up to this day, political historians and sociologists have also seen in the reparations planned by the Versailles Treaty an "unambiguous form of 'victor's justice', which were resented accordingly" (Torpey 2003:4) by the Germans, and which were dictated by the populist sentiments agitating the British and French politicians and their public opinions.

Not all scholars, however, agree with this view of the reparations settlement as too punitive, and too one-sided in its assignment of responsibility and guilt. In contrast to long-held interpretations of these financial provisions, Sally Marks (1978, 2013) argues persuasively that the financial obligations that the Allies asked Germany to recognize were not as extravagant as the Germans claimed they were, and that they were actually quite commensurate both with what the Germans could pay and also with what they needed to pay for European recovery. Here, along with Mallard (2011), we argue that the reparations philosophy, which was translated into action by the *Reparations Commission*, did not involve the German admission of guilt, but instead, the recognition of some collective responsibility among European nations in repairing the war damages caused to Allied populations. The *duty to repair* that Germany as well as the Allies (like France) recognized was established not on the prior existence of a convention – or a pact, which warring parties would have signed prior to entering into the war – but on the commonly held assumption – at least since the times when Bodin and Grotius re-discovered Roman principles of contractual law and applied them to the realm of international politics (Bernardini 2007) – that a duty such as the duty to repair originates from the acknowledgement of a tort made to one aggrieved party.

In fact, this legal understanding of the states' duty to repair and the idea that each warring nation would be responsible vis-à-vis its civilian population was first turned into law at the national level in France. In October 1915, the French Parliament enacted a law that proclaimed "the equality of all Frenchmen and the solidarity of nations in supporting the costs of war," and "the right to a complete reparation" for the "damages caused in France to the movable properties and real estate property, by acts of warfare" (Gide 1932:22). Charles Gide, a lawyer by training, and a professor of political economy in the faculty of law at Montpelier and then Paris who promoted the "economic program of solidarists" before he represented France in the Reparations

Commission since its creation in 1919, applauded this French law because it expressed a form of "national solidarity, which had never before been expressed in such an affirmative way by France" – after previous wars, like in 1870, "it was said that the victims of the war might be compensated for their loss, but nothing was done, and nobody had raised the possibility of complete reparation."

When the war ended, it was not a surprise if those Frenchmen who had lobbied in favor of the recognition of their state's *duty to repair* favored the establishment of multilateral rather than purely national organizations to ensure the financial sustainability of the reconstruction efforts that aimed at reducing socio-economic inequalities between the European populations who had suffered from the war and those who did not. For instance, Léon Bourgeois had become the first President of the League of Nations in 1919 after a long-lasting effort in favor of obligatory arbitration of interstate conflicts in The Hague conferences, an activity for which he received the Nobel Peace Prize in 1920 (Blais 2007:237). For him, the establishment of the Reparations Commission complemented the efforts to manage world affairs on a multilateral basis and it prolonged the national recognition of a right for civilians to be insured against the risk of war. Quite characteristically, Léon Bourgeois, the rapporteur on the Versailles Treaty to the French Parliament, and a lawyer by training, an essayist and the founder of the "Radical Socialist" Party, argued that with the reparations provisions, the Allies did not ask "any indemnity from Germany in compensation for the military expenses and the exceptional civilian expenses which the state of war required them to pay" (Bourgeois 1919:82).[7] Bourgeois evaluated that such indemnities would have amounted for France up to 143 billion francs, and France only asked Germany to pay to compensate the French population for damages directly caused by bombardments (85 billion) and pensions to war invalids and widows (60 billion).[8] For Bourgeois and other supporters of Versailles, the reparations simply aimed at diminishing the socio-economic inequalities that the war had created between European citizens: indeed, the citizens of Germany, the South of France and Italy for instance, did not suffer from the war as much as the French citizens in the North, who had lived where the

[7] The exception is Belgium, which required that Germany pay her inter-allied war debts, which helped Belgium pay for ammunitions.

[8] Even though President Wilson initially opposed the inclusion of pensions, they were eventually introduced in the bill after British lobbying (Trachtenberg 1979:45).

trenches had been built.[9] Thus, for Bourgeois, states and inter-state cooperation mechanisms, should be set up to distribute more evenly the loss of private citizens due to the risk of war, according to a logic of collective responsibility and collective insurance (rather than because of a specifically German demonstration of immorality during the conduct of war).[10]

Thus, we take the analysis of reparations architecture away from the political debates about the alleged German "guilt" that both promoters and critics of the Versailles Treaty read in the text, and place the analysis of the treaty back in its proper context: the interwar creation of a body of international law concepts (such as collective responsibility, duty to repair, collective insurance). In many ways, the attention placed on this notion of guilt is a reconstruction that does not translate the real motivations of the authors of the reparations provisions. Most economists, diplomats and lawyers who negotiated the Reparations settlement shared the opinion that Germany did not believe that the payment of reparations should be tied to the admission of such "metaphysical guilt." The negotiation process of the Versailles Treaty was such that the 16 articles (articles 231–247, and all the annexes), which spelled out the reparations claims, were distinguished from those that concerned the individual responsibility of the Kaiser himself. When read closely, these sixteen reparations articles suggested that the responsibility lay on the side of "Germany and her allies," but that at the same time, Germany and her allies could not be held responsible for all the destruction of the war, but for the majority of it, and that the responsibility of the victors should also not be evaded. Indeed, if the Allies planned that Germany would "make a special issue of bearer bonds" (Article 232) to restore the properties of civilians, it also said that the final amount as well as the schedule of payments of these reparations, depended on the recommendation of the Reparations Commission (Article 233),[11] which shall "give to the German Government a just opportunity to be heard," and which shall compute a fair price for the loss of property incurred by the Allied civilian populations during the conduct of the

[9] Therefore, the reparations promoters imposed that Germany's taxation should be indexed on the highest taxed population in Europe (Bourgeois 1919:92).

[10] For instance, to justify the reparations provisions, the leader of the French socialist party, Léon Blum told his fellow European socialists in 1923 that the reparations were the first pan-European re-distribution policies that took seriously for the first time the existence of a collective mechanism against the risk of war. (Blum 1972[1923]:273).

[11] The Reparations Commission could change the deadline of payment (art. 234).

war. Quite characteristically, the word "guilt" did not appear in Article 231, which established instead the "responsibility" of Germany in the destruction of the property during the war: the lawyers and diplomats who dealt with financial questions carefully avoided to base claims of reparations on admission of "guilt" of one individual (the Kaiser), representing one people (Germany), whose (aggressive) intentions during the war they would have needed to assess.

In doing so, these diplomats departed from the opinion of the legal scholars who participated in *Commission on the Responsibilities of the Authors of War and the Enforcement of Penalties* (hereafter, Commission on Responsibilities), and who (like Ferdinand Larnaude, the very influential French expert in that Commission) came to the conclusion that Germany was fully responsible for the war (de Lapradelle 1918:20), and recommended the prosecution of the German Emperor for the violation of "international morality and the sanctity of treaties" – a demand that was included in article 227 of the Treaty. The story of the aborted attempt to put to trial the Kaiser finds its proper context in national politics, international alliance politics and transnational efforts to criminalize certain warfare practices (Mallard and Holthoefer forthcoming). It was in such demands to charge the Kaiser with war crimes that the German public saw an attribution of a moral, or as Martti Koskenniemi (2001:292) argues, a "metaphysical guilt," mostly understood in moral terms – for example, moral obligations (to respect human life) that were assumed to be widely shared among humanity's civilized nations. But the reparations articles were based on a different philosophy of international law, one, much more classical, which sought to derive states' duties either from explicit contractual (or conventional) commitments, or from the reported wronging of citizens' private rights. The reparations provisions of the Versailles Treaty thus did not make any claim that reparations should be paid because of a collective guilt of the German people in occasioning the war – or, in the sense of Karl Jaspers, in the sense of a passive guilt, one which expressed the fact that some Germans did not intentionally or directly provoke some harm to Allied civilians, but that they still benefitted from a system that was based on the production of such harm.

In fact, the philosophical outlook of the reparations "contract" – as we may call these sixteen provisions of the Versailles Treaty – was deeply prospective rather than retrospective: by paying reparations, the Germans did not expiate for a collective crime, but made sure that Europe would not fall again in the cycle of financial disorder and chaos that would lead to a new war. For the French members of the Reparations Commission in particular, reparations would then express a renewed sense of transnational social "solidarity," a key concept for the *solidarist* intellectuals active in the work of the Reparations Commission, like Léon Bourgeois, Charles Gide, but also Durkheim's nephew, Marcel Mauss and his friend Léon Blum (Mallard 2011). In fact, such a philosophy of financial responsibility was not only asked from Germany by the Allies: in fact, the Versailles Treaty also asked that the new countries that included territories formerly under German control accept to repay the debts that Germany had contracted when it administered these territories (Article 255).[12] In the Versailles Treaty, past German financial obligations were thus transmitted to the new states which now controlled these territories whose infrastructure had benefitted from German administration and financing: they were neither unilaterally cancelled, nor placed to the debit of the new Weimar Republic.[13] Other treaties, like the Treaties of Saint-Germain and Trianon, which liquidated the war assets and territories of the defunct Austro-Hungarian empire, followed the same logic: they also urged the new states to endorse past debts of the Empire.

Thus, the reparations scheme was not an exceptional bilateral measure placed upon Germany's finances, but it illustrated the broad philosophy of financial responsibility that the architects of peace asked all European nations to observe.[14] This reference to the successor states' "responsibility" or Germany's responsibility to honor past debts and new reparations debts therefore meant both the recognition of a new status (with statehood came the responsibility to honor one's debt), and an injunction to act "responsibly." In Alexander Sack's systematization of the philosophical principles behind the Versailles Treaty and other contemporary treaties, debt contracts between nations could be restructured only in extreme circumstances. In the Versailles Treaty, the implicit use of the doctrine of "odious" debt that Sack later tried to systematize, was extremely rare: the only example that Sack (1927:159) finds is the example of Poland (a new state created out of the association

[12] As Germany lost about 13 percent of its territory.

[13] As Alexander Sack writes, to impose all war debts onto the newly created (and diminished) Austria and Hungary, would have de facto meant the cancellation of all these debts, as the two states would have defaulted (Sack 1927:177).

[14] The burden of proving that debt contracts or reparations obligations were odious was quite high, much higher than present-day calls for the cancellation of the debt of Third World nations, as expressed by the Jubilee network of legal activists (Gulati and Ludington 2008).

of territories formerly under either German or Russian authority and control), which was relieved from a small part of the previously German debt (an amount to be fixed by the Reparations Commission) that the Germans had created to fund their occupation and colonization of Polish lands (Article 254). The experts sitting in the Reparations Commission thus saw in the peace settlement with Germany (and Austro-Hungary) the illustration of how one could apply the legal concept of collective responsibility into international law: each state was asked to act responsibly in order to maintain the collective order and to accept some redistribution to equalize the burden of war debts among nations. For Charles Gide (1932), to repudiate debts in a unilateral way – as the Bolsheviks had done – would have been typically a crime against the principle of reciprocity, or inter-dependence.

Crafting new instruments of macro-economic governance in the reparations "laboratory"

Now, we would like to move one step further and argue that as the reparations provisions were turned into a set of instruments of financial transfer, they were seen as one of the most – if not the most – essential mechanisms of macroeconomic regulation: in fact, that they were conceived as a multilateral instrument of financial stabilization at a time of opening markets and European-wide investments in reconstruction efforts. This is why we claim that reparations provisions fully participated in the establishment of a common legal architecture governing financial flows, and that they were assumed to play that role for a long period of time – in the same way the International Monetary Fund (IMF) played the role of ensuring currency stabilization from World War II to the dismantlement of the Bretton Woods system that occurred with the end of convertibility dollar-gold. Here, we thus analyze how the Reparations Commission worked to design new instruments in the same way as Bruno Latour (1987) when he analyzes how "laboratories" work to create new instruments in isolation from society, so as to later colonize their social environment with the spread of these instruments – and the rearticulation of social relations that such a spread engenders.

The legal understanding of "collective responsibility" that was taken up by the members of the Reparations Commission meant that the extent to which Germany should be asked to pay reparations would be determined by economists according to their own instruments rather than either by theologians or historians. Indeed, the compensation that

Germany had to pay for the civilian destructions did neither depend on the value given to a human life by various theological doctrines, or on the history of Germany's wrong deeds during the war, but rather, on the financial consequences that Germany's reparation debt would have on the national budgets of Germany, France, Belgium and other Allied nations, and on the overall macro-economic equilibrium of Europe's finances. This is why economists were brought to the center of such debates: the international experts who gathered during the first Conference, held in Brussels in December 1920 to determine the amount of the reparations, included Irving Fisher from New York, Charles Gide from Paris, Arthur Cecil Pigou from Cambridge, and their work consisted in trying "to fix a rational reparations policy based on a reasonable estimate of the credit and debit of each warring party to devalue depreciated moneys in proportion of that estimate; and in the meantime, to find enough international capital in order [for central banks] to let enough gold circulate to restore the gold-standard" (Mauss 1997 [1922]:481).

In that sense, the "reparations contract" was assessed according to instruments of macroeconomic governance – such as national account systems – that were used by international experts in macroeconomic stabilization, just like any other new sovereign debt contract that was under discussion at the time. Charles Gide and the other experts inferred the reparations from the overall credit and debit of each nation after the Great War,[15] as reparations were meant to fairly balance the price of the war among the warring parties so that European solidarity could be reconstituted on sustainable grounds. Therefore, they looked for an overall estimate of all the wartime debts contracted to domestic and international actors. As Charles Gide noted, "[a]mong the damages resulting from the war, we have the debts that each warring party has contracted (which weigh to a greater extent on the victors than on the vanquished)" (Gide and Oualid 1931:3). For example, the experts determined at the Brussels Conference "that France owes 219 billion pre-war francs in loans," mostly borrowed on French capital, and to a small extent (about a sixth, or 38 billion), on foreign (British and American) creditors. Seeing the extent of the wound the war brought to France, it then made sense that Germany would help France shoulder

[15] Gide was also commissioned by the Carnegie Endowment of International Peace to participate in the collaborative study of the costs of the Great War, charged with independently assessing a "reasonable estimate of the credit and debit of each warring party " (Gide and Oualid 1931).

its debt by paying reparations. The experts calculated that Germany would need to pay annual payments of three billion gold marks each year for forty-two years. After these calculations were made, it appeared that each nation could not reevaluate the extent to which it would pay back its debts on a unilateral basis, but that the "reparations contract" would play the role of a macroeconomic system of debt cancellation and redistribution, not unlike those put in place after a sovereign country defaulted on its obligation – here, it was *as if* France defaulted ex ante on its obligation to pay the costs of reconstruction, and if it asked Germany to help share that burden.

The Reparations Commissions thus became the official institutional conduit where the harmonization of national accounts were made in Europe as well as where negotiations of sovereign default in a globalizing world economy were conducted across the Atlantic. It was the place where new macroeconomic instruments of measurement were developed to assess the health of each national economy in a context of transatlantic interdependency: the discussions focused on the consequences of Germany's default on other European economies, but also on the role that the United States should play in the prevention of global financial crises.[16] Keynes, who participated in the Brussels Conference of 1920, was the first to make the linkage between European (reparation) debts and interallied debts (that involved the United States): for him, the reparations that the Allies asked Germany to pay were too high, and, since the end of the war, he had proposed that the Americans should cancel the interallied debts that France (and to a lesser extent the United Kingdom, Belgium and Italy) owed them,[17] as the reparations to be paid by Germany to France could then be scaled back to a reasonable level (Carabelli and Cedrini 2010:317). Unfortunately, the Americans ignored Keynes's call for debt forgiveness in 1920 and 1922, and the US bankers and the US government warned various times the French representatives on the Reparations Commission that they may agree to lower the inter-allied debts in the future, but that "if French leaders were to wait for this before their own revision of reparation, they shall wait in vain" (cited in Maier 1988:289).

16 The sovereign obligations contracted by new Central European states were administered under the auspices of the League of Nations.

17 As Marc Trachtenberg (1979:29) shows, like Keynes, during the Peace treaty negotiations, the French Minister of Commerce has hoped to reapportion inter-allied debts and to maintain Allied control of raw materials (coal), a position that he shared with his young advisor, Jean Monnet, who then created the European Coal and Steel Community after WWII.

Indeed, the United States did not want to be the first ones to devalue the worth of their loan to the French, and they insisted that the French should adopt a stabilization plan first, a legal change in the value of the money, a "euphemism" for the re-evaluation of the reparation debt, as Gide wrote (Gide and Oualid 1931:3). The economists in the Reparations Commission thus tried to find a scheme by which every country (France included, and not just Germany) should be encouraged to pay its debt, even if scaled back to a realistic level (like half or a third of its prewar value), with real money, rather than just pay the interests of the debt with fake money artificially created by the printing press, which the German government started to manipulate in 1920 and 1921.

In the next section, however, we show how the ambiguity over the question of responsibility (and its relation to the notion of "guilt," which existed at least in the mind of the German public) resurfaced as the instruments of financial stabilization were re-interpreted "in the wild" – for example, outside the laboratory of the Reparations Commission – and how such ambiguity affected the German, French and British attitudes toward sovereign default.

Experimenting with new financial instruments in the wild: the sanctions debate

The notion that economists and financial experts could settle disputes about war reparations in what sociologists would call a "laboratory-like" (Latour 1987) setting was not of the liking of the right-wing legal commentators and politicians from both France and Germany. The right-wing politicians in both France and Germany blocked the working of the Reparations Commissions: when the time came to pay the 1921 annuity, Germany did not have enough foreign currency to pay reparations with French and Belgium francs and British pounds. As a result, Germany had to sell marks (rather than exported goods, which they did not have) to buy foreign moneys, and the speculation against the mark led to further depreciation (Maier 1988:244).[18] The French government then agreed to re-assess the amount of reparations once more, but it asked that its own creditors, the British and the American banks (especially J.P. Morgan, which floated loans to the British and the French for almost half a billion dollars in 1915 and 1916)

[18] To bypass the German problem of buying foreign currencies, the French government agreed to be paid in kind (in coal), or in cession of shares of the industrial coal conglomerates upon which France's steel industries depended. But German industrialists, aided by the British opposed the creation of large Franco-German cartels in the coal sector.

first cancel part of the French debts.[19] J.P. Morgan refused: instead, he agreed to float a loan to Germany so that it could avoid a default for 1922, and proposed that, in exchange, France write off some of the amount of reparations.[20] But the new French government of Raymond Poincaré opposed the stabilization plan proposed by Gide as his government refused to lower the reparations that France asked Germany to pay (in exchange of a promise of reduced interallied war debts). As a result, the Reparations Commission found Germany in default of its coal payments in January 1923.

From becoming a site from where new macro-economic theories were debated, with the politicization of the debate about the notion of collective responsibilities and the origins of the German default on its reparations obligations, the Reparations Commission tried to move to become the authority in charge of deciding when a "credit event" (a default in modern parlance) occurred. Still, it failed to impose its authority on this issue: the Reparations commission had not been granted by the Versailles Treaty the authority to establish the penalties and sanctions against the defaulter, and to establish an order of priority among the creditors whose interests were harmed by the default. After Germany defaulted on its reparation debt, France unilaterally claimed authority to decide on sanctions, and the government of Raymond Poincaré immediately sent French troops to occupy the Ruhr in retaliation to the default. The French right-wing politicians expressed highly principled moral calls for Germany to pay whatever formidable sum the French would ask, as they insisted that German reparations were a sanction that only Germany had to pay because of its collective guilt, and that a failure to do so meant that Germany needed to be occupied again. To this extent, they gave fuel to the interpretation of the reparations provision crafted by right-wing legal scholars in Germany, like Carl Schmitt (2003[1950]:268), who encouraged the German government not to pay reparations (as they refused the notion that Germans shared some metaphysical guilt associated with the Great War, from which the Allies were exempted), to default on the payment of reparations, and to refuse the necessary stabilization of the mark – and of the franc. Indeed, the French occupation of the richest Western German

[19] Already in 1918, Gide had written that at some point, inter-allied debts needed to be cancelled; or that, if their total was re-negotiated, a lesser amount could be reimbursed for instance by the creation of a pan-European loan, "un grand emprunt international solidaire" (cited in Pénin 1997:185).

[20] Maier 1988, op. cit., p. 287.

regions confirmed the German interpretation of reparations as indemnities, and responsibility as guilt: as Marcel Mauss (1997[1924]:580) noticed, the militarization of the French response to German default meant that the reparations paid by Germany "went to the bailiff [the French occupying armies] rather than to the victim," that is, the Belgian and French families whose properties were destroyed.

The Ruhr crisis finally gave the experts of the Reparations Commission the opportunity to test "in the wild" the validity of the new instruments that they had designed in their "laboratory-like" setting, when they compared national accounts and deducted the amount of debt transfers that needed to be effectuated to ensure the stability of the European economic and financial area. After the German default, followed by the French sanction in the form of the occupation of the Ruhr, the experts initially failed to impose their views. But the failure of the French sanctions policy helped the experts impose their stabilization plans on France (and Germany). After the US and British bankers started buying some francs to help France redress its parity,[21] putting an end to the depreciation of the franc, Raymond Poincaré moved toward the acceptance of the stabilization plan drawn by a committee of experts (known as the "Dawes Plan," written under the Chairmanship of the US vice-president Charles Dawes), to review Germany's capacity to pay reparations and France's capacity to pay inter-allied debts. Putting an end to the Ruhr crisis, the three main points of the Dawes plan of August 1924 were: the end of the French occupation, the immediate payment of 1 billion marks and the Allied supervision of the Reichsbank (Maier 1988, op. cit.:418).

Finally, the authority of economists and the usefulness of their instruments to assess the level at which reparations should be established (and the resulting level at which the franc should be priced against the gold) was recognized by the French government. As Léon Blum (1972[1924]) wrote in April 1924, at last "the experts, disavowing the policy of Poincaré, declared themselves in favor of a moratorium" along the lines that the experts of the Reparations Commission advocated: "during the first years, limited contribution of the Germans to

[21] The occupation of the Ruhr in retaliation to the German default not only drew the two countries further apart, but it also exported the financial crisis in Germany to France: indeed, after the German government finally stabilized the mark by creating a devalued new money – the Rentenmark – in November 1923, the franc suffered in January 1924, as "the Germans who were full of francs [which was used by the French occupying armies], now sell [the francs]" (Mauss 1997[1924]:580).

the Allied reparations effort by payments in kind" until the Germans could accumulate enough money to start paying back. As Mauss (1997 [1924]:680) wrote, Poincaré "was forced to change his general policy, and to adopt the principle of increased taxation [on income and profits], reaching budgetary equilibrium, paying back debts rather than inflating the printed money." France had to accept the notion that Germany did not have to pay reparations because of a metaphysical guilt, but that reparation debts should be reassessed with an eye for their consequences on Europe's financial equilibrium. Of course, this demonstration had repercussions on national elections, as ultimately, the solidarists' efforts were rewarded when the "Cartel des gauches" won the election in May 1924, with Blum's SFIO as the first party in the new parliamentary majority. But here, we emphasized the significance that the specific notion of collective responsibility espoused by the Reparations Commission had for efforts aimed at regulating global financial flows (and involving currency stabilization for example); from the adoption of the Dawes plan to the end of the 1920s, economists in the Reparations Commission continued to serve as the conduit for negotiations of sovereign debt restructuring (Schuker 1988).

Of course, the geo-political and financial context in both Europe and the United States was such that the authority of the experts and their instruments was short-lived, in the sense that the mechanisms of macro-economic governance proposed in 1924 did not survive the Great Depression and the rise to power of the National Socialist Party in 1933. By then, Germany then defaulted on both reparations and foreign debts.[22] This decision contrasted with most of the successor states of Eastern Europe, which had been "hesitant to interrupt service [of the debt] on the grounds that much of their debt had been arranged under League of Nations auspices" (Eichengreen and Portes 1987:29). The German default showed to Germany's creditors that it rejected the whole system of macro-economic governance that had been based upon the work of the Reparations Commission and the legal philosophy behind the Reparations contract: the German state did not see itself responsible for the fate of non-German populations in the post-war era, and Hitler claimed that the new Reich had a higher responsibility (beyond that recognized by treaties) to defend and protect the interests of all Germans, wherever they might be situated (especially

[22] This leads Stephen Schuker (1988) to claim that the Weimar Republic paid almost no reparations at all, since it had largely paid the interest on its reparations debts with US loans.

in new states with large population of German-speaking minorities), thus ignoring the sanctity of territorial boundaries drawn by the post-war treaties. Thus, the system of sovereign debt negotiation, which continued to be heavily politicized, as the interpretation of the reparations provisions included the Versailles Treaty had not stabilized around one common notion of "responsibility," collapsed. When the latter collapsed, it was not a coincidence if the interesting discussion of a collective responsibility in the post-war context was thrown like the baby with the water's bath.

RESPONSIBILITY AND GUILT IN THE 1990S HOLOCAUST CLAIMS FOR REPARATIONS

After WWII, debates about the legal concept of collective responsibility that justified reparations claims made by various civilian populations (especially European Jews, who were the most severely touched victims of the conflict) resurfaced. Immediately after WWII, West Germany agreed to pay reparations to the state of Israel;[23] to the Jewish victims in the diaspora; and to Jews of these nations of twelve Western European states – most of the NATO countries as well as Switzerland, Austria and Sweden (Colonomos and Armstrong 2006:406). These reparations were inspired by the consequentialist logic of responsibility not unlike that defended by the solidarists in the interwar period. Indeed, the reparations were paid to states with which the new Germany felt a community of destiny, and therefore, a responsibility to share financial burdens in times of hardship and reconstruction: the Germans' reparations policy carefully maintained the boundary between the West (the United States, Western Europe and Israel), and Eastern European states, which Germany refused to include into this web of interstate contracts. If the West German taxpayers' acceptance of an extensive program of reparations could be seen as an implicit "acceptance of its collective responsibility," (Colonomos and Armstrong 2006:412) Chancellor Adenauer consistently refused to explicitly acknowledge a "collective responsibility" – in the sense meant by Karl Jaspers of a collective even if passive "guilt" – for the Holocaust. It is plausible that

[23] The 1952 Luxembourg Agreement had the effect that most capital intensive investment in the steel and energy sectors in Israel originally came from Germany and that when the program was officially terminated in 1965, Germany had become Israel's third trading partner, although diplomatic relationships were not yet established between the two countries (Colonomos and Armstrong 2006:409).

Chancellor Adenauer's reluctance to acknowledge collective responsibility for the crime might have been motivated by the interwar confusion that reigned over whether collective responsibility meant retrospective shame and guilt or prospective responsibility.

In this section, we show how this paradigm was completely overhauled by the expression of new claims for restitutions in the post-Cold War context, when the fall of the Berlin Wall liberated new claims for reparations of the atrocities committed during WWII. During the Cold War a number of voices had been raised in denunciation of the limits of the reparations paid by Germany to specific communities, or by French Vichy government or neutral (but somewhat collaborating) Switzerland, but such calls went entirely unheeded, as the security dimension of East-West relations and the friend/enemy division prevented communal demands from crossing national barriers. It would have been unthinkable for American lawyers to endanger trade or good relations between the United States and Switzerland, Germany or France.[24] But for some victims of the Holocaust and mostly for the descendants of those who were assassinated by the Nazis, the books were not closed with the first wave of the 1950s reparations agreements. Many victims appealed for justice and called for new financial compensation schemes to be set up. Among those involved were Jews demanding that Swiss banks, European insurance companies and German industry restore their goods to them and pay them compensation.[25]

The global call for a tribunal of history: the case of the Holocaust era assets scandal

Here, we show that the restitutions claims expressed after the end of the Cold War manifested a change in the social fabric of restitutions claims. From the interwar to the Cold War, reparations claims had remained largely produced in the conclaves of inter-state negotiations, in the European chancelleries where economic and financial experts could argue about numbers without being subjected to the scrutiny of the public eye. In contrast, after 1989, new claims were directly voiced in the public sphere, in the form of public accusations of responsibility

[24] This chapter focuses on the Swiss case. However, other claims for reparations and restitutions were addressed at French companies such as, for example, the French railroad company. German companies that benefitted from slave and forced labor were also targeted by activists and lawyers.

[25] Other communities that were victims of the Second World War also received compensation, most notably the Slavic populations.

(in the sense of complicity) against the states and corporate actors that had supposedly benefitted from the Holocaust. The public calls for restitutions expressed in the post-Cold War era were initiated by individuals and groups (in the context of class actions lawsuits) external to the state who demanded either from governmental bureaucracies or from large private companies that past injustices committed against them should be fully brought to light. Here, again, to understand how reparations claims operated, and the role they played in the establishment of larger schemes of global governance, it is important to pay attention to the transnational roots behind the proliferation of restitutions claims that originated from North America in the 1990s, in a context where access to US currencies on the New York financial scene had been increasingly important since the 1980s. Indeed, it would be a mistake to reduce this story to a purely bilateral fight between what was pictured as the "US Jewish community" represented by US diplomats, and Swiss nationals represented by the Swiss Federal government. In this story, most of the claims started directly in the public sphere, and used some of the instruments of public relations first crafted by human rights NGOs, which operated to mobilize public opinion.

Among the transnational actors that operated in these very public transatlantic arm-wrestles, the most important one was undoubtedly the World Jewish Congress. This organization had already been involved in negotiations with Germany and, as early as 1944, pronounced itself in favour of an economic settlement made within an international system of justice. However, the World Jewish Congress was not the most active movement in The Hague negotiations that gathered representatives from Israel and West Germany in 1952 and when reparation payments to Israel were discussed. During the Cold War, it devoted its energies to assisting Jews in the Soviet Union. The organization changed character in the 1980s when the Canadian magnate Edgar Bronfman took over its leadership and attempted to give its activities greater public visibility. Shortly after his appointment, the industrialist launched an international campaign against the nefarious figure of Kurt Waldheim. In the exposure of the UN Secretary General's Nazi past, we see three characteristics that were present in the scandal of the Swiss banks and the European companies: public harm done to the reputation of an organization by the exposure of shameful behaviour; revelation of an unknown aspect of the Second World War; and the establishment of a campaign that is global in its scope, resources and consequences. With this first success behind it, the World

Jewish Congress now had resolutely global ambitions, which it sought to accomplish by using the same kind of public relations instruments – for example, unearthed archives about a shameful past, accusatory op-eds, effective lobbying of transnational organizations.

The reparations and restitutions demanded by Jewish groups revealed a clash of *ethos*, reflecting a sharp contrast between past Cold War defenders of Westphalian secret state diplomacy, and non-state actors who operated transnationally and very publicly in the context of global financial capitalism. The new leaders of the World Jewish Congress and the lawyers condemned the disdainful behaviour of many of the Swiss – and, subsequently, French – dignitaries who took the view that money was not the best way to assuage the pain of memory and that the burden of these reparations could not be imposed on them.[26] The pugnacity of the former clashed with the defensiveness or the arrogance of the latter – and their "art of not paying their debts"[27] – and the variety of resources they used to publicly prove their point: at the beginning of the scandal of the Swiss banks and the unclaimed accounts, the lawyers and the World Jewish Congress employed researchers who were sent in public archives in Washington, where they found access to documents that had been until then unexploited. They wanted to prove the existence of accounts that had been opened in Switzerland by Jews who had perished in the camps. Working for the law firm of Cohen, Milstein, Hausfeld and Toll, Miriam Kleiman was one of the first to exhume from the Washington archives a list of names of account holders that was compromising for the Swiss bankers. That list had a spectacular impact in the media, even though the descendants of the persons listed were unable to obtain restitution of the moneys deposited by their relatives.[28] Both the claimants' lawyers and the companies accused – the banks, insurers and industrial companies – drew on the services of historians and archivists who worked as "genealogists" to get to the bottom of a potentially ignominious past.

[26] At the end of WWII, both in Israel and in the diaspora, many Jewish voices were critical of those who accepted tainted "blood money." The victims felt shame at the idea of making a request to their former persecutors. For instance, Menahem Begin opposed the West German reparations paid to Jews by the 1952 Luxembourg Agreement precisely for the reason that, for them, the German debt could not be paid off, and they preferred instead to quarantine Germany (Colonomos and Armstrong 2006:397). More than forty years later, this shameful restraint was no longer so widely shared.

[27] This is one of the possible interpretations of Don Juan's behavior and aristocratic attitude when he is confronted with his creditors (Kofman 1991).

[28] The various Swiss establishments imposed very strict rules; death certificates were required.

Still, faced with the denial showed by Swiss bankers in the responsibility of the Holocaust, lawyers had difficulties convincing themselves that they could win a fight against such powerful (and foreign) institutions. Like other non-governmental organizations which resorted to the exercise of "naming and shaming" in the human rights campaigns of the 1980s against abuses of dictators in Latin America (Risse and Sikkink 1999), law firms that defended those who wanted to have access to the dormant accounts in Swiss banks wanted to imprint the mark of shame on their targets.[29] The very first act of the World Jewish Congress and the lawyers who took this case was to attack the European companies, asserting that they had grown rich out of the war. The persons harmed by this illegal, immoral conduct had to be compensated for this "unjust enrichment."[30] In the name of principles inspired by a philosophy of property and restitution, the Swiss banks were obliged to make a reasonable offer. The tactic assumes a division of roles between the denouncer and the accused. The denouncer attacks the accused, employing blackmail by threat of defamation and a boycott of the companies that are said to have denied their misdeeds. He awaits the accused's offer. If it turns out to be small, the accused is suspected of dishonesty or avarice and ill-will.

This tactic, however, completely changed the rules of the game: the notion of responsibility that restitutions claimants implicitly assumed was very different from that assumed in the interwar period. When proferring these kinds of accusations, restitutions claimants did not ask former enemies to accept to share the burden of responsibility, whatever their level of guilt and association in the crime, but based on a comprehensive assessment of the capabilities of everybody. Rather, they assigned guilt and direct complicitly in a crime onto a suspect, based on newly released evidence, like a prosecutor accusing a suspect of a violent crime, although an old one. In so doing, these transnational organizations departed from the role of neutral observers that the Reparations Commission experts had tried to play in their "laboratory-like setting," when they strictly limited their role to assessing the financial capabilities of each party to the war to pay reconstruction costs. Lawyers

[29] The denunciation of a particular case must always be articulated to general and universal conditions of injustice (Garfinkel 1956).

[30] One finds this notion in American law; it also corresponds to an Aristotelian conception of property – see Aristotle (1988:5–7). In French, the notion of "biens mal acquis" covers some of the same ground.

and activists besieged bankers, insurers, industrialists and states in the attempt to lay bare the shameful dimension of their history.

This quest to have nations and companies confess is a singular event of enormous scope: it is one of the essential vehicles of the expansion of transitional justice and the repentance model. The accusers-lawyers wanted to induce financial establishments to carry out an introspective self-examination, which were buttressed by institutional assessments, as for example in Switzerland where was convened the Bergier Commission in Geneva, was set up to examine Switzerland's role and its responsibility in the war. In this commission, historians accepted to frame the responsibility of the Swiss in the context of debates about collective guilt (in the Jasperian sense of "moral taint"). Indeed, as the Bergier report clearly indicated, anti-semitism was widespread in Switzerland during the war, and it played a role in the way Swiss neutrality was practiced during the war.[31] It must be underlined that this initiative, a country that investigates its past and, as such, makes some amendments to the national official narrative, was not isolated. In the context of claims for reparations, France was also forced into revisiting parts of its past (notably the behavior of its corporate agents, such as, for example, the national railroad company, the SNCF).[32]

To the extent that the historical episodes to which they referred had already been the subject of legal, political and, also, economic agreements, the victims were not asking that a wrong committed in the immediate past be repaired – as in the earlier Reparations Debate – but they were reopening old cases that had long seemed closed because of a lack of access to archives. But after the fall of the Berlin Wall, lawyers hoped to benefit from the release of a massive number of documents archived in Moscow on the Nazi crimes. The campaign against the Swiss banks involved two aspects of their wartime activities that are often confused with one another. The World Jewish Congress set out to look for evidence of the existence of unclaimed accounts in Switzerland's banks and claimed to have made such a discovery in late 1995 – although they were not able to make a total estimate of all the accounts that still had balances in Swiss coffers without the depositors'

31 *Final Report of the Independent Commission of Experts Switzerland – Second World War*, pp. 122–124.

32 A country official narrative indeed also includes an account of large corporate agents. To this extent, the role of several German industries was also scrutinized and revisited. In another setting, in the context of debates about post-sionism, a critique of national official narrative was also to be found in countries such as Israel.

descendants being able to claim them. They were also trying to establish a relation of causality between the banking activities of Switzerland and the sustainability of the Third Reich during the war. In doing so, they challenged the official historical narrative of Switzerland, which was that Switzerland had been forced to accept the Nazis' requests because, and that had it failed to do so, the country would have been invaded. Such deterministic view was challenged in the Eizenstadt's US official report that activists – Jewish organizations such as the World Jewish Congress and their laywers – referred to: after 1943, according to this report and based on evidence found in the correspondence of some Swiss leaders of the time, Swiss statesmen were aware that Germany would have not invaded their country had they failed to accept their requests, since German troops were stuck in their fighting on the Eastern front. Morever, Eizenstadt argued that Switzerland helped prolong the war (State Department 1997), taking an approach akin to virtual or counterfactual history (Tetlock and Belkin 1996), which identifies the alternatives that a bank, company or industry faced when they rubbed shoulders with a dictatorial power such as the Nazis. In this climate of suspicion, historians were even given a new role. Indeed, historians were hired by lawyers to establish evidence of the responsibility of a particular entity, to evaluate a decision-making process in a group, company or bank, by reconstituting its various sequences. Their findings reconstructed the historical trajectory, and it led them to asking such questions as whether one modification in the sequence underlying a particular set of decisions would have led to different outcomes. The aim of this counterfactual operation was to provide an explanation of history, here by asking the question: *what would have happened if* the Swiss banks had not contributed to financing the Nazi war economy? If the Swiss had refrained from all trade with the Germans, the war would perhaps have been shorter; this can be said, therefore, to prove a causality that rationally establishes Swiss responsibility. Of course, it is extremely difficult to prove the validity of this counterfactual, so this reasoning was not used in a legal setting and had no legal role as such. But it was widely appealing socially and publicly for those who wanted states and companies to "pay" for their misdeeds.

This type of counterfactual history thus fed into a process of denunciation and renewed suspicion: by suggesting that things could have been otherwise – that the Swiss banks made a decision that commits them directly, that Switzerland adopted a very specific policy towards refugees, that German industrialists could have not used the forced labour of prisoners – these "new historians" and their followers hinted at a moral offence of substantial magnitude deriving from a collective decision. Historians tried to show that the decisions of Swiss profiteers had the effect of reinforcing or extending the harm suffered by a group that suffered an injustice for which the profiteers were not directly responsible. This moral accusation had a particular voice in a context where the "guilt of nations" (Barkan 2001), that is, i.e. the collective guilt of state entities that, however, could also include corportate agents of those nations – became a focal point of attention in the United States. Paradoxically, in comparison with the interwar period, when the debate placed at the center the victims of the war (those populations of Northern France and Belgium whose houses were destroyed), here, the victims were less central in the debate, as the focus was placed on understanding the degree of intentionality, and the degree of complicity, demonstrated by those who benefitted from an unequal and oppressive politico-economic system. In this case, reparations and restitutions claimants started by assuming that there existed a collective responsibility in the sense of a collective guilt (French 1974; Barry 1981), and they soon overcame the obstacles raised by the fact that it is logically impossible for a collective to feel guilt, by individualizing the instances of guilt in their search for historical evidence of direct implications in a crime. Then, guilt became the verdict of a Tribunal of History (Fletcher 2002).

From public campaign to legal action: the US extra-territorial competence in the context of financial globalization

The Swiss were the first to experience the cost of a useless, expensive denial, at a time when the global integration of banking activities made Swiss banks vulnerable to US attacks.[33] In 1995, Swiss bankers felt they were able to resist the demands formulated by Edgar Bronfman. Over the next two years, they countered the Jewish demands with a massive denial, which prompted the lawyers and leaders of the World Jewish Congress to display an ever more aggressive attitude. Several American lawyers delivered an ultimatum to the bankers, threatening to restrict their activities in New York or California; this threat turned out to be

[33] Because of Germany's role in the war, the sensitivity of opinion in that country about the Shoah, and the demonstration of force by American lawyers and the World Jewish Congress, German industrial companies accepted the principle of compensation more easily and quickly. The more astute entrepreneurs went along with the campaign, participating in the disclosure of a shameful past: a number of German business leaders adopted this line of conduct.

decisive in concluding an agreement. In a context of globalization and interdependence between economies and financial centres, European companies were threatened as a consequence of their interests in the United States. Both in the industrial and financial sectors, many mergers and acquisitions had taken place in the 1980s and '90s, as a result of which links between the European and American economies were strengthened. A very large number of British and American shareholders now had holdings in Swiss companies, which did not want to risk losing their clients and shareholders.

Furthermore, from 1996 to 1998 the World Jewish Congress and a number of American lawyers exerted pressure on Switzerland by bringing a series of class actions in the American courts. The World Jewish Congress also explored the possibility of laying the matter before the American Congress in order to attack Switzerland with economic sanctions: this possibility was the focus of discussions with Republican senator Al D'Amato, who initiated the embargoes on Libya and Iran in 1996, but a measure of this kind targeted against Switzerland was never adopted, and the plan was quickly abandoned. Instead, the World Jewish Congress and the lawyers opted for the application of legal pressure, the main protagonists in this being the courts and the various bodies charged with regulating commercial activity at the local level. In so doing, they took their lead from the kinds of pressure that had been exerted on the oil and textile multinationals over human rights issues. They also seized the option offered by the Alien Tort Claims Act, an old law of 1789, which gives the possibility for any citizen of any nation to sue before a US court any non-American entity for a crime committed outside the United States against the "law of nations" – originally, it was meant to be used against acts of piracy.[34] In that sense, the accusations proferred by the World Jewish Congress and their attacks "*tous azimuts*" before US courts, characterized by their strongly adversarial culture, moved the notion of Swiss reponsibility closer to the notion of a Swiss guilt, of either direct crime, or complicity in the crime.

The World Jewish Congress and those who filed class action lawsuits against Swiss banks used courts as a public arena in order to put pressure on corporate agents. Faced with the pressure of legal action, the final settlement came out of negotiations between the banks, the WJC

[34] During the last decade, several groups tried to use the same legal instruments, including some who suffered from Apartheid in South Africa, or African Americans who have begun the battle for compensation for slavery in the United States (Torpey 2006: 149).

and the American Under-Secretary Eizenstat. As the banks accepted to pay 1.25 billion dollars, this sum not only covered an estimate of the amount of money in dormant accounts, but also served to compensate those persons who attempted to find refuge in Switzerland and who had been denied admission and some persons who had been forced into slave labor. Therefore, by agreeing to settle, Swiss banks implicitly accepted some responsibility in harming some of the victims of World War II. It is the reflection of a form of collective responsibility and agency on the part of these corporations.

In many ways, the paradigm that emerged from the restitutions claims campaign, which was characterized by the mobilization of US courts (or the threat to go to court), the adoption of an accusatory position, the equation between responsibility and guilt (either direct or indirect), the use of counterfactual history to prove one's point, has had far reaching consequences beyond the restitutions debate. There was a new development in this mirror-play between past and present when the NGO Jubilee 2000, which argues for the cancellation of the debt of the countries of the South,[35] formed an alliance with the American lawyers who brought the cases against the Swiss banks and German industry, and also with South African activists. The studies carried out as part of the Jubilee 2000 campaign picked up the thread of virtual economic history, attempting to show that the activities of the Swiss and German banks that did business with the Apartheid regime extended the life of that political system.[36] Actions were brought in the American courts to demand that Swiss and German banks (soon to be followed by French and American ones) give an account of the business they had done with the South African Apartheid regime. The legal actions taken by this triumvirate coincided with the Durban Conference; taking their lead from the actions formulated around the Second World War, their frame of reference was slavery and the domination suffered by black people. Slavery, ancient and modern, and also genocide were all brought into the question.[37] This Möbius strip of references

[35] Particularly by calling for cancellation of the debt.

[36] http://journal.probeinternational.org/2003/07/30/southern-africa-calls-reparations-apartheid/

[37] The question of slavery re-surfaced both in the United States and internationally. In 2000 a class action was brought in America against the Aetna insurance company with which the bodies of slaves had been insured, as freight, when, in the nineteenth century, they were transported by rail from city to city in the north-eastern United States.The action against Aetna was the first in a series of lawsuits against many companies that had guilty links with the slave trade in their pasts. Five companies are directly concerned by these trials: Aetna, New York Life, AIG, J. P. Morgan Chase and First Boston Principal Group.

lent the accusation substantial weight. These actions echoed the campaigns against multinationals that violated human rights law, such actions being based on the exposure of transgressions of UN embargo rules. Most recently, US judicial authorities have claimed jurisdiction on cases of violations of US embargoes (not UN ones) by European banks – and particularly, Geneva-based branches, as Geneva is the main hub of oil trade and financing – based on the fact that transactions were priced in US dollars. For instance, like Federal and New York (NY) state prosecutors imposed high penalties against France's biggest bank BNP-Paribas, which recently fined 8.9 billion dollars in a NY criminal court case, which involved oil deals with Sudan and Iran (Ayad 2014).

More generally, the category of "profiteer" has been found in many exposés of international wrongdoing. The same paradigmatic features as found in the restitutions public relations campaign also characterize some of the main actions taken by various governments and publics in response to the financial crisis that followed the times of relative prosperity of the 1990s. Many of the actions undertaken by various governments in reaction to the financial practice – the United States in particular – have aimed at finding the guilty parties and at bringing them to prosecution rather than at changing the institutional (global and domestic) architecture of inter-state sovereign debt negotiations, which could help equalize the burden of the crisis for most citizens and nations. Rather than trying to set up a new inter-state negotiating forum, as the solidarists had vainly tried to do in the interwar period, most of the actions for instance directed against the Swiss tax laws, aim at finding and punishing the individuals and corporations that have practiced tax evasion (in the case of the companies located in Switzerland), or those corporations or individuals who practiced insider trading (in the case of hedge funds like SAC Capital and its founder Steve Cohen); or those banks and individuals in specific banks (like Fabrice Tourré of Goldman Sachs) which traded against the interests of their clients, by encouraging them to buy toxic products which they put back on the market; or those mortgage companies (like Wells Fargo) accused of predatory lending practices, which are the objects of class actions against them. Here again, responsibility in the financial crisis meant the admission of guilt in criminal practices that have led to escalate or aggravate the effects of the crisis, and from which the accused have benefitted. Thus, again, the notion of "unjust enrichment" is central in this paradigm, which states have adopted to respond to the unjust increase of inequalities. The relative ease with which the G20 summit of September 2013 has adopted measures which criminalize tax evasion[38] by which they will force Swiss banks to open their accounts to the investigative campaigns of cash-starved European states only prolongs the successes achieved by US lawyers who pursued the Holocaust era assets in the prior period of relative prosperity.

There are, however, some problems associated with the fixation on the guilt of profiteers manifest in the paradigm of restitutions. The exclusive focus on "unjust enrichment" can be deplored as it goes hand in hand with the absence of any reflection that does not associate responsibility with guilt, *duty to repair* with the punishment of individuals with evil (collective or individual) intentions. The risk is that restitutions demands (or financial compensations to assuage the burden of the victims of a financial crisis) would always have to demonstrate the existence of a minimal intention to harm, without which no compensation could be obtained. As the latter is always hard to prove, especially fifty years after the fact in the case of the Holocaust era assets, the hegemony of this paradigm of collective responsibility risks to condemn victims to an elusive quest for a just order. In other cases, the profiteer can always claim that he has derived advantage from a situation for which he is not directly responsible, even if he admits that he was not unaware that there was great injustice in the situation. Unlike the accomplice, the profiteer can claim that he was not a perpetrator of the great crime; he did not participate in it; his is a case of vicarious responsibility, which makes calls for justice harder to receive. And in the meantime, the focus has moved from that of understanding the wrongs done to the victims, or by the flawed architecture of a system of economic exchange, to the degree of intentionality demonstrated by some profiteers in an unjust system.

CONCLUSION

Over a hundred years of reparations claims, we see a radical move this chapter has tried to account for. In a context of growing financial integration, the claimants' direct access to US courts claiming extra-territorial jurisdiction – a process of joint judicialization and re-nationalization of international negotiations – has had major effects on the political and legal understandings of the *duty to repair*. Indeed, the evolving practice of reparations cases has facilitated a move from a

[38] www.g20.org/news/20130828/782201775.html.

negotiated settlement within the limits of an inter-statist "laboratory-like" forum – in which experts design new computational instruments to justify the amount of financial transfers – to new forms of non-state and transnational public relations campaigns, in which the reliance on US courts serves to threaten non-cooperative parties. The adoption of new instruments coming from the field of human rights in the form of public campaigns aimed at "labeling and shaming" – with its extensive use of investigative (both archive-based and counterfactual) history – and the heavy reliance on threats to go to courts has been at the heart of the process of moralization of international affairs (Colonomos, 2008). Whereas the socio-legal scholarship often offers a positive view of such a process of judicialization (Moravcsik 2000; Chorev 2009), as the process of going beyond inter-state mechanisms of cooperation and giving direct access to courts to individuals is often seen as a positive step toward the acquisition and protection of new rights, we come up with a more balanced perspective on this process. We underline that the choice of instruments used in such a process of "moralization" (accusatory defamation campaigns, threats to use criminal courts to extort financial profits, etc.) have reduced the scope of cases in which a duty to repair could be exercised. Indeed, the "moralization" of public campaign means that guilt became prevalent over mere responsibility, and that far from bringing closure, the last debates have generated spirals of suspicions. True, these aggressive campaigns have also relied on the unveiling of historical evidence and therefore have contributed to historical knowledge, however, they have also spurred a "competition between victims" (Chaumont 1997), which is very characteristic of the 1990s and that has prolonged itself in Western democracies.

Our focus on the level of instruments associated with the *duty to repair* also highlights the growing significance of the United States in the governance of financial flows and legal adjudication. From the interwar period, when the United States largely refused its responsibilities in the governance of capitalism, which suffered as a result, the post-Cold War has seen the joint erosion of the norm of sovereign equality and the rising hegemony of the US legal system. This is particularly striking in the Holocaust era assets episode, during which Switzerland has been constrained in its banking policy and has had to elaborate a new official history of its involvement in World War II. But this decline of small states' sovereign autonomy should not be read as the consequence of the rising power of US diplomacy abroad. In fact, US diplomats were caught off guard by the World Jewish Congress action against the

Swiss banks, and in the aftermath of the crisis with Switzerland, further claims against German companies that used forced and slave labor during WWII started jeopardizing US foreign policy objectives in Europe. The joint processes of Americanization and judicialization of reparations dispute settlements was therefore not only turned against foreign diplomats but also against the classical agents of US hegemony: the State Department. Thus, reparations are one of the most paradigmatic cases of the broader shift from a Cold War vision of international politics where states are the sole players of international politics reduced to the rationalist game of the pursuit of national interest to a more complex vision of global politics where norms, instruments and concepts are constraining both state and non-state actors. Judicialization is a market based process whose epicenter is American society and that is spurred by communitarian politics in an era of accrued fluidity of ideas, identity and investments at the global level.

Twenty years later, the lesson seems to have been learnt by the US Federal government, whose foreign policy is increasingly performed, not by the State Department, but by the Treasury Department and the judiciary authorities in charge of exerting pressures on foreign banks so that they comply with a host of new global governance rules and policies put in place by the US Treasury. As said, the recent case against BNP-Paribas, which led to a record settlement, may be exemplary of the new instruments by which the US seeks to regulate global capitalism. In many ways, this chapter has thus described at the level of the instruments what other contributors to this volume (Dezalay and Garth 2002) have called the "dollarization" of the world economy.

References

Abend, Gabriel. 2014. *The Moral Background: An Inquiry into the History of Business Ethics*. Princeton: Princeton University Press.

Aristotle. 1988. *The Politics*. Cambridge: Cambridge University Press.

Ayad, Christophe. July, 2, 2014. "Pourquoi BNP Paribas a été prise au piège soudanais." *Le Monde*.

Barry, Brian. 1981. "Do Countries Have Moral Obligations? The Case of World Poverty." *Tanner Lectures on Human Values*. www.tannerlectures.utah.edu/abcd.html/

Bernardini, Bruno. 2007. *Le principe d'obligation*. Paris: Vrin.

Blais, Marie-Claude. 2007. *La solidarité: Histoire d'une idée*. Paris: Gallimard.

Blum, Léon. 1972. [1923]. "Discours du 24 mai 1923 au Congrès de l'Internationale socialiste à Hamburg," In *L'oeuvre, t.2*, 272–288. Paris: Albin Michel.

1972 [1924]. *Le populaire*. "M. Poincaré et les experts. Réponse au discours de Luna Park," 18 avril 1924. In *L'oeuvre, t.2*, 326–328. Paris: Albin Michel.

Bourgeois, Léon. 1919. *Le Traité de paix de Versailles*. Paris: Alcan.

Carabelli, Anna and Mario Cedrini. 2010. "Global Imbalances, Monetary Disorder and Shrinking Policy Space: Keynes' Legacy for our Troubled World." *Intervention* 7:303–323.

Chaumont, Jean-Michel. 1997. *La Concurrence des victimes génocide, identité, reconnaissance*. Paris, La Découverte.

Chorev, Nitsan. 2009. "The Judicial Transformation of the State: The Case of U.S. Trade Policy, 1974–2004." *Law & Policy* 31(1): 31–68.

Colonomos, Ariel and Andrea Armstrong. 2006. "German Reparations to the Jews After World War II: A Turning Point in the History of Reparations," pp. 390–419 in *The Handbook of Reparations*, edited by P. de Greiff. Oxford: Oxford University Press.

Colonomos, Ariel. 2008. *Moralizing International Relations – Called to Account*. New York: Palgrave.

Dezalay, Yves and Bryant Garth. 2002. *The Internationalization of Palace Wars: Lawyers, Economists, and the Contest to Transform Latin American States*. Chicago: University of Chicago Press.

de Lapradelle, Geouffre. 1918. *Examen de la responsabilité pénale de l'Empereur Guillaume I*. Paris: Imprimerie Nationale.

Eichengreen, Barry and Richard Portes. January 1987, "The Anatomy of Financial Crises." NBER Working Paper No. 2126, http://papers.ssrn.com/sol3/papers.cfm?abstract_id=227380

Feinberg, Joel, 1968, "Collective Responsibility," *Journal of Philosophy*, 65: 674–688

Flandreau, Marc, Carl L. Holtfrerich and Harold James. (eds.) 2003. *International Financial History in The Twentieth Century: System and Anarchy*. Cambridge: Cambridge University Press

Fletcher, George. 2002. *Romantics at War: Glory and Guilt in the Age of Terrorism*. Princeton: Princeton University Press.

French, Peter. 1974. "Morally Blaming Whole Populations," pp. 266–285 in Virginia Held, Sidney Morgenbesser, Thomas Nagel (eds.), *Philosophy, Morality and International Affairs*. New York: Oxford University Press.

Garfinkel, Harold, "Conditions of Successful Degradation Ceremonies," *American Journal of Sociology*, vol. 61, 5, March 1956: 420–424.

Gide, Charles. 1932. *La solidarité, Cours au collège de France 1927–8*. Paris: PUF.

Gide, Charles and William Oualid. 1931. "Le bilan de la guerre pour la France," pp. 1–34 in J. Shotwell (ed.), *Histoire économique et sociale de la guerre mondiale*. Paris: PUF and Carnegie Endowment for International Peace.

Goldhagen, Daniel. 1996. *Hitler's Willing Executioners: Ordinary Germans and the Holocaust*. New York: Knopf.

2002. *A Moral Reckoning: the Role of the Catholic Church in the Holocaust and its Unfulfilled Duty to Repair*. New York: Knopf.

Gulati, Mitu and Sarah Ludington. 2008. "A Convenient Untruth: Fact and Fantasy in the Doctrine of Odious Debts," *Virginia Journal of International Law* 48: 595–639.

Hall, Peter A. (ed.) 1989. *The Political Power of Economic Ideas: Keynesianism across Nations*. Princeton, NJ: Princeton University Press.

Jaspers, Karl. 2001. *The Question of German Guilt*. New York: Fordham University Press.

Kofman, Sarah. 1991. "L'art de ne pas payer ses dettes," pp. 97–100, in Sarah Kofman, Jean-Yves Masson (eds.), *Don Juan ou le refus de la dette*. Paris: Galilée.

Koskenniemi, Martti. 2001. *The Gentle Civilizer of Nations. The Rise and Fall of International Law*. Cambridge: Cambridge University Press.

Latour, Bruno. 1987. *Science in Action: How to Follow Scientists and Engineers through Society*. Cambridge, MA: Harvard University Press.

Maier, Charles. 2003. "Overcoming the Past? Narrative and Negotiation, Remembering and Reparations Issues at the Interface of History and the Law," pp. 277–294 in J. Torpey (ed.), *Politics and the Past: On Repairing Historical Injustices*. New York: Rowman & Littlefield Publishers.

Maier, Charles. 1988. *Recasting Bourgeois Europe: Stabilization in France, Germany and Italy in the Decade after World War I*. Princeton, NJ: Princeton University Press.

Mallard, Grégoire. 2011. "The Gift Revisited: Marcel Mauss on War, Debt and the Politics of Reparations." *Sociological Theory* 29(4): 225–247.

Mallard, Grégoire and Anne Holthoefer. Forthcoming. "Responsible or Guilty? Interpretive Polysemy in the German Reparations Debate," in Adam Seippe and Pierre Purseigle (eds.), *Oxford Handbook of the First World War*. Oxford: Oxford University Press.

Marks, Sally. 1978. "The Myth of Reparations," *Central European History*, 11: 231–255.

2013. "Mistakes and Myths: The Allies, Germany, and the Versailles Treaty, 1918–1921." *The Journal of Modern History* 85.

Mauss, Marcel. 1997 [1922]. "Les changes 2. Une politique, un exemple sinistre, l'Autriche." *Le populaire*, December 5, 1922, pp. 480–483 in *Ecrits politiques*, p. 481.

1997 [1924]. "Les changes 4. Comment le gouvernement a exporté des francs. Les dépenses militaires et impériales." *Le populaire*, January 22, 1924, pp. 579–582 in *Ecrits politiques*, p. 580.

1997 [1924]. "Les changes. L'inflation fiduciaire." *Le populaire*, March 17, 1924, pp. 647–650 in *Ecrits politiques*, p. 652.

May, Larry. 1992. *Sharing Responsibility*, Chicago, University of Chicago Press.
Moravcsik, Andrew. 2000. "The Origins of Human Rights Regimes: Democratic Delegation in Postwar Europe." *International Organization* 54(2): 217–252.
Risse, Thomas and Kathryn Sikkink. 1999. "The Socialization of Human Rights Norms into Domestic Practices: An Introduction," pp. 1–38, in Thomas Risse, Stephen C. Ropp, and Kathryn Sikkink (eds.), *The Power of Human Rights: International norms and domestic change*. Cambridge: Cambridge University Press, 1999.
Sack, Alexander. 1927. *Les effets des transformations des Etats sur leurs dettes publiques et autres obligations financières: traité juridique et financier*. París: Recueil Sirey.
Schmitt, Carl. 2003[1950]. *The Nomos of the Earth in the International Law of the Jus Publicum Europaeum*. New York: Telos Press.
Schuker, Stephen A. 1988. *American "Reparations" to Germany, 1919–1933*. Princeton, Princeton University Press.
State Department. 1997. *U.S. and Allied Efforts To Recover and Restore Gold and Other Assets Stolen or Hidden by Germany During World War II*, prepared by Dr. Greg Bradsher, for The Interagency Group On Nazi Assets, Coordinated by Stuart E. Eizenstat, Under-Secretary of State for Economics, Business, and Agriculture, Special Envoy of The Department of State on Property Restitution in Central and Eastern Europe. National Archives and Records Administration, College Park, Maryland.
Tetlock, Philip and Aaron Belkin (eds.). 1996. *Counterfactual Thoughts Experiments in World Politics*. Princeton: Princeton University Press.
Torpey, John. 2003. "Introduction: Politics and the Past," pp. 1–36, in J. Torpey (ed.), *Politics and the Past: On Repairing Historical Injustices*. New York: Rowman & Littlefield Publishers.
2006. *Making Whole What Has Been Smashed: On Reparations Politics*. Cambridge, MA: Harvard University Press.
Trachtenberg, Marc, 1979. "Reparation at the Paris Peace Conference." *Journal of Modern History* 51: 24–55.
Wasserstrom, Richard. "The Responsibility of the Individual for War Crimes" pp. 47–70, in Virginia Held , Sidney Morgenbesser, Thomas Nagel (eds.), op. cit.

CHAPTER EIGHT

THE CHANGING IDEAS ABOUT VALUATION MECHANISMS IN THE INTERWAR PERIOD: TOEPLITZ, MARLIO AND THE "GREAT TRANSFORMATION"[1]

Marco Bertilorenzi and Giuseppe Telesca

Many analysts of markets see in prices a mechanism of coordination between buyers and sellers of goods. Neoclassical economists believe that for market coordination to be efficient, prices have to freely fluctuate (Officer 2014). But not all agree that markets work efficiently when prices are freely floated. Sociologists have demonstrated that the valuation of goods in markets is not always free from administrative or social imperatives, nor that it should be (Callon et al. 2007; Callon 1998). On the contrary, many alternative valuation devices work more efficiently than the determination of prices based on comparisons between quantities of goods demanded and supplied. Famous sociologists like Karl Polanyi warned their contemporaries that this was even truer when markets became global. According to Polanyi, in the second part of the nineteenth century it was the *Haute Finance* that assured the good operation of markets on a world scale. The author, in a book highly critical of the opaque idea of self-regulating markets, imagined the global markets of the late nineteenth centuries as loosely regulated by what he defined a "powerful social" instrument, flexible and very effective, which was able to remain "independent of single governments, [but] in touch with all; independent of the central banks, even of the Bank of England, [but] closely connected with them" (Polanyi 1944:10). During normal economic times, the *Haute Finance* provided a loose form of

[1] The authors contributed to the writing of this chapter in an equal way. Marco Bertilorenzi wrote sections 3 and 4, while Giuseppe Telesca is the author of sections 1 and 2; introduction and conclusion were written together.

coordination, reinforced by the tight sociability of elite bankers (the *entre-soi* that Bourdieu talks about), which allowed markets to operate quite efficiently even when crises associated with the making of global markets emerged, as in the case of Baring's bail-out in 1890 for instance (Ford 1956; Mitchener and Weidenmier 2008; Cassis 2011:9–13).

It has been correctly pointed out that Polanyi's idea about the *Haute Finance* is postulated rather than demonstrated. Polanyi, for instance, does not offer any insights on the mechanism through which the *Haute Finance* managed to grant "the hundred years' peace" to the world – a research question that has fascinated economists working on the theory of group and organization (Olson 1965), political scientists working in the field of international relations (Kirshner 2007; Tomz 2007), and economic historians (Flores and Flandreau 2012). Polanyi does not explain either the structure or the composition of the *Haute Finance*, limiting himself to mention the House of Rothschild as the pillar of this "mysterious institution." In spite of this vagueness, one of the main heuristic insights of Polanyi's book is that markets' self-regulation is an historical construction and not a natural fact. The real breakthrough of Polanyi was to consider the creation of a *laissez-faire* economy as the outcome of deep interventions by governments, and its continuation as a real commitment by economic and financial elites. Polanyi was struck by a paradox of the liberal economic thought that, from the enclosures onwards, had consistently failed to recognize that "the introduction of free markets, far from doing away with the need of control, regulation, and intervention, enormously increased their range. [...] This paradox was topped by another. While *laissez-faire* economy was the product of deliberate state action, subsequent restrictions on *laissez-faire* started in a spontaneous way. *Laissez-faire* was planned; planning was not" (Polanyi 1944:140–141). If the affirmation of the liberal economy was led by the *Haute Finance* in the nineteenth century, the commitment of financial and industrial elites was decisive in the attempt of "recasting bourgeois Europe" after the shock of the Great War (Maier 1975). The financial dogma to stabilize currencies, which spread throughout the 1920s and captured the energy of governments, central banks and new intergovernmental agencies, was highly engaging for private bankers committed to this economic paradigm. Likewise, the return to prewar free trade, advocated by national and international public powers as a medium/long-term goal of the international polity after the Treaty of Versailles, became an explicit commitment for the industrial elites.

Like Polanyi, we are interested in the question of valuation in global markets. Also like Polanyi, we are interested in the shattering effects of the Great War on the forms of market coordination that were held legitimate before the conflict. For this reason, we investigate the transition from the late nineteenth century forms of regulation of these global markets to the interwar period, with the goal of providing a better understanding of the mechanisms that affect the legitimacy of various valuation devices over time.

This scrutiny provides insights into the process of valuation: while advocating the free market and market self-regulation as crucial for the creation of value in their business, financial and business elites created more or less informal coordination tools that, deeply altering the free market process, ended up becoming the new devices presiding over the process of valuation of both financial products and commodities. In some cases, this movement produced even paradoxical ideas: for instance that financial speculation could help the currency stabilization or that cartels could help the settlement of free trade (Hara 1994; Barjot 1994, 2013). In this paper, we ask: after the First World War (WWI), what happened to the informal mode of regulation which had allowed prices to be sustained artificially when markets failed and prices plummeted? Did the legitimacy of this informal mode of regulation resist the sweeping changes introduced in the economy by its total mobilization for the war effort?

To answer these questions, we adopt a Bourdieuan approach to the sociology of valuation devices, based on methods that are close the prosopographic approaches of elites. Among the groups that we identify as having a key influence on the choice of valuation devices during the transition that interests us, we focus on the *Haute Finance* and the elite industrialists. We identify both groups as strong supporters of the idea of self-regulation of markets, a concept which was understood very differently from today. Far from meaning that prices should never be the object of interventions by powerful market actors, this idea of self-regulation meant that some interventions on prices were legitimate when conducted by powerful private global forces (cartels of producers for instance) while others (conducted by the state in particular) were not. Central in this question of legitimacy of pricing techniques was the boundary drawn between social groups, as the sociology of valuation and boundary-making tells us (Lamont 2012).

Section one and two of this paper deal with a case study in the world of high banking to illustrate the pre-war financial elites' initial resilience, and then adaptation, to the transformations in the forms of regulation of global markets after WWI. These sections are centered around the figure of Józef Leopold Toeplitz (1866–1938), the *Banca Commerciale Italiana* (BCI's) executive director from 1915 to 1933. Founded in Milan in 1894, within a few decades the BCI became the Italian universal bank prototype and the most important bank in the country.[2] The third and fourth sections look at Louis Marlio (1878–1952), executive director of *Pechiney*, the French aluminum champion of which he became president in 1939.

Building on Pierre Bourdieu's theory of human capital, the first section explores Toeplitz's "set of the usable resources and powers" acquired before WWI – an endowment probably inadequate to deal with the challenges spawned by the "Great Transformation." However, Bourdieu's observation that individuals can convert one type of capital into another, and hence modify the volume and distribution of their assets over time, offers a possible explanation for Toeplitz's post-war resilience (Bourdieu 2010:119–126). Generalizing Toeplitz's experience, one can assume that, even though, in the face of the interwar financial disturbances, the loose and informal regulation of markets of the late nineteenth century was no longer efficient, older bankers still abided by the old rules. In section two we will see this in relation to Toeplitz and the currency market during the 1920s.

The third and fourth sections show, starting from the example of Marlio, how industrialists confronted with a deep economic crisis innovated by formalizing new rules of valuation. In particular, it explores the way in which Marlio, one of the main representatives of the industrial elite who participated in the process of legitimation of cartels, interacted with a new group of technocrats within newborn international organizations such as the International Chamber of Commerce (ICC) and the League of Nations (LoN). These institutions and their forbearers made clear their intention to both come back to economic orthodoxy and free trade, and ease the re-integration of the markets after the shock of the war. As these sections demonstrate, the perception of cartels changed during the interwar years, as they moved from being seen as institutions of international economic self-regulation during the 1920s, to being perceived as instruments

[2] In 1929, the BCI's total assets were equal to 10,358 million lire, compared with the 6,748 of the *Credito Italiano*. In continental Europe, only the *Deutsche Bank* (with 13,669 million) and the *Darmstädter* (10,721 million) fared better than the BCI (Confalonieri 1994:245).

which governments supported, endorsed, or even controlled during the 1930s.

THE TRAJECTORY OF JÓZEF TOEPLITZ: A PRIVILEGED SON OF THE FIRST GLOBALIZATION

Toeplitz was born in Zychlin, near Warsaw, on 10 December 1866. Fifth of eleven children, he was part of an influential Polish-Jewish family with interests in agriculture, trade and banking. Since a Polish national state did not exist in 1866, Toeplitz acquired Russian nationality. The wealthy status of his family gave him the opportunity to enjoy a cosmopolitan education in Mitau, Gand and Aachen. Although he did not finalize his master's in engineering, the experience gained abroad during these years would prove crucial for his career (Telesca 2010: 19–21).

In 1890, Toeplitz moved to Genoa with the aim of learning the banking profession by exploiting both his qualities and his family ties with the then director of the *Banca Generale* (BG) Genoa subsidiary, Otto Joel.[3] A few years later, in 1893–1894, the Italian banks went through difficulties both due to internal factors, their tendency to over-invest in real estate assets, and external shocks – a typical episode of capital outflows from periphery to core countries (De Cecco 1990:22–23). This turmoil led to the salvaging of one of the then existing issuing institutes, the *Banca Romana*, and the collapse of the two biggest banks inspired by the Péréire brothers' model, the *Credito Mobiliare* and the BG (Quilici 1935; Pantaleoni 1977). A momentous change in the Italian banking system ensued, and was built on a reorganization of the issuing institutes and the founding of universal banks inspired by the German model.[4] Joel, who was general inspector at the BG when it collapsed, played a crucial role in the months that preceded the founding of the BCI (October 1894) and, together with his German colleague Friedrich Weil, he was appointed as a BCI executive director (Garruccio 2002).

After a brief adventure as director at the newly established Genoa subsidiary of the *Banca Russa* (BR) – a choice prompted by a desire to

[3] Toeplitz's uncle, Benedikt, was married to Joel's aunt, Friederike.

[4] In August 1892 the *Banca Nazionale del Regno*, the *Banca Toscana di Credito* and the *Banca Nazionale Toscana* merged into the *Banca d'Italia*. The law provided for the newly established bank a prominent status with respect to the already existing issuing institutes: *Banco di Napoli* and *Banco di Sicilia* (Bonelli and Cerrito 2003:103–106).

move closer to Poland, the BR headquarters being located in St Petersburg – in June 1895, Toeplitz joined his mentor at the BCI (Toeplitz 1963:32–33). The move to Milan inaugurated Toeplitz's slow ascent to the BCI's summit. Initially, the banker flanked Joel in a series of minor affairs and merchant banking activities (Confalonieri 1979:339–349). Afterwards, Toeplitz was entrusted with the opening of two crucial subsidiaries in Naples and Venice, making him a key protagonist of the BCI's territorial expansion through the country. In Naples, he built up crucial relationships, among others with Giuseppe Volpi and Dannie Heineman, which we will return to later. Toeplitz's return to Milan in 1903 resulted in a growing involvement in the BCI's industrial business and marked a further step toward top-tier positions. On the one hand, he was appointed fiduciary on the boards of an increasing number of BCI's client firms (in 1930 Toeplitz was member of forty-five boards of directors in both firms and banks);[5] on the other hand, when a consortium of banks headed by the Bank of Italy (BoI) saved the *Società Bancaria Italiana* (SBI) from bankruptcy in 1907, Toeplitz was entrusted with scrutinizing the SBI's balance sheets on behalf of the BCI. When the BCI's governance reform eventually materialized – establishing a functional separation between the headquarters and the Milan offices – Toeplitz was called to the helm of the branch and subsidiary inspection services, thus attaining the crucial role of coordinating between the bank's centre and its periphery. This took place in November 1907, and Toeplitz's ascent indicated a future succession to his mentor. During his apprenticeship at the BCI, Toeplitz had learned how to perform the four roles that, according to information economics, characterize financial intermediaries: monitoring, coordination, control and commitment (Bhattacharya and Thakor 1993).

Before WWI, Italian bankers' practical knowledge was not framed in any theoretical scheme, nor was such a pattern uncommon in other countries, except for France, where the education of bankers was a more formalized process (Cassis 1991:67–68). A move in the1890s from the *Crédit Mobilier* to the *Kreditbanken* model, combined with a shift from unit to branch banking, induced the newly established Italian banks to look for a set of skills that academia was still unable to supply. To fill this gap, the new banking elite was partly recruited from abroad, and partly selected among Italian bankers whose know-how was obtained

[5] Archivio Storico Intesa-Sanpaolo (hereafter ASI-BCI), Database fiduciari Banca Commerciale Italiana in progress.

on the job (Piluso 1998). The considerable number of foreign directors and managers at the BCI can be justified on this ground, rather than relying on the nationalists' mystifications against the "German banks". The foreign bankers granted to the Italian universal banks a competitive advantage consisting of the transfer of financial technology, networks and information (Goldshmit 1969:363).

Toeplitz, who had become an Italian citizen in January 1912,[6] succeeded *de facto* to Joel at the helm of the BCI in spring 1915, amid the trouble instigated by the Italian intervention in WWI and a hidden struggle for control of the BCI (Montanari 1995:23). His leadership, together with the Italian Fenoglio, became official only in March 1917.[7] Three years later when Fenoglio resigned, Toeplitz became "the boss" of the BCI.[8] He remained at the helm of the bank until March 1933, when he was obliged to resign.[9] Afterwards, Toeplitz served another year as deputy President of the board, before abandoning the BCI and the scene of the Italian economy. In 1938, following Benito Mussolini's order to give no relevance to the news of his death, only obituaries in the national newspapers briefly acknowledged the end of a banker who, *The New York Times* emphatically recalled, once had "his finger on the pulse of three-quarters of the nation's largest firms."[10]

Bourdieu explains that a similar quantity of cultural capital produces a different yield according to the social agent's possibility of mobilizing a network of more or less institutionalized relations. Toeplitz's cultural capital – already above the average because of his cosmopolitan education – was strengthened by the "multiplier effect" of his prestigious social capital (Bourdieu 1980). It has already been mentioned that he was Joel's cousin; it must also be specified that his father, Bonawentura, was a correspondent of the Rothschild Frankfurt branch and his uncle, Henryk, was among the founders of the most important commercial bank in Warsaw, the Bank Handlowy (Toeplitz 2004:363–368). In other words, Toeplitz's family was part of the "*comédie financière*" that, "from the titans of the City or the *Chaussée d'Antin*, to their trusted correspondents in the great ports and entrepôt, to small local bankers

6 Archivio di Stato di Milano, Gabinetto Prefettura I, 532, Ufficio di Stato Civile di Milano, 1 February 1912.

7 ASI-BCI, Verbali Consiglio di Amministrazione (hereafter VCA), 27 March 1917.

8 *Il padrone* was the epithet which designed Toeplitz among his inner circle of collaborators (Malagodi 1999:73).

9 ASI-BCI, Verbali Assemblea Generale, vol. IV, ff. 68–69, 25 March 1933.

10 "Giuseppe Toeplitz, Financier, is Dead," *The New York Times*, 30 January 1938.

in manufacturing centers and agricultural markets," distinguished the different tiers of the *Haute Finance* (Landes 1958:16). Toeplitz's status was not comparable, either in terms of social prestige or in terms of political influence, with that of the "aristocratic bourgeoisie" which had dominated international finance before 1914 (Harris and Thane 1984; Cassis 1994), however, by means of his origin and education, his position and functions within the BCI, and the ties built with the Italian business community and abroad, Toeplitz had a significant amount of human capital at his disposal from which most of his colleagues were precluded.

Bourdieu's human capital can be seen as the "aces in a game of cards" that define the chances of an individual of "profiting in a particular field" (Bourdieu 1985:724). Some individuals have better chances of being prominent in a certain field because they are endowed with more capital than others – this was the case of Toeplitz before WWI. An individual's process of capital formation, however, is a dynamic one that can experience both accumulation and erosion. After WWI, the bankers of Toeplitz's generation were confronted with an erosion of their capital, namely the cultural one acquired on-the-job training and inadequate to deal with the completely new scenario. The stabilization of the currencies during the 1920s, analyzed in the next section, exemplifies this process of loss. This case study can be seen as a sort of natural experiment to test a broader reality, which, during the interwar years, confronted a generation of top-league bankers obliged to adjust to the new climate.

TOEPLITZ'S CAREER DURING THE INTERWAR YEARS: A PAINFUL PROCESS OF APPRENTICESHIP

After WWI, returning to the same path of the *belle époque*'s economic growth by simply imitating the pre-war recipes proved to be damaging. In particular, the persistence of a gold standard *mentalité* became the symbol of the stubborn resolution with which the post-war imbalances were treated. The commitment to gold convertibility, rather than to domestic fundamentals such as employment and growth, far from unraveling the problems, added new obstacles to their solution (Eichengreen 1992; Eichengreen and Temin 2000). The "erratic and perverse" behavior of capital movements did the rest (Bloomfield 1950).

A few nonconformist economists and publicists dared to indicate a different way out of the crisis. Inspired by the success of Keynes' *The*

Economic Consequences of the Peace (1919), this group of intellectuals deployed a remarkable activism in promoting appeals, conferences and other initiatives. If the unorthodox stances of these iconoclasts rendered them "*persona non grata* in orthodox banking circles during the 1920s" (Schuker 2003:65–66), their proposals received a good deal of attention both within international organizations such as the LoN and the ICC, and in the specialized press. In November 1921, for instance, the *Rivista Bancaria* (RB) – founded one year before under the auspices of the newly established Italian banking association – published Gustav Cassel's report on currency stabilization, presented at the LoN Financial Committee in September 1921. The document invited, *inter alia*, to ignore the pre-war parity of currencies in order to escape the deflationary effects of a painful adjustment. Cassel suggested the adoption of some form of managed currency stabilization, a solution which would have implied the direct intervention of the governments (Cassel 1921).

Commenting on Cassel's report, the director of the RB, Attilio Cabiati, included in his article the anonymous opinions of two prominent Italian bankers. As emerges from the BCI's archives, Toeplitz was one of them.[11] In his contribution, the banker dismissed Cassel's ideas as "utopias" destined to thrill "the large public" but which fell short in the eyes of both rational scholars and wise practitioners. Toeplitz defined "harmful" and "artificial" Cassel's plan, adding sarcastically that its "only positive aspect consisted in the difficulty to turn it into practice." Only the reliance on "old formulas" and "permanent principles" could have produced the conditions for a real economic recovery according to the banker, who assigned a crucial role to the speculation which "cooperated to the balance of payment's equilibrium of the countries, namely the ones with a weak currency" (Cabiati 1921:597–598).

Toeplitz's enthusiasm for speculation can be understood not only in light of his mindset firmly grounded in the *laissez-faire* era, but also if one considers the remarkable profits realized by the BCI in currency arbitrations during that period.[12] Having outlined Toeplitz's initial perspective, two attempts of currency stabilization in which the BCI played a significant role – the Polish loan (1924) and the maneuvers for the stabilization of the Italian lira (1925–1926) – will provide the base for

[11] Toeplitz sent a letter to Cabiati which was partially reproduced in the article (ASI-BCI, Copialettere Toeplitz (hereafter CpT) 17, ff. 1–3).

[12] In 1925, faced with the first signs of a deflationary twist, Toeplitz told his board of directors that the new governmental policy would mean less profits in currency arbitrations, a situation that everyone had to "peacefully accept" (ASI-BCI, VCA, 30 June 1925).

exploring Toeplitz's difficult process of adaptation to the new reality during the 1920s.

The appointment of Wladyslaw Grabski as prime minister, in December 1923, created the conditions for the launch of a BCI Polish loan. Grabski, convinced that Poland was able to stabilize the currency without being obliged to endure the severe prescriptions of the LoN, at the beginning of 1924 established a central bank independent of the government (Bank Polski) and withdrew the worthless Polish mark, replacing it with the *zloty*. Grabski's maneuver, consisting of introducing a new currency without previously balancing the budget, was built on Poland's capacity to negotiate a series of piecemeal loans, which were less costly in political terms (Pease 1986:22–25). The BCI was the first bank to buy into this strategy, with the offer of a 400 million lire loan for twenty years at 7 per cent.[13] The negotiations ended in March 1924 and the loan was floated in two tranches: three hundred million lire were offered on 18 April and the remaining hundred million by the end of October. The loan, officially devoted to the constitution of the Polish tobacco monopoly and the modernization of the sector, established that 60 percent of the imported tobacco should come from Italy. Its alleged commercial purpose, however, did not remove the risk that the loan could be used – and was used, indeed – to buy foreign reserves, in the case of difficulties of the *zloty* (Asso 1993:123–142). This risk was stressed upon by the Director of the BoI, Bonaldo Stringher – unaware of the negotiations and finding himself faced by a *fait accompli* – in an irritable letter to the then Finance Minister Alberto De Stefani, on 8 March 1924 (De Cecco 1993:755).

Toeplitz saw in the Polish loan the first of a series of ambitious stabilization loans led by the BCI in Eastern Europe. Well aware of the risks connected to the loan, however, he had conditioned the conclusion of the negotiations on an Italian government assurance of intervening in the case of war and replacing the Polish government in the payment of the interest.[14] Surprised by such an atypical axis between the government and the BCI, not always on good terms, the American

[13] With the lira floating around quota twenty-three against the dollar, the loan was worth more than seventeen million dollars.

[14] The performance of the BCI Polish loan, despite the success of the placement of the first *tranche* (with a demand ten times greater than the supply), faded when the weakening of the *zloty* and the failure of Grabski's political attempt urged the Polish government to use the Italian currency to defend the Polish currency. At the end of 1931, the BCI portfolio was still engulfed with seventy million lire of the 1924 Polish loan (Asso 1993:331–335).

ambassador in Rome wrote to his secretary of state that Toeplitz had obtained Mussolini's guarantee on the Polish loan in return for BCI support in the impending elections of April 1924 (De Cecco 1993:755–756). The reality is simpler than that. We have seen how bankers of Toeplitz's generation saw currency stabilization as a process to be worked out by private capital markets rather than by (and through) the LoN. Moreover, since the Polish loan was functional to Mussolini's political interests, Toeplitz's pragmatic strategy was to take advantage of his influence in his motherland to negotiate a loan meant to strengthen his frail relations with the *Duce* and lessen the authority of the Italian central bank.

Apart from personal divergences, which are not surprising if one considers the *milieu* from which they came, there were objective reasons for the Stringher-Toeplitz conflict. Stringher had been general director of the Treasury before running the BoI. A convinced nationalist, at the beginning of the 1920s Stringher understood his role as central banker in a different way to that set out at the 1922 Genoa international monetary conference (James 2001:33–34). By mid 1920s, however, the wave of stabilization programs related to international cooperation schemes to which the BoI had been called to take part, and the moral suasion of Montagu Norman (governor of the Bank of England) and Benjamin Strong (governor of the New York Fed), had the effect of slowly converting Stringher to the doctrine of central banking.[15]

The BCI Polish loan was at odds with the enforcement of central banks international cooperation supported by Norman. It was considered a premature move also by private bankers such as Russel Leffingwell of the House of Morgan which, in 1923, had rebuffed an attempt by the Polish government to negotiate a small loan. While the English central banker refused the logic of Toeplitz's artificial stabilization of the *zloty*, the American private banker was concerned by the depressing outlook of the Polish economy, worsened by the geopolitical fragility of the country and the unsolved problem of its war debts towards the United States. In the wake of the BCI, in February 1925 the American bank Dillon, Read and Co. negotiated another unsuccessful loan with

[15] That the process was far from being concluded is confirmed by an editorial of *The Banker*. In assessing the functioning, power and independence of different central banks around the world, the prestigious review considered the central banks of France and Belgium as "more or less willing instrument of weak financial Governments." The BoI was considered in the same terms, even though, the editorial added, "to a lesser extent" ("A Survey of World Banking," *The Banker*, June 1926:443–448).

Poland that "far from furnishing Poland with her coveted breakthrough loan,...stigmatized the Polish state in the eyes of financial community" (Pease 1986:39). It was only after the coup d'état staged by Józef Piłsudski in May 1926, that an improved economic situation stimulated a growing inflow of foreign capital (Landau and Tomaszewski 1990: 275). In this climate, the American bank Blair and Co., through the intermediation of its French subsidiary led by Jean Monnet, negotiated with the Polish government a stabilization loan that presented more than a similarity with the BCI loan. In a context of declining mutual trust between central banks, the Polish loan became another source of tension between the Bank of England, the Banque de France and the Federal reserve of New York (Meyer 1970).

From an internal perspective, the 1924 Polish loan exposed dramatically the BoI and BCI's contrasting opinions about the hierarchy within the Italian banking system. In Stringher's view, the BoI, as systemic "bank of the banks," was called on to manage the reserves which, together with savings, represented the measure of liquidity. Toeplitz considered the BoI a mere "bank among banks." In his scheme, the universal banks "created" money and the central bank had to provide lending of last resort in cases of liquidity shortage (Piluso 2011). This actually happened in June 1925, when the BCI underwent serious liquidity difficulties due to a massive withdrawal of foreign deposits, and the BoI was forced to inject liquidity to the tune of 30 percent of the bank's total fund raising (Toniolo 2003:325). In July 1925 Volpi replaced De Stefani as Minister of Finance. The move was likely due to the mounting hostility of the business community against De Stefani – namely against his controversial decree to curb the exuberance of stock markets (February 1925) that, coupled with the increase in the discount rate from 5.5 to 6 percent, triggered a bourse collapse which anticipated the 1926 deflationary turnaround (Baia Curioni 1995:330–342).

The entry of Volpi in the control room of the Italian economy represented good news for Toeplitz and the BCI. The Count of Misurata, the city in Libya where Volpi had resided as Governor of Tripolitania, had maintained an excellent relationship with Toeplitz after meeting him in Naples at the end of the century (see section one). In particular, the arrival of Volpi provided a competitive edge to Toeplitz against Stringher when, between August 1925 and May 1926, the control of the Italian currency passed into the hands of Volpi at the expense of the BoI. In an endeavor to strengthen the lira, Volpi sought the help of the BCI, which had already received authorization to intervene in matters regarding the currency in June 1925 and could put at the disposal of the minister its inestimable treasure of know-how and information. During the 1920s, the BCI was the Italian bank with the most sophisticated multinational network (D'Alessandro 1998; Di Quirico 1999; Piluso and Toninelli 2002). The London and New York branches, opened respectively in 1911 and 1918, represented a key tool for Volpi to defeat speculation. In a context of mounting instability, the BCI could play a key role in organizing the defense of the lira through reducing the asymmetry of information. For this reason, immediately after his appointment Volpi asked Toeplitz to keep him posted "on a daily basis," about any significant movements related to the currency market.[16] The maneuver, based on a document produced by the BCI in May 1925, envisaged a shift in the defense of the lira from the spot to the forward markets.[17] Yet, the most remarkable feature of the combined action of Toeplitz and Volpi in defense of the lira was that it entailed a large use of speculation in order to beat private investors on their own ground.

Volpi's aim was to get the course of the lira under control before discussing the inter-ally debt agreements with the United States and the United Kingdom (Romano 1979:131–141). The containment of inflation through a capping of salaries, and the possibility of getting credit from abroad, following agreements reached with the United States (November 1925) and the United Kingdom (January 1926) on the repayment of the inter-ally debts, represented the ingredients of the successful currency management carried out by Toeplitz and Volpi until spring 1926. Subsequently, the lira, which had remained for a while in the region of 120 against the British pound, lost 18 percent of its value between April and August. This deterioration pointed to the necessity of stabilizing "twin currencies" such as the French and Belgian franc, strictly linked to the lira and the Italian economy. Moreover, it urged Mussolini – pressed by the international financial community– to give a new governance to the currency.

The Polish loan and the facts of 1925–1926 had reinvigorated Stringher's determination to defend the BoI's autonomy, not only against the government, but also against the claims of the commercial banking system. In this process Stringher became, in the eyes of Strong,

16 ASI-BCI, Segreteria Toeplitz (hereafter ST) 82, fasc. 5, Baracchi's letter to Toeplitz, 13 July 1925. Toeplitz did inform Volpi on a regular basis about movements on the currency market (ASI-BCI, ST 82, Toeplitz' letters to Volpi, 1, 8 and 13 August 1925).

17 The document of 26 May 1925, entitled "Mutamenti nelle tendenze del mercato dei cambi e causa della mancanza di divise estere in Italia," is in De Cecco (1993:940–943).

"a thoroughgoing central banker," able to "talk the language in orthodox style."[18] Meeting the Duce in May 1926, Strong was adamant about the fact that a stabilization plan could not disregard Stringher and the BoI, which had to be the pivot of the maneuver (De Cecco 1993:64–67). Mussolini's speech in Pesaro, on 18 August 1926, sent a strong signal to the international markets and launched a dramatic appreciation of the lira. While Mussolini was launching his "battle for *quota* 90," a series of reforms related to the stabilization of the lira and the adoption of the gold standard were implemented. In July 1926 a Royal Decree granted the BoI the monopoly of note issuing. In September 1926 a law was passed for the protection of savings conferred to the BoI supervisory powers on the Italian banking system (Conti 2008:435–437). The lira was eventually stabilized at 92.46 sterling in December 1927. Toeplitz was obliged to cheer Mussolini when *quota* 90 was achieved.[19] In the months which preceded the stabilization, however, he did not conceal his frustration with the monetary policy pursued by the regime. The critiques were directed not against the stabilization *per se*, but against the level of the lira's appreciation.[20] While the strategic defeat of Toeplitz was taking place, Stringher could proudly write to his "colleagues" Norman and Strong that the BoI had "enter[ed] into absolute possession of the reserves" and had "assume[d] the responsibility of maintaining the gold value of the lira."[21]

Did the events of the mid 1920s affect Toeplitz's original beliefs on currency stabilization? A letter of the Polish-born banker provides an enlightening answer to this question. The letter, written in February 1931, was addressed to his old friend, the engineer and industrialist Heineman, who he met in Naples at the end of the nineteenth century (see section one). During the 1920s this cosmopolitan businessman, at the helm of the electrical multinational holding *Société financière de transports et d'entreprises industrielles* (Sofina), had been among the main supporters of Pan-Europa, the movement founded by Richard de Coudenhove-Kalergi. In the second part of the decade, he had argued for an international cartel of electricity producers and distributors. In

18 [Strong to Harrison, May 1926].

19 This achievement, in the affected wording of the banker "represented the basis for a steady and effective development of the Italian economy and the banking system" (See ASI-BCI, CpT 57, f. 19, telegram to Mussolini, 22 December 1927).

20 A large part of the Italian business community considered *quota* 120 the threshold below which the appreciation of the lira could harm the Italian economy (Baffi 1973:115).

21 [December 1927].

November 1930, Heineman was invited to Cologne by the then burgomaster Konrad Adenauer to give a talk on the future of Europe. On that occasion he presented the idea of a European federation – a plea which inspired similar events in Barcelona and Paris. Heineman's speeches were published in a pamphlet in English, French and German (Ranieri 2005:334–335). In *Outline of a New Europe*, Heineman built on the idea elaborated by the German engineer Oskar Oliven for a European electric network intended to create a bridge between the industrialized western Europe and the agricultural eastern Europe (Schot and Lagendijk 2008:207–201). To overcome the dualism between what Heineman defined as the "horse-power Europe A" and the "draught-horse Europe B," and to overcome the crisis in which it was engulfed, Europe had to find inspiration from the United States, and build its reconstruction on three pillars: one technical, the already mentioned electric network; one administrative, the removal of administrative barriers to trade; one financial, the free circulation of capitals (Heineman 1931).

Toeplitz received the French version of the pamphlet (*Esquisse d'une Europe nouvelle*) and wrote a long letter to his friend which contained a good deal of skepticism toward Heineman's ideas. Toeplitz conceded that in Europe there were twenty-seven countries whose borders represented an obstacle to business, but he invited his friend to consider that there were also about thirty different languages and seven religions to take into account, together with the strength of traditions and affinities that, in spite of Heineman's dreams, "paraît être plutôt en train de s'accroître que de diminuer." According to Toeplitz, Heineman's new Europe could work as a federation of engineers, but not as a federation of bankers. The bankers, as long as depositors give them not a single currency but "des lires, des livres, des francs ou des florins, symbols de particularismes nationaux, " would always stand "plus ou moins du côté des politiciens."[22]

This prescient letter was written in 1931. While in September, the gold exchange standard revealed the contradiction at the very core of the system, when the British Pound was obliged to abandon its ill-conceived parity, during the same year a systemic banking crisis involved several European countries: Austria, Germany, Hungary and Italy. In particular, the Credit-Anstalt's collapse, which triggered the trouble in May, marked the *nadir* of financial globalization, as Baring's

[22] Cfr. ASI-BCI, CpT 71, ff. 432–435, letter to Heinemann, 2 February 1931.

salvage had epitomized its zenith. Established by the Rothschilds during the middle of the 1850s, the glorious Viennese bank, chaired by Louis Von Rothschild, since the moment of its foundation "stood in the forefront of international finance" (Schubert 1991:11). With the solidarity within the international banking community weakened after WWI, as exemplified by the figures on the collapse of foreign bankers sitting in the board of directors of other countries' banks, the Credit-Anstalt's crisis proved that bankers could no longer save banks through informal late-night meetings in the secluded world of London clubs: new forms of regulation and valuation techniques were badly needed. The bankers, as Toeplitz bitterly acknowledged, had to sit on the side of politicians – a rather surprising change of perspective for a banker that, in 1916, had declared to the British ambassador in Rome that he did not believe in "political banks," and that banks "should confine [themselves] to business affair."[23]

LOUIS MARLIO. THE ACCUMULATION OF A HUGE HUMAN CAPITAL UNTIL THE GREAT WAR

Born on 3 February 1878, Marlio came from a relatively wealthy Parisian family which, however was not part of the French elite. His father studied law and was an official auctioneer (*commissaire priseur*) of the art and antiquities district of Paris, around *rue Drouot*, where the family lived until the death of Marlio's mother, in 1890. Marlio's social promotion passed through a successful education and then – as in the case of Toeplitz – by the Bourdieuan "multiplier effect" of his conspicuous social capital. When he was twenty years old, Marlio won the public competition to enter the *Ecole Polytechnique*, the leading French engineering school that formed a large part of the French administration and business elites. Marlio's classmates were, *inter alia*, the future car industrialist André Citroen and the pioneer of well logging industry Conrad Schlumberger (Pose 1955). According to the informal rules that governed the carriers of the graduates from the *Ecole Polytechnique*, the first ten of them usually continued their education at the *Ecole des Mines de Paris*, in order to enter in the *Grand Corp* of state engineers of mines, also known as X-Mines. The former *Polytechnique* students

[23] National Archives, Foreign Office, 368/1540, memorandum of James Rennell Rodd to the Foreign Minister Edward Gray, 1 June 1916.

ranking from the eleventh to the twentieth position were instead destined to the *Ecole des Ponts et Chaussées*, to then become members of the *Grand Corps* of state engineers of bridges, also known as X-Ponts (Joly 2013). Marlio ranked sixteenth and, following the classic *excursus honorum* of his education, became an X-Pont and passed through the different echelons of this administrative body from 1904 to 1910.[24]

At *Ponts et Chaussées*, Marlio became a disciple of the famous liberal economist Clement Colson, he too a former *X-Ponts*, who merged the classical liberalism of Jean-Baptiste Say with the marginalist approach of Léon Walras. Colson was a fine expert of the pricing of services under monopolies, such as railways and transports (Picory 1989; Le Van-Le Mesle 2005). This encounter not only crafted the political views of Marlio in the field of liberal economy; it also shaped the early career and the first orientation of the future *Grand Patron*. Actually, Marlio focused his main scientific interests into railways and waterways – the main interest of Colson as a scholar and state engineer. After his graduation at *Ponts et Chaussées*, Marlio undertook, like Colson, a further specialization in law (Pose 1955; Morsel 1987). He obtained a PhD in 1907 with a thesis dedicated to German policy of national water transportations, which was published a year later (Marlio 1908), and which he completed following a series of field trips he made to Germany as a state engineer.[25] After his PhD, he achieved an impressive career in the administration. In 1909 he served as *Chef du Cabinet Technique* of the Minister of Public Works Alexandre Millerand – a future President of the Republic during the 1920s. In 1910, when he was only thirty-two, he won the competition to become *Maître de Requêtes* (counsel) at the Council of State, one of the highest positions that a young officer could achieve within the French administration (Pose 1955; Morsel 1987; Hachez-Leroy 2010).

In parallel to his impressive career in the public administration, Marlio started also a brilliant career as professor in the Parisian academic field thanks to Colson's guidance and reputation. In 1908 he became professor of transports at the *Haute Ecole du Commerce* (HEC), in which Colson had taught until 1905. In 1910 he also obtained the

[24] Archives de l'Ecole Nationale des Ponts et Chaussées, Personal Documents of Louis Marlio. Archives nationales, fonds des membres de la légion d'honneur (base Léonore), file 1980/0035/11386.

[25] Archives nationales, fonds des membres de la légion d'honneur (base Léonore), file 1980/0035/11386.

chair of political economy (*économie politique*) at Sciences Po, in which Colson had become professor in 1905. In 1919, thanks to Colson, he was designed to substitute Charles Gide, one of the fathers of the corporatism in France who was opposed to liberalism (Pénin 1997), for the chair of social economics at the *Ecole des Ponts et Chaussées*. He also continued teaching at the HEC and at Sciences Po (international business) until the eve of the 1930s. In 1934, Marlio obtained also the chair in the section of economics at the *Academie des Sciences Morales et Politiques*, where both Colson and Millerand were already members.[26]

If the liberal economist Colson crafted Marlio's orientation at the University and his career in the administration and academia, the encounter with the socialist Millerand was decisive for his shift to the private business, where his experience of public servant emerged as a crucial factor. Between August 1914 and October 1915, Millerand served as Minister of War and Marlio, in his quality of top-level civil servant already implicated with Millerand when the latter was Minister of the Public Works, was mobilized at the center of the French war effort: the *Grand Quartier Général*. Once there, he occupied relevant positions in the administration of the transports and of the war supplies, getting in touch with the big French private business. As reported by Marlio himself (1927, 1938), the progressive impoverishment of public officers during the inflation years was the main cause of his shift to the more remunerative private business. Yet, the knowledge of the public machine matured during the war, his proximity with the Ministry of War, and his former experience as state engineer and top-level counsel, became a crucial competitive advantage for the firms that hired Marlio. Actually, in 1916, Marlio entered the board of governors of *Produits Chimiques d'Alais et de la Camargue* (PCAC), one of the leading French aluminum and chemical company. One year later, he was called to replace PCAC's general director, Adrien Badin, who died abruptly. At the same time, Marlio became the executive director of *Aluminium Français*, the French national cartel of the aluminum producers that served as the principal market organizer of the French aluminum market during WWI and afterward (Hachez-Leroy 1999).

The arrival of a high-level public servant at the head of both the main French aluminum producer and the commercial entity of this metal, epitomized the stronger bonds established, because of the war, between

[26] Archives de l'Ecole Nationale des Ponts et Chaussées, Personal Documents of Louis Marlio. ENPC, Enseignements, modules, professeurs, 1747–1992, ≪Economie≫

private business and public administration (Cailluet 1997). Moreover, in the specific field of aluminum, Marlio participated into the organization and the coordination of the whole Allied war efforts, dealing directly with his American and British homologues. The French production of aluminum was not fully deployed during the war because a great part of the hydroelectricity needed for this production was utilized for realizing explosives. That pushed France to become a big importer of this metal from the United States and exposed the French war market to the high price of aluminum due to the inflation and the general shortage of this commodity. In the first part of the war, the competition between France, Britain, Italy and Russia to obtain the American metal provoked further distress to the war effort. Soon after the entry of the United States into the conflict, and the creation of the Interallied Munition Board, this industry was reorganized, according to a direct observer of the aluminum business, as a kind of "cartel de guerre" through which the administrators of the aluminum firms in the belligerent countries stabilized prices and allocated resources (Pitaval 1938).

The role of Marlio during WWI led him to continue his frequentation with the Ministers of War who succeeded Millerand – Albert Thomas and, especially, Louis Loucheur – and to become acquainted with other highly influential politicians such as Etienne Clementel. Loucheur played a crucial role in the settlement of the French war effort. Inspired by the German Walter Rathenau, Loucheur reorganized the French production for the war effort as a system of cartels and interfirm networks – an experience which continued after the war to help the transition to peace economy (Loucheur took the position of Minister for the Industrial Reconstruction). As Dominique Barjot points out, the war experience of Loucheur was decisive to craft his 1925 proposal, to use international cartels to promote the return to economic normalcy after the shock of the war and the unification of the European market (Barjot 2013). Clementel was founder and president of the ICC and contributed, as Minister of Finance, to the achievement of the Dawes Plan for Germany's reparations and to the normalization of the relationships between France and Germany during the 1920s. For Clementel as well, the return to normalcy after the shock of the war passed thought the recasting of the commerce, of the free trade and the return to the free-enterprise; these ideas explain why he took an active role in the creation of ICC in 1919 (Kuisel 1981; Godfrey 1987; Rousseau 1998).

EXPERT OR OPINION MAKER? MARLIO AND THE INTERNATIONAL DEBATE ON CARTELS

The career of Marlio in the private business rose after the war, when he took on prestigious roles in the French national industry. In 1921, when PCAC merged with the other leading French aluminum firm, *Société Electrométallurgique Française* (SEMF), Marlio became the chief executive officer of the new firm, *Alais, Froges et Camargue* (AFC, which after the Second World War was renamed *Pechiney*). In 1939 he became also the president of AFC. In 1924, Marlio entered in the board of governors of the *Société des Chemins de Fer de l'Est*, one of the six leading railways companies in France, and in 1934 he became its president. In 1938, when SNCF was created, Marlio became vice-president of the new company that represented a joint venture between the state and the already mentioned six leading French railways. Apart from SNCF's first executive director, Robert Le Besnerais, Marlio was the only top manager of the railways company who came from the private sector (SNCF's president, Pierre Guinand, and a second deputy president, were both nominated as representatives of the French government) (Caron 2005). Marlio became the president of some electrical companies as well, and he entered the board of directors of the *Union pour l'Industrie et l'Electricité*, whose chairman was Ernst Mercier. Marlio played also a big role within the French business organizations and in the more or less informal business meetings organized during the interwar period. In 1921, he was appointed president of the *Chambre Syndicale des Forces Hydroliques* and was named vice-president of the *Union des Industries Minières et Métallurgiques*, while he participated at the meetings of the movement "*Redressement français*," of X-Crises and he collaborated with the *Comité Franco-Allemand* (Morsel 1987; Fraboulet 2007).

Endowed with a background of economic liberal ideas, Marlio passed directly through a process of apprenticeship in a high-cartelized industry in which private business and public powers interacted intensively to put in place a sort of industrial diplomacy for the allocation of resources. He became aware of the new phenomenon of interplay between state and industry through his participation into the organized interests of the French electrical and metallurgical firms. His beliefs about the desirability of a free and competitive economy were reinforced by his experience. In his visions, the price settled by a cartel was closer to the market price than the prices fixed by governmental authorities. In this respect, the influence of Loucheur was decisive to consider cartels as a means of efficiency that could reduce the distortions of state intervention. In his activity as a businessman, he promoted this kind of approach to aluminum industry at the international level. Marlio worked, since November 1918, with other Allied aluminum producers in order to set cartel agreements to help the return to normalcy and to use them to recast an open market for this metal. These efforts, however, were frustrated by the dismal state of the monetary system and the persistence of the state controls over the production and trade of aluminum. According to Marlio, state intervention in monetary and industrial matters had the effect of completely altering, the international competition between firms (Bertilorenzi 2015).

Marlio tried to recast a more liberal attitude toward the aluminum trade after WWI acting at the political level. In his role as President of the *Chambre Syndicale des Forces Hydroliques*, Marlio obtained from the French government the suppression of political controls over the aluminum trade between 1921 and 1922, in order to help British and Swiss producers to gain back control over their properties of the bauxite resources in the southern part of France. Once back to a more "normal" business economy in aluminum, Marlio led the process to create an international cartel, with the idea to reduce the international price of this metal and harmonize the global output with its demand. Since 1922, Marlio also worked to involve the German producers into the regular meetings held between ex-Allied firms. This was a first real attempt of appeasement between Germany and France, which anticipated the Dawes Plan and the Loucheur proposal to use cartel for the creation of a true European market. Like Loucheur, Marlio thought that private agreements could help the market economy to reemerge from the political control: this vision inspired his leadership of the international aluminum oligopoly. Even if they were an emendation to the market economy, the cartel prices for aluminum were considered as efficient because they were linked to the producing costs, which were falling due to technological progress and the rapid increase of the scale economies. In 1926, when finally the European cartel (Aluminium-Association) was formed, Marlio was called to preside it. He kept the role of president also in 1931, when a new global cartel, Alliance Aluminium Compagnie, was founded (Bertilorenzi 2015).

At the end of the 1920s, the debate over cartels allowed Marlio to play new important roles in international politics. The Loucheur proposal to use cartels as means of economic recovery and reunification was highly endorsed by Clementel at the ICC, and became one of the leading themes at the 1927 LoN Economic Conference.[27] After the Conference, the debate about cartels was linked to the proposal to reduce tariff barriers and promote effective market integration in Europe (Bussière 1994). The LoN and the ICC continued to put at the center of their analyses the theme of cartels even after the Economic Conference, when they settled a special committee to promote the adoption of cartels as a means to both self-regulate the industry and help the transition to a more free-trade economy. Cartels were considered as a way to revive liberal principles within the international economy after WWI shock. Since cartels were "voluntary" institutions, merely responding to economic needs, any mandatory involvement by political powers in national or international cartels was considered as highly perverse.

A joint ICC-LoN agency, the *Comité des Ententes Industrielles* (CEII), was created in 1928 in order to undertake the "promotion" of cartels and their use for the purpose of trade barrier reductions. The CEII gathered prestigious industrialists from cartelized industries. Marlio was among them because of his role as president of the Aluminium-Association, because of his double reputation as businessman and member of the academia and because of his intimacy with the leaders of the ICC.[28] Other top cartelists of the interwar period were involved in this initiative. Aloys Meyer was invited because of his chairmanship of the *Entente Internationale de l'Acier*, while Harry McGowan, chairman of Imperial Chemical Industries and member of the boards of many cartels in the chemical industry, replaced Alfred Mond, who was initially designed for the CEII, after his death. Gino Olivetti, a prominent Italian industrialist and president of the ICC, also served as an expert in this committee, as did Clemens Lammers and Antonio Stefano Benni. If the former was a leading member of the German *Reichsverband der deutschen Industrie*, the latter was the president of the *Confederazione Generale Fascista dell'Industria Italiana*,[29] and both were already engaged in several committees at the LoN economic conference (Curli 1990; D'Alessandro 2007). During 1930 and 1931, the CEII organized four conferences to study the problem of cartels. They resulted in the publication of two reports, edited by the LoN. The first, titled *Etude*

[27] Archives ICC, Procès-Verbal du 21 Conseil, 25 June 1926.

[28] Archives LoN, R.2857, file 16770, Consultation d'Experts en matière d'ententes industrielles. Service d'un expert Français, 29 December 1929.

[29] Archives LoN, R.2829, file 13731, Ententes Industrielles, Collaboration de MM Lammers et Benni, 1929.

(Benni et al. 1931a), included specific case studies; the second explored the general nature of cartels and was titled *Rapport Général* (Benni et al. 1931b).[30] The group of experts claimed to present the theme of cartels from an objective point of view. It was argued that the experts' reputation, along with their inner knowledge of cartels, represented the best guarantee for the quality of the information provided.[31]

For the writing of the *Etude* and the *Rapport Général*, the CEII made use of Marlio's 1930 article (Marlio 1930), in which the author argued in favor of cartels for the rationalization of the European economy. According to the CEII, the above mentioned studies provided evidence that cartels could serve to reduce costs and to stabilize prices. These publications defined cartels as "des associations entre des entreprises indépendantes de la même branche ou de branches analogues, crées en vue d'une amélioration des conditions de la production ou de la vente" (Benni et al. 1931b:8).[32] Cartels were also presented as beneficial to public welfare because they sought to "éviter les conséquences désastreuses de la concurrence déréglée entre de très grandes usines qui, dans les périodes de dépression économique ou en cas de surproduction, ne peuvent plus marcher qu'à allure réduite" (Benni et al. 1931b:36–37). Cartels, for instance, could fight inflation through the process of stabilization of commodity prices, and restrain the adoption of trade barriers and bilateral agreements, limiting the role of the state into trade and monetary controls.[33] Furthermore, it was argued, cartels could serve a political purpose, namely the resumption of liberal economy. Fitting perfectly with Polanyi's narrative, the debate about cartels demonstrated that its leading protagonists were considering market manipulations as a necessary tool to bring back free market economy.

In spite of these ideas, the international economic panorama changed abruptly on the eve of the 1930s, as a consequence of the Great Depression. Cartels did not prove very useful in this circumstance, while governmental policies produced more effective result. Marlio observed directly this transition in the sector of the aluminum industry. Since 1931, the abandonment of the parity by the British

30 Archives Lon, R.2830, file 20773, Ententes Industrielles. Pubblications de Monographies, 1930.

31 Archives ICC, Procès-Verbal du 32 Conséil, 4 March 1930.

32 "Cartels are associations in which independent firms, either of the same industrial branch or of similar branches aim to ameliorate production or sales conditions."

33 "Avoid the ruinous consequences of cutthroat competition amongst large producing units that, during periods of economic depression or during periodical over-production crises, can no longer work at economics of scale."

Pound put in jeopardy the international pricing model for aluminum, which until then was expressed in £/ton. A complicated system of conversion between £-paper and £-gold was settled, while the Swiss Franc was adopted for the internal transactions (metal swaps and stocks controls) of the cartel. Nevertheless, the new monetary instability drove the former international trade in aluminum industry to an end and brought about the reemergence of governments as actors of the economic regulation. After Hitler's takeover and, above all, after the new monetary and trade policies set by Hjalmar Schacht, the German Minister of Economics and *Reichbank*'s president, the German delegates claimed the need to change the working of the aluminum cartel. They proposed a system of national monopolies, in order to free German aluminum industry from any limitation related to the quotas.[34] Louis Marlio, as president of the Alliance, was directly involved in the search for a compromise between the different components of the cartel. During 1935, Marlio negotiated with Schacht in person, granting the German group some exceptions to the output limitation with respect to the cartel rules. These exceptions, however, put in jeopardy the cohesion of the cartel. The British delegates asked for the same exceptions and, in 1936, a general negotiation started in order to settle a new system based on the "home markets." The rush to rearmament finally hampered the continuation of the negotiations and the cartel was put on hold in 1938 (Bertilorenzi 2014).

Aside aluminum, in other three cases the transition toward a new and growing role of politics into the international cartelization movement took place. The steel cartel, which worked between 1926 and 1931 by means of production quotas, was not able to cope with the Great Depression and with the development of national policies to support steel production. The tension between the international self-regulation and the national policies drove the cartel to an end in 1931. After about a couple of years of negotiations, a new cartel was created with a system of reservations for "home markets" of its members. Each group was completely free to produce for the domestic market without quotas, while the cartel only fixed export quotas (Hexner 1946:82–83;

[34] C'était une erreur de penser de régler le marché de l'aluminium par l'entremise de l'Alliance. Le cartel international de l'acier a commis la même faute [...]. C'est pourquoi je suis decidé d'organiser tout d'abord l'exportation dans mon pays, afin de pouvoir vous demander ensuite de nous arranger sur les marches d'exportation – Rio Tinto Archives Paris, Pechiney Documents, 00–2–15929, Alliance, Comité de Direction, "PV 15ème Réunion du Board of governors," 10 February 1934.

Barbezat 1989; Berger 2000). In the case of tin and rubber, new types of agreements emerged to reduce outputs and stockpile excess. These agreements, reached under the control of political authorities, were very innovative because governments played a relevant role in the management of the stocks and the buffering of the market. This kept some of the unsold stocks outside the market, allowing for minimizing the output and manipulating the prices (Coates 1987; Hillman 2010). The main problem for programs of output restriction was that the general economic crisis of the 1930s made the acceptance of sacrifices even difficult. The earlier definition of cartels as voluntary and private organizations, did not suit anymore this new scenario.

Louis Marlio tried to use the CEII to promote a vision according to which only private cartels could have solved the economic turmoil of the Great Depression and to criticize state intervention in the management of cartels as a source of further disequilibrium. Even within the CEII, however, a new vision about the political intervention into cartelization slowly emerged. Lammers, for instance, became a supporter of the role of governments which, according to him, had the merit of making cartels more cohesive and effective. Benni pointed out that the crisis was changing the range of cartels. In his opinion, while during the 1920s cartels served to provide governance to the international markets, the crisis of the 1930s called for the adoption of new regulations at a national level that compelled governments to intervene in the promotion of cartels, like in the Italian and German cases.[35] This internal debate about the nature of cartels did not know a definitive solution during the 1930s. The 1937 congress of the ICC, which was largely devoted to Lammers' group on international cartels, discussed three possible models of cartels. The aluminum industry, described by Louis Marlio, was presented as the *Idealtypus* of the private cartel, in spite of its on-going transformation toward new forms of governance. The tin and rubber industries, by contrast, were described by Sir John Campbell, who according to Hillman (2010) was their leading crafter, as examples of agreements under strict governmental control. Between these two categories, Meyer described the steel industry as a combination in which public powers endorsed and helped the establishment of the cartel (International Chamber of Commerce 1937).

[35] Procès-Verbal de la Commission des Ententes Industrielles Internationales, 27 and 28 June 1934, Archives LoN, serie 11803, file 13855.

Marlio's failure in imposing his views to the CEII pushed him to shift from the level of expert maneuvering behind the scenes, to the role of the expert who openly defends his opinions about the desirability of the liberal economy. Already in 1934, when these transformations were only at the beginning stage, he took part in the debate about the "économie dirigée" of André Siegfried, condemning the irrationality that led governments to elaborate economic and military plans (Marlio 1934). Perhaps, Marlio decided to become a member of the *Academie des Sciences Morales and Politiques* in 1934 to carry out more efficiently his battle for liberalism against state interventionism. The authority provided by the acquired membership of this cultural institution pushed him to undertake an intense activity as essayist, with the publication of a half of dozen books which he signed as proud "membre de l'Institut." In 1935 Marlio published an *essai* about the Treaty of Versailles (Marlio 1935), in which for the first time he talked openly about the failure of the supra-nationalism of the LoN. In spite of the fact that he had believed in the LoN-ICC methods – to which he also contributed – he considered the nationalism contained in the fourteen points of Wilson, in particular the one on the self-determination of nations, detrimental to the free market economy, to internationalism and, as a consequence, to peace. This ideas were also developed in his last book, *Le Cercle Infernal*, where he wrote : "C'est un paradoxe de baser la paix des nations sur l'association des nations qui sont, par essence, les plus belliquesuses de toutes collectivités" (Marlio 1951:278).

In 1938, Marlio published his first book as businessman "engagé" titled *Le sort du capitalisme* (Marlio 1938). His thought about the liberalism evolved toward a more social vision of the economy. While the old liberalism of Adam Smith was not applicable to the new big business economy, Marlio did not consider "dirigisme" and state interventionism as the solution to the economic crisis. His vision shifted toward some form of "capitalisme organisé" in which, while cartels were fundamental to self-regulate the international economy, organizations of employers and workers should have self-managed the resolution of their conflicts in the national fields, without state intervention. *Le sort du capitalisme* granted to Marlio the invitation to the *Colloque* Lippmann which, held in Paris in 1938, was often considered the birth of the neo-liberal movement and which was motivated by the journey to France of Walter Lippman, the author of *The Good Society* – a first criticism to the New Deal. *The Colloque* gathered the main personalities of the future intellectual movement that led to the creation of the

Mont Pelerin Society: Aron, Marjolin, Von Hayek, Von Mises, Ropke, Van Zeeland and many others (Denord 2007; Audier 2012, 2014) Some scholarly studies assume that Marlio himself, on that occasion, coined the term "neo-liberalism." His "néo-libéralisme" was synonym of a more social vision of the liberal economy, in which organizations were considered as elements of self-regulation. While he agreed with the other participants about the aberration of state intervention into economy, Marlio also defended cartels as means of self-regulation. After the conference, Marlio became the first president of the ephemeral *Centre international pour la renovation du libéralisme* (CIERL), an initiative which ran only for one year and which aimed to promote the recasting of liberism. In *Dictature ou Liberté* (Marlio 1940), Marlio saw state intervention into economy as a form of dictatorship, strictly linking general freedom to the freedom of economic and social actors to settle private agreements.

These beliefs were reinforced during World War II, when Marlio left France and moved to the United States (in June 1940). According to Henri Morsel (1987), Marlio obtained permission to be sent to the United States with an official mission to promote the image of France there and to help the trade of foodstuff between France and the United States. In fact, the secret purpose of Marlio's mission was to push the Americans to enter the conflict.[36] When he arrived in the United States, Marlio got to know the Brookings Institution, a powerful American counseling agency close to the Democratic Party that supported the American intervention in the war. As requested by its president, Harold Moulton, Marlio was hired by Brookings as an expert in economics and international affairs. The think tank financed the publication of several studies on the possibility that the United States could enter the war, the military superiority of Americans compared to dictatorships and which strategy to adopt toward Japan and Germany.[37] Thanks to the intermediation of the Brookings, Marlio took an active role in the rapid rearmament of the American industry. The US government commissioned two studies to Marlio: one on the production of aluminum in the United States and the other on the electrical energy for the American military production. Marlio served as

[36] TNA, FO 371/24354, Sir Samuel Hoare, (British ambassador in Madrid), Reported mission of M. Marlio to United States of America, 30 June 1940.

[37] Brookings Institution Archive, Washington D.C. (ABI), Personal documents of Mr. Louis Marlio, Harold G. Moulton to Louis Marlio, 25 August 1941. Harold G. Moulton to Louis Marlio, 22 August 1944.

economic advisor for a new entrant in the American aluminum market, Reynolds Metals Company.[38] In the United States, Marlio's ideas further evolved into which he called "liberalism social." To this theme Marlio dedicated three books (Marlio 1943, 1944, 1951) and one public conference (Marlio 1946), while on his ideas about cartels published his "version" of the history of the aluminium cartel (Marlio 1947). His interwar liberalism, which saw cartels as the kernel of the future international trade, and his aversion to the active role of the state in the economy, were implemented by new social visions and political proposals. He became very critical toward the controls over trade, people and currencies which characterized the Bretton Woods post-WWII global scenario. Instead of the state, Marlio proposed the foundation of a world government inspired by the theories of Wendell Willkie (1943), which would have terminated the supra-nationalism of the LoN and ONU. In each state, he proposed the creation of a *Fédération sociale*, in which trade unions and trade associations would be responsible for the economic regulation. This model differed from the corporatist one, because the state had no role to play. Marlio also criticized one of the pillars of the modern welfare state, arguing that employers should have taken the burden to subside the jobless through private foundation. Again, as in his vision about cartel, the *Fédération* was a tool meant to save the fundamental mechanism of the market economy from the ineffectiveness of the state (Marlio 1951).

CONCLUSION

Our article purported to show that we gain a better understanding of regulatory approaches to markets by analyzing the spread of new types of valuation devices across the worlds of high bankers and industrialists. If the Great War weakened the "international" of financiers and, more generally, the pre-war economic elites, the bankers and industrialists who promoted international cooperation across national borders to regulate the growth of global markets in the interwar years did not take stock immediately of the profound transformations that WWI had brought about. They realized the magnitude of the change through a long and painful process of apprenticeship, as we have seen in the case

[38] National Archives and Records Administration, RG 107, War Department. Office of the Under Secretary of War, box 4, Louis Marlio (Brookings Institution) to Mr. Robert P. Patterson (Under Secretary of War), 12 January 1942. ABI, Personal Documents of Mr. Louis Marlio, Marlio to Moulton, 5 February 1942.

of Toeplitz. Moreover, they saw in very negative terms the move toward a larger role of the state in the economy, even though the state was the main source of their personal and professional achievements, as we have seen in the case of Marlio. To use Pareto's image of "history as the graveyard of elites" – an image elaborated having in mind the carnage of WWI – this paper demonstrated that economic ideas and forms of ideal market mechanisms survive for some time before everyone realizes they have long been dead. After WWI, a mounting tension emerged between the bankers' and elite industrialists' beliefs on the one hand, and the necessity to make use of new forms of regulation and valuation techniques – once verified the ineffectiveness of the old one – on the other. If the 1920s witnessed an attempt to restore the international liberal economy after the shock of the Great War, the Great Depression showed the impossibility of "recasting bourgeois Europe" (Maier 1975). The impact of state regulation in key economic activities such as monetary policy, industrial production and international trade, put an end to the liberalism as it was understood before 1914. This "Great Transformation" was not without oppositions and adaptations, as this chapter has demonstrated.

To analyze changes in valuation devices that were being considered legitimate during both times of normal economic exchange and times of crisis, we distinguished between two levels: their efficiency and their legitimacy. We argued that valuation devices can still be held legitimate, especially by aging elites, during times when they no longer work well to coordinate markets. We showed that the mounting tension between efficiency and legitimacy may originate from the slow replacement of older elites, who were used to interact with markets in their own way, based on prior experience of a world whose rules they still hold to be valid long after market mechanisms have changed (Mallard 2014). This process, which evokes Polanyi's paradox mentioned in the introduction, gave legitimacy to speculation, providing arguments to prove its efficiency in the process of currency stabilization, and to cartels, presenting them as necessary instruments of price valuation at times of multiplying market failures, and as virtuous examples of self-regulation in opposition to state interventionism. Both devices (speculation and cartels) were part of a specific narrative about the "return" to liberal economy, an illusion that delayed the understanding of the real reach of the "Great Transformation," as we have seen in the specific case of Toeplitz and Marlio. Both devices (speculation and cartels), lost efficiency in setting prices, paving the way, during the 1930s, to new forms of market regulation in which the state emerged as a new, effective and legitimized actor.

Józef Leopold Toeplitz, the protagonist of the first part of this chapter, epitomizes the international high financier of his time. Louis Marlio, analyzed in the second part of this work, is more than a simple representative of the interwar industrial world. His activities included also academia, public administration and top-level consultancy for governments, such as the French and the American ones, and international organizations, such as the ICC and the LoN. This latter utilized Toeplitz's expertise as well, though not systematically as in the case of Marlio. As emerges clearly from his comments on Cassel's non-orthodox approach to the post-war problems of currency stabilization, Toeplitz was a practitioner who had learned his profession on-job-training and was not particularly concerned to elaborate a vision for the future. Marlio's vision, as businessman, consultant within the ICC and the LoN, chairman of the interwar cartels of the international aluminum industry and prolific publicist, was projected to the future. In Marlio's view, cartels were an answer to the current crisis but also a first step toward the resumption of liberal economy. Yet, in spite of the differences, Toeplitz and Marlio – the latter twelve years younger than the former – had to deal with the same post-war scenario and respond to the same tough challenges: namely, the creation of some form of "organising power" in a period of declining profits and the emergence of new forms of governance for the national and international economies. These challenges were complicated by the intrinsic liberalism of the two protagonists of this story.

If we look at the Polish-born banker and the French industrialist from the standpoint of valuation, we find in both the same tension between beliefs and actions. In the case of Toeplitz, this tension clearly emerges if we look at his "struggle" against Stringer – a civil servant who, during the 1920s, can be considered as a central banker "in progress." During the mid 1920s, the banker did not hesitate to build a temporary alliance with the politics – namely his old friend Volpi, the then Minister of Finance – in order to take over the Italian central bank role in stabilization policies. Toeplitz, a private actor of the banking world, carried a specific vision of market regulation according to which speculation could help stabilization, incidentally offering to "his" bank the possibility to realize profits (or vice versa). In the case of Marlio, there is a continued tension between the strong connections of this businessman with the liberal field in economics, on the one hand, and his belief in cartelization as the best tool of market "self-regulation", on the other. His opposition to state intervention in economy, which made him diverge to other French *Grand Patrons* of his time, lured by the so-called "*dirigisme*" (Morsel 1987), is even more surprising if one considers that Marlio spent a big part of his career in the public administration. At first sight, Marlio's contradictions are striking: a cartelist who defends the market economy; a civil servant who does not trust the public administration; a consultant of the LoN and ICC who did not like supra-national organizations, a determinant player in the US war efforts who did not approve the Bretton Woods architecture. In reality, all these tensions reveal the complexity of the adaptation of economic actors to the institutional economic change (North 1990).

WWI served as main crafter of the careers of Toeplitz and Marlio. Toeplitz became, *de facto*, the number one of the BCI in 1915 after a long process of apprenticeship. Toeplitz, a former Russian citizen who had obtained the Italian citizenship in 1912, succeeded to the "German" (even though "Italianized") Weil and Joel in a situation of rising nationalism, which to some extent announced the post-war advent of fascism. Marlio arrived at the chairmanship of the PCAC in a difficult moment for the firm, when new commitments with the French governments linked to the war effort were crafting the relationship between business and politics within the aluminum industry. When the *Ingénieur Civil des Mines* Adrien Badin died in 1917, the state engineer member of the *Grand Corps des Ponts* Louis Marlio was considered the best choice to embody the new proximity of business to politics. In the merger of 1921 with the second largest French aluminum company, Marlio again was called to play the role of business continuator. In spite of what Toeplitz and Marlio embodied during WWI, a period of extremely complex transition, they spent the rest of their lives as advocates of the old world that they had contributed to replace. They climbed to top-level roles when nationalism was at its peak. Aware of this tendency – as clearly emerges from Toeplitz's comments to Heimeman's *Esquisse d'une Europe nouvelle* and from the critiques of Marlio to the potential aberrations related to the Wilsonian principle of self-determination of nations – they proudly maintained an international profile on the eve of globalization sunset. Both well equipped and positioned during the 1920s, they did not fully understand the 1930s. Toeplitz, displaced by the move of the fascist government toward autarky as a response to the Great Depression, had been already weakened in the second part of the 1920s by the "paradigm shift" in banking partially described in section two. His defence of a (loose) regulatory framework, a business model (the universal bank) and an interpretation of banking activity that were destined to be reversed, contributes to turning him into the "old" banker *par excellence*, confronted with major institutional, operational and cultural transformations. Marlio, displaced by the wave of nationalizations, "dirigisme" and "plannisme" experienced at a global scale during the 1930s and after WWII, continued to argue against any form of state intervention in economy, in opposition to other French *Grand Patrons* of his time, lured by these formulas (Morsel 1987) and in opposition to the post-1945 Bretton Woods order. All this considered, it is not surprising that both Toeplitz and Marlio, as collateral damages of the "Great Transformation," died emarginated and almost forgotten.

References

Audier, Serge 2012. *Le Colloque Lippmann. Aux origines du néo-liberalisme*. Paris: Le Bord de l'eau éditions.

Audier, Serge 2014. *Néo-Libéralisme(s). Une archéologie intélectuelle*. Paris: Grasset.

Asso, Pier Francesco 1993. "Finanza internazionale, vincolo esterno e cambi. 1919–1939," in *Ricerche per la storia della Banca d'Italia*, 10 vols. vol. III, edited by Gabriella Raitano. Roma-Bari: Laterza.

Baffi, Paolo 1973. "La rivalutazione del 1926–27, gli interventi sul mercato e l'opinione pubblica," in *Nuovi studi sulla moneta*, edited by Paolo Baffi. Milan: Giuffrè, 1973.

Baia Curioni, Stefano 1995. *Regolazione e competizione. Storia del mercato azionario in Italia: 1808–1938*. Bologna: il Mulino.

Barbezat, Daniel 1989. "Cooperation and Rivalry in the International Steel Cartel, 1926–1933," *The Journal of Economic History*, vol. 49, no. 2.

Barjot, Dominique 1994. "Introduction", in *International cartels revisited. Vues nouvelles sur les cartels internationaux, 1880–1980*, edited by Dominique Barjot. Caen: Editions du Lys.

Barjot, Dominique 2013. "Les cartels, une voie vers l'intégration européenne? Le role de Louis Loucheur (1872–1931)", *Revue économique*, vol. 64, no. 6: 1043–1066.

Benni, Antonio, Louis Marlio, Clemens Lammers, and Aloys Meyer 1931a. *Etude sur les aspects économiques de différentes etentes industrielles internationals*. Geneva: League of Nations.

Benni, Antonio, Louis Marlio, Clemens Lammers, and Aloys Meyer 1931b. *Rapport Général sur les aspects économiques des ententes industrielles*. Geneva: League of Nations.

Berger, Françoise 2000. *La France, l'Allemagne et l'acier (1932–1952), De la stratégie des cartels à l'élaboration de la* CECA, Ph.D thesis, Université Paris I Panthéon-Sorbonne.

Bertilorenzi, Marco 2014. "Business, Finance, and Politics. The rise and fall of the International Aluminium Cartels, 1914–45," *Business History*, vol. 56, no. 2: 236–269.

Bertilorenzi, Marco 2015. *The International Aluminium Cartel, 1886–1978. The Business and Politics of a cooperative industrial institution.* London & New York: Routledge.

Bhattacharya, Sudipto and Anjan V. Thakor 1993. "Contemporary Banking Theory," *Journal of Financial Intermediation*, vol. 3, no. 1: 2–50.

Bloomfield, Arthur 1950. *Capital imports and the American balance of payments, 1934–39: A study in Abnormal Capital Transfers*. Chicago: Chicago University Press.

Bonelli, Franco and Elio Cerrito 2003. "Momenti della formazione di una banca centrale in Italia, 1894–1913," in, *La Banca d'Italia. Sintesi della ricerca storica 1893–1960*, edited by Franco Cotula, Marcello De Cecco and Gianni Toniolo. Roma-Bari: Laterza.

Bourdieu, Pierre 1980, "Le capital social. Notes provisoires," *Actes de la recherche en sciences sociales*, vol. 31: 1–4.

Bourdieu, Pierre 1985. "The social space and the genesis of groups," *Theory and Society*, vol. 14, no. 6: 723–744.

Bourdieu, Pierre 2010. *Distinction. A Social Critique of the Judgement of Taste.* London & New York: Routledge.

Bussière, Eric 1994. "La SDN, les cartels et l'organisation économique de l'Europe entre les deux guerres," in *International cartels revisited. Vues nouvelles sur les cartels internationaux, 1880–1980*, edited by Dominique Barjot. Editions du Lys, Caen.

Cabiati, Attilio 1921. "Come si risanerà il cambio?" *Rivista Bancaria*, vol. 2, no. 11: 593–601.

Callon, Michel (ed) 1998. *The Laws of the Markets*. Oxford: Blackwell.

Callon, Michel, Yuval Millo and Fabian Muniesa (eds) 2007. *Market Devices*. Oxford: Blackwell.

Caron, François 2005. *Les Grandes compagnies des chemins de fer en France, 1823–1937*. Geneva: Droz.

Cassel, Gustav 1921. "I problemi monetari mondiali," *Rivista Bancaria*, vol. 2, no. 11: 538–546.

Cassis, Youssef 1991. "Financial Elites in Three European Centres: London, Paris, Berlin 1880s–1930s," *Business History*, vol. 33, no. 3, 53–71.

Cassis, Youssef 1994. *City Bankers 1890–1914*. Cambridge: Cambridge University Press.

Cassis, Youssef 2011. *Crises and Opportunities, The Shape of Modern Finance.* Oxford: Oxford University Press.

Confalonieri, Antonio 1979. *Banca e industria in Italia, 1894–1906*, 3 vols. Bologna, Il Mulino 1979, vol. III.

Confalonieri, Antonio 1994. *Banche miste e grande industria in Italia, 1914–1933*, 2 vols. Milano: Banca Commerciale Italiana, vol. II.

Coates, Austin 1987. *The Commerce in Rubber. The First 250 years*. Oxford: Oxford University Press.

Conti, Giuseppe 2008. "Banca centrale e politica monetaria tra le due guerre", in, *Storia d'Italia. La Banca*, edited by Alberto Cova et al. Torino: Einaudi.

Curli, Barbara 1990. "L'Italia, la Società delle Nazioni e la disucssione sugli accordi industriali internazionali, 1927–1931," *Rivista di Storia Economica*, vol. 7, no. 1.

D'Alessandro, Michele 1998, "L'organizzazione delle reti estere. Comit e Credit nei centri finanziari internazionali (1910–1935)," *Archivi e Imprese*, no. 9: 245–289.

D'Alessandro, Michele 2007, "Seeking governance for world markets. The League of Nations between corporatism and public opinion, 1925–1929," EBHA annual conference paper, Geneva.

Denord, François 2007. *Néo-libéralisme version française*. Paris: Demopolis.

Di Quirico, Roberto 1999. "The Initial Phases of Italian Banks' Expansion Abroad, 1900–1931," *Financial History Review*, vol. 6, no. 1: 7–24.

De Cecco, Marcello 1990. "Introduzione," in *L'Italia e il sistema finanziario internazionale, 1861–1914*, edited by Marcello de Cecco. Roma-Bari: Laterza.

De Cecco, Marcello 1993. "Introduzione', in *L'Italia e il sistema finanziario internazionale 1919–36*, edited by Marcello de Cecco. Roma-Bari: Laterza.

Eichengreen, Barry 1992. "The Origins and Nature of the Great Slump Revisited," *Economic History Review*, vol. 45, no. 2: 213–239.

Eichengreen, Barry and Peter Temin 2000. "The Gold Standard and the Great Depression," *Contemporary European History*, vol. 9, no. 2: 183–207.

Flores, Juan and Marc Flandreau 2012. "Bondholders vs. bond-sellers? Investment banks and conditionality lending in the London market for foreign government debt, 1815–1913," *European Review of Economic History*, vol. 16, no. 4: 356–383.

Ford, Alec G. 1956. "Argentina and the Baring Crisis of 1890," *Oxford Economic Papers*, vol. 8, no. 2: 127–150.

Fraboulet, Danièle 2007. *Quand les patrons s'organisent. Stratégies et pratiques de l'Union des industries métallurgiques et minières, 1901–1950*. Presses Universitaires du Septentrion: Villeneuve-d'Ascq.

Garruccio, Roberta 2002. *Minoranze in affari. La formazione di un banchiere: Otto Joel*. Soveria Mannelli: Rubettino.

Godfrey, John F. 1987. *Capitalism at War. Industrial Policy and bureaucracy in France, 1914–1918*. New York: Berg.

Goldshmit, Raymond 1969. *Financial Structure and Development*. New Haven-London: Yale University Press.

Hachez-Leroy, Florence 1999. *L'Aluminium français. La création d'un marché, 1911–1981*. Paris.

CNRS Editions

Hachez-Leroy, Florence 2010. "Louis Marlio 1878–1952," in *Dictionnaire historique des patrons français*, edited by Jean-Claude Daumas. Paris: Flammarion, 459–462.

Hara, Terushi 1994. "La conférence économique internationale de 1927 et ses effets sur la formation des cartels internationaux," in *International cartels revisited. Vues nouvelles sur les cartels internationaux*, 1880–1980, edited by Dominique Barjot. Editions du Lys, Caen.

Harris, José and Pat Thane 1984. "British and European Bankers: An Aristocratic Bourgeoisie?," in *The Power of the Past. Essays for Eric Hosbawm*, edited by Pat Thane, Geoffrey Grossick, and Roderick Floud. London; New York: Cambridge University Press, 215–234.

Heineman, Dannie 1931. *Outline of a New Europe*. Brussels: Vromart & Co.

Hexner, Ervin 1946. *International Cartels*, Chapel Hill: North Carolina University Press.

Hillman, John 2010. *The International Tin Cartel*, London: Routledge.

International Chamber of Commerce 1937. *Ententes Internationales – Congrès de Berlin – 1937*, International Chamber of Commerce, Paris, Document no. 4.

James, Harold 2001. *The End of Globalization. Lessons from the Great Depression*. Cambridge-London: Harvard University Press.

Joly, Hervé 2013, Diriger une grande entreprise au XXe siècle. L'élite industrielle française. Tours: Presses Universitaires François-Rabelais.

Kirshner, Jonathan 2007. *Appeasing Bankers. Financial caution on the road of war*. Princeton: Princeton University Press.

Kuisel, Richard F. 1981. *Capitalism and the State in modern France. Renovation and economic management in the twentieth century*. London: Cambridge University Press.

Landau, Zbignev and Jerzy Tomaszewski 1990. "Foreign Policy and International Business in Poland: 1918–39," in *Multinational Enterprise in Historical Perspective*, edited by Alice Teichova, Maurice Lévy-Leboyer, and Helga Nussbaum. Cambridge: Cambridge University Press 271–285.

Landes, David 1958. *Bankers and Paschas. International Finance and Economic Imperialism in Egypt*. Cambridge: Cambridge University Press.

Lamont, Michèle 2012. "Toward a Comparative Sociology of Valuation and Evaluation". *Annual Review of Sociology* 38(21): 201–221.

Le Van-Le Mesle, Lucette 2005. "Cauwès et Colson, le juriste et l'ingénieur: une ou deux conceptions du service public?" *Revue d'histoire moderne et contemporaine*, vol. 2005/3, no. 52–53, 75–87.

Maier, Charles 1975. *Recasting Bourgeois Europe*. Princeton: Princeton University Press.
Malagodi, Giovanni 1999. "Mattioli banchiere," in *La figura e l'opera di Raffaele Mattioli*. Milan-Naples: Ricciardi.
Mallard, Gregoire. *Fallout: Nuclear diplomacy in an age of global fracture*. Chicago: Chicago University Press, 2014.
Marlio, Louis 1908. *La politique allemande et la navigation intérieure*. Paris: Larose et Tenin.
Marlio, Louis 1930. "Les Ententes Industrielles," *Revue de Paris*, vol. 37, no. 1: 829–852.
Marlio, Louis 1934. "URSS. Allocution de Louis Marlio," in *L'économie dirigée. Conférences organisées par la Société des anciens élèves de L'École libre des sciences politiques*, edited by André Siegfried. Paris: Alcan.
Marlio, Louis 1935. *L'Armistice de Versailles*. Paris: Domat-Montchrestien.
Marlio, Louis 1938. *La sort du capitalisme*. Paris: Flammarion.
Marlio, Louis 1940. *Dictature ou Liberté*. Paris: Flammarion.
Marlio, Louis 1943. *La révolution de hier, d'aujourd'hui et de demain*. Montréal: Brentano's.
Marlio, Louis 1944. *Problèmes d'aujourd'hui*. Montréal: Parizeau et co.
Marlio, Louis 1946. *Le Liberalisme Social*. Paris: Fortin.
Marlio, Louis 1947. *The Aluminum Cartel*. Wahsington DC: Brookings Institution.
Marlio, Louis 1951. *Le Cercle inférnal*. Paris: Flammarion.
Meyer, Richard Hemming 1970. *Bankers' Diplomacy. Monetary Stabilization in the Twenties*. New York and London: Columbia University Press.
Mitchener, Kris James and Marc Weidenmier 2008. "Trade and Empire," *The Economic Journal* vol. 118, no. 533: 1805–1834.
Montanari, Guido 1994. "Introduzione," in *Segreteria dell'amministratore delegato Giuseppe Toeplitz, 1916–34*, edited by Alberto Gottarelli and Guido Montanari. Milano: Banca Commerciale Italiana.
Morsel, Henri 1987. "Louis Marlio, position idéologique et comportement politique d'un dirigeant d'une grande entreprise dans la première moitié du XXe s." in *Entreprises et entrepreneurs XIXe-XXe siècles*, edited by François Caron. Paris: Presses de l'Université Paris-Sorbonne.
North, Douglass 1990. *Institutions, Institutional Change and Economic Performance*. Cambridge: Cambridge University Press.
Olson, Mancur 1965. *The Logic of Collective Action. Public Goods and the Theory of Groups*, Cambridge: Harvard University Press.
Officer, Lawrence H. 2014. *Pricing Theory, Financing of International Organisations and Monetary History*. London & New York: Routledge.
Pantaleoni, Maffeo 1977. *La caduta della Società Generale di Credito Mobiliare*, Milano: Guiffrè [1893].

Pease, Neal 1986. *Poland, the United States, and the Stabilization of Europe, 1919–1933*. Oxford: Oxford University Press.

Pénin, Marc 1997. *Charles Gide 1848–1932. L'Esprit critique*. Paris: L'Harmattan.

Picory, Christian 1989. "Othodoxie libérale et hétérodoxie marginaliste: Clément Colson," *Revue économique*, vol. 40, no. 4: 679–708.

Piluso, Giandomenico 1998. "Per una storia della cultura economica dei banchieri 'milanesi': formazione, culture e istituzioni (1890–1914)," *Milano e la cultura economica del XX secolo* 2 vols, edited by Pier Luigi Porta. Milano: Franco Angeli, vol. I.

Piluso, Giandomenico 2011. "L'Italia e il gold standard: genesi e razionalità del modello Beneduce, 1905–1935," *Imprese e Storia*, vol. 41–42: 13–33.

Piluso, Giandomenico and Pier Angelo Toninelli 2002. "Managing a Multinational Network: Organization, Training and Accountancy in Italian Multinational Banking (1910–1933)," *Transnational Companies: 19th–20th centuries*, edited by Hubert Bonin. Paris: Plage.

Polanyi, Karl 1944. *The Great Transformation*. New York: Farrar & Rinehart.

Pose, Alfred 1955. *Notice sur la vie et les travaux* de Louis Marlio (1878–1952). Paris: Firmin-Didot.

Quilici, Nello 1935. *Fine di secolo*. Banca Romana. Milano: Mondadori.

Ranieri, Liane 2005. Dannie Heineman. *Un destin singulier* 1872–1962. Bruxelles: Racine.

Romano, Sergio 1979. Giuseppe Volpi. *Industria e Finanza da Giolitti a Mussolini*. Milano: Bompiani.

Rousseau, Guy 1998. *Étienne Clémentel (1864–1936). Entre idéalisme et réalisme, une vie politique: essai biographique*. Clermont-Ferrand: Archives départementales du Puy-de-Dôme.

Schot, Johan and Vincent Lagendijk 2008. "Technocratic internationalism in the interwar years: building Europe on motorways and electricity networks," *Journal of Modern European History*, vol. 6, no. 2: 196–200.

Schubert, Aurel 1992. *The Credit-Anstalt Crisis of 1931*. Cambridge: Cambridge University Press.

Schuker, Stephen A 2003. "Money doctors between the war. The competition between central banks, private financial advisers, and multilateral agencies 1919–39," in *Money Doctors*, edited by Marc Flandreau. London & New York: Routledge.

Telesca, Giuseppe 2010. Il mercante di Varsavia. Giuseppe Toeplitz: un cosmopolita alla guida della Banca Commerciale Italiana. Unpublished PhD thesis, Università degli Studi di Firenze.

Toeplitz, Ludovico 1963. Il banchiere. Milano: Ferro.

Toeplitz, Krysztof Teodor 2004. "Rodzina Toeplitzów." *Ksiązka mojego ojca*. Warsaw: Iskry.

Tomz, Michael 2007. *Reputation and International Cooperation: Sovereign Debt Across Three Centuries* Princeton: Princeton University Press.
Toniolo, Gianni 2003. "La Banca d'Italia e il sistema bancario 1919–1936", in *La Banca d'Italia. Sintesi della ricerca storica 1893–1960*, edited by Franco Cotula, Marcello de Cecco and Gianni Toniolo. Roma-Bari, Laterza.
Willkie, Wendell 1943. *One World.* New York: Lippincott.

PART THREE

STRUCTURING FIELDS: MARKET DOMINANCE, COMPLEMENTARITY AND DIFFERENTIATION IN COMPLEX INSTITUTIONAL ECOLOGIES

CHAPTER NINE

THE RISE AND FALL OF TRADE AND MONETARY LEGAL ORDERS: FROM THE INTERWAR PERIOD TO TODAY'S GLOBAL IMBALANCES

Gregory Shaffer and Michael Waibel

Many analysts of globalization see in the process of 'legalization' (Abbot and Snidal, 2000) the tendency of informal rules to harden over time, either because practice clarifies ambiguous rules over time, or because institutions for dispute resolution are created to interpret and apply them – a characteristic in the evolution of international legal orders. The poster child for this development is the World Trade Organization (WTO) and its Appellate Body created in 1995. In this chapter, we take issue with this account of the purposeful character of the evolution of transnational legal regimes at two levels.

First, we find that not all regimes of rules harden over time, but that a process of de-legalization and the turn to informal law can weaken or even eclipse hard multilateral rules. To illustrate this first point, we trace the process of legalization of the monetary order from the League of Nations to the creation of the International Monetary Fund (IMF), which was followed by a process of de-legalization when the dollar lost its parity to gold in the 1970s and the IMF had to re-invent a role for itself other than that of the arbiter of a system of fixed exchange rates. The post-1973 IMF has, or more precisely its member states have, limited interest in law, preferring instead to rely on soft law such as standards and codes to safeguard international financial stability. Formalized dispute settlement has never featured prominently in the monetary sphere.

Second, multilateral institutions often have overlapping jurisdiction. We argue that the dual processes of legalization and de-legalization can challenge existing settlements and complementarities between international organizations, and that these changing equilibriums can add another source of complexity (and sometimes uncertainty) to the governance of the international economic system. To illustrate this second point, we tell the parallel story of two organizations with overlapping mandates but opposite trajectories: the WTO, where the creation of a strong mechanism of dispute resolution started a process of judicialization in the global trade regime in the mid 1990s and the IMF, whose function shifted in the 1970s from being a multilateral institution charged with currency stabilization to an institution charged with the surveillance of country-specific macro-economic policies. The paper shows that, the degree of legalization today differs significantly within the trade and monetary spheres, ranging from the use of formal legal norms to informal means of cooperation. We argue that the dual processes of judicialization and de-legalization have created zones of obscurity in the overlapping areas where each organization could claim jurisdiction before those shifts occurred.

To demonstrate these points, this chapter charts the rise and fall of the legal orders in the trade and monetary spheres, the turn from discretion and informal means for macro-economic policy coordination up to World War II and the gradual legalization of the trade legal order until its rapid legalization and institutionalization in the WTO. The first section shows that jurisdictional overlaps are largely a product of the post-World War II era, as the League of Nations provided a comprehensive framework for both monetary and trade oversight, although one that was not very legalized and was incapable of avoiding the backlash against free trade in the wake of World War I and the onslaught of the Great Depression. We address the absence of lawyers within the offices of the League in relation to the League's failure to legalize its regulatory regime, which reflected the fact that there was little positive law upon which legal arguments could be based during the interwar period, such that international economic law did not yet exist as a distinct discipline. Indeed, there were virtually no legal rules governing international economic exchange aside from bilateral commercial treaties.

The chapter shows why the architects of the post-World War II order had good reasons to opt for greater legalization and for creating two separate but interrelated transnational legal orders at the multilateral level: one for international monetary matters, and the other for international trade. Such functional legal differentiation was supposed to encourage institutions to focus on their comparatively narrow mandates, which they could then implement according to hard rules, creating two effective transnational legal orders for ordering international trade and monetary affairs. By a transnational legal order, we refer to a collection of formalized legal norms and associated organizations and actors that authoritatively order the understanding and practice of law across national jurisdictions (Halliday and Shaffer, 2015). The second section shows that the decision by the Nixon administration to delink the dollar from the price of gold and let the US currency float effectively broke the system of hard rules that the IMF was to police. The IMF had to reinvent a role for itself. This process of de-legalization had implications that we explore in the third section.

The third section shows that at the same time that the IMF lost its hard law jurisdiction over currency stabilization, and as it moved into macro-economic policy advising, lending, and technical assistance (functions which included advising countries on their specific trade policies), the WTO evolved into an increasingly legalized and judicialized institution for dispute resolution in the field of global trade. The dual move of the IMF toward trade and macro-economic policy, coupled with its de-legalization, and the judicialization of the WTO, increased the uncertainty over the coherence of the system of international economic rules. It raises the specter of misalignment between the two transnational legal orders with real potential consequences. More recently, bilateralism and new challenges arising at the interface of the trade and monetary legal orders (such as currency misalignment) have raised questions regarding the effectiveness of the trade legal order. We argue in this section that the uneven effectiveness of the trade transnational legal order is partly due to the trade order's deference to the (now weak) monetary legal order on issues regarding monetary relations and the monetary legal order's relative silence on the issues of exchange rate undervaluation and capital controls on the capital account.

TRADE AND MONETARY DISORDER BEFORE WORLD WAR II

The first era of globalization and its demise

The volume of world trade grew at a rapid and unprecedented pace in the nineteenth century. The period 1870–1913 saw the birth of the first era of trade globalization and the period 1914–1939 its death (Estevadeordal, Frantz and Taylor, 2003). Great Britain moved to free trade in the

1840s, most notably with the repeal of the Corn Laws and the Anglo-French Cobden-Chevalier Treaty of 1860 that included a most favored nation (MFN) clause. A network of similar bilateral trade treaties followed, covering most of Europe. Free trade became the dominant doctrine. Before 1870, only a few countries adopted the gold standard. As more countries adopted this multilateral commitment device, the multilateral payments system based on gold convertibility underpinned trade liberalization.

In the second half of the nineteenth century, the international trade and monetary order rested on established norms of international conduct, rather than legal norms. The best example of the informal arrangements that ordered the international economic system was the gold standard. It 'tended to make international payments more or less automatic' (Vagts, 2006, p. 770). At that time, international economic law did not exist as a separate field. As a corollary, 'exchange controls were more or less unknown' (Cooper 1967, p. 1276; Vagts, 2006, p. 772). In the first golden era of global capital, from 1870 to 1914, 'the flows of economic factors were largely unregulated' (Vagts, 2006, p. 782). That system of spontaneous international cooperation coupled with the stability resulting from Great Britain's financial hegemony (Kindleberger, 1981) came to a sudden stop with World War I.

With the outbreak of World War I, tariffs, quotas, and other barriers to trade multiplied (Findlay and O'Rourke, 2007, p. 430). Concomitantly, World War I brought about a wave of exchange restrictions, such as in German legislation of November 1915 (Gesetz über Verbot der Ausfuhr und Durchfuhr von Gold, 1915). The war wreaked havoc on the open international economic order. Blockades hampered trade not only among belligerent countries, but also affecting neutral countries. Shipping, central to the transportation of goods, was under constant threat of attack, especially from German submarines. Transportation and insurance costs rose sharply. Even Great Britain broke with free trade by introducing the McKenna Tariff in 1915.

The gold standard and the international payment system it underpinned had ceased to function. When peace returned to the European continent, a legacy of protectionist policies hampered economic reconstruction in Europe. Views among economic historians differ as to whether the 1920s saw a normalization of trade policy towards greater openness (Kindleberger, 1989). Some hold the view that 'normalization in commercial policy was more hoped for than achieved' (Kindleberger, 1989, p. 163). After a brief sense of normalcy in the mid 1920s, the

Great Depression delivered the deathblow to the first period of globalization. The international trade and monetary system based on the pre-war gold standard was gone by the mid 1930s. In 1933 the United States went off the gold standard. Countries increasingly resorted to exchange controls. If law played a role in dealing with these difficulties, it was private international law, involving domestic courts hearing commercial disputes among parties from multiple jurisdictions, rather than public international law.

The debt overhang left behind by World War I

The cost of World War I was enormous and the treasuries of the countries that fought in it were severely depleted by 1919. Germany's currency totally collapsed, triggering hyperinflation. The Versailles Treaty failed to create the conditions for macroeconomic stability in Europe. Many sectors of the economy were keen to retain the protection for domestic production dating back to the war (Findlay and O'Rourke, 2007, p. 439). Most importantly, the Versailles Treaty failed to deal decisively with the large debt overhang left by World War I. Unsustainable levels of debt cast a long shadow over post-war economic recovery. The protracted dispute over German reparations prompted France to occupy the Ruhr in 1923. Germany and Austria then experienced further hyperinflation. In Eastern Europe too, macroeconomic instability was the order of the day. Against the background of these severe tensions in the international economic system, central banks found it much harder to cooperate compared to the pre-World War I period.

The US Congress created the World War Foreign Debt Commission in February 1922 to offer a solution to the rapidly growing problem of inter-governmental indebtedness (US Congress, 1922; United States World War Foreign Debt Commission, 1927, pp. 1–10). Due to the prevailing economic conditions, many governments could not pay their debts according to their terms. The United States realised it needed to make some adjustments in the form of definite settlements to allow national economies to recover. The Commission reduced the interest payable and stretched the maturities. As a rule, however, it did not write off any principal.

During the Great Depression, all European countries, with the exception of Finland, defaulted on loans advanced by the United States to aid their war effort. Many debtor governments pleaded their inability to pay the full face value of their debts due to the effects of the worldwide economic depression, which commenced in 1929. The capacity of the Allies to repay the United States depended on receiving German war reparations, which were not forthcoming as promised. The financial quagmire illustrates the vicious circle of borrowing and inability to pay that bedeviled inter-governmental fiscal relations in the interwar period.

Bilateralism was also the order of the day in debt renegotiations. The Commission's task was not to supervise and implement a general debt cancellation scheme, especially of the various European countries among themselves. A global debt settlement could have achieved equal treatment of debtor countries, and could have taken equitable considerations related to these interlinkages into account in drawing up the settlement (United States World War Foreign Debt Commission, 1927, pp. 1–10). An alternative to bilateral debt negotiations would have been a multilateral joint settlement – an option that was less attractive to the United States that wished to preserve its own bargaining power.

The debt overhang from World War I was partly responsible for a series of banking crises in the late 1920s and early 1930s. This led to a wave of sovereign defaults in Latin America. In early 1932, there were isolated yet ultimately unsuccessful attempts to break with growing protectionism, most importantly in the World Economic Conference of 1933 in London. Globalization's demise, however, was sealed with Hitler's rise to power in 1933, and Germany's gearing up for war and self-sufficiency. The underdeveloped international economic law of the time was incapable of defusing these macro disputes – but the same could also be said in respect of modern international trade law, which has on the whole been able to resolve micro-level trade disputes focused on specific sectors or products, but much less successful in dealing with macro-level disputes such as global imbalances.

A tentative return to economic openness

The victorious Allies insisted in the peace negotiations on the inclusion of provisions regarding economic openness. In the Versailles Treaty, Germany undertook not to discriminate against the Allies and Associated States in respect of tariffs, customs regulations, internal charges, export duties, and import as well as export prohibitions. The League of Nations was an important player, especially its Economic and Financial Organization which moved quickly to re-establish some degree of economic openness after the war had left the international economy shattered by restrictions on trading with the enemy and other impediments to trade.

This pattern of liberalization continued in the interwar period, not just through the League of Nations but also more generally. A striking feature of the work of the League of Nations in the economic and financial sphere was the absence of formal legal ordering. Lawyers played a very limited role in the League's operation. Even though the League in general had a Legal Advisor who was a senior staff member, the Economic Relations section was staffed virtually exclusively by non-lawyers. In the interwar period, international lawyers produced no textbook or other significant piece of writing on international economic law. For all practical purposes, the discipline came into being only after World War II.

Promises to abolish quantitative restrictions and lower tariffs given in Brussels in 1920 and in Portorose in 1921 were not realized however. Not a single country ratified the Portorose Protocol (League of Nations, 1944; Kindleberger, 1989; James, 2001; Findlay and O'Rourke, 2007, p. 443). The Genoa conference of 1922 urged a return to non-discrimination and tariff barriers instead of quantitative barriers, but without success. The League took up the subject, but to no avail. It summarized the interwar experience with rising protectionism in the following words: 'the international conferences unanimously recommended, and the great majority of Governments repeatedly proclaimed their intention to pursue, policies designed to bring about conditions of "freer and more equal trade;" yet never before in history were trade barriers raised so rapidly or discrimination so generally practiced' (League of Nations, 1944, p. 101). The Great Depression only increased demand for tariff protection in many countries, both industrialized and commodity producing ones. Deflation increased the barriers because tariffs were fixed in nominal terms (Findlay and O'Rourke, 2007, p. 447).

The League of Nations Covenant was not entirely silent on trade, and the League did regularly produce studies on trade. Article 23(3) of the Covenant bound member states to 'maintain freedom of communications and of transit and equitable treatment for the commerce of all Members of the League'. However, this provision was an empty shell given the qualification of the obligation in the chapeau of Article 23, which provided that this obligation was 'subject to and in accordance with the provisions of international conventions existing or hereafter agreed upon'. Thus, not only did the Covenant grandfather existing commercial treaties, it also placed no restrictions whatsoever on the ability of governments to enter into bilateral and preferential trade and financial agreements. Many governments availed themselves of this opportunity in the 1930s.

Furthermore, the League of Nations lacked compulsory, binding dispute settlement, unlike the WTO today. Article 14 of the Covenant of the League of Nations mandated the Council to develop plans for a standing international court. The parties established a Permanent Court of International Justice (PCIJ) three years later in 1922, but its name was soon to prove inauspicious. The League could request advisory opinions from the PCIJ, though they were only advisory, and not binding on the parties, and were not backed by enforcement measures. In practice, only one out of twenty-one advisory opinions rendered by the PCIJ arguably concerned economic or financial matters. That judgment, the PCIJ's Advisory Opinion in *Customs Regime between Germany and Austria*, centered on the question of whether Germany's and Austria's plans to enter into a customs union at the height of the Great Depression breached Austria's obligations under Article 88 of the Saint-Germain-en-Laye Peace Treaty designed to guarantee Austria's political independence.

In addition, some of the Court's contentious (non-advisory) cases concerned economic and financial matters, most famously the *Serbian and Brazilian Loans* cases. These two disputes, however, exclusively concerned the application and interpretation of national law governing sovereign bonds. Given the absence of economic and financial provisions in the Covenant itself, the Court's case law in the economic and financial sphere bore mostly on the interpretation of the economic and financial clauses of the Peace Treaties. Formalized legal dispute settlement in general, and in economic and financial matters in particular, played little role during the interwar period.

When the League sponsored new conventions that sought to facilitate the expansion of trade, the latter failed to be adequately implemented. For instance, in 1927, countries signed an ambitious agreement on the Abolition of Import and Export Prohibitions and Restrictions, following a resolution of the League Assembly and a recommendation of the International Economic Conference held at Geneva in May 1927 (Convention for the Abolition of Import and Export Prohibitions and Restrictions, 1927; Vagts, 2006, p. 774). All major developed states, including non-members of the League itself, such as the United States, were signatories. The Convention contained a general prohibition on prohibitions and restrictions on importation (Article 1) and provided for dispute settlement, but only with the agreement of the parties after a dispute had arisen (Article 8). But the Convention was undermined by a series of exceptions, including the general exception in Article 5 that allowed countries to restrict imports or exports 'in extraordinary and abnormal circumstances', in order to protect 'the vital interests of the country'. States also attached a significant number of reservations. The Convention was short-lived. For example, the United States and the United Kingdom withdrew from the Convention in the summer of 1933 (United States Department of State, 1933, pp. 783–786; Irwin, 2011).

Backlash and retreat into economic autarky and bilateralism in the interwar period

The Great Depression further revealed the weakness in the legalization of the multilateral trade and financial orders provided by the post-WWI treaties and League's statutes. As regards trade, in the United States, the Smoot-Hawley Tariff Act of 1930 increased the barriers on imports. It had a domino effect in other countries, leading to further tariff increases. Great Britain increased tariffs on many imported goods in 1932 to 10 percent. Even before Adolf Hitler came to power in 1933, Germany curtailed imports through exchange controls and licensing. Autarky became in vogue virtually everywhere.

Up to the Great Depression and the banking crises in many countries in its wake, most countries refrained from adopting capital controls. However, capital controls mushroomed from the early 1930s, particularly in response to capital flight related to banking crises. Argentina, Austria, Brazil, Czechoslovakia, Germany, Greece, Hungary, Uruguay, and Yugoslavia all adopted capital controls in 1931 (Mitchener and Wandschneider, 2013). China and Italy followed in 1934, and the United States applied capital controls from March 1933 to November 1934. Italy, for instance, introduced systematic capital controls to alleviate a sustained balance of payments deficit. Even though countries such as Australia, Canada, India, Mexico, South Africa, Sweden, Switzerland, and the UK refrained from using capital controls in the interwar period, by World War II, 'hardly a country [was] without exchange restrictions' (Nussbaum, 1939, p. 448).

Neither formal nor informal norms were able to substantially stem the rising tide of capital controls during this period. In reaction to the growing number of capital controls, a couple of Friendship, Commerce, and Navigation Treaties limited the freedom of states to adopt capital

TABLE 9.1 Selected capital controls in the interwar period (United States Tariff Commission, 1943)

Country	Types of capital controls introduced
Italy	In 1925, initial curbs on speculative capital movements through regulation. In May 1934, Italy prohibited any transaction in foreign exchange except for the purpose of financing effective trade and industry requirements or for travelling abroad. Any purchase by Italian investors of stocks and bonds issued abroad, as well as export of banknotes and checks, were also prohibited. Increased utilization of bilateral clearing agreements as a device for circumventing the restrictive effects on international trade of quotas and exchange rate controls.
Bulgaria	In 1933, the Bulgarian National Bank raised interest rates imposing further import restrictions to keep foreign capital in Bulgaria and halt depletion of foreign reserves. Bulgaria also concluded a series of bilateral clearing agreements.
Germany	During the early 1930s, Germany created a complex system of bilateral trade clearing agreements. German capital controls were initially imposed to curb capital outflows and maintained in order to keep the official foreign exchange rates for the Reichsmark at the old parity; thereafter, an extensive trade clearing system was created to offset the distortions of the capital controls. In 1931, Germany also introduced a flight tax to limit capital outflows.

controls (e.g. Greece–UK Treaty 1938). Others provided for the non-discriminatory application of exchange restrictions, or most-favored nation treatment with respect to foreign exchange restrictions (Shuster, 1973, pp. 98–100). The inclusion of these clauses was a response to the rising tide of unilateralism in international monetary affairs in the interwar period, including through capital controls. A small number of treaties prohibited the use of capital controls entirely, such as the Czechoslovakia–US Trade Agreement (Article X, Czechoslovakia–United States Trade Agreement, 1938), the Ecuador–US Trade Agreement (Article X, Ecuador–United States Trade Agreement, 1938), the Liberia–US trade agreement (Liberia–US Trade Agreement, 1938) and the Greece–US Trade Agreement (Article X, Greece–US Trade Agreement, 1938), but overall they had little global impact.

To be able to maintain trade relationships with countries that had imposed capital controls, countries increasingly entered into various clearing and transfer arrangements that 'facilitated the transfer of funds from one country to another in such a manner as to maintain the balance of payments between the two countries in a state of reasonable equilibrium'. (Hahn, 1990, pp. 310–313, p. 128.) Countries competed with one another to enter into bilateral clearing agreements to preserve their export market shares. Increasingly, capital controls not only supported the balance of payments. Governments also relied on them to give preferential treatment to certain sectors of the economy, and to restrict expensive imports.

As the multilateral regime fractured, countries increasingly turned to bilateral agreements to preserve their export markets. For example, in the United States, the Reciprocal Trade Agreements Act of 1934 gave authority to the President to negotiate agreements for the reciprocal reduction of tariffs. Renewed in 1937, 1940, 1943, and 1945, the United States entered into thirty-two such agreements under this authority (Vagts, 2006, p. 775). In the 1930s, Germany entered into a series of preferential agreements for the supply of raw materials, especially with countries in Eastern and Southern Europe that suffered from balance of payments difficulties. In this way, Germany secured access to raw material at preferential prices. This web of bilateral trade deals proliferated, involving Germany and other colonial empires such as Great Britain, including under Great Britain's Imperial Preference system established at Ottawa in 1932. This 'pernicious bilateralism' left the MFN principle as an empty shell (Findlay and O'Rourke, 2007, p. 451). As the League of Nations reported, ruefully looking back at the limited impact of the MFN clause in the interwar period: 'instead of facilitating, the [MFN] clause tended to obstruct the reduction of tariffs by means of bilateral or multilateral agreements, owing to the reluctance of governments to make concessions which would be generalized by it. This was the result, mainly of two causes: first, the refusal of the United States to reduce its own very high tariff by negotiation while claiming to benefit from any tariff reduction negotiated between European countries; secondly, the opposition of certain countries – notably the United Kingdom, the United States, and the British Dominions – to derogations from strict MFN practice permitting the conclusion of regional or similar agreements for tariff reduction, the benefits of which would be limited to the participants' (League of Nations, 1944, p. 119).

The Tripartite Agreement of 1936, under which France, Great Britain, and the United States agreed to consult on any changes in exchange rates, was a very soft precursor to the Bretton Woods System of fixed exchange rates. The three signatory countries pledged to consult with one another in advance. The IMF, by contrast, would later establish hard legal obligations on countries to adhere to fixed exchange rates backed by gold, and have a much broader membership.

To sum up, following the catastrophic experience of World War I and the enormous human and economic costs of the war, countries struggled to return to the pre-war normalcy in international economic relations. They succeeded somewhat at first, however imperfectly, but within the space of a bit more than a decade, the economic and political challenges became almost insurmountable, and the world economy relapsed into autarky. Despite being a comparatively strong international institution for its time, the League of Nations was ultimately powerless to prevent the backlash against economic openness in the interwar period. As we have seen, this failure may have been linked to the fact that international economic law as a distinct discipline did not exist in the interwar period, and that there were virtually no legal rules governing international economic exchange, aside from bilateral commercial treaties. To the extent formalized legal rules existed in the interwar period in the monetary and trade sphere, they were bilateral in character. The absence of multilateral disciplines led to widespread beggar-thy-neighbor policies. Non-discrimination, which had been central to the first golden era of globalization before World War I, was emasculated by the proliferation of bilateral trade agreements. The international trading system was dominated by an economic system based on preferential agreements – the most notorious example being Britain's imperial preferences for trade with its colonies and dominions.

Even though the contours of a distinct field started to emerge in the early twentieth century, the world had to wait until the institutionalization of the Bretton Woods institutions following World War II, for international trade to receive a multilateral legal frame.

THE RISE AND DECLINE IN LEGALIZATION OF THE MONETARY LEGAL ORDER: FROM WORLD WAR II TO THE 1970S

From the disastrous turn towards autarky and economic nationalism in the trade and monetary sphere during the interwar period, a strong commitment to a multilateral monetary order emerged after 1945. Leading policy makers, led by those in the United States and UK such as Harry Dexter White and John Maynard Keynes in particular, found that a robust multilateralism was necessary for prosperity and growth. Out of the ashes of World War II arose a new spirit of cooperation, not only in the political sphere with the creation of the United Nations as successor to the League of Nations, but also in international economic relations with the establishment of the Bretton Woods institutions. The trade regime followed, but took longer than the monetary regime to be formalized, with the World Trade Organization only being formed in 1995 as the successor to the 1948 General Agreement on Tariffs and Trade (GATT) following the Cold War's end.

The legalization of the monetary and trade orders from 1945 to the 1970s

In the preparations for the Bretton Woods conference, policymakers considered a unified organization for global economic governance on the model of the League of Nations (Dubin, 1983). In the Interwar Period, in some sense a peak organization (the League of Nations) addressed the different, but complementary, functions of international monetary stability and trade liberalization. The Economic and Financial Organization persistently advocated trade liberalization and the coordination of member state policies in the monetary sphere, but also without much success (Clavin, 2013). But it largely operated in the absence of formalized legal rules in either the trade or monetary sphere. Moreover, the organization was not universal and did not include all the important powers, most importantly, the United States, but also Germany and Italy after their withdrawal from the organization in 1933.

Thus, the Bretton Woods architects concluded that the League may not be the best model to replicate after World War II, as the trade and monetary non-order of the interwar period was characterized by 'competitive currency devaluations, excessive tariff barriers, uneconomic barter deals, multiple currency practices and unnecessary exchange restrictions' (U.S. State Department, 1948, p. 1226). The stated aim of the peak organizations of the trade and monetary legal orders since World War II – the GATT/WTO and the IMF – is to confine these 'desperate tactics of the past' to the dustbin of history. Instead of one, the framers of the Bretton Woods financial and trade framework decided to create two separate organizations, the IMF and an International Trade Organization, the latter not being formed because of US resistance and being substituted by the 'provisional' GATT. This decision would raise issues regarding the interface of these two legal orders and how they align in areas of overlapping jurisdiction, as Article I of the IMF Articles of Agreement includes not only financial stabilization, but also trade expansion, among the 'purposes' of the IMF: its goals are 'to promote international monetary cooperation through a permanent institution', 'facilitate the expansion and balanced growth of trade', 'promote exchange stability', 'maintain orderly exchange arrangements among members', and 'avoid competitive exchange depreciation'. This definition parallels the purpose of the GATT, and its successor, the WTO, which is to facilitate agreement among the organization's members for a liberalized trading order, and to oversee, monitor, and facilitate the maintenance of such order, including through legalized dispute settlement.

Still, the decision of states to opt for functional differentiation into separate trade and monetary regimes was largely due to the lessons that the architects of Bretton Woods drew from the comprehensive failures of macro-economic policy coordination in the interwar period. Functionally differentiated regimes, built on a higher degree of formalization, were to provide a stronger foundation for effective international economic governance. The IMF during the Bretton Woods system was at the center of overseeing and policing a system of fixed exchange rates. As the guardian of international monetary stability and the central mechanism for exchange rate coordination, the IMF had a comparatively narrow mandate. The greater focus of its work, compared to the League of Nations, may well have been an important ingredient in its higher degree of effectiveness as an international organization. Vesting narrow mandates in separate peak organizations is a perfectly understandable strategy in light of the failure of the League of Nations in the economic and financial sphere. Furthermore, following World War II, the new international monetary system was underpinned by a series of multilateral legal commitments, embodied chiefly in the IMF Articles of Agreement. This new monetary order was placed on a treaty footing, in contrast to the League, which had pinned its hopes for macroeconomic policy coordination on informal coordination by providing economic expertise and a forum for political exchange among national economic policymakers. The contemporary Bank for International Settlement, created in 1930, and to a significant degree the IMF after 1971, fit into the same mould.

The original architects of the Bretton Woods system, in particular, were wary of unchecked capital flows, and wished to retain room for states to address financial instability and crises. But they did not vest such authority in the IMF, partly because there was consensus among professional economists regarding the desirability of capital controls (Chwieroth, 2010). Nurske, the leading economist at the League of Nations working on the international monetary system in the interwar period, commenced in 1942 to write 'an historical account of the interwar experience of monetary problems ... with the objective of determining some principles of future monetary arrangements' (Clavin, 2013, p. 309). This led to Nurske's famous work *International Currency Experience: Lessons of the Interwar Period* (1944).

His book was highly influential and played a central role in shaping the Bretton Woods negotiations for creating the IMF and World Bank. It establishes the need for monetary order, and sought to avoid a repeat of the spaghetti bowl of capital controls and bilateral clearing agreements that had helped unravel the international economic system in the interwar period. Even more so than Nurske, the lead negotiators at Bretton Woods, Harry Dexter White for the United States and Keynes for the British, had long been concerned about the risks of 'hot money' to national and global financial stability, based primarily on the disastrous experience with free capital mobility in the 1920s in the lead up to the Great Depression. Keynes and White were both particularly suspicious of private capital flows. According to Keynes 'control of capital movements, both inward and outward, should be a permanent feature of the post-war system', a sentiment echoed by White who thought 'a good case could be made for ... the [government's] power to control the influx and efflux of capital' (Steil, 2013, p. 145). U.S. Secretary of the Treasury Henry Morgenthau even rejoiced that the IMF was located at a distance from Wall Street, and thus would 'drive ... the usurious money lenders from the temple of international finance' (Steil, 2013, p. 167). Morgenthau and his fellow New Dealers wanted an international financial system centered on the US Treasury, rather than one in the hands of private financiers, either on Wall Street or in the City of London.

The original IMF Articles of Agreement thus prioritized currency stability over capital mobility, and left untouched the ability of countries to regulate and restrict capital account transactions. Accordingly, the IMF Articles subject only current account transactions to the IMF's jurisdiction (such as those related to trade in goods), so that IMF members are free to restrict all capital account transfers (such as portfolio investment), provided these restrictions do not unduly delay current transactions (Article VI.3). The IMF Articles did not formally recognize the ability of states to impose capital controls in hard law, but permitted their introduction by their silence.

The framers of the Bretton Woods architecture knew that the establishment of a legalized framework facilitating the expansion of global trade would be arduous. In effect, it took several decades to dismantle the protectionist legacy of the two world wars and the interwar period, and the IMF was only one cause among many others (including, decolonization). One contemporary commentator wrote of the newly established International Monetary Fund: 'World trade cannot be restored and expanded unless the United Nations abandons the restrictive and discriminatory currency practices that became so prevalent in the 1930's. Their very existence is a threat to friendly economic relations. The International Fund, established to deal with this problem of currency warfare, is intended to facilitate the full flow of trade by promoting stable and orderly exchange arrangements. The members of the Fund have undertaken to maintain fair currency standards, under which trade can expand and grow' (Pehle, 1946, pp. 1127–1139, 1129).

But as long as imperial states (such as the UK and France) maintained systems of preferential trade with their colonies, the IMF could do little, and promoters of free trade would need to use various policy instruments. For the United States, one of the key objectives at the Bretton Woods conference was the abolition of imperial preferences and the creation of a level playing field. Britain fought a rearguard and ultimately an unsuccessful action to defend the colonial system and imperial preferences. The United States used its leverage from its lending to Britain under the Lend-Lease program to pressure the UK to abandon these preferences that privileged trade between the UK and its colonies. With the GATT, the United States aimed to institutionalize the removal of such trade discrimination, although it would take some time (Zeiler, 1997).

Between 1945 and 1971, the IMF was in many ways the world's most influential and independent international organization. It oversaw an exchange rate system in which all currencies were pegged to the US dollar, which was, in turn, backed by gold at $35 per ounce. Under the Bretton Woods system, coordinated activist monetary and fiscal policy with a view to remedying balance of payments imbalances replaced gold flows under the gold standard to which countries had tried to return during the interwar period, or automatic adjustment through floating exchange rates. By and large, the Bretton Woods system managed to internalize the externalities arising from monetary policy.

In the words of its former General Counsel Joseph Gold (1990, p. 2), the original par value system overseen by the IMF was 'unprecedented as a system for regulating the exchange rates of currencies under a multilateral treaty administered by an international organization'. The IMF rules on exchange rates were strict and states generally abided by them. Central banks regularly intervened in foreign exchange markets to maintain the pegs, and in practice, the pegs were rarely changed. The government treasury/central bank (depending on the national system) committed to exchange domestic currency for foreign currency at the par value. With a system of pegged exchange rates, there was no room for currency manipulation, unlike in the interwar period and from the 1970s onwards. Under the policies of embedded liberalism of the Bretton Woods system, countries maintained capital controls to provide stability and enhance their ability to develop social welfare systems.

The trade order was longer in the making than the monetary legal order, but its establishment also originated from the immediate post-war context. Unlike the IMF, the GATT was a weak organization when it began in 1948 as a 'provisional' agreement. The GATT nonetheless contained a series of detailed legal rules on trade in goods, as well as clear non-discrimination provisions (GATT Articles I on MFN treatment and GATT Article III on national treatment) that over time helped bury the preferential, bilateral legacy of the Interwar Period for trade in goods. The GATT brought about a secular decline in applied tariff rates through negotiated tariff ceilings.

The de-legalization of the monetary order and the collapse of the Bretton Woods system

The Bretton Woods system collapsed in the early 1970s when the United States unilaterally ended the dollar's convertibility to gold and imposed an across-the-board tariff increase of 10 percent (Gardner, 1985). The dollar, as a result, became a fiat currency, one no longer backed by gold or any other precious metal. The Bretton Woods system of pegged exchange rates rapidly gave way to a world of national choice of exchange arrangements, with the United States and other major economies moving to floating exchange rates, subject to periodic government interventions.

Europe was more ambivalent about the move to floating exchange rates, at least insofar as it concerned fluctuations of European currencies against each other. In 1969, the heads of state of the EEC first called for the progressive creation of an economic and monetary union, and the

EEC Council created the so-called 'snake' in 1972, which operated outside the formal EEC Treaty. Pursuant to it, the members' central banks were to coordinate the management of their currencies within narrow margins of fluctuation against the dollar. The 'snake' quickly failed, a casualty of the breakup of the Bretton Woods system, but it represented a predecessor of the European Rate Mechanism of the European Monetary System (EMS) established in 1978, to be subsequently followed by the creation of a single currency for seventeen European states, the Euro.

Another way of viewing the change following the collapse of the Bretton Woods system is that political and market ordering displaced legal ordering. Legal ordering of trade and monetary relations, certainly on a multilateral level, was substantially new following World War II. As we have seen in Section I, no comparable legal order existed in the interwar period; and the stability of the pre-World War I system resulted from informal cooperation, largely among central banks, rather than legalized ordering in the modern sense. Pre-1914 and post-1989, markets determined the value of floating currencies, although with important exceptions, such as the People's Republic of China on account of its market interventions.

Following the collapse of the Bretton Woods system, the IMF's role significantly decreased as regards developed economies. This secular decline of the monetary legal order echoes the weakening of the informal monetary legal order that developed in the first golden period for global capital in the late nineteenth century. The Banque de France, the Bank of England, and the German Reichsbank were the central decision-makers in international economic affairs at the beginning of the twentieth century. At the beginning of the twentieth century, the United States was absent from this exclusive club as Congress established the Federal Reserve system only in 1913.

The percentage of lawyers among the staff of an international organization provides a rough proxy for the degree of legalization of a legal order. In the case of the League of Nations – apart from its work in the political sphere where lawyers played at times an influential role – the number of lawyers providing legal advice was close to zero. A substantial percentage of League staff had trained as lawyers. Yet their role at the League, by and large, was not to provide legal advice. Rather, like all other staff, they were mostly engaged in providing policy advice and report on the state of the economies of League member countries. A good example is Leon Bourgeois, a lawyer by training who was elected the first President of the Council of the League. For the IMF today (which has been the case since its creation in 1945), the percentage of lawyers working for the organization is around 3 percent (around fifty lawyers out of a total professional staff of about 2,000).

Another way of evaluating the role of law in an international organization is to attempt to measure the influence of lawyers on the policy-making process. There is little doubt that lawyers influence the policy-making process more directly and more frequently at the WTO than at the IMF or in the League of Nations. On the whole, the IMF Legal Department is not centrally involved in the formation of policy-making at the Fund, even though it plays a central role in ensuring compliance with Fund policies and has increasingly been involved in providing technical assistance to IMF member countries on matters as diverse as effective corporate insolvency frameworks, the formulation of central banking statutes, and financial regulation. Economists play the dominant roles in the IMF on matters of policy generally and for the IMF surveillance missions in particular.

From the early 1970s, the IMF's primary function changed from being coordinator and potential enforcer of an international monetary system of rules-based pegged exchange rates, to being a surveillance organization that issues country reports regarding a country's economic and balance-of-payments situation, and a lender and adviser for developing countries facing balance-of-payments problems. In the contemporary world of floating exchange rates, there are few monetary rules left for the IMF to police and enforce. This return of the monetary legal order to informality and central bank coordination harks back to the interwar period.

Whereas the creation of the IMF resulted in considerable exchange rate stability for the duration of the Bretton Woods system of fixed exchange rates so that the interface of the trade and monetary legal orders raised a few questions, that interface became much more challenging as regards global imbalances and exchange rates following the collapse of the Bretton Woods arrangement and the turn to floating exchange rates by the world's major economies in the 1970s. IMF Article IV now permits countries to choose their exchange arrangements, subject to IMF surveillance and member compliance with a series of principles that are rather soft in nature and in practice. As Andreas Lowenfeld (2010, p. 582) writes, 'the *fundamental rule* [of pegged exchange rates] was *replaced by a non-rule*' (emphasis added). Law receded as a means to resolve conflicts between debtor and surplus countries.

The revised IMF Articles (of 1978) create only minimal legal requirements, ones that are difficult to apply and enforce in practice. The preamble to revised Article IV provides that 'each member undertakes to collaborate with the Fund and other members to assure orderly exchange arrangements and to promote a stable system of exchange rates'. Section 1(iii) of Article IV provides, 'in particular', that members shall 'avoid manipulating exchange rates or the international monetary system in order to prevent effective balance-of-payments adjustment or to gain an unfair competitive advantage over other members'. The legal standard for showing 'manipulation' is a delicate one because it includes both objective and subjective criteria – that of government intervention in exchange markets, and that of a country's intent. The IMF has never made such a finding.

Pursuant to Article IV, the IMF adopted a surveillance system to ensure members' compliance with their obligations, and thereby protect the stability of the global monetary system. Article IV, Section 3(a) mandates that the IMF shall 'oversee the international monetary system in order to ensure its effective operation, and shall oversee the compliance of each member with its obligations under Section 1 of this Article'.

Members are to cooperate fully with the IMF and, to this end, 'shall provide the Fund with the information necessary', and 'when requested by the Fund, shall consult with it on the member's exchange rate policies' (Article IV.3.b.). In 1977, the IMF Executive Board adopted a 'Decision on Surveillance over Exchange Rate Policies' which established several factors that the Fund must consider 'which might indicate the need for discussion with a member' (IMF Executive Board Decision 1977). Included in these factors is 'protracted large-scale intervention in one direction in exchange markets'. In this way, the IMF can attempt to use the shadow of IMF rules to persuade countries to change their behavior.

As Rosa Lastra writes, '[f]rom being a virtually self-enforcing arrangement subject to *strict rules*, surveillance now becomes a function in which judgment is of the essence. Surveillance is no longer a rules-based regime but a "*discretion based regime*"' (emphasis added) (Lastra, 2006, p. 400). The monetary legal order for exchange rate governance had largely folded. That left it ill-equipped to deal with new challenges, such as increasingly frequent allegations of currency misalignment and manipulation. Currency misalignment and manipulation was a central factor in the fracturing of international cooperation in the interwar period, and would once more pose a major challenge following the financial crisis and so-called Global Recession of 2008.

In practice, the role of the IMF has been very limited, leaving an important gap in the institution whose mandate is to safeguard global financial stability. The Fund has initiated and conducted formal consultations with members regarding their exchange rate policy only twice, on an ad hoc basis, with Sweden in 1982 and South Korea in 1987 (Goldstein, 2006, p. 150). In both cases, the IMF did not make a finding that the country was unlawfully manipulating its currency, but only consulted with it in order to induce it to change its domestic practices. On global imbalances, the world similarly lacks hard legal rules, just like in the interwar period. When disputes arose following the collapse of Bretton Woods system of fixed exchange rates, governments used diplomacy and political pressure to coordinate a realignment of exchange rates, as reflected in the 1985 Plaza Accord – similar to the 1936 Tripartite Agreement for exchange rate coordination between the UK, France, and the United States.

Under the Plaza Accord of 1985, the United States, United Kingdom, France, Japan, and West Germany collectively intervened in currency markets to induce an appreciation of the yen and deutsche mark, and thereby help stem protectionist pressures from the private sector for restrictive trade measures in the United States. They did so, however, in a particular geopolitical context in which Japan and Europe depended on the US security umbrella in the context of the Cold War, and the United States exercised greater market power than it does today.

Formal dispute settlement likewise plays no role in international monetary law under the IMF today. Even though the IMF Articles contain binding rules, and the IMF in theory can impose sanctions to enforce them, such as withdrawing eligibility of a member's access to Fund resources, suspending its voting rights, or even compelling it to withdraw from the Fund, in reality, ineligibility for funds and suspension of voting rights are rare occurrences in Fund practice, and no country has yet been forced out of the IMF. The Fund, moreover, lacks a formal dispute settlement system. Rather the Fund relies on consultations with IMF members where IMF authority is based on Fund professional 'expertise', and, if applicable, any leverage the Fund has over a country in financial difficulty, as in the context of IMF financing arrangements. Although some of the IMF's legal provisions are formally hard, they are in practice rather soft, in particular because their enforcement depends on consultations (Gold, 1982).

Although IMF members attempted to elaborate new rules to address exchange rate controversies in the 2000s, the rules remained weak in practice. There has been a similar turn towards informality in international finance more generally. Even though international monetary law retains a bedrock of hard legal rules, international monetary law is curiously silent about the major risk to global monetary stability – private international finance, where soft law predominates.

POST-1989: MISALIGNMENT, FRAGMENTATION AND POSSIBLE ECLIPSE

After 1989: the judicialization of WTO and the de-legalization of the IMF

When the Berlin Wall fell and the Soviet Union collapsed, ideas of market liberalization triumphed, reflected in the rise of the 'Washington consensus', a term coined in 1989 regarding neoliberal reform packages advocated by international financial institutions and other policy makers for developing countries to become more market-oriented (Williamson, 1990). The Uruguay Round of trade negotiations, which had been initiated in 1988, concluded with the agreement to create, for the first time, a formal international trade organization, the WTO, in 1995. Following the WTO's formation, the trade legal order reached the height of its influence. The WTO expanded the trade order's legal scope to include an array of new agreements covering non-tariff barriers, services, and intellectual property protection. The WTO's geographic scope continued to expand significantly, as its membership grew to 161 by May 2015, including China and Russia that joined in 2001 and 2012 respectively.

Under the post-Cold War trade legal order, WTO dispute settlement panels and the WTO Appellate Body issue legal rulings are binding on the parties to the dispute. These rulings are likewise regularly cited for their interpretations and applications of WTO law in subsequent disputes and rulings. If the respondent fails to comply with a ruling, the complainant has the option to enforce it through withdrawing trade concessions in an equivalent amount, something unthinkable in the IMF context. The WTO system also provides mechanisms for consultations and peer review that can facilitate compliance, but they exist and operate in parallel and in the shadow of the formal WTO dispute settlement system.

The WTO system has become much more legalized than the original GATT and is now built on a hard law model that can affect deliberations in its soft law-type forums. WTO members filed 492 cases before the WTO dispute settlement system as of May 2015. WTO hard law thus exercises a much greater shadow effect on interactions within the WTO committee system. This judicialization of the trading order has curtailed the power of diplomats in favor of lawyers (Weiler, 2002), and potentially made it more challenging to reconcile the trade and monetary organizational cultures.

This increased legalization is reflected in the rising percentage of lawyers among the staff of the WTO: the percentage of lawyers at the WTO today is higher than before (WTO Annual Report, 2013). The number and role of lawyers has risen significantly within the WTO secretariat compared to under the GATT. With the decline of negotiating activity in the WTO and the ongoing importance of formalized dispute settlement, the WTO's Legal Affairs division (servicing all dispute settlement panels other than for import relief matters), the Rules division (servicing all panels on antidumping, subsidy, and safeguard relief matters), and the Appellate Body division (hearing appeals of all panel decisions), have risen in importance.

The rise of the influence of lawyers in the modern trade legal order is a recent phenomenon. The GATT Director General laid the seeds for the increasing influence of legal professionals when he created a small legal affairs division of three lawyers within the secretariat in 1982. This staffing of GATT dispute settlement panels with lawyers reflected and facilitated the move towards a more legalized dispute settlement system. With the WTO's creation in 1995, WTO members created a compulsory dispute settlement system to interpret and apply its legal requirements and authorize enforcement measures. No longer could a defendant unilaterally block the creation of a panel or the adoption of a panel report. The role of lawyers in the WTO secretariat accordingly rose.

Both the WTO agreements and the IMF Articles – whose reach was widest during the Bretton Woods period – formally imposed hard law obligations, but today, the density of hard rules differs considerably. Whereas the WTO agreements contain hundreds of pages of legal rules, backed by a formalized dispute settlement system, the number of hard law obligations in the IMF Articles is small. The result has been coordination challenges in key areas affecting the interface of the two regimes, and in particular regarding the issue of currency manipulation when a WTO member intervenes on the currency markets or otherwise engages in macro-economic policies that depreciate its currency and provide commercial advantages to its domestic producers in international trade.

In contrast to the process of judicialization that has taken place in the WTO, the IMF has been more and more sidelined as a possible third party in international financial and commercial disputes over issues that fall under its jurisdiction, as illustrated by the recent evolution of the regulatory framework over capital controls. As said before, the founders of the Bretton Woods architecture had been very wary about the destabilizing effects of the free flow of capital, but the IMF did not create a clear system of hard law over the issue. Over the last decade, the implied authorization for capital controls that is inscribed in the IMF Articles has been increasingly overridden by bilateral free trade and investment agreements. The first step in this turn to bilateralism was a generalized move away from capital controls. During the 1970s and 1980s, US officials reversed their views on capital controls. In 1972, the United States announced for the first time at an IMF meeting that it opposed capital controls and would remove its own by the end of 1974. US officials then led a movement to overturn Keynesian views towards capital controls in the IMF and abroad. In the 1990s, the United States targeted controls that particularly affected the US financial sector (Chwieroth, 2010, p. 146).

This shift of views in the United States would soon lead to a domino effect in Europe and subsequently elsewhere. During the late 1980s and the 1990s, a new regional legal order emerged in Europe that provided for the elimination of capital controls. Under the Maastricht Treaty on European Union in 1993, European Union Law prohibited capital controls, and free capital mobility has since been further entrenched in EU law (now Article 63 of the Treaty on the Functioning of the European Union (TFEU). Today, 'the very definition of a "European" state includes a commitment to capital mobility' (Abdelal, 2007, p. 83). This prohibition of capital controls underpins the European Monetary Union.

During the 1990s, the IMF too became increasingly receptive to the liberalization of global finance. IMF management and staff appeared to lead the charge as part of a neoliberal ideological turn, despite resistance from some of the IMF's membership, especially developing countries (Abdelal, 2007). First, the Second Amendment to the IMF Articles in 1978 partially constrained countries' seemingly unqualified right to impose capital controls (under Article VI) by extending the IMF's surveillance function (under Article IV) to address the implications of national measures for global financial stability in a system without multilaterally fixed exchange rates. In its surveillance and technical assistance, IMF staff advocated and spurred countries to liberalize their capital controls, as well as to adopt financial standards and codes built largely from US and UK models (Chwieroth, 2010).

In the mid 1990s, IMF management, supported by developed country members of the Executive Board, pushed for an amendment of the IMF Articles to grant the IMF explicit jurisdiction over capital account transactions. The Executive Board approved a mandate to work on a new amendment to promote capital account liberalization through which countries' capital accounts would be progressively liberalized, just as their current accounts had been earlier (Fischer, 1998). The East Asian crisis of 1998 undermined these efforts. Developing countries opposed the IMF initiative almost in block. In September 1998, Malaysia banned all international capital transfers for one year to prevent contagion from the devaluation of the Thai baht. Its decision attracted considerable controversy, as it went against economic orthodoxy of the time, but the decision is now widely considered to have been a prudent measure (Kaplan and Rodrik, 2001). India and China continued to maintain limited openness in their capital account, and unlike many of their Asian peers, were spared serious banking and financial crises. The IMF quietly shelved its initiative and then altered its position over capital controls after being severely chastened for its handling of the crisis (Blustein, 2012).

When multilateral initiatives to guarantee free capital mobility failed to make much headway, the United States and some countries in Europe, lobbied by their financial sectors, became active in negotiating mostly bilateral free trade and investment agreements that restrict the use of capital controls and lead to patchwork liberalization of capital accounts through the backdoor (Waibel, 2009). Bilateral investment treaties (BITs) and free trade agreements (FTAs) with free transfer clauses are misaligned with the monetary legal order when it comes to addressing financial crises. Unlike the WTO's General Agreement on Trade in Services (GATS), the great majority of these clauses do not refer to the IMF Articles of Agreement, nor foresee any role for the IMF and its expertise in assessing whether restrictions on capital account are justified on balance-of-payments grounds. German and US BITs typically do not even contain a balance-of-payments exception. By contrast, ASEAN member countries learned painful lessons in the Asian financial crisis of 1998, and these lessons are reflected in the detailed exceptions to the free transfer provisions in the ASEAN Comprehensive Investment Agreement of 2009 (Desierto, 2012). The agreement contains extensive references to the IMF Articles in order to justify the imposition of capital controls.

These BITs and FTAs also grant private rights to investors to enforce the commitments through investor-state arbitration, so that host states become liable for compensation to investors when they impose transfer restrictions. The threat of such investment disputes can change the calculus of governments and chill the use of capital controls. The turn away from informality and towards enforceability of norms of free capital mobility in BITs and FTAs risks restricting policy space for governments. Provided these norms guaranteeing free capital mobility are effective, they will prevent a vicious circle of capital controls. Notwithstanding, on the basis of the experience in the interwar period, these bilateral agreements may go too far by ruling out an instrument of macro-economic policy management that may be necessary, in extreme cases, to prevent rapid capital flight, such as in Iceland in October 2008. It also leads to fragmentation in the international monetary order based on competition for market access rather than policy coordination.

Thus, today, we observe further differentiation on geographic lines within the trade and monetary legal orders, resulting in growing fragmentation. Regional and bilateral alternatives and complements to the multilateral regime have risen to prominence, especially since the Doha Round of trade negotiations stalled and since the failure to create a multilateral regime for investment – the Multilateral Agreement on Investment, or MAI). For example, today the WTO, the EU, US, and other nations' bilateral free trade and investment agreements address capital transfers and capital controls in different ways (Shaffer and Waibel, 2015).

Even though bilateralism in trade and finance is not nearly as pervasive in trade and monetary affairs today as it was in the interwar period, the rise of bilateralism in trade and investment agreements over the last decade in particular poses challenges to both the modern trade and monetary legal orders, and their interface. Both the trade and the monetary transnational legal orders may now be past their peaks. The monetary regime, whose rapid decline – compared to the former glory of the IMF under the Bretton Woods system – came with the transition towards floating exchange rates by the world's major economies, may provide a crystal ball into the future of the trade regime.

The failure to deal with disputes between debtor and creditor states

Post-1989, the functional differentiation between the IMF (whose main purposes, although they include the expansion of global trade, focus on financial issues dealing with balance of payments imbalances) and the WTO may have become the Achilles heel of the trade and monetary transnational legal orders. New challenges have arisen at the interface of the trade and monetary legal orders that neither order is able to satisfactorily resolve, such as the issues of exchange rates and global imbalances. These challenges of institutional interaction are substantially new since the WTO, the peak organization for the trade regime, was established only in the mid 1990s, and informal policy coordination has become more challenging with the diffusion of economic power, reflected in the rise of China and other emerging economies and the relative decline of US and European economic power.

Over the last decade, global imbalances and associated allegations of currency misalignment and manipulation have become one of the most pressing issues facing the international community. What role can the trade and the monetary legal orders play in ensuring the orderly unwinding of global imbalances? This unwinding poses a major threat to not only cross-border trade in goods and services, and cross-border financial transactions, but to the stability of the international economic system as a whole. Thus far the monetary and trade legal orders have not assisted countries in alleviating these global imbalances, as actors have considered but so far been unable or unwilling to use law for such ends. These global imbalances are widely seen as one of the proximate causes of the global financial crisis that started in 2008.

It is a time-honoured pattern that surplus and deficit countries tend to disagree about the solution to global imbalances, one that goes back to the interwar period involving disputes among debtor and surplus countries (Meissner, 2010). Debtor countries tend to advocate multilateral solutions that require creditor countries to assume some responsibility for limiting global imbalances. Yet time and time again, surplus countries, whose identity has changed over time, resist such moves. As a result, we presently have no hard rules and preciously little soft law that could help with unwinding global imbalances resulting from exchange rate misalignment. Germany in the interwar period, and the UK following World War II, adopted the position characteristic of the deficit countries, contending that part of the burden of adjustment should fall on surplus countries, such as the United States. At Bretton Woods, the United States, which was the major surplus country at the end of World War II, blocked Keynes' initiatives for multilateral rules to be introduced which imposed obligations on both surplus and deficit countries to adjust imbalances (Steil, 2013, p. 208).

In the intervening decades, the United States has become the world's largest deficit country, and China the world's largest surplus country. Not surprisingly, in the last decade, the United States has pressed the IMF to interpret and apply IMF rules to induce China to change its exchange rate policies so as to reduce China's surplus, and has toyed with the idea of imposing sanctions on China for deliberately undervaluing its exchange rate through interventions on the currency markets. More recently, Germany has come under pressure from its Eurozone partners and the US government, among others, to do its part in reducing imbalances by boosting domestic demand and investment, and as a consequence, at least partly unwinding its sizeable trade surplus.

Because China is the largest creditor in the world and has a huge trade surplus, China became a center of concern in the United States during the 2000s regarding the interface of trade and monetary policy. China has actively and regularly intervened on foreign exchange markets to stem the likely appreciation of its currency (the renminbi, or yuan). China's foreign exchange reserves have risen in the process from $403 billion at the end of 2003 to over $3.3 trillion by the end of 2011 (CIA). US policy makers have responded by raising allegations of currency manipulation, as reflected in the 2012 US political campaign in which Republican candidate Mitt Romney proclaimed that he would declare China a currency manipulator on his first day of office.

In comparison, the relationship between the United States and China in the trade legal order has been considerably less contentious. The approach of China to the WTO has been largely cooperative. As of May 2015, China has been complainant in thirteen cases, and respondent in thirty-three cases before the WTO's Dispute Settlement Body (WTO website). The United States brought fourteen of the cases against China. As a rule, China has complied with panel reports and Appellate Body decisions, with the recent exception of the *Publications and Audiovisual Products* (WTO, DS363) where China only implemented the AB's ruling with a delay of two-and-a-half years (Zhang and

Li, 2014). Since 2008, China has proactively used WTO dispute settlement, increasingly also acting as a complainant as a result of rising legalism and socialization (Harpaz, 2010; Huang and Ji, 2012).

The US government's attempt to press the IMF to be more aggressive towards China in its Article IV surveillance, aiming to induce the IMF to pressure China to permit the renminbi to appreciate. These actions divided IMF staff, some of whom found 'that the US Treasury wanted them to do its dirty work' (Blustein, 2012, p. 11). The IMF staff felt under considerable pressure from the US Treasury to find that renminbi was fundamentally misaligned, allegedly even sparking remarks from IMF Managing Director Dominique Strauss Kahn that it was 'blackmail' because the IMF needed Congressional votes to maintain the Fund's financial viability (Blustein, 2012, p. 21).

In 2007, the IMF staff prepared and the Executive Board adopted a revision to the IMF's surveillance guidelines, called 'Decision on Bilateral Surveillance over Member's Policies'. Controversially, the IMF Decision adopted 'fundamental exchange rate misalignment' as its key term for surveillance, which was the very language used in a US Senate bill sponsored by Senators Charles Grassley and Max Baucus, the Republican and Democratic leaders of the Senate Finance Committee. The IMF Executive Board adopted the principles despite China's vote to the contrary, after considerable IMF and US efforts at persuading non-OECD members of the Executive Board who initially opposed it. This 2007 Decision could be read as tempering the reference to 'currency manipulation' (the 'scarlet M' in the words of U.S. Treasury Under Secretary Timothy Adams) (Blustein, 2012, p. 12) with the less politically-charged language of 'fundamental exchange rate misalignment', and to do so in the context of an open-ended, but formally binding IMF Article IV undertaking.

The Fund's staff attempted to implement the Decision in preparing the next Article IV report on China in September 2008, finding that 'there are significant concerns that the exchange rate may be fundamentally misaligned and exchange rate policies could be a significant contributor to external instability'. However, the IMF did not publicly release the report in light of the bankruptcy of Lehman Brothers that catalyzed the global financial crisis. It was an inopportune time to pick a fight with China (Blustein, 2012, p. 21).

China reacted vigorously to the IMF Decision and draft surveillance report. It was particularly concerned that such a report could provide ammunition for a WTO complaint against it, as well as justification of unilateral protectionist measures. China stopped high-level contacts with the IMF. The IMF eventually backed down and, abandoned use of the term 'fundamental misalignment'. It quickly adopted a 'revised operational guidance' for its 2007 decision that it put on its website, noting: 'The attempt to apply exchange rate-related "labels" – for instance the use of specific terminology such as "fundamental misalignment"... has proved an impediment to effective implementation of the Decision'. The IMF acknowledged that this episode had been 'damaging [to] the Fund's credibility' (Blustein, 2012, p. 23). It abandoned the use of the term 'fundamental misalignment' and rather used terms such as 'under-or overvaluation' in its ensuing country reports under Article IV (IMF 2009, [8]).

In light of the United States failure to enlist the IMF in challenging China's exchange rate policy, the handling of the issue of global imbalances and currency valuations shifted to the G20, reflecting the rise of emerging economies in global governance and a move away from international law and independent international institutions such as the IMF. The G20 launched a new process at its Pittsburg summit in September 2009, entitled a Framework for Strong, Sustainable, and Balanced Growth. Under the framework, members agreed to a multilateral Mutual Assessment Process under which they identify objectives, policies to achieve them, and a peer-review monitoring process. Positions, however, continue to divide, such as between the United States, which wants quantitative benchmarks and a peer-review mechanism for assessing currency misalignment, and China, which resists constraints on it. In short, law has played little role, and the turn to political ordering has been unsuccessful.

CONCLUSION

In the 1940s, the United States and UK took the lead in creating new international institutions to address international monetary and trade issues through law. They created two distinct trade and monetary legal orders, one governing monetary affairs through the IMF, and the other governing trade matters through the GATT. How they interact, and how the terms of this interaction have changed over time, tells us something important about the history of economic globalization.

However, when the international economy moved towards floating exchange rates and free capital mobility in the 1970s and with increasing liberalization post-1989 with the collapse of the Berlin Wall symbolizing the end of the Cold War, the interface between the monetary and trade legal orders became more conflicted. In particular, the issue of exchange rates is a non-law area today, much like during the interwar period. The fragmentation of law reflected in the rise of bilateral trade and investment agreements further opens up the prospect of conflict on the issue of capital controls, curtailing government policy space to prudentially address financial stability and to respond to financial crises. As the monetary legal order under the IMF has become less legalized, the trading order has become more so under the WTO and bilateral agreements, with many of the latter guaranteeing the free movement of capital and thus countering the implied authorization for capital controls under the IMF Articles.

The misalignment of the two legal orders on exchange rates, in turn, spurs demands for trade protectionism, in a global economy still dealing with the hangover of the global financial crisis of 2008, much like the overhang of debt in the interwar period that was intimately linked to the issues of exchange rates, balance of payments, and the use of capital controls to stem capital flight. The absence of third party dispute settlement leaves the issue of exchange rate coordination entirely to negotiations between governments. Similar to the interwar period, both surplus and deficit countries struggle to fashion solutions in multilateral and bilateral negotiations to unwind global imbalances.

In the interwar period, the collapse of the gold standard and the rise of currency instability affected trade and investment with a lag. A repeat of this experience is a possibility. Dark clouds stemming from the backlash against financial globalization are likely to hang over the contemporary international economic system for some time. The resilience and adaptability of the trade and monetary legal orders are likely to face particular challenges in the coming years. The interwar experience points to the limits of political ordering. Diplomacy cannot substitute for weak legal ordering in all circumstances. The shadow of international economic law can provide useful stimulants for governments to reach cooperative solutions to some of the gravest challenges facing the world economy, such as global imbalances and high levels of private and public indebtedness. But there is no guarantee that it will do so.

Bibliography

Abbott, Kenneth W., Duncan Snidal. 2000, "Hard Law and Soft Law in International Governance." *International Organization*. 54 (3): 421–456.

Abdelal, R. 2007, *Capital Rules: The Construction of Global Finance*, Harvard University Press, Cambridge, MA.

Ahamed, L. 2009, *Lords of Finance: The Bankers who Broke the World*, William Heinemann, London.

Bhagwati, J. 1998, "The Capital Myth: The Difference between Trade in Widgets and Dollars." *Foreign Affairs*, May/June, pp. 7–12.

Blustein, P. 2012, "A Flop and a Debacle: Inside the IMF's Global Rebalancing Acts," in CIGI Papers No. 4, Centre for International Governance Innovation, Ontario, Canada.

Boughton, J.M. 2004, "The IMF and the Force of History: Ten Events and Ten Ideas That Have Shaped the Institution," Working Paper WP/04/75, International Monetary Fund, Washington DC.

Brummer, C. 2012, *Soft Law and the Global Financial System: Rule Making in the 21st Century*, Cambridge University Press, Cambridge, UK; New York, NY.

Chwieroth, J. 2010, *Capital Ideas: The IMF and the Rise of Financial Liberalization*, Princeton University Press, Princeton, NJ.

Clavin P. 2013, *Securing the World Economy: The Reinvention of the League of Nations, 1920–1946*, Oxford University Press, Oxford.

Cooper, R.N. 1967, "National Economic Policy in an Interdependent World Economy." *Yale Law Journal*, vol. 76, no. 2: 1273–1298.

Convention for the Abolition of Import and Export Prohibitions and Restrictions, 1928, signed at Geneva on Nov 8, 1927, 25 AJIL (1931), 9 League of Nations O. J. 728.

Czechoslovakia-United States Trade Agreement 1938, 200 LNTS 87.

Desierto, D.A. 2012, "Investment Treaties: ASEAN" in Gochoco-Bautista, M. Socorro (ed.) *Asia Rising Growth and Resilience in an Uncertain Global Economy*, Edward Elgar, Cheltenham/Northampton, MA, 184–212.

Dubin, M. 1983, "Transgovernmental Process in the League of Nations." *International Organization*, vol. 37: 469–493.

Ecuador-United States Trade Agreement 1938, 193 LNTS 85.

Eichengreen, B. 2008, *Globalizing Capital: A History of the International Monetary System*, 2nd edn, Princeton University Press, Princeton, NJ.

Eichengreen, B. 2011, "Why the Dollar's Reign is Near an End," *Wall Street Journal*, www.wsj.com/articles/SB10001424052748703313304576132170 18101324.

Einzig, P. 1934, *Exchange Control*, Macmillan, London.

Estevadeordal, A., Frantz, B. and Taylor A.M. 2003, "The Rise and Fall of World Trade, 1870–1939," *The Quarterly Journal of Economics*, vol. 118, no. 2: 359–407.

Findlay, R. and O'Rourke, K.H. 2007, *Power and Plenty: Trade, War, and the World Economy in the Second Millennium*, Princeton University Press, Princeton, NJ.

Fischer, S. 1998, *Should the IMF Pursue Capital-Account Convertibility?* International Finance Section Department of Economics, Princeton University.

Gardner, R.N. 1985, "Sterling-Dollar Diplomacy in Current Perspective," *International Affairs*, vol. 62: 21–33.

Gesetz über Verbot der Ausfuhr und Durchfuhr von Gold, 13 November 1915, *RGBl* 1915, 763 (Germany).

Greece-United States Trade Agreement 1938, 195 LNTS 145.

Gold, J. and International Monetary Fund 1990, *Legal Effects of Fluctuating Exchange Rates*, International Monetary Fund, Washington DC.

Gold, J. 1983, "Strengthening the Soft International Law of Exchange Rates," *American Journal of International Law*, vol. 77: 443–489.

Goldstein, M. 2006, "Currency Manipulation and Enforcing the Rules of International Monetary System" in Truman, E. (ed.) *Reforming the IMF for the 21st Century*, Institute of International Economics, Washington D.C.

Hahn, H.J. 1990, *Währungsrecht*, Beck, Munich.

Halliday, T. and Shaffer, G. 2015, *Transnational Legal Orders*, Cambridge University Press, Cambridge.

Harpaz, M.D. 2010, "Sense and Sensibilities of China and WTO Dispute Settlement." *Journal of World Trade*, vol. 44: 1155–1186.

Huang, C. and Ji W. 2012. "Understanding China's Recent Active Moves on WTO Litigation: Rising Legalism and/or Reluctant Response?" *Journal of World Trade*, vol. 46: 1281–1308.

IMF Executive Board Decision No. 5392-(77/63) 29 April 1977.

Irwin, D.A. 2011, *Peddling Protectionism: Smoot-Hawley and the Great Depression*, Princeton University Press, Princeton, NJ.

Irwin, D.A. 2012, *Trade Policy Disaster: Lessons from the 1930s*, MIT Press, Cambridge, MA.

James, H. 2011, *The End of Globalization: Lessons from the Great Depression*, Harvard University Press, Cambridge, MA.

Kaplan, E. and Rodrik, D. 2001, 'Did the Malaysian Capital Controls Work?', National Bureau of Economic Research NBER Working Paper No. 8142.

Kindleberger, C.P. 1981. "Dominance and Leadership in the International Economy: Exploitation, Public Goods, and Free Rides," *International Studies Quarterly*, vol. 25: 242–254.

Kindleberger, C.P. 1989, *Manias, Panics, and Crashes: A History of Financial Crises*, 2nd edn, Macmillan, London.

Lastra, R.M. 2006, *Legal Foundations of International Monetary Stability*, Oxford University Press, Oxford.

Laughlin, J.L. 1927. "The Gold-Exchange Standard," *The Quarterly Journal of Economics*, vol. 41, no. 4: 644–663.

League of Nations, 1944, *International Currency Experiences: Lessons of the Inter-War Period*, League of Nations: Economic, Financial and Transit Department.

Liberia-United States Trade Agreement, 1938, 201 LNTS 163.

Lipson, C. 1985, *Standing Guard: Protecting Foreign Capital in the Nineteenth and Twentieth Centuries*, University of California Press, Berkeley, CA.

Lowenfeld, A. 2010, "The International Monetary System: A Look Back Over Seven Decades," *Journal of Economic International Law*, vol. 13, no. 3: 575–595.

Meissner C. 2010, "Surplus Reversals in Large Nations: The Cases of France and Great Britain in the Interwar Period" in Claessens S, Evenett S and Hoekman B (eds.), *Rebalancing the Global Economy: A Primer for Policymaking*, Centre for Economic Policy Research.

Mitchener, K.J. and Wandschneider, K. 2013, "Capital Controls and Recovery from the Financial Crisis of the 1930s," Centre for Competitive Advantage in the Global Economy, University of Warwick, No 132.

Nussbaum A. 1939, *Money in the Law*, Foundation Press, Chicago, IL.

Pehle, J.W. 1946, "The Bretton Woods Institutions," *Yale Law Journal*, vol. 55: 1127–1139.

Ruggie, J.G. 1982, "International Regimes, Transactions, and Change: Embedded Liberalism in the Postwar Economic Order," *International Organization*, vol. 36 no. 2: 379–415.

Shaffer, G. and Waibel M. 2015, "The (Mis)Alignment of the Trade and Monetary Legal Orders" in Halliday, T. and Shaffer, G. (eds.), *Transnational Legal Orders*, Cambridge University Press, Cambridge, UK.

Shuster, M.R. 1973, *The Public International Law of Money*, Clarendon Press, Oxford.

Smoot Hawley Tarrif Act, Pub. L. 71–361, June 17, 1930 46 Stat. 590.

Spiermann, O. 2005, *International Legal Argument in the Permanent Court of International Justice: The Rise of the International Judiciary*, Cambridge University Press, Cambridge, UK; New York, NY.

Steil, B. 2013, *The Battle of Bretton Woods: John Maynard Keynes, Harry Dexter White, and the Making of a New World Order*, Princeton University Press, Princeton, NJ.

United States Congress. 1922, "An Act to Create a Commission Authorized Under Certain Conditions to Refund or Convert Obligations of Foreign Governments Held by the United States of America, and for Other Purposes," February 1922, 42 Stat. 363.

United States Department of State, 1933, *Foreign Relations of the United States Diplomatic Paper. General Part*, U.S. Government Printing Office, Washington DC.

United States Department of State, 1948, *Proceedings and Documents of the United Nations Monetary and Financial Conference*, U.S. Government Printing Office, Washington DC.

United States Tariff Commission, 1943, *Foreign-Trade and Exchange Controls in Germany*, U.S. Government Printing Office, Washington DC.

United States World War Foreign Debt Commission 1927, *Combined Annual Reports of the World War Foreign Debt Commission with Additional Information Regarding Foreign Debts Due the United States*, United States Government Printing Office, Washington DC.

Vagts, D.F. 2006, "International Economic Law and the American Journal of International Law," *American Journal of International Law*, vol. 100: 769–782.

Waibel, M. 2009, "BIT by BIT – The Silent Liberalization of the Capital Account" in Binder, C; Kriebaum, U; Reinisch A and Wittich S (eds.), *International Investment Law for the 21st Century – Essays in Honour of Christoph Schreuer*, Oxford University Press, Oxford, pp. 497–518.

Williamson, J. 1990, "What Washington Means by Policy Reform," in *Latin American Adjustment: How Much Has Happened?* Ed. John Williamson. Institute of International Economics, Washington DC.

Weiler, J. 2002, "The Rule of Lawyers and the Ethos of Diplomats: Reflections on the Internal and External Legitimacy of WTO Dispute Settlement," *American Review of International Arbitration*, vol. 13: 177–196.

Wilson, R.R. 1960, *United States Commercial Treaties and International Law*, Hauser Press, New Orleans, LA.

WTO Annual Report 2013, World Trade Organization, Geneva.

WTO, *China – Measures Affecting Trading Rights and Distribution Services for Certain Publications and Audiovisual Entertainment Products*, AB-2009-3.

Zeiler, T. 1997, "GATT Fifty Years Ago: U.S. Trade Policy and Imperial Tariff Preferences," *Business and Economic History*, vol. 26: 709–17.

Zhang, X. and X. Li 2014, "The Politics of Compliance with Adverse WTO Dispute Settlement Rulings in China," *Journal of Contemporary China*, vol. 23: 143–160.

Zimmermann, C.D. 2011, "Exchange Rate Misalignment and International Law," *American Journal of International Law*, vol. 105: 423–476.

CHAPTER TEN

CREDIT RATINGS AND GLOBAL ECONOMIC GOVERNANCE: NON-PRICE VALUATION IN FINANCIAL MARKETS

Bruce G. Carruthers

Rating agencies figured prominently in the global financial crisis of 2008. But how did ratings become so important? Bond ratings were traditionally used by investors as independent measures of credit risk that would improve private investment decisions. Ratings were a form of information that helped to deal with the information asymmetries that plague credit markets. But today, ratings play an important role in the more general governance of credit relations and global capital flows. In addition to their traditional function as an evaluation of a financial risk, ratings are widely inscribed into private financial contracts, prudential regulations, and bank capital standards. Why would so many non-investors use ratings? The 2008 financial crisis revealed the importance of high credit ratings, as documented by the extreme and sometimes highly creative measures undertaken by those who engineered structured financial instruments like CDOs (collateralized debt obligations) and RMBS (residential mortgage-backed securities),[1] in search of "AAA" ratings from agencies like Moody's and S&P. Good ratings were highly sought-after. Despite the poor performance of ratings during the crisis (MacKenzie 2011), and despite strong evidence that the rating agencies were vulnerable to serious conflicts of interest due to their "issuer pays" business model (SEC 2008), credit ratings continue to play a central role in capital markets. They were disgraced, but not

[1] CDOs and RMBSs are two types of structured financial instruments. Generally, they are created out of underlying financial assets, like home mortgages or credit card receivables, and involve complex pooling and tranching of cash flows.

displaced. In this paper, I consider how an evaluative method originally devised by a small private firm to assess U.S. railroad bonds came to assume such a dominant position in global finance, to the point where it functioned as an alternative to what is arguably the most self-evident form of valuation, namely, market price.

In times of crises, ratings have served as an important substitute for market valuation: for instance, during the last Greek sovereign debt crisis, when Greece could not borrow on financial markets, the measure of Greece's creditworthiness was set by credit rating agencies (CRAs), whose evaluations were incorporated into the rules used by financial institutions like the European Central Bank to determine whether it could buy Greek bonds on the secondary market (Pénet and Mallard 2014). Building on the concept of "placeholder," proposed by Annelise Riles (2010: 803, 2011: 169),[2] to designate "a technique for working with and in the meantime," Pénet and Mallard (2014) claim that ratings produced by Moody's during the Greek sovereign debt crisis were deliberately kept high in order to mask market uncertainty and avoid worsening the crisis.

In this paper, I study situations where ratings have been used as alternatives to market valuations, sometimes even when markets still produced prices. In cases where investors and regulators had access to multiple valuation techniques at the same time – producing different values for the same asset – it is puzzling that market actors would not use market prices to compute asset values but rather turn to alternatives produced by small and privately owned companies like Moody's or Standard Statistics and Fitch. How could market prices be displaced as the canonical measure of value? Did users emphasize the *pragmatic utility* of ratings or did they ground their use of ratings on other criteria, such as their *accuracy* or *objectivity*?

I address such questions by focusing in particular on two episodes: in the 1930s, when ratings were first given regulatory standing in the United States, and starting in the 1990s, when ratings were given contractual standing in the global financial derivatives market. The paper shows that in the 1930s, and later in the 1990s, ratings expanded significantly in two new directions. Starting in the Great Depression ratings were incorporated into financial regulations, first by US federal banking regulators but expanding to other kinds of federal, state and (eventually) international regulations. As the first section of the paper shows,

[2] Thanks to Gregoire Mallard for reminding me of the relevance of Riles' work.

regulators mixed pragmatic concerns with claims of scientificity, when they started using ratings as regulatory instruments: ratings not only helped them to stem a tide of bankruptcies among financial institutions by recognizing the alternative value – for example, non-market value – of their assets in the hope that market prices would soon recover, but they were also used to impose more scientific and uniform standards of asset valuation in financial institutions such as banks and insurance companies.

The second section of the paper focuses on a period from the 1990s, when ratings were incorporated into a wide variety of private financial contracts, especially as a legal trigger or threshold device. The inclusion of ratings into financial contracts was related to the unregulated nature of new financial markets, in particular, the financial derivatives and futures that developed starting in the 1980s. In this section, I note that whereas some new financial derivatives contracts were traded on exchanges, and so were heavily regulated by US statutory and administrative law dating back to the Great Depression era (e.g., the Commodity Exchange Act of 1936), over-the-counter (OTC) derivatives markets were essentially unregulated in the United States. Furthermore, the international nature of these transactions – when big international banks entered into currency swaps with their counterparties – created additional legal uncertainty in cases of contractual breach: it was unclear in which jurisdiction to litigate contractual disputes *ex post* (after breaches occurred). For OTC financial derivatives, then, model contracts were produced by industry representatives, who addressed the problems raised by legal uncertainty by asking trading partners to agree *ex ante* on the price of the penalty for contractual breach (by posting collateral). As Annelise Riles (2010, 2011) argues, such collateral served as a placeholder for regulations, and ratings were used to fix the amount of collateral (i.e., the magnitude of the penalty for contractual breach). Here again, the choice of ratings as a valuation technique for collateral was justified mostly on pragmatic grounds: ratings offered a credible and independent (from the two parties to the financial transaction) measure of value.

These two periods were thus both marked by a substantial expansion in the non-investment use of credit ratings. The two episodes, which greatly magnified the significance of credit ratings, helped set the stage for the global financial crisis of 2008. The third and closing section of the paper compares the two periods of expansion, and considers their causes and consequences: in particular, the unintended effects of the actions of pragmatic regulators and market actors who used ratings to innovate.

FROM INFORMATIONAL COMMODITIES TO REGULATIVE INSTRUMENTS: THE GREAT DEPRESSION AND THE USE OF RATINGS

Ratings as informational commodities: their pre-war use

Moody's rating agency began publishing rating manuals in 1909,[3] and these offered a new service to railroad bond investors: "The fundamental idea at the base of this book is to establish a standard for measuring railroad security values" (Moody 1913: 97). The premise behind the new business was that since bond investors faced an almost overwhelming number of options, Moody would sell them useful and independent information to assist with their investment decisions. Ratings were to be an informational commodity whose value pertained to the measure of value. Although the service was new, the form of the rating information was not. John Moody explicitly adopted an ordinal category format in 1909 as he began to publish his ratings of railroad bonds (Harold 1938: 6–7, 11; Partnoy 1999: 637–638; Sinclair 2005: 24). This rating system had been previously developed and refined by mercantile agencies (e.g., R.G. Dun and Bradstreet's) for the assessment of trade credit (Norris 1978; Olegario 2006). It was already widely known, a part of standard business practice for the management of credit, and so it provided an obvious and credible template. Many of the banks that purchased bonds already subscribed to the service of mercantile agencies, and so bank officials were familiar with the assessment of creditworthiness in terms of ordered categories. It was easy to translate that idiom from the evaluation of small businesses to bonds.

In a Moody's Manual, railway bonds were rated and listed alongside descriptive information about the railroad that issued them. An index enabled any user to look up a particular bond with little trouble. "A complete record of every railroad bond issue of each system is furnished, the different issues being listed according to their priority and general security. A Rating, based on the relative strength of each issue, is then given. These ratings are presented on a plan similar to that employed by mercantile agencies in rating the credit of merchants. Thus, a very

[3] Flandreau et al. (2011: 502–3) provide a useful summary of the origins of the modern bond rating industry.

high-grade bond, such as Lake Shore 3½s, is rated Aaa; one of lower grade, like Baltimore & Ohio Southwestern 3½s, is rated Aa; Erie consol. 4s are rated A; Missouri Pacific refunding 5s, Ba; while much lower grade issues, such as Erie convertibles, get a rating of B, and much more speculative bonds, with doubtful futures, are rated Ca, C, D, etc." (Moody 1913: 18). Initially, Moody devised an eleven-category ordinal framework, ranging from "Aaa" at the top to "D" at the bottom (with an even lower category, E, for defaulted bonds). From the outset, Moody's ratings were understood to offer more than just a compilation of existing information; rather, they reflected "scientific" deductions drawn from that information (Johnson 1909).[4]

Moody's new service succeeded to such an extent that its subscriber base soon moved beyond banks, insurance companies, and other financial institutions. The immediate demand for John Moody's bond ratings was such that the initial print run of his 1909 edition sold out, and it was updated and reprinted that same year (*Wall Street Journal* December 1, 1909). For example, even public libraries far from Wall Street obtained subscriptions to the manuals.[5] Moody's also expanded its coverage to include utility and industrial bonds starting in 1914, and sovereigns in 1918. By 1920, Moody's issued four separate manuals (for railroads, industrials, utilities, and sovereigns), rating over 50,000 different securities.[6]

Competing agencies issued their own ratings, but *all* agencies adopted some version of alpha-numerically labeled ordinal categories, with good investments placed at the top and bad ones at the bottom (Flandreau et al. 2011: 509). Poor's rated bonds from all industries, beginning in 1922, and Standard Statistics and Fitch covered all industries after 1924 (Hickman 1958: 143). Standard Statistics and Poor's merged in 1941, and so for most of the twentieth century, bond rating was dominated by three agencies. By the mid 1920s, bond ratings were widely used by investors (West 1973: 161), and the number of households investing in

[4] Consider the discussion entitled "The Scientific Test for a Railroad Bond," which is part of the introductory material in Moody's 1909 Manual, in a larger section called "The Principles of Analysis."

[5] An announcement in the *Salt Lake Tribune*, August 6, 1911, p.14, noted that the public library received its new copy of Moody's Manual. That same year, the Arizona Railway Commission paid for its own subscription to Moody's, as noted in the *Arizona Republican*, September 12, 1911, p. 8.

[6] As the Moody's ad claimed: "Every stock or bond you own or are thinking of purchasing is 'rated.' At a glance you can tell whether your investments are good, bad or 'indifferent.'" *Philadelphia Evening Public Ledger*, April 20, 1920, p. 20.

bonds grew rapidly during and after World War I (Ott 2011: 2). Thus the demand for such information came from both financial institutions and individual investors. Financial policy-makers also heeded the rating agencies' information, as indicated by the fact that the Federal Reserve Board itself subscribed to Moody's manuals (Federal Reserve Board 1920: 947). As occurred with trade credit during the nineteenth century, in the twentieth century a relatively stable category system was used to classify the credit risks associated with an ever-expanding universe of debtors and the financial instruments they issued.

For a long time the rating industry was dominated by a small number of small-scale firms. Rating bonds was a highly-specialized activity with little potential for market growth. Hence, once the "big three" were in place (Moody's, Fitch, and S&P), there were few attempts by new entrants to get into the market. Even as late as the mid 1990s, the biggest rating agency had fewer than 800 employees, and Fitch only had around 200 (Cantor and Packer 1994: 2). And before then, rating agencies had analysts numbering only in the tens. The biggest opportunities for expansion didn't come until after the switch to a new business model in the early 1970s, and the growth of securitization in the 1980s and 1990s. But by then, the SEC restricted entry into the industry by selectively conferring NRSRO (Nationally Recognized Statistical Rating Organization) status.

Ratings into regulations: an alternative to market valuation

At the start of the Great Depression, corporate bonds were a significant part of U.S. bank assets. As the economy crashed, bank solvency depended on the value of the assets on bank balance sheets, and as the value of those assets decreased (as bond prices collapsed, or as loans became delinquent or non-performing), growing numbers of banks failed. Following the emergency bank holiday of March 1933, 3,460 banks were suspended in the third quarter of 1933, and the number of banks within the Federal Reserve System declined from 8,929 in 1928 to 5,606 in 1933. At the same time, the number of non-member banks declined from 16,869 to 8,601. The collapse of the market value of bank assets, and the subsequent collapse of many banks, put tremendous pressure on the US financial system and on the regulators and politicians who oversaw it. Something had to be done, quickly.

Before the era of federal deposit insurance, it was the job of federal and state bank examiners to assess the financial status of a bank, to appraise its assets and liabilities, and to close down banks that were technically insolvent or which failed to meet regulatory standards (Jones 1940: 183). But by weakening the standards they imposed, bank regulators could introduce a measure of forbearance that would make it easier for marginal banks to survive. And if such flexibility allowed an insolvent bank to remain open (without starting a panic among the depositors) then it was possible for bank management to make necessary changes and return the bank to positive net worth. Before 1930, the Comptroller of the Currency recorded bank-owned securities (like bonds) at their market value when calculating the overall worth of bank assets during a bank examination. As market prices plummeted, the value of total bank assets declined and more banks had negative worth (liabilities greater than assets). And with the collapse of the stock market, it was obvious that bank balance sheets could not be strengthened by having banks raise more capital from investors.

Both the Hoover and Roosevelt administrations enacted a variety of policies to try to resolve the financial crisis that opened the Great Depression. One response involved a change in bank examination rules. Starting in 1931, the Comptroller initiated a new policy that made use of the ratings produced by agencies like Moody's, Poor's Publishing, and Standard Statistics. This change adopted a new valuation method, devised by the Federal Reserve Bank of New York, to use bond ratings to estimate the overall quality of a bank's bond portfolio (Harold 1938: 160–161).[7] With the Comptroller's new policy, bonds rated "BBB" or higher could be valued at their *historical cost* (i.e., what the bank paid for them) rather than at their current market value (Harold 1938: 26; Morton 1939: 277; Jones 1940: 187). In 1933, the Federal Reserve Board bolstered official recognition of bond ratings when it started to publish tables that showed how current bond yields varied across different ratings, using Moody's system of Aaa, Aa, A, and Baa for "investment grade" securities (see Federal Reserve Board 1933: 483). To that extent, the Federal Reserve Board started using ratings

[7] Flandreau et al. (2011) examine the poor performance of bond rating agencies during the 1930s and wonder how ratings could have been given regulatory standing in precisely the same decade. But this move was not unprecedented for the New York Federal Reserve Bank, perhaps because of its close ties to Wall Street and familiarity with current financial practices. Issued soon after the founding of the Federal Reserve System, a New York Fed circular on the topic of eligible paper (i.e., what member bank assets could be brought to the Fed discount window for rediscounting) shows that mercantile agency credit ratings factored into the determination of eligibility (Federal Reserve Bank of New York 1915). This was done without strong evidence of the predictive accuracy of credit ratings. Furthermore, rating agencies were increasingly a point of reference in US courts (Flandreau and Sławatyniec 2013).

as pragmatic "placeholders" (Riles 2010, 2011): ratings were compensatory instruments used to weaken the effect of depreciating bond prices on bank failures.

Many state bank regulators followed the Comptroller's new policy. Indeed, in 1938 the National Association of Supervisors of State Banks affirmed the use of bond ratings to group bank bond holdings into four different classes, with the highest rated bonds (i.e., given "AAA," "Aa," "A" or "Baa" ratings) being valued at their historic cost (Morton 1939: 280; Jones 1940: 194). Highly-rated bonds would no longer be marked to market, and this innovation quietly spread.[8]

New Deal bank regulations also focused on low rated bonds. The Banking Act of 1935 gave to the Comptroller of the Currency the power to restrict the kinds of securities a national bank could purchase on its own account. In early 1936, the Comptroller applied this power when prohibiting the purchase of securities that were "distinctly or predominantly speculative," or of an even lower standard (Atkins 1938; Palyi 1938: 70; Comptroller of the Currency 1937: 21–22). The real problem with U.S. banks, the Comptroller asserted in a speech to the California Bankers Association in May 1936, lay on the asset side of their balance sheets rather than on the liability side. During the 1920s, too many banks had invested in "speculative" bonds, and they had to be stopped from doing so again (Federal Reserve Board 1936: 422–423). The new rule referred to the rating agency manuals when defining terms like "speculative" or "predominantly speculative," (which, in the Moody's rating scale, meant ratings below the "Baa" level). Since bank examiners were inexperienced in the detailed assessment of financial securities, the application of ratings to bond portfolios was done quite mechanically (Atkins 1938: 14). Most state bank regulators followed the federal lead and adopted similar rules (Palyi 1938: 73). Although bond ratings had been used by institutional and individual investors since 1909, their direct incorporation into bank regulatory machinery greatly increased their significance. Low-rated bonds were sanctioned as much as high-rated bonds were encouraged.

Another important step occurred in 1938, when the Uniform Agreement on Bank Supervisory Procedures attempted to standardize bank examination procedures across multiple regulatory agencies, including the Federal Reserve, the Comptroller of the Currency, and the

[8] In addition to protecting bank assets from the collapse of the bond market, this measure also put a premium on high ratings.

Federal Deposit Insurance Corporation (FDIC). U.S. financial institutions were governed by a patchwork of different regulatory agencies that didn't always apply the same standards, thus encouraging regulatory arbitrage (Federal Reserve Board 1938b: 8–10). The new common standard put bank assets into overall categories, depending on the bank examiner's judgment of the level of risk or impairment. Assets in the highest category were recorded at book value, without adjustment for market depreciation (Simonson and Hempel 1993: 255). In appraising assets, examiners were to consider them: "...in the light of inherent soundness rather than on a basis of day to day fluctuations" (Federal Reserve Board 1938a: 564). More generally, regulators asserted that the overall condition of the banking system: "...should not be measured by the precarious yardstick of current market quotations which often reflect speculative and not true appraisals of intrinsic worth" (Federal Reserve Board 1938a: 564). In this respect, the Federal Reserve Bulletin utilized uncharacteristically vivid terms to distinguish market prices from "intrinsic worth" or "inherent soundness," and to downplay market price. When these different measures didn't align, the agreement clearly signaled to regulators and examiners that they should overlook low market prices and emphasize "intrinsic worth."[9] However, the Federal Reserve Board was emphatic that ignoring market price did not entail a "relaxation of standards" (Federal Reserve Board 1938b: 39).

Since bond market prices had declined at the beginning of the Depression, these new valuation policies allowed bank regulators to overlook that decline and so treat banks as if they were in better financial shape than signaled by the old valuation policies. Market valuation of bank bonds was partly suspended, contingent on the evaluations of the bond rating agencies. Under these special circumstances, the valuational authority of rating agencies displaced that of the market. In addition, new prudential standards for banks excluded assets that were "below investment grade," again relying on the rating agencies (Fons 2004). For the first time, bond ratings were given regulatory standing in order to protect banks from the uncertainties of the bond market and to prevent insolvency. Such regulatory forbearance kept a bank open until a future time when, it was hoped, its assets would return to their "true" value. Yet this change was not simply an ad hoc measure, for as Jones

[9] Bach (1949: 275–6) also notes the regulatory difference between "intrinsic soundness" and "current market value," and the importance of recognizing the former during a recessionary period.

(1940: 186) explained: "...bank assets have a particularly indeterminate value in periods of crisis. Current market prices cannot be accepted because markets are demoralized, and many classes of bank assets, e.g., most bank loans and real estate, cannot be sold at any price." In other words, during a crisis, previously accurate market signals became misleading measures of value, reflecting the "demoralized" state of the market. Since market price is often the default measure of value, departure from this standard required special circumstances. However, once the change was made, it wasn't readily reversed.

The regulatory use of ratings wasn't confined to banking. Starting in the 1930s, the state agencies and commissions that regulated U.S. insurance companies (which were chartered by states, not by the federal government) began to use ratings to calculate the amount of capital that insurance companies would have to set aside to cover potential losses on their assets, with higher required capital for lower rated bonds (Cantor and Packer 1994: 6). In 1932, for example, the New York Insurance Department explicitly set the valuation rules for life insurance company bond holdings according to the ratings given by one of the four main bond rating agencies (O'Leary 1954: 164–165). Then in 1951 the NAIC (National Association of Insurance Commissioners) established uniform asset categories based on bond ratings (West 1973: 162), and ratings continue to play an important role in insurance regulation today (Hunt 2011). Ratings were also incorporated into federal regulation of money market funds. The Investment Company Act of 1940 mandated that such funds could only invest in high-quality short-term financial instruments, where the criteria were set using agency ratings (SEC 2003: 7). Although US mutual funds were not particularly numerous or large in the early 1940s, they grew to great size as time passed and so this ratings-based restriction became increasingly important. The general point of these kinds of rules was to impose uniform standards on the assets of various financial institutions in order to ensure some measure of safety and soundness for banks, money market funds, and insurance companies (Hunt 2011).

After World War II, many US state banking authorities followed the lead of federal regulators and henceforth the distinction between "investment grade" and "below investment grade" became enormously consequential. When the Federal Reserve Board reconsidered the Uniform Agreement in 1949, during the postwar boom, the insulation of highly rated bonds from valuation by market price was simply continued (Clayton 1949).[10] Starting in 1975, the SEC began to use bond ratings in setting net capital rules for broker-dealers (SEC 1994). The U.S. Department of Education used ratings to set financial standards for educational institutions that sought to participate in various student financial assistance programs (SEC 2003: 8). Despite the absence of public accountability, notwithstanding the opacity of rating methods, and despite little rigorous evidence of their validity, ratings were given public regulatory significance starting in the 1930s (Harold 1938: 72; Palyi 1938: 92). And the process of regulatory incorporation continued so that by the early twenty-first century eight Federal statutes, forty-seven Federal rules, and one hundred state laws made reference to ratings (Langohr and Langohr 2008: 431–433; see also Sinclair 2005: 42–44). As required by the Dodd-Frank Wall Street Reform and Consumer Protection Act, the Federal Reserve Board had to determine where its own regulations made reference to credit ratings, and the Board found no less than forty-six such references (Federal Reserve Board 2011: 1, 6–7). Contemporary international financial regulations (such as the Basel II bank capital standards) also make use of credit ratings (Abdelal 2007: 193; Singer 2007: 64; Weber and Darbellay 2008), and a number of countries follow the United States in using ratings in their banking or financial regulations (Sinclair 2005: 47–49).

From the beginning, Moody's bond ratings were perceived to be "scientifically" based (Johnson 1909), and were advertised by Moody himself as a way to avoid investment errors (e.g., *New York Times* April 6, 1917, p. 18).[11] Interestingly, it wasn't until the late 1930s that a proper "scientific" study was done of the performance of bond ratings. Gilbert's 1938 study was based on his Columbia University dissertation, and used a medium-sized sample of bonds to calculate their average performance and see if this varied by rating class. Not until the 1940s was a truly large-scale statistical study of ratings undertaken in cooperation with the rating agencies, the NBER, and the FDIC, with the published results not coming out until the 1950s (Pogue and Soldovsky 1969). Before then, the accuracy of ratings was largely taken on faith, and the

[10] There were some minor modifications of the labels of different groups of bonds, and group 2 ("substandard" quality) securities were to be valued at market prices rather than at an 18-month moving average of market prices (Federal Reserve Board 1949: 776–7). Most importantly, however, highly rated bonds were not to be valued at their market prices.

[11] Consider a Moody's newspaper ad from the early 1920s which states: "Long experience, careful study and conscientious effort have made our opinions reliable and our ratings accurate." (*Atlanta Constitution* February 14, 1923, p. 14).

prevalence of ratings was assumed to reflect their informational value. Indeed, as Flandreau et al. (2011) show, during the 1930s ratings were adopted into financial regulations at the very same time when their performance in predicting sovereign bond defaults was anything but reassuringly positive.

The decision to incorporate credit ratings directly into US financial regulations ultimately proved to be a fateful one, for as US financial markets grew to world dominance over the course of the twentieth century, some of their institutional idiosyncracies assumed greater importance. Adoption of ratings by regulators followed an uneven process of diffusion where the high status of the first adopting agency made it easier for others to follow suit. In the United States, the Federal Reserve Bank of New York was the most prestigious of all the regional banks, in part because of its close links to Wall Street. A valuational method that used ratings enjoyed the imprimatur of the New York Fed, and so offered a credible and accessible "placeholder" tool to be adopted by the Comptroller of the Currency in 1931 as it reconciled its statutory duty to examine US banks while at the same time trying to minimize bank insolvency during a financial crisis. Distributing the valuation of assets between public and private organizations increased the significance of the judgments made by bond rating agencies, and magnified the effect of "mistaken" ratings. Following the lead of federal bank regulators, many other regulatory agencies in and outside of the United States adopted ratings to set prudential standards, protect investors, and govern market access (Grant 1941; Langohr and Langohr 2008: 430–439; FCIC 2011: 119).

INCORPORATING RATINGS INTO OVER-THE-COUNTER DERIVATIVES

Regulative diversity in financial derivatives markets

A second major episode involving expansion in the importance of ratings occurred with the growth of financial derivatives markets. In finance, a derivative is an "arrangement or instrument (such as a future, option, or warrant) whose value *derives* from and is dependent upon the value of an underlying variable asset, such as a commodity, currency, or security" (Oxford English Dictionary). Derivatives, including financial derivatives, are generally traded either on an organized exchange (like the Chicago Mercantile Exchange, or CME) or over-the-counter (OTC). Exchange-traded derivatives (like options, or futures) are standardized and fungible contracts. Trade on an exchange allows for high levels of liquidity and transparency (including "price discovery"). Who is doing what and at what price becomes public knowledge. Exchanges also enable clearing, an arrangement under which the exchange itself guarantees that transactions between buyers and sellers will be finalized and executed.[12] The OTC market, by contrast, involves private, customized, bilateral exchanges between dealer-banks and clients.[13] There is much less transparency in OTC markets and much more information asymmetry.

Derivatives markets can be used to hedge various risks, but also to speculate. A U.S. firm that trades internationally might worry that the US dollar will drop in relation to other currencies, and so it might use foreign exchange futures or options to protect itself against FX risk. Or a firm may simply wish to speculate on the future value of the US dollar. Whether for hedging or speculation, activity in both exchange-traded and OTC derivatives markets grew dramatically at the end of the twentieth century. For example, the total notional value of OTC interest rate and currency swaps grew from US $865 *billion* in 1987 to $426 *trillion* in 2009. In the latter year, the addition of credit default swaps and equity derivatives put the overall OTC total at $463 *trillion*. Exchange-traded derivatives markets also experienced substantial growth, especially as markets like the Chicago Board of Trade (CBOT) and Chicago Mercantile Exchange (CME) shifted away from commodity-based derivatives (like wheat and "pork belly" futures and options) and toward financial derivatives (foreign exchange, interest rate, and equity index contracts). According to the BIS (Bank for International Settlements), the total notional value of financial futures traded globally on organized exchanges was about $3.7 trillion in March of 1993, and about $24.3 trillion in March of 2012. Growth in financial options traded on organized exchanges was comparable over the same period.

If market activity requires a functioning legal framework, then that requirement was evidently satisfied in abundance in the case of modern financial derivatives markets, but not evenly so. Exchange-traded derivatives were a form of contract, and hence governed by whatever contract law applied in the jurisdiction in which the exchange was

[12] Clearing mitigates so-called "counterparty risk" because for sellers, the exchange assumes the buyer position, and for buyers it assumes the seller position. Neither buyers nor sellers have to worry that their counterparty will fail to live up to their obligations (unless the exchange itself fails).

[13] Without clearing, counterparty risk is a serious problem in OTC markets.

domiciled. Exchanges based in the United States were subject to US law, for example. Furthermore, trading in such contracts in the United States was governed by the Commodity Exchange Act of 1936, regulated first by a bureau in the Department of Agriculture (because the early market was dominated by derivatives based on agricultural commodities), and then regulated by the Commodities Futures Trading Commission (CFTC), founded in 1974. The earliest derivatives contracts were simple futures and options with a commodity "underlying." Market innovation was constrained by the requirement that new contracts had to have prior CFTC approval before they could be introduced on to the exchange. Thus, only about five new contracts were introduced annually during the 1970s (Gorham and Singh 2009: 186). But with financial deregulation in the 1980s and 1990s, such constraints were loosened, and after passage of the Commodity Futures Modernization Act of 2000 it became much easier for the exchanges to innovate, and the rate of new contract introduction increased. Overall, the legal framework for exchange-traded derivatives is clearly situated in statutory, administrative and case law.

The legal status of over-the-counter transactions has been much less straightforward. As the global OTC market emerged in the 1980s, OTC derivatives transactions often involved institutions that spanned different legal jurisdictions. So although OTC derivatives were clearly a type of contract, it was uncertain which national body of contract law was applicable. The London branch of a US bank might enter into a pound-deutschmark currency swap with a French institution, and so potentially either US, British, German or French law might apply. A particularly worrisome consequence for market participants was that important contractual provisions might not be valid or enforceable in all jurisdictions (e.g., netting provisions), and both procedural and substantive law varied from one country to the next. Since OTC derivatives are "bespoke" and subject to near-continuous innovation, new provisions and contractual obligations were created all the time and so the question of their enforceability was constantly being revisited (Awrey 2013). Even if a simple interest rate swap was deemed enforceable, what about a "collar," or a "swaption" or some more complex hybrid contract? In addition, the market was jarred early on by surprising court rulings about the enforceability of derivatives contracts, unclear standards for the liability of dealer-bankers for customer losses, uncertain rules about the capacity of market participants, and plagued by concerns about the applicability of statute-of-frauds measures (Lynn 1994).

One of the biggest legal questions concerned whether OTC derivatives were subject to the same public regulatory oversight that applied to exchange-traded derivatives, and it remained open for some decades (Morgan 2010). The swaps market started in something of a regulatory void. To be sure, the market players were themselves regulated as institutions (banks were overseen by bank regulators), but the market itself was not. Should the CFTC, which regulated exchange-traded derivatives, also regulate the OTC market? The OTC market was and is highly concentrated (Stulz 2004), highly profitable (FCIC 2011: 50–51), and core market participants have wanted to minimize public oversight. Furthermore, OTC derivatives consisted of private financial arrangements between sophisticated traders, which undermined the case for public oversight. Nevertheless, reasonable interpretations of the Commodity Exchange Act and the Commodity Futures Trading Commission Act suggested that OTC derivatives might be regulated by the CFTC.

At first, swaps occurred outside of any regulatory framework. This exclusion was reinforced by a specific regulatory intervention made by the US Treasury Department when the CFTC was established in 1974. The Congressional bill establishing the CFTC was amended in accordance with the wishes of Treasury that all foreign exchange (FX) transactions in over-the-counter market (then primarily based in New York City) be exempted from CFTC oversight (Harvey 2013). Only exchange-traded currency futures were to be regulated. The "Treasury Amendment" was justified on the grounds that FX market participants were large, experienced institutions that knew what they were doing, and furthermore that they were already regulated by the Federal Reserve and the Comptroller of the Currency. As the OTC market grew, the issue of its regulatory status was revisited several times during the 1990s. Always, however, market participants successfully resisted regulatory oversight, using a combination of political clout and neo-liberal arguments (Carruthers 2013).

Collateral: fixing *ex ante* the penalty of breach

If OTC derivatives markets are not publicly regulated through statutory law or a federal agency, then what creates the legal certainty and predictability that Max Weber (and others) believed to be necessary for a functioning market? In this case, private rule-making and regulation were centrally important (Shaffer 2009). The dealer-bankers are formally organized through an industry association founded in 1985, the

International Swaps and Derivatives Association (ISDA). The founding members included both US commercial and investment banks that were also the major dealers in the swaps market. ISDA offers various services to its members, but the most important involves the provision of highly standardized contractual language in the form of a Master Agreement (Flanagan 2001: 23; Riles 2011: 57–61). Before undertaking any swaps transactions, two parties will typically first enter into a Master Agreement that sets the overall framework for their relationship. Such Agreements are not invented *de novo* each time, but are based on an ISDA prototype. They provide legal building blocks that can be assembled and combined in different ways to create the "bespoke" derivatives that can hedge idiosyncratic risks in "innovative" ways.[14] Once in place, even a high volume of swaps transactions becomes much easier to manage.

The first such Master Agreement was created by ISDA in 1987, with updates in 1992 and 2002 to reflect the evolution and growth of the market. Its provisions were clearly designed to fit within British and American law, but since London and New York are the two main locations for global derivatives market participants, such affinities are no surprise (Biggins 2012: 1316). ISDA's documentation now governs about 90 percent of the transactions in the OTC derivatives market (Braithwaite 2012: 784). With standardized forms and legal templates, OTC dealer-bankers can more easily build the customized swaps that constitute the market (Suchman 2003: 101–102). By creating a common contractual language in the form of legal boilerplate, ISDA in effect set forth the rules of the OTC game (Choi and Gulati 2006). This formal legal language provided the basic contractual infrastructure of the market.

OTC derivatives involve significant counter-party risk (because of the absence of clearing): what happens if the counter-party in a swap is unable to meet its contractual obligations? Such risk is dealt with by the "credit support annex" attached to a Master Agreement. In situations where market prices are frequently hard to determine, credit ratings are used to measure counter-party risk, to set levels of collateral, and to value collateral when it consists of financial securities (Cunningham and Werlen 1996; ISDA 1996: 11,20,49–50; Gregory 2010: 65–66). As early as 1996, ISDA proffered guidelines that recognized two key roles for credit ratings in derivatives contracts: to gauge the value of assets

[14] By contrast, exchange-traded derivatives are highly standardized contracts.

offered as collateral (securities with low ratings should be given low value), and to gauge the magnitude of counter-party risk in order to mitigate it (counterparties with lower ratings would have to post more collateral, see ISDA 1996: 20,50). A 1999 ISDA review of collateral practices by derivatives market participants observed that private contractual requirements to post collateral according to the credit rating of counterparties were an "…increasing and prudent trend." (ISDA 1999: 8). Credit ratings had the advantage of being familiar and widely available, independent of the two parties to a contract, and legitimized by virtue of being "market based." The development of these practices broadened the OTC market by making it easier to include counterparties whose credit standing wasn't of the highest order, because the risks of contractual breach were mitigated by collateral.

ISDA's review also recommended that contractual agreements use credit ratings in appropriate thresholds to calibrate the amount of collateral to be posted (ISDA 1999: 31,45). An internal survey conducted soon after estimated that core ISDA member organizations (the so-called "dealer banks") collateralized around 55 percent of their OTC derivative trades, already had established collateral programs and formal procedures (ISDA 2000: 2,17), and most often relied on credit ratings to set thresholds for collateral (ISDA 2000: 47). More recent evidence (ISDA 2010, table 4.2) underscores that, *even after the financial crisis of 2008*, derivatives market participants continued to rely on credit ratings in their contracts to set levels of collateral. This is especially true of the biggest market players, the dealer-banks, and despite the discrediting of the rating agencies during the crisis. For example, a November 3, 2011 ISDA press release announced a Standard Credit Support Annex for OTC derivatives, intended to make global derivatives markets "safer and more efficient." This Annex includes a set of thresholds derived explicitly from Moody's, S&P, or Fitch ratings.

The project to create standardized financial contracts was successfully pursued by ISDA, and this undergirded tremendous growth in the market. Given the high concentration of the OTC derivatives market and the central role played by the biggest market actors in ISDA, ISDA's incorporation of credit ratings into its legal boilerplate meant that ratings became part of the market standard. The absence of public oversight meant that ISDA was not accountable to anyone except its own membership. In one quick and definitive move, credit ratings entered into the private contractual governance of financial transactions notionally worth hundreds of trillions of dollars. For many years, this private "regulation" weakened the political case for public regulation. And as compared to the public regulatory adoption of ratings, the diffusion process through the OTC derivatives market was rapid and nearly complete. Here again, the choice of ratings as a valuation technique for collateral was justified mostly on pragmatic grounds, and the spread of ratings had less to do with their inherent efficiency or accuracy, and more to do with the highly centralized position of the adopters and their ability to dictate market practices to other market participants.

THE TWO EPISODES COMPARED: THE UNINTENDED EFFECTS OF REGULATORS' PRAGMATIC CONCERNS

Drawing on the evaluative methods previously developed by mercantile agencies like R.G. Dun, bond ratings were invented in the early twentieth century to satisfy investor demand for credible information about bonds. But ratings expanded beyond this original usage in two ways: starting in the 1930s, ratings were widely incorporated into public financial regulations. And then, starting in the 1990s, ratings were widely incorporated into standardized private financial contracts within the burgeoning OTC derivatives market. Together, the two episodes made credit ratings much more consequential. A ratings downgrade, for example, would not simply send a cautionary signal to investors. It would also force multiple institutional investors to sell off assets if their ratings fell below the "investment grade" threshold enshrined in regulatory standards. It might contractually oblige participants in the OTC derivatives market to post collateral, or to post additional collateral. Ratings, and ratings changes, became amplified through the regulatory and contractual machinery.

These two episodes differed in some important ways. The first unfolded during the Great Depression, a period of acute global economic crisis which drove the expansion of U.S. financial regulations as the government dealt with the near total collapse of the domestic banking system. Ratings were incorporated into a growing public regulatory apparatus, providing a credible and tractable "market based" measure of credit risk.[15] The first regulatory use of ratings didn't

[15] It is interesting that ratings were widely used and highly regarded even though there was, until 1938, no systematic statistical evidence on their accuracy.

anticipate subsequent adoptions, and there was no "grand plan" for overall regulatory architecture. Rather, ratings were a practical solution to a series of practical problems, aimed overall at stabilizing the financial system. As the United States became the world's dominant capitalist power, however, some of its institutional features were transferred outward (to other countries) and upward (to the global level) and affected finance outside of the United States. Ratings were no longer just an American peculiarity, but rather something that affected debtor sovereign nations around the globe (e.g., Greece, Argentina).

The second episode, by contrast, occurred during a period of intense "financialization" at the end of the twentieth century, in which global financial activities expanded and the entire financial sector grew (Krippner 2011). Furthermore, it was a period marked by widespread deregulation and the ascendency of neo-liberal policy ideas, and so many parts of the New Deal regulatory apparatus were weakened or even abolished. Widespread financial disintermediation shifted the balance away from "bank-centered" financial systems to the "market-centered" systems that traditionally characterized Anglo-American finance (Allen and Gale 2000; Davis 2009). Market governance became increasingly private rather than public, and ISDA lawyers quite intentionally crafted the basic contractual elements for the entire derivatives market. Indeed, effective private governance was supposed to show that public regulation wasn't needed for OTC derivatives, and that deregulation was a good thing. In some respects, the second episode attempted to undo what had been accomplished during the first. In the 1930s, regulators used ratings to help protect banks from the market, while in the 1980s and 1990s ratings were used by dealer banks to protect the OTC market from regulation. In both instances, ratings constituted a valuational alternative to market price.

Rating agencies have always been run as "for profit" enterprises that sold commodified information, but their "business model" changed between the two periods. Initially, John Moody and his competitors sold their information to investors, that is, to people who used that information to make decisions. Rating agencies had a reputational incentive to provide accurate and useful information, because otherwise the user/subscriber wouldn't pay. But the rating industry changed in the 1970s and shifted from a "user pays" to an "issuer pays" model. Henceforth, rating agencies charged bond issuers to be rated, and so the borrowers, not investors, became agency customers. Furthermore, the SEC officially recognized some rating agencies, but not others, by selectively granting NRSRO status. As became clear during the 2008 financial crisis, rating agencies sought to please their customers by giving higher ratings to structured financial instruments (like CDOs) than was justified. A reputational interest in accuracy had become a conflict of interest, and ratings mistakes were magnified by the regulatory and contractual use of ratings.

During the period of regulatory adoption, use of ratings was largely a matter of convenience, simplicity, and legitimacy: here was a pre-existing, "market based" measure of credit risk that could easily be incorporated into simple and mechanical regulatory rules. As categorical information, ratings were highly portable: without difficulty they could be incorporated into new bureaucratic procedures, formal criteria or decision rules. Bond ratings had been available to investors for more than twenty years and were thought to be useful and accurate. Mercantile credit ratings had been in use for almost seventy-five years, "proven" their value in the marketplace, and had already been included in the financial criteria of the New York Federal Reserve Bank. In similar fashion, ratings were widely incorporated into financial contracts because of simple availability: ratings may not be the perfect measures of risk, but they were readily available, and possessed the legitimacy and familiarity of long-use. Certainly by the 1990s their predictive value for ordinary bonds had been amply demonstrated, and ratings constituted "third party" information that was ostensibly independent from the two parties to a financial contract.[16] Similarly, ratings were a convenient and discrete way to calibrate financial contractual provisions, and the shift during the 1970s from a "user pays" to an "issuer pays" business model for rating agencies made the ratings themselves available for usage by anyone (i.e., unprotected by intellectual property rights). So it was easy to incorporate a rating into the standard contractual language of a credit default swap.

In both episodes, the supply side of the market for credit information remained remarkably small and concentrated. There have been only a handful of rating agencies for many, many decades, and this was only reinforced with the application of the formal NRSRO status starting in the mid 1970s. Such high levels of concentration belied the image of the free market as a place with decentralized, diffuse, and multiple sources of information, which may be aggregated into overall signals

[16] Of course, by itself the "issuer pays" business model raised serious conflict-of-interest issues for rating agencies.

like market price but which nevertheless are beyond central control. It turns out that contemporary financial capitalism has its own private "central planners."[17]

The spread of ratings was driven by different kinds of standardization and standard-setting. Direct evidence is largely absent for why so many sellers adopted trade credit ratings during the nineteenth century, or for the adoption of bond ratings by individual investors in the twentieth century, but extensive commentary suggests that use of these two kinds of ratings became part of standard business practice, and hence were embraced by "proper," "bona fide" decision-makers who acted in a "business-like" manner. In other words, use of ratings by these groups became a kind of informal norm or part of prudent "best practice." And once this type of information was part of normal business in the private sector, it was easy to justify its adoption by public regulators.[18] On the regulatory use of ratings, it is clear that, in the United States, the practice spread after it was first adopted by a prominent actor, in this case the federal government. Once bank examiners working for the Office of the Comptroller of the Currency or the Federal Reserve System embraced bond ratings, this became a standard that other regulators copied. The status order among regulators underpinned a pattern of diffusion that started in the center and went to the periphery. The use of ratings in financial contracts was almost certainly encouraged by the "boiler plate" tendency of contractual standardization. Indeed, ISDA now promulgates a standard credit support annex that explicitly incorporates ratings, but this kind of standard-setting has been going on since ISDA was founded. In such a highly centralized market as OTC derivatives, once the core participants agree to a standard then others must almost certainly embrace it, and so it quickly becomes the market standard.

Ratings proved to be a remarkably pliable regulatory instrument. In the 1930s, they were adopted into U.S. public governance as an alternative valuational device to escape the constraints of market appraisal. Strict adherence to market standards for bank assets would have led to even more bank failures, so regulators imported ratings in order to relax their examination standards and allow more banks to survive. These alternative valuations were not arbitrary or illegitimate, nor beholden

[17] Thanks to Jerome Sgard for this point.

[18] In a similar fashion, grain standards were first set privately by organizations like the Chicago Board of Trade, and later on were enshrined in public law and regulation. See Hoffman and Hill (1976).

to regulatory discretion, so they could justifiably be used to mitigate the effects of plunging market prices. Ratings in regulations helped insulate financial institutions from problematic market volatility. In the 1990s, however, ratings were partly used as "placeholders" to help ensure that derivatives markets escaped public regulation (Kroszner 1999). Ratings imported into derivatives contracts (and elsewhere) enabled advocates of deregulation to argue that private risk management had achieved such a high level of sophistication and efficacy that public oversight was no longer needed. In other words, ratings helped to bolster market valuation and private governance. Again, this was because ratings were seen as a legitimate and "market based" form of information, and by the 1990s, their predictive accuracy for traditional kinds of bonds had been well-established. Even during the 2008–2009 financial crisis, central banks continued to rely on ratings as a way to qualify bank assets as collateral for liquidity support.[19]

Different groups adopted ratings in different contexts and for different reasons, but both changes moved in the same direction in greatly increasing the non-investment use of ratings. When combined together, regulatory and contractual incorporation of ratings had the unintended effect of making an already complex global financial system even more "tightly coupled," with ratings doing the coupling. These largely invisible links joined financial markets through their inscription into regulatory and contractual infrastructure. A ratings change could now trigger automatic and highly synchronous responses that would cascade through the entire system. Crossing the "investment grade" threshold, for example, would force pension funds and insurance companies to unload securities all at the same time, driving down prices. Compliance with prudential regulations necessitated that fiduciaries alter their portfolios, but in a highly correlated fashion. Ratings downgrades, especially changes from "AAA," forced derivatives counterparties to post more collateral (which is usually cash, see Gregory 2010: 63; ISDA 2010: table 2.1), and in effect unleash the equivalent of a bank run as derivatives market participants rushed to seize liquidity. Obviously, the effect of standardized contractual provisions grew with the increasing overall size of the OTC derivatives market. But if modern financial risk management is undermined by overlooked or underestimated correlations, widespread reliance on credit ratings as a *de facto* coordination device had the effect of engendering highly

[19] My thanks to Jerome Sgard for pointing this out.

correlated market actions and reactions. Ratings inadvertently coordinated capital market activity, around the globe.

References

Abdelal, Rawi. 2007. *Capital Rules: The Construction of Global Finance*. Cambridge: Harvard University Press.

Atkins, Paul. 1938. "The official supervision of bank security portfolios," *Bankers' Magazine* July 1938: 13–19.

Allen, Franklin and Douglas Gale. 2000. *Comparing Financial Systems*. Cambridge: MIT Press.

Awrey, Dan. 2013. "Toward a Supply-Side Theory of Financial Innovation," *Journal of Comparative Economics* 41(2): 401–419.

Bach, G.L. 1949. "Bank Supervision, Monetary Policy, and Governmental Reorganization," *Journal of Finance* 4(4): 269–285.

Biggins, John. 2012. "'Targeted Touchdown' and 'Partial Liftoff': Post-Crisis Dispute Resolution in the OTC Derivatives Markets and the Challenge for ISDA," *German Law Journal* 13(12): 1297–1328.

Braithwaite, Joanne P. 2012. "Standard Form Contracts as Transnational Law: Evidence from the Derivatives Markets," *Modern Law Review* 75(5): 779–805.

Cantor, Richard and Frank Packer. 1994. "The Credit Rating Industry," *Federal Reserve Bank of New York Quarterly Review* 19(2): 1–26.

Carruthers, Bruce G. 2013. "Diverging Derivatives: Law, Governance and Modern Financial Markets," *Journal of Comparative Economics* 41(2): 386–400.

Choi, Stephen J. and G. Mitu Gulati. 2006. "Contract as Statute," *Michigan Law Review* 104(5): 1129–1173.

Clayton, Lawrence. 1949. *Memorandum to Board of Governors*, from The Marriner S. Eccles document collection, accessed November 8 2013 from FRASER, http://fraser.stlouisfed.org/docs/historical/eccles/046_20_0002.pdf.

Comptroller of the Currency. 1937. *Seventy-Fifth Annual Report of the Comptroller of the Currency*. Washington DC: US Government Printing Office.

Cunningham, Daniel and Thomas Werlen. 1996. "Derivatives and the reduction of credit risk," *International Financial Law Review* 15: 35–36.

Davis, Gerald F. 2009. *Managed by the Markets: How Finance Reshaped America*. Oxford/New York: Oxford University Press.

Federal Reserve Bank of New York. 1915. "Eligible Paper," Circular No. 25, June 19, 1915. New York: Federal Reserve Bank of New York.

Federal Reserve Board. 2011. *Report to the Congress on Credit Ratings*. Washington DC: Federal Reserve System.

Federal Reserve Board. 1949. *Federal Reserve Bulletin July 1949*. Washington DC: US Government Printing Office.

Federal Reserve Board. 1938a. *Federal Reserve Bulletin July 1938*. Washington DC: US Government Printing Office.

Federal Reserve Board. 1938b. *Twenty-Fifth Annual Report of the Board of Governors of the Federal Reserve System*. Washington DC:

Federal Reserve Board. 1936. *Federal Reserve Bulletin June 1936*. Washington DC: US Government Printing Office.

Federal Reserve Board. 1933. *Federal Reserve Bulletin August 1933*. Washington DC: US Government Printing Office.

Federal Reserve Board. 1920. *Federal Reserve Bulletin September 1920*. Washington DC: US Government Printing Office.

Financial Crisis Inquiry Commission [FCIC]. 2011. *The Financial Crisis Inquiry Report*. New York: PublicAffairs.

Flanagan, Sean M. 2001. "The Rise of a Trade Association: Group Interactions Within the International Swaps and Derivatives Association," *Harvard Negotiation Law Review* 6: 211–263.

Flandreau, Marc, Norbert Gaillard and Frank Packer. 2011. "To err is human: U.S. rating agencies and the interwar foreign government debt crisis," *European Review of Economic History* 15: 495–538.

Flandreau, Marc and Joanna Kinga Sławatyniec. 2013. "Understanding Rating Addition: US Courts and the Origins of Rating Agencies' Regulatory Licence (1900–1940)," Working Paper No.11/2013. Geneva: Graduate Institute of International and Development Studies.

Fons, Jerome S. 2004. "Tracing the Origins of 'Investment Grade'," *Special Comment*, New York: Moody's Investors Services.

Grant, Daniel L. 1941. "The Problem of Security Ratings," *Bankers' Magazine* May: 378–382.

Gregory, Jon. 2010. *Counterparty Credit Risk: The New Challenge for Global Financial Markets*. New York: Wiley.

Harold, Gilbert. 1938. *Bond Ratings as an Investment Guide: An Appraisal of Their Effectiveness*. New York: Ronald Press.

Harvey, Rachel. 2013. "The Legal Construction of the Global Foreign Exchange Market," *Journal of Comparative Economics* 41(2): 343–354.

Hickman, W. Braddock. 1958. *Corporate Bond Quality and Investor Experience*. Princeton: NBER and Princeton University.

Hoffman, Kathryn J. and Lowell D. Hill. 1976. "Historical Review of the U.S. Grades and Standards for Grain," *Illinois Agricultural Economics* 16(1): 1–9.

Hunt, John Patrick. 2011. "Credit Ratings in Insurance Regulation: The Missing Piece of Financial Reform," *Washington and Lee Law Review* 68(4): 1667–1697.

International Swaps and Derivatives Association [ISDA]. 2010. *ISDA Margin Survey 2010*. New York: ISDA.

International Swaps and Derivatives Association. 2000. *ISDA Collateral Survey 2000*. New York: ISDA.

International Swaps and Derivatives Association. 1999. *ISDA 1999 Collateral Review*. New York: ISDA.

International Swaps and Derivatives Association, Inc. 1996. *Guidelines for Collateral Practitioners*. New York: ISDA.

Johnson, Emory R. 1909. "Review of Moody's Analyses of Railroad Investments, by John Moody," *Annals of the American Academy of Political and Social Science* 34(1): 210–211.

Jones, Homer. 1940. "An Appraisal of the Rules and Procedures of Bank Supervision, 1929–39," *Journal of Political Economy* 48(2): 183–198.

Jones, Homer. 1938. "Some Problems of Bank Supervision," *Journal of the American Statistical Association* 33(202): 334–340.

Krippner, Greta R. 2011. *Capitalizing on Crisis: The Political Origins of the Rise of Finance*. Cambridge: Harvard University Press.

Kroszner, Randall S. 1999. "Can the Financial Markets Privately Regulate Risk? The Development of Derivatives Clearinghouses and Recent over-the-Counter Innovations," *Journal of Money, Credit and Banking* 31(3): 596–618.

Langohr, Herwig M. and Patricia T. Langohr. 2008. *The Rating Agencies and Their Credit Ratings*. New York: Wiley.

Lynn, David M. 1994. "Enforceability of Over-the-Counter Financial Derivatives," Business *Lawyer* 50(1): 291–337.

MacKenzie, Donald. 2011. "The Credit Crisis as a Problem in the Sociology of Knowledge," *American Journal of Sociology* 116(6): 1778–1841.

Moody, John. 1913. *Moody's Analyses of Investments, Part I – Steam Railroads: Containing in Detailed Form a Comparative Analysis of Each of the Railroad Systems of the United States, with Careful Deductions, Enabling the Banker and Investor to Ascertain the True Value of Securities*. New York: Analyses Publishing Co.

Morgan, Glenn. 2010. "Legitimacy in financial markets: credit default swaps in the current crisis," *Socio-Economic Review* 8(1): 17–45.

Morton, Walter A. 1939. "Liquidity and Solvency," *American Economic Review* 29(2): 272–285.

Norris, James D. 1978. *R.G. Dun & Co. 1841–1900: The Development of Credit-Reporting in the Nineteenth-Century*. Westport: Greenwood Press.

O'Leary, James. J. 1954. "Valuation of Life Insurance Company Holdings of Corporate Bonds and Stocks – Some Recent Developments," *Journal of Finance* 9(2): 160–177.

Olegario, Rowena. 2006. *A Culture of Credit: Embedding Trust and Transparency in American Business*. Cambridge: Harvard University Press.

Ott, Julia C. 2011. *When Wall Street Met Main Street: The Quest for an Investors' Democracy*. Cambridge: Harvard University Press.

Palyi, Melchior. 1938. "Bank Portfolios and the Control of the Capital Market," *Journal of Business* 11(1): 70–111.

Pénet, Pierre and Grégoire Mallard. 2014. "From Risk Models to Loan Contracts: Austerity as the Continuation of Calculation by Other Means." *Journal of Critical Globalization Studies* 7: 4–50.

Pogue, Thomas F. and Robert M. Soldofsky. 1969. "What's in a Bond Rating," *Journal of Financial and Quantitative Analysis* 4(2): 201–228.

Riles, Annelise. 2011. *Collateral Knowledge: Legal Reasoning in the Global Financial Markets*. Chicago: University of Chicago Press.

Riles, Annelise. 2010. "Collateral Expertise: Legal Knowledge in the Global Financial Markets." *Current Anthropology* 51(6): 795–818.

Securities and Exchange Commission [SEC]. 2003. *Report on the Role and Function of Credit Rating Agencies in the Operation of the Securities Markets*. Washington DC: SEC.

Securities and Exchange Commission [SEC]. 1994. Nationally Recognized Statistical Rating Organizations, Concept Release 34–34616. Washington D: SEC.

Shaffer, Gregory C. 2009. "How Business Shapes Law: A Socio-Legal Framework," *Connecticut Law Review* 42(1): 147–183.

Simonson, Donald G. and George H. Hempel. 1993. "Banking Lessons from the Past: The 1938 Regulatory Agreement Interpreted," *Journal of Financial Services Research* 1993: 249–267.

Singer, David Andrew. 2007. *Regulating Capital: Setting Standards for the International Financial System*. Ithaca NY: Cornell University Press.

Sinclair, Timothy J. 2005. *The New Masters of Capital: American Bond Rating Agencies and the Politics of Creditworthiness*. Ithaca: Cornell University Press.

Stulz, Rene M. 2004. "Should We Fear Derivatives?" *Journal of Economic Perspectives* 18(3): 173–192.

Suchman, Mark. 2003. "The Contract as Social Artifact," *Law and Society Review* 37(1): 91–142.

West, Richard R. 1973. "Bond Ratings, Bond Yield and Financial Regulation: Some Findings," *Journal of Law and Economics* 16(1): 159–168.

Weber, Rolf H. and Aline Darbellay. 2008. "The regulatory use of credit ratings in bank capital requirement regulations," *Journal of Banking Regulation* 10(1): 1–16.

CHAPTER ELEVEN

CONTRACTS AND PRIVATE LAW IN THE EMERGING ECOLOGY OF INTERNATIONAL LAWMAKING

Susan Block-Lieb and Terence Halliday

The creation of global markets rarely proceeds without the creation of institutions to enable and set parameters around global market actors, whether multinational companies, seafaring carriers, international banks or other private global investors. And yet little is known about the institutional matrix of lawmaking organizations on which markets depend. What is known about the proliferation of international institutions to rationalize the legal framework for global trade has prompted socio-legal scholars to question whether this accumulation of organizations creates legal fragmentation (Koskenniemi 2002), complexity (Alter et al. 2009; Kennedy 2006), harmonization or subversion (Shaffer and Pollack 2010; Mallard 2014), the institutionalization of transnational legal orders (Halliday & Shaffer 2015; Block-Lieb & Halliday 2015), or contestations among their proponents (Halliday & Shaffer 2015.

This paper provides the long view of a complex of international lawmaking organizations that emerged over 150 years, ultimately to constitute an ecology of international trade lawmaking. Among other goals and practices of these organizations, the formation and evolution of this ecology turned substantially on negotiations and disputes among lawmaking IOs about which of them had the authority to formulate international instruments governing private parties' contractual practices, a broad terrain of law that is characterized most commonly as international private law.

More particularly, we examine the emergence of three principal organizations over more than a century – the Hague Conference on

Private International Law, the International Institute for the Unification of Private Law (first known as the Rome Institute and later renamed UNIDROIT) and the UN Commission on International Trade Law (UNCITRAL) – in order to advance an ecological theory of international organizations (Block-Lieb and Halliday 2011a and b; Abbott et al. 2013). Such a theory would explain the emergence of these organizations and the lawmaking ecology in the geopolitical and economic contexts and conditions of their respective foundings. It would identify how each IO demarcated its boundaries vis-à-vis other IOs and claimed niches to ensure resources sufficient minimally for survival and optimally for competitive advantage.

By employing ecological theory in the analysis of institutional complexification, we shift the central focus of socio-legal analyses of global legal complexity from an emphasis on textual interpretations of rules (Koskenniemi 2002; Shaffer and Pollack 2010; Mallard 2014) to a focus on assertions of competence, claims of legitimacy, and other boundary-marking practices leading to more or less settlement of relations among potentially competitive international trade lawmaking bodies. Hence we will pay less attention to the substantive law created by the Hague Conference, UNIDROIT, and UNCITRAL for the governance of global trade and more to their claims to authority over a specific territory in the terrains of contractual law.

Building upon studies of professional conflicts and settlements in an ecological setting (Abbott 1988:69), we distinguish among different ways in which IOs have managed territorial conflicts so that their constellation formed a moving equilibrium which itself was constrained, enabled, and propelled by historical events. These settlements variously involved: *full authority*, when an IO successfully asserts its exclusivity over an issue area; *subordination*, when various IOs recognize each but understand their relationships hierarchically; *division of labor*, when IOs choose cooperation over direct competition in an horizontal playing field that involves the differentiation of tasks; and *segmentation*, when IOs cooperate to divide the global terrain according to issue areas of particular salience.

There are two innovations we offer in this theoretical orientation. On the one hand, ecology theory has rarely been applied to the social space of international organizations (although cf. Abbott et al. 2013). On the other hand, ecology theory in general has attended relatively less to the emergence of ecologies than the dynamics of already functioning ecologies. We argue, in this chapter, that ecology theory holds important insights for understanding the interactions of IOs and focus especially on the emergence, not only of such organizations, but also more fundamentally of an ecology of interconnected IOs engaged in international lawmaking.

We advance this conjunction of ecological explanations with the institutionalization of meta-law governing contractual practices in four steps. First, we step back into the nineteenth century to sketch the origins of an impetus toward the unification of private and other international law standards, not least with the conferences convened as the Hague Conference on Private International Law. Second, we observe in more detail the emergence of an entity, the Rome Institute, later renamed UNIDROIT, as a product of the League of Nations between World War I and II. Third, we demonstrate that a seeming settlement of "jurisdictions" among international lawmaking IOs was disturbed by the founding of new IOs in the economic and geopolitical turbulence of the 1960s, most notably with the contested founding of UNCITRAL in 1964. Each of these sections describes the emergence of another IO designed to pursue distinct goals or quests – international organization and legalization; international unification of private law; inclusiveness in international lawmaking – yet finds that none of the three IOs (Hague Conference, UNIDROIT or UNCITRAL) sat in full authority over international private lawmaking. Instead, they cohabited an emerging ecology of international lawmaking in which their relative positions shifted to accommodate new entrants. In the fourth section of this chapter, we describe how the fall of the Soviet command economies and the subsequent debt crises of the 1990s disturbed more than three decades of lawmaking co-existence, thereby pressing the actors in the lawmaking ecology to reconstitute themselves, and their relations with each other, to justify their salience in a new geopolitical and economic world order. The paper concludes with a retrospective long view of the ways ecological processes shaped both the institutional and substantive parameters of contracting in increasingly globalized markets.

THE QUESTION OF INTERNATIONAL LAW

Private organizations and proto organization

The idea that international organizations should work toward the unification and codification of international law began to emerge in the 1860s when David Dudley Field first applied the philosophical insights of Jeremy Bentham by attempting to codify a single, unified "international law" (Moore 1937; Janis 2010). Field's efforts at codification, in turn, inspired the formation of private advocacy associations in the late nineteenth and early twentieth centuries, such as the International Law Association (ILA) in 1873; *Institut de Droit International* in 1873; *Committee Maritime International* (CMI) in 1897; American Society of International Law in 1906; and the International Chamber of Commerce (ICC) in 1919.

These private organizations brought together lawyers, academics and philosophers, traders, financiers and commercial leaders (on the ICC, see the chapters by Lemercier and Sgard as well as Dezalay and Garth in this volume). Private groups advocated the development of international law on a broad range of topics, some proposals governing states' interactions and some governing the interactions of private actors whose commerce had become increasingly global. Organizations of business leaders focused particularly on the codification of uniform rules to govern global trade, transport, and communications.

While initiatives for private law reform were more often organized along issue areas than the claim that one international law should govern commercial practices, proponents of the codification of international laws on private and public actors aspired to both the greater certainty and predictability that the codification and unification of law would endow on an increasingly global commerce (Demogue 1927; Dubinsky 2005). Perhaps the most important accomplishment of these private organizations was their success in obtaining states' involvement in the making of international law – an essential step as only states could adopt international legislation.

By the latter half of the nineteenth century, nations, including many of the Great Powers, were themselves convinced to attempt to bring order through the codification of international law, and diplomatic conferences on a range of public and private law topics began to get organized. National interests in the development of legal order were driven by a quest for peace and for extensions in trade, yet there was little understanding of the complex relationships among coordination and codification, conflict and commerce (see, e.g., Abbot 1988; Halliday and Shaffer 2015).

Initially, governmental efforts at the codification of international law involved ad hoc meetings at which delegations of states were invited to address calls for reform along specified issue areas. These ad hoc meetings, generally called conferences, sometimes succeeded in negotiating multilateral treaties or conventions. Increasingly in the nineteenth

TABLE 11.1 Varieties of international law conferences, 1877–1914

	Meeting dates	Issues addressed	Resulting conventions
Lima Congress of Jurisconsults	1877	Extradition; uniform rules for legal conflicts in commercial matters	None
Brussels Conference on Bills of Exchange	1885 and 1888	Uniform rules on bills of exchange and like	None
South American Congress on Private International Law	1888, 1889	Various issues of private int'l law	Montevideo treaties on private int'l law
International Conference of American States	1889, 1902, 1906, etc.	Unif. rules on private int'l law on civil and commercial laws, and on legalization of documents	None
Hague Conference on PIL	1893, 1894, 1900, 1904	Private int'l law	Civil procedure; legal conflicts and jurisdiction on marriage; legal conflicts on divorce, separation, custody of minors, matrimonial property
Hague Peace Conference	1899 and 1907	First Peace Conf. (limits on arms buildups; arbitration; other issues of law and customs of war); Second Peace Conf.	First Peace Conf. led to creation of Permanent Court of Arbitration and 3 conventions on laws and customs of war; Second Peace Conf. resulted in no diplomatic conventions
Brussels Maritime Conference	1905, 1909, 1910	Uniform rules on various maritime issues	1910: Int'l Conv. for Unif. Rules on Collisions bet. Vessels; Int'l Conv. for Unif. Rules of Law on Assistance and Salvage at Sea
Hague Conference on Bills of Exchange	1910 and 1911	Uniform rules on bills of exchange and like	None
International Commission of Jurists	1912, 1914	Code of private int'l law and enforc't of foreign judgments	None

century, international conferences sought agreement on states' regulation of private activity, either in terms of coordination of the substance of regulation of private transactions, or coordination of the procedures to be followed when a dispute arose involving a private transaction. As early as 1864, conferences were convened to reach agreement on telegraphy and postal delivery that crossed national borders, on cross-border rail, road and river transport, and to coordinate on the weights and measures, monetary standards, customs and tariffs governing the terms of cross-border trade, etc. (UN 1947: 33–34; Northedge 1986). By the last decade of the nineteenth century, these conferences mostly were organized substantively around a range of issue areas, and temporally in terms of an understanding that, in the absence of unanimous agreement upon the terms of a convention, conferees would agree upon the next meeting date for the diplomatic conference. Often the inspiration and preparation for these diplomatic conferences emanated from international organizations of private actors, such as the *Association Internationale pour le Progrès des Sciences*, ILA, ICC or CMI.

The Hague Conference

Political entrepreneurs argued that the production of international texts (or international laws) would facilitate international trade. Although these efforts were ad hoc, and generally organized along issue areas, such as maritime trade and bills of exchange, the Hague Conference on Private International Law, first convened in 1893, was distinct in that its potential reach included all areas of private law where it sought to unify the procedural rules applicable to resolution of any cross-border private dispute. The Hague Conference on Private International Law organized several ad hoc conferences in the pre-WWI period in 1893, 1894, 1900 and 1904, which produced a handful of international conventions on disparate topics that were ratified only in continental Europe (Gutteridge 1951; van Loon 2007). Its breadth of vision was expansive: Hague Conferences sought greater predictability and transparency in the enforcement of virtually any sort of cross-border contractual arrangement or private relationship. Moreover, the Hague Conference's focus on uniform procedural rules looked to de-emphasize politics and legal difference by instead emphasizing neutral, process-oriented principles, a focus which gave it generic scope over any area of private law, not least in areas of private commercial law where contracts are pervasive.

The frequency and breadth of topics covered at ad hoc conferences held by the Hague Conference and other bodies should not be understood as an indication of their success (Table 11.1). The Hague Peace Conferences failed to reduce armaments, as had been hoped (Higgins 1909). The Montevideo Treaties, also on topics of private international law, also received only limited regional accession (Nadelmann 1954). The most successful of these early issue-oriented diplomatic conferences were the Brussels Maritime Conferences, which produced conventions that survived into the late twentieth and early twenty-first centuries (Sturley 1991; Block-Lieb and Halliday 2015). While the Hague Conference on Private International Law produced half a dozen conventions at the very beginning of the twentieth century, there were virtually no other diplomatic agreements reached in its subsequent meetings until the early 1950s (see Table 11.6, infra).

Governments from continental Europe discovered that the need for coordination among states created collective action problems and incentives for states to hold out – that is, to threaten to veto conduct otherwise consistent with their interests in order to gain disproportionate advantage in multilateral negotiations. The collective action problems that infected these gatherings should have been manageable since there were only a handful of Great Powers, but a demand for unanimity subverted the prospect of successful production of law. Importantly, the two most powerful common law nations, the United Kingdom and United States, generally did not sign early private international law conventions or even attend the conferences (Gutteridge 1951; Nadelmann 1964).

More than simply a failure of consensus, ad hoc conferences suffered from a lack of preparation and coordinated effort. Although the Dutch government had assisted with the administration of conference settings, and academics were appointed to assist as reporters and even the titular heads of the meetings, political actors alone were charged with decision making. A paucity of administrative assistance that had been provided proved to be insufficient for the tasks at hand.

Looking to achieve international agreement within an issue area held numerous benefits and detriments, but subject-specific diplomatic conferences assisted only one industry at a time, not commerce overall. Although the focus of the Hague Conferences on Private International Law on procedural matters seemed strategically wise, since procedure more readily can be styled as mere legal technicalities, this single-minded focus on procedure also faltered, and for two reasons. First, politics and power can never be eviscerated from negotiation of transnational legal orders (or indeed any transnational negotiation) (see Halliday and Shaffer 2015); countries found that negotiations over international conventions on procedural rules were as contested as other sorts of international instruments. Second, governments learned that international conventions crafted as uniform rules on topics of procedure are inherently limited in that they work best in adversary disputes that the two or more parties look to resolve before courts. They are less effective where adjudication is not sought (i.e., arbitration) or where multiple parties' interests or wider markets concerns are at stake (i.e., insolvency laws or trade policies).

By the outset of WWI, when globalization of trade reached levels not to be attained again until a half-century later, private actors, associations of legal specialists and a handful of states focused on the production of international conventions persistently demanded international economic order through law. Their energies led to a growing determination to replace ad hoc responses with permanent well-resourced organizations committed to ideals not only of more open trade and commerce, but also a more expansive ideal of legal order. War would shake but ultimately strengthen the belief that international organization would lead the world away from chaos and toward peace, prosperity and the rule of law. But the importance of international law to the emergence of international trade nevertheless remained underdeveloped in the absence of a stable international organization. The lack of standing lawmaking IOs left the terrain of lawmaking unsettled.

THE QUEST FOR UNIFICATION OF PRIVATE LAW

Ecological theory proposes that the stabilization of relationships within an emerging ecology of actors-in-relations may take the form of "settlements" between and among actors to resolve what might otherwise endure as unstable or destabilizing "territorial" disputes. For international private lawmaking those disputes might break out over either the substance or procedure of law to govern a narrower or wider expanse of economic, trade and other contract-related issues to be ordered through lawmaking.

Two provisional settlements marked the emergence of the first enduring IO dedicated to international lawmaking. The first settlement marked the founding of a League of Nations entity, the Rome Institute, in the interwar period.[1] The second settlement, an inter-governmental organization formed out of the reconstituted residue of this League of Nations entity, uncoupled from the United Nations, arose in the early 1950s. One organization in two guises adapted to radically different multilateral and geopolitical landscapes, in each case dedicated to the unification of private law.

The first settlement: between the League of Nations and UNIDROIT

Created in the wake of WWI, the League of Nations (LoN) was "intended to serve as an umbrella, under which a more orderly management of all world affairs, political, economic, financial, cultural and so on, would develop" (Northedge 1986: 1). It established a wide range of auxiliary organizations to address international questions on transit and communications, labor, health, education and cultural affairs (Covenant, Articles 9, 23, 25). It also sought to formalize the conference system that had occurred on an ad hoc basis in the nineteenth century (Id., Arts. 18–21, 24). With each of these moves, the League of Nations established a shift from a belief in the coordinating effects of law to an emphasis on the possibility of coordination through institution building (Kennedy 1987).

The codification of international law increased substantially under the direction of the League. Although the League convened important diplomatic conferences for the drafting of international conventions,[2] it did not purport to act as the exclusive source of international law, often deferring to pre-existing channels that had been created for the development of international instruments on issues of private law. Whether because the League of Nations did not enjoy universal membership among even the Great Powers of the time,[3] or because the momentum for the continuation of earlier diplomatic conferences proved substantial, the Hague Conference on Private International Law

[1] The League of Nations International Institute for the Unification of Private Law was referred to as the "Rome Institute" until the close of WWII, the "International Institute" for roughly a decade thereafter, and "UNIDROIT" beginning in 1964. We use all three names as temporally appropriate.

[2] Between 1920 and 1939, about 120 international instruments were concluded under the auspices of the League of Nations (UN 1947: 49).

[3] At its height, sixty-three nations were members of the League of Nations. For a variety of reasons, countries drifted in and out of League membership (Northedge 1986).

and the Brussels Conference on Maritime Law continued to meet independently of the League during the interwar period, as did regional conferences involving the North and Latin Americas (Table 11.2).[4]

The League's deference to these earlier, more established conferences on private lawmaking was partly a consequence of questions regarding the competence of the LoN to draft any international legislation (LoN, Advisory Committee of Jurists 1920; LoN 1921). Because the Covenant did not establish a lawmaking institution within the League,[5] the lawmaking practices of the League evolved organically.

Clarification of the League's authority in the finding and making of international law was sought in the first days of its existence. The Covenant called for the creation of a Permanent Court of International Justice, but left the details of its organization for the League of Nations (Covenant, Art. 14). The Advisory Committee of Jurists, appointed by the League's governing Council to draft an international agreement to establish the Permanent Court of International Justice, also forwarded to the League's governing council a corollary resolution recommending that the work begun at the First and Second Hague Peace Conferences should continue under the auspices of the League of Nations (LoN, Advisory Committee of Jurists1920). The Council adopted this recommendation as its own, but before the Assembly could ratify the recommendation, disagreement arose between the Council and the Assembly on how this work should proceed.

The Assembly was reticent to create any sort of formalized lawmaking organization within the auspices of the League of Nations. It rejected the idea of establishing an additional organization within the League for these purposes, on the grounds that "the Assembly itself was continuing the work of the Hague Conferences" (LoN 1921). It also rejected the idea of relying on existing (private) institutions devoted to the study of international law, such as the ILA and *Institut de Droit International* (id.). Until the mid 1920s and the creation of its own

4 The International Conference of American States and the International Commission of Jurists, which had been established in Rio de Janeiro in 1912, continued to meet throughout the interwar period. A Cuban jurist, Dr. Antonio Sanchez de Bustamante y Sirven, produced a draft code on private international law in 1925, which was adopted by the International Conferences of American States in 1928 (Nadelmann 1954).

5 That the Covenant did not spell out the League's role in the finding and making of international law had been, from its inception, a disappointment for many, especially for lawyers and others confident in the coordinating affects of the law (ABA 1919). While this disappointment was placed mostly on the Covenant's failure to address what would now be considered questions of public international law, the distinction between international laws pertaining to public or private spheres of actors was still ill-defined at the time.

TABLE 11.2 Varieties of international law conferences, 1920–1931

	Meeting dates	Issues addressed	Resulting conventions
LoN Conference on International Labor	1921, 1922, 1923, to date	Labor conditions and related issues	Numerous
Brussels Maritime Conference	1922, 1926	Bills of lading	1924: Int'l Conv. for the Unif. Of Certain Rules of Law on Bills of Lading
Hague Conference on PIL	1925, 1928	Bankruptcy, family law, etc.	
LoN Conference on Bills of Exchange, Promissory Notes and Cheques	1930, 1931	Bills of exchange, promissory notes, cheques	LoN Conv. on Unif. Rules Relating to Bills of Exchange, Promissory Notes and Cheques
LoN Conference on Progressive Codification of Int'l Law	1930	Nationality; territorial waters; responsibility of states for dgs to property caused by war	One convention and several protocols and related international agreements on nationality; thirteen articles on territorial waters, but no convention

lawmaking institute, it was the Assembly of the League that presented itself and itself only to the community of nations as the source of expert advice on legal matters.

Yet, as ecological theory has previously shown, claim to full authority over an issue area can distort the reality of everyday practice in its rejection of coordination with other organizations in their efforts to diagnose problems and propose solutions. Quickly, the League learned that it would be unable to address the breadth of issues it had taken on unless it organized itself to work on parallel tracks on various issues and to create pockets of assistance from "non-political" actors. Within a short time it agreed to create subsidiary organizations and institutes with a range of responsibilities. Eventually, in 1923 and 1924, the League organized two committees of experts and another international institute to assist it with lawmaking projects.

For instance, in 1923, the League had created a committee of experts to comment on the advisability of convening an international conference on an issue of private law. This decision followed from an earlier international conference that the League had convened in Brussels in 1920, less than a year after its inception, to address problems of finance. Although eighty-six delegates attended the conference from thirty-nine different countries, this was not a diplomatic conference since national leaders did not attend. Instead, individuals with private and official experience participated as "experts and not as spokesmen of official policy" (LoN, International Finance Conference 1920). Delegates were comprised mainly of prominent bankers and business leaders (Pauly 1996). As a result of its unofficial delegates, the Brussels Finance Conference could not produce a formal international agreement to react to the dire economic circumstances that confronted the world, and especially Europe, following WWI.

The delegates to the Brussels Finance Conference nonetheless urged international action. They published recommendations advising national actors to balance their budgets and, in particular, to reduce expenditures on armaments; to curb inflation and stabilize currency fluctuations; to abolish "artificial" restraints on trade; to take steps to restore market confidence and liquidity. They offered specific recommendations for law reform, including proposals that the laws of bills of exchange and bills of lading should be unified, that bondholders claims and loss of securities in international finance required international legal governance, and that double taxation, too, should be removed so as to facilitate international investment (LoN, International Finance Conference 1920: 237).

Recommendations to unify national laws important to market liquidity and international trade did not originate with the Brussels Financial Conference.[6] The ILA and the *Institut de Droit International* had worked on the topic of bills of exchange at the turn of the century, convincing the Belgium government to convene an international conference in 1885 and 1888 and the Netherlands government to do the same at The Hague in 1910 and 1912 (Table 11.1). When the Conference recommended reaching international agreement on the laws of bills of exchange, unification of the law on this issue appeared feasible given earlier efforts.

Prompted to act, the League created a committee of experts on bills of exchange in 1923, comprised of four academics involved in the earlier diplomatic conferences, to advise the Council and Assembly on bills of exchange and related financial instruments (LoN, Economic Committee 1923).[7] The committee recommended the convening of a conference, despite understanding that unanimous diplomatic agreement on substantive unification of the civil and common laws on the topic was nearly impossible; the UK and US were unlikely to agree to be party to a convention harmonizing private law understood to sit within the competence of the common law, the experts understood, but nonetheless might be encouraged to attend and, if possible, reach at least an agreement on the procedural aspects of a convention. In this way, the experts argued, "*almost complete* uniformity will soon be secured" (id. at 23). Experts also agreed that the conference should invite private actors to observe the proceedings – the bankers and other commercial actors with economic interests in the lawmaking.

Even during a period in which the League's Assembly claimed principal authority over the codification of international legal matters, there was slow movement toward coordination of the diversity of the

6 Work on bills of lading had begun in previous international conferences on maritime law held in Brussels in 1905, 1909 and 1910 (see Table 11.1).

7 Based on the reports offered by these experts, by 1930, the League's Section on Economics and Finance convened a diplomatic conference to consider an earlier draft convention on bills of exchange. It opened the conference to all states, regardless of their membership in the League. It also followed the expert committee's advice to include financiers and lawyers as observers. Although, predictably, the United States and UK did not accede to the terms of the treaties on payments law, the League of Nations Conferences on Bills of Exchange, Promissory Notes and Cheques succeeded in securing the agreement of more than forty nations to a handful of substantive and procedural conventions on these issues (Gutteridge 1951; LoN 1930a, 1931).

ecological milieux in which legal work was performed on an everyday basis. The League defined its relationship with the committees of experts it had created as one of *subordination* (Abbott 1988). Moreover, pre-existing diplomatic conferences on topics of private law continued to convene without LoN involvement – the Brussels Maritime Conference in 1922 and 1926; the Hague Conference on Private International Law in 1925 and 1928 (Table 11.2).

This movement eventually led to the creation of more permanent institutes, however. While initially the League created an array of permanent committees, institutes and other organizations devoted to examining various policy initiatives,[8] it quickly expanded the reach of permanent organs to address first the codification of (public) international law[9] and later an institute devoted to the unification of private law.[10] The move from temporary and ad hoc organizations to those of increasing permanence, thus, followed a parallel shift from policymaking organs to include organizations dedicated to providing expert advice to the League on its emerging lawmaking functions.

On September 26, 1924, Italy proposed the foundation in Rome of an Institute to study and promote the unification of private law on an international basis.[11] In making this offer, the Italian delegate drew a parallel between the work of a new Rome Institute and that of the Committee on Intellectual Cooperation and its sister Institute, which the French government previously had "magnificently" offered to host and fund "in perfect good faith" (id., at 168). In like manner, Italy offered to create an institute in Rome intended to "show the world" in a practical way that "Signor Mussolini's Government" was committed to the ideals of international peace and international coordination. More

[8] By the mid-to-late 1920s, the League had created, the Committee on Intellectual Cooperation and its related French Institute, the Economic and Financial Committees, the Organization for Communications and Transit and the Health Organization.

[9] The Committee of Experts for the Progressive Codification of International Law was first created in 1924, but did not achieve more permanent status until after the First Codification Conference held in 1931.

[10] The creation of the Rome Institute on the Unification of Private Law and the French Institute on Intellectual Cooperation would be followed, in 1927, with the creation of two additional institutes: the International Institute of Educational Cinema and the Institute of the Scientific Organization of Labor (LON 1927).

[11] Three Assembly delegates joined to second Italy's offer: France, acknowledging the connection between the French and now the Rome Institute; Belgium, demonstrating the unqualified support of this government, despite its own longstanding interest in the development of international treaties on maritime law; Uruguay, referring to its country's "special satisfaction" with the project given that "we in America were the first to undertake a work of this nature, which was brought to a concrete conclusion in the Montevideo Treaties of 1869" (id., at 169).

broadly, the Italian government's interest in the unification of private law was justified as a continuation of earlier efforts undertaken during the war to address "the great problem on the unification of private law" (id.).

During the debates in the League's Assembly, representatives from continental European powers and Latin America spoke in favor of the creation of a new Institute in Rome as a way to convert earlier ad hoc diplomatic conferences into a permanent structure, although one subordinated to the ultimate authority of the LoN. The proposal met with principled opposition from common law countries like Great Britain, which argued that the creation of a new institution simply added legal complexity since it would create a "problem of double employ or overlapping jurisdiction in two organizations" (id.). "I do not for a moment suggest that there is not ample room for the new Institute, but this problem of overlapping must be settled" (id., at 169–170).

Implicitly, the British delegate would also have been concerned about the relationship between this Institute and pre-existing diplomatic conferences on topics of private law, such as the Brussels Maritime Conferences.[12] For common law countries, some areas of private law sat within the competence of subnational actors, such as the procedural matters addressed in the various Hague Conferences, which would have raised questions as to the Crown's authority to regulate on a topic subject to common law courts' inherent jurisdiction. More generally, opponents to the new committee on legal codification criticized the new Institute simultaneously for increasing legal complexity and blurring existing boundaries that present IOs maintained around their law-making jurisdictions.

The constitutive Statute of the Rome Institute ensured that the work of the Institute would both be *subordinated* to that of the Assembly and *differentiated* from that of other League entities. It specified that the Rome Institute would work "under the direction" of the League and "in connection with, and with due regard for the work of, the Committee on Intellectual Coordination, the International Labour Office and the technical organizations of the League" (id.). Effectively, this differentiation was directed at the *segmentation* of distinct issue areas (Abbott 1988): labor law and policy as distinct from issues of

[12] Great Britain first attended the Hague Conference on Private International Law in 1925, and then only on one topic, that is bankruptcy, and only for a limited time, in that it left mid-way through these proceedings (Block-Lieb 2015).

intellectual property rights and cultural cooperation; international rules for the unification of private law as distinct from both.

The Statute carefully defined territorial boundaries surrounding the Institute, specifying that it should "study methods for the assimilation and coordination of private law as between States or groups of States, and to prepare for the gradual adoption by the various States of uniform private law legislation" (Institute Statute, Art. 2, 1926). The Statute also specified the responsibilities of the Institute's governing body, a standing committee and secretariat (id., Arts. 3–10), including especially the governing body's control over the Institute's agenda and objects of work (id., Art. 7), approval of draft proposals for submission to the Council (id., Art. 9), and the determination to suggest to the Council that the convening of an international conference was desirable (id., Art. 10; see also Peters 2012).

Despite the limits contained in its constitutional document, the Institute's governing body acted with a degree of independence. Early reports provide little indication of influence on the Institute's agenda from the League's governing council. Nor do the Assembly's records contain direction for the Institute. The precise nature of the relationship among the Assembly, Council and the Institute may well have been subject to conflicting pressures. On the one hand, League actors would have been conscious of a danger that limiting too severely the authority of this "committees of experts" might have the effect that their very expertise was neutered.[13] On the other hand, experts were understood not to be decision-makers. Care was taken in drafting the Institute's constitutive Statute to demarcate a subordinate role for the Institute. This statement of hierarchy nonetheless confirmed the League's understanding of the Institute as constituting a distinct international organization, that is, its status as an *agent* of the LoN.

[13] The work of the Committee of Experts on the Codification of International Law had been especially controversial. The Assembly had asked the Committee to propose topics "desirable and realizable" for international codification, and to draft questionnaires and a report on governments' responses to this questionnaire, but consciously determined not to ask it to prepare draft conventions for consideration at the conference. When the Codification Conference produced little concrete agreement, this lack of preparedness was criticized by several national delegations. As a result of this criticism, by the end of the First Codification Conference in 1931, the League's Assembly moved to strengthen the influence of governments at every stage of the codification process, while at the same time making permanent the Committee of Experts on the Progressive Codification of International Law (LoN 1931: 9). Although this deliberation on the composition and mandate of the Permanent Committee of Experts would not have influenced the Assembly's decision to create the Rome Institute, because these second thoughts arose in 1931, years after it had begun its work, actors within the Institute would have been aware of this equivocation.

From its inception in 1928, the Rome Institute worked with the skeleton of an inter-governmental organization and the heart of a scholarly institution. With no IO template on which to model its organizational structure and work practices, the Institute functioned like an academic conference or institution of higher learning, although its governance structure nominally resembled the League of Nations. Like the League, the Institute's member states met periodically as an Assembly. As with the League, the Institute's Assembly was its ultimate decision-making organ, annually approving the budget and electing a President of the Assembly and governing council from among its ranks. Periodically, it voted on the Institute's program of work, although it is not clear if this was entirely pro forma.

In many ways, the subordination of the Rome Institute to the League's Assembly allowed technical work on unification of national laws governing contractual relationships to move rapidly ahead, without interference from politics between 1930 and 1939.[14] The pace of this work also was enabled by the Institute's methods of work. Working groups were small (four or five principal negotiators, with an equal number of "assistants," were engaged in work on a convention on the sale of goods, for example); the members of these groups endeavored to harmonize based on "scientific" comparative analysis of discordant laws rather than on political or ideological grounds.

From its first sessions, work proceeded on a draft convention on the sale of goods, procedures for arbitration of private disputes, hoteliers responsibilities, insurance law, copyright and other intellectual property laws, and so on. Although this range of work included both procedure and substance, the Institute first completed two substantive draft

[14] The relationship between the Rome Institute and organizations other than those within the LoN, including especially other organizations involved in the drafting of international instruments on private law (i.e., the Hague Conference on Private International Law and the Brussels Maritime Conference), was complicated by several factors. These other "conferences" were no more than ad hoc diplomatic events; lack of agency would have precluded any formal agreement on the hierarchy among them. Moreover, the location of the precise boundary between private and public law was unclear: the Brussels conferences on maritime law had addressed contracts (producing the Hague Rules on bills of lading), but also a range of public law topics (Yiannopoulos 1965: 372 n. 12); the Hague Conference on Private International Law sought to unify international procedural law, which governed private disputes before public adjudicative organs (Baty 1914). The Brussels and Hague Conferences met during the interwar period, including after creation of the Rome Institute (Table 11.2). Clarification of these boundaries would cause the Institute's leadership to reach agreements with the interested private organizations, such as the CMI and ICC, regarding the breadth and location of their work (Institute 1946–56), and to hold conferences dedicated to the coordination of organizations engaged in the unification of law (Note 1950).

legal conventions: a draft convention on the international sale of goods and another on hoteliers' responsibilities. But the outbreak of WWII created a context in which the world was in no mood for uniform rules governing international sale of goods. The draft was put in a locked drawer for safekeeping until after the War.

The second settlement: the UN and UNIDROIT

In the ten years following the founding of the UN in 1945, a more complex international lawmaking ecology began to take shape around several international organizations that were either created or recreated in the postwar period. While during the interwar period, the Rome Institute, the Hague Conference on Private International Law, the Brussels Maritime Conference and the League's Committee of Experts on the Codification of International Law divided among themselves work on the codification of various aspects of international law, this settlement did not survive the dissolution of the LoN.

The new settlement among organizations engaged in the codification of international law, which emerged after WWII, involved more than the subordination of a technical body (like UNIDROIT) to the authority a political body (like the Assembly of the League now turned into the Assembly of the UN), but also the establishment of a tacitly agreed-upon *division of labor* and *segmentation* of areas of expertise among technical bodies. The "market" for international lawmaking more clearly divided between the formulation of public and private laws, a segmentation that recognized the distinct clientele (states versus commercial and other private parties) and policy issues (peace versus prosperity). In addition, within a short time after the creation of the United Nations, a division of labor resumed within private lawmaking entities, which divided procedural from substantive questions.

This resettling of roles and of work occurred in reaction to tectonic political and economic shifts following the close of WWII. Mostly, however, this proto-ecology of international lawmaking organizations unsettled and resettled in the immediate postwar years because the very idea of international law, and thus also the processes for its formation, remained contested, even as related to the private law governing commercial and contractual relationships.

Like the Covenant of the League of Nations, the United Nations Charter did not create a lawmaking entity under the aegis of the UN, providing only that the General Assembly should "encourag[e] the progressive development of international law and its codification"

(UN Charter, Art. 13, para. 1). The Charter appeared to differentiate between the "development" of international law and its "codification." When the UN General Assembly established the International Law Commission (ILC) in 1947, it perpetuated this usage, despite debate on the meaning of this language (UN General Assembly Resolution 1947).

The language employed in their constitutive Statute created at least two unsettling uncertainties regarding the breadth of the new ILC's competence. First, there was the distinction between the "development" and the "codification" of international law. Second, there was the question of the breadth of "international law" that the ILC could develop and codify. As to the first question, the Statute reiterates that the "Commission shall have for its object the promotion of the progressive development of new international law and codification" of existing law (ILC Statute, Art. 1, para. 1).[15] On the second issue, the Statute provides that the Commission would "concern itself primarily with *public* international law" (ILC Statute, art. 1, para. 2). Although this Statute expressly did not preclude the ILC from "entering the field of private international law" (id.), it became clear that the ILC would rely on the Hague Conference to continue its deliberations on questions of private international law (PIL) – that is, conflicts of law, jurisdiction, enforcement of foreign judgments, and the like. By 1953, the United Kingdom had joined the Hague Conference, signaling a resolution of questions about the relevance of international conventions on PIL to common law countries.

Settling the ILC's role vis-à-vis the Hague Conference resolved only some questions about the contours of this emerging ecology. If the ILC worked primarily on the codification of *public international law* and the Hague Conference confined itself to the procedural questions of *private international law*, this left an important role for the Institute: international law concerning the *substance* of private contractual interactions. The Hague Conference historically had focused exclusively on matters of procedure; its newly ratified constitutive Statute did not expand its mission to include the unification of substantive private law. But

[15] It goes on to distinguish "for convenience" between "progressive development," which it refers to as the formulation of a draft convention on a subject that is neither the subject of existing international law nor "sufficiently developed in the practice of States," and "codification," which it defines as referring to "the more precise formulation and systematization of rules of international law in fields where there already has been extensive State practice, precedent and doctrine" (id., Art. 15).

neither did the ILC's Statute. The UN had not expressly vested in the ILC authority to formulate private law. This narrow construction of the work of the ILC and Hague Conference permitted the Institute to struggle to survive in a *segmented* ecology of international lawmaking organizations so long as it confined itself to the unification of the *substance* of private law.

The intellectual *segmentation* of the emerging lawmaking ecology did not involve a *division of labor* as relates to methods of work, however. Table 11.3 reveals one important constant: the Institute remained locked into a single legal technology.[16] The ILC, the Hague Conference and the Institute all worked exclusively to draft multilateral treaties (i.e., conventions) in their distinct issue areas. While the Institute's Secretariat produced studies and similar reports, the Institute itself produced only draft international conventions until the final decade of the twentieth century (see Table 11.5). The drafting of an international convention is time-consuming. Much of the Institute's work on early drafts of these conventions had begun in the interwar period. Its simultaneous work on so many issues is, thus, partly explained by the long arc of time required for each final product. A preference for multilateral conventions did not distinguish UNIDROIT from the other lawmaking IOs in the ecology at the time. The ILC and Hague Conference also worked exclusively in this formal medium (see, e.g., Table 11.6).

Although the methods of work followed by the ILC, UNIDROIT and the Hague Conference were similar, one fundamental structural difference distinguished the three lawmaking IOs. Although the ILC clearly fitted under the UN umbrella organization, in that it reported to the Sixth Committee of UN's General Assembly, neither the Hague Conference nor the Institute were subsumed into the UN. Ultimately, the UN failed to embrace the Institute as an UN-related entity, although it had adopted the International Labor Organization, World Health Organization and the International Committee on Intellectual Cooperation, later to become UNESCO. And because the Institute/UNIDROIT held out the hope of being embraced by the UN organization, it delayed

[16] While the term "technology" might appear cumbersome, we use it deliberately to evoke the political and technical elements of the formal means by which legal norms were drafted both to solve internal political difficulties in the deliberative process and to meet external political challenges of key implementing audiences and bodies inside states. Like mechanical technologies, legal technologies can be created, adapted and manipulated, and these expressions of creativity become crucial aspects of transnational and global normmaking (see Block-Lieb and Halliday 2006).

in reconstituting itself as an independent IO until the 1950s. It survived on scarce resources – member states' voluntary contributions, 500 Swiss Francs at a time, supplemented with the volunteer efforts of a network of "correspondents" that had been established during the interwar period.

Perhaps because neither the Hague Conference nor the Institute reported to an umbrella IO (like the United Nations) and, thus, lacked a overseeing parent organization, neither overtly coordinated with nor deferred to the other. In the late 1940s and early 1950s the Institute had its hands or its eyes on virtually every international and transnational initiative involving private law. Most of these topics involved *substantive* private law issues, but some pushed on the line between substance and procedure. The Institute's work on arbitration and on the enforcement of maintenance obligations treads closely to the *procedural* work of the Hague Conference on Private International Law. The Institute's work was also partly international and partly regional as it became enmeshed in the construction of a common market within Europe, a project that was heavily related to the unification or harmonization of at least some laws.[17]

Although its status as an orphaned IO left the Institute outside the embrace of the UN, it frequently worked in tandem with international organizations, including UN-related entities such as the UN's Economic and Social Council (ECOSOC), Economic Commission on Europe (ECE) and Education, Scientific and Cultural Commission (UNESCO), or through regional actors, such as the Council of Europe or Benelux, often at the request of these entities (Table 11.3). Such formal partnerings, which may have effectively functioned as a survival strategy, were also supplemented by informal coordination with international professional and industrial organizations. Institute reports frequently refer to meetings and other coordinative work with the International Chamber of Commerce, *Committee Maritime International*, International Law Association and other organizations.[18]

[17] There is little coherence in the variety of private international law topics covered by the Institute's early conventions. They cover a wide range of private laws, arguably because its need to survive gave it less choice over the work it took on board. The Institute appeared rarely to turn away requests to take up a topic. For example, although it was an "International Institute," it assisted the Italian government in designing national law governing their post-War equity markets and stockbrokers' conduct.

[18] The Institute actively worked to avoid duplication of effort with other IOs. For example, its reports refer to negotiations with the CMI to divide work on issues of maritime law, resulting on its focus on inland waterways and inland navigation vessels (see Table 11.3). Beginning as early

TABLE 11.3 International instruments drafted with UNIDROIT's assistance but adopted under the auspices of other IOs or regional actors

Date	Title of convention	UNIDROIT partners
1954	UNESCO Convention for the Protection of Cultural Property in the Event of Armed Conflict	UNESCO
1955	Benelux Treaty of 1955 on Compulsory Insurance against Civil Liability in respect of Motor Vehicles	Benelux
1955	European Convention on Establishment	adopted under auspices of Council of Europe
1956	Convention on Contract for International Carriage of Goods by Road (CMR)	adopted under auspices of UN's Economic Commission for Europe (ECE)
1958	Hague Convention concerning Recognition and Enforcement of Decisions relating to Maintenance Obligations towards Children	adopted under auspices of UN Economic and Social Council (ECOSOC)
1959	European Convention on Compulsory Insurance against Civil Liability in respect of Motor Vehicles	adopted under auspices of Council of Europe
1961	Int'l Convention for the Protection of Performers, Producers of Phonograms and Broadcasting Organizations	adopted under auspices of ILO, UNESCO and WIPO
1962	European Convention on Liability of Hotel-keepers concerning the Property of their Guests	adopted under auspices of Council of Europe
1965	Protocol No. 1 concerning Rights in Rem in Inland Navigation Vessels, annexed to 1965 Convention on Registration of Inland Navigation Vessels	adopted under auspices of UN's Economic Commission for Europe (ECE)
1965	Protocol No. 2 concerning Attachment and Forced Sale of Inland Navigation Vessels, annexed to 1965 Convention on Registration of Inland Navigation Vessels	adopted under auspices of UN's Economic Commission for Europe (ECE)
1973	Convention on Contracts for Int'l Carriage of Passengers and Luggage by Road (CVR)	adopted under auspices of UN's Economic Commission for Europe (ECE)
1980	UN Convention on Contracts for Int'l Sale of Goods (CISG)	UNCITRAL began work on CISG with 1964 Hague Convention relating to Uniform Law on Int'l Sale of Goods, based on 1939 UNIDROIT draft

By 1951, hopes of incorporation into the UN organization seem to have cooled within the Institute, while at the same time opportunities for survival as an independent international entity tasked with the unification of private law appear to have solidified. Refounded as an independent inter-governmental organization in 1951, the statute of the reconstituted body clarified its purposes by providing that "the purposes of the International Institute for the Unification of Private Law are to examine ways of harmonising and coordinating the private law of States and of groups of States, and to prepare gradually for the adoption by the various States of uniform rules of private law" (Institute Statute, Art. 1).[19] Its League of Nations task of "assimilation" gave way to the more expansive possibility of "harmonization." Curiously, in 1951, the Institute's refounding coincided with the reawakening of the Hague Conference on Private International Law, which resumed meeting for the first time since its inter-War sessions held in 1925 and 1928.

The reconstitution of the Hague Conference did not precipitate overt competition with the ILC or the Institute. The Hague Conference never challenged the ILC's claim to work in the area of public international law. Nor did it overtly challenge the authority of the Institute to work on unification of substantive private laws. Instead, beginning in 1951 the Hague Conference on Private International Law resumed production of procedurally focused conventions ranging from topics on marriage, family and children to commercial law. Differentiating itself from both the ILC and Institute, the Hague Conference emphasized questions of jurisdiction, procedure and applicable law, such as which court should hear an issue, which countries' law should apply in case of litigation, which law would be applied in the forum court, rather than the substance of a legal issue. The Hague Conference differentiated between the labors of procedural and of substantive lawmaking, and took the former for itself.

At this juncture, three organizations divided international lawmaking among themselves along three familiar boundaries. One entity, the ILC, sat fully within the UN, and exercised jurisdiction over public international lawmaking. The Hague Conference sat outside the financial and political protection of the UN, exercising jurisdiction over

as 1950, the Institute convened an International Congress of Private Law (UNIDROIT 1950). By 1956, it convened the First Meeting of the Organizations Concerned with the Unification of Law (UNIDROIT 1956: 43), which met on and off for less than a decade.

19 Despite its reconstitution in 1951, the Institute did not rename itself as UNIDROIT until later, in 1964 (UNIDROIT 1964).

questions of private international law of a procedural and jurisdictional nature. The Institute was nestled in another corner of the international lawmaking ecology, content to work on the substantive unification of private law. It, too, sat outside the UN tent. Only the Institute exercised authority over the development/codification/unification of globalized contractual practices, that is, the substance of private law. All three claimed full authority over their segment of the ecology.

A settled ecology?

This historical sketch, which seeks to identify great currents of change discernible beyond the eddies of fine detail, reveals several shifts in a slowly emerging international lawmaking ecology: first, the shift from nineteenth century ad hoc lawmaking and one-off international conferences toward the establishment of an organization devoted permanently to the making of international law; second, the shift from silos of consideration (distinct conferences for various issue areas) to uniformity of approach (organizational effort); and, third, the shift from seeking to achieve uniformity in international procedural norms toward also looking to craft uniformity in substantive laws. The latter shift from procedure to substance involved a division of labor and products, as well as an expansion of horizons. Although the emerging ecology of international lawmaking organizations now included three standing organizations with competence over broad segments of issues (public and private law) and distinct strategies (procedural and substantive law), none was organized to resolve the problems found within a narrow issue or industry (such as maritime law, for example, which might involve questions of public and private international law, depending on the topic of the problem).

The separation of public international from private international lawmaking, and of procedure from substance, held many benefits, but the division of labor and segmentation of lawmaking space were especially important for commercial interests. That uniform rules on law should be preferred over uniform rules of enforcement seems clear when looking to enable global trade and globalized trade practices, because procedural laws only clarify what countries' court and law will govern in a dispute. Procedural law, even international agreement on uniform rules of procedure, does not obviate commercial actors' needs to assess the consequences of distinct courts and distinct laws, an assessment that is likely to be costly and filled with uncertainty.

Each of the three post-WWII lawmaking IOs looked to depoliticize their work by looking to subordinate themselves to an umbrella organization (whether formally or otherwise) and to specify in their constitutive statutes that delegates should expect to work in their personal capacity as experts and not as state representatives.

Deference to the LoN or the UN need not have signaled a lack of interest in securing *full authority* over international lawmaking on a global scale, however. When the Hague Conference emerged in the latter years of the nineteenth century, no other lawmaking arena asserted competence over all private law. When the Rome Institute was created under the auspices of the League, the Hague Conference, which had convened briefly and unproductively in 1925, waited more than twenty-five years to reconvene. The Rome Institute might well have asserted competence over procedural and substantive areas of private law, but chose mostly to deliberate on issues of substance.

Full authority had been within the reach of each and neither succeeded in fully grasping this brass ring. The ILC, by contrast, secured what the Rome Institute had long sought – the protection and imprimatur of the UN – but in doing so renounced claims to stewardship of either private law or private international law. As a result, the international lawmaking ecology was comprised of three distinct entities, each claiming "full" authority over a section of the whole. But was the ILC's failure to assert authority over private international law a rejection by the UN of the importance of private international lawmaking, or a recognition by it of the expertise situated within other lawmaking IOs?

THE QUEST FOR INCLUSIVENESS AND REPRESENTATION: THE UNITED NATIONS, WORLD POLITICS AND PRAGMATISM

The tripartite division of labor in international lawmaking institutions was thrown into disarray roughly ten years later. In 1964 the convergence of three events resulted in the creation of a new UN commission to address issues of international trade and development.[20]

[20] This is the same year in which the Institute's governing council determined to rebrand itself as UNIDROIT (UNIDROIT 1964). The name was not an acronym, but rather an abbreviated reference in French to its mission of private law unification – a mission that would eventually, it was hoped, lead to "one law." That the term held open the likely possibility of confusion with other UN-related entities could not have been lost on the Institute, however.

In that year, a diplomatic conference at The Hague finally succeeded after a dozen years of effort to produce two conventions on the international sale of goods (Farnsworth 1962; Honnold 1959 and 1965).[21] Although these conventions were traceable to a draft convention first produced by the Rome Institute in the 1930s, few viewed the convention as likely to bring uniformity to the law governing international sales contracts of goods mostly because very few countries had been involved in the diplomatic conference.

Also in 1964, the UN's General Assembly responded to developing countries' claims of worsening global trade conditions by agreeing to host a single conference on trade and development (Rajagopal 2003). Developing countries, organized as the Group of 77, demanded that this UN Conference on Trade and Development (UNCTAD) receive permanent status as a UN entity. Perhaps most importantly, Hungary proposed in that same year that the UN General Assembly "consider the steps to be taken" to create another UN-affiliated entity alongside UNCTAD, which would be dedicated to "progressive development in the field of private international law with a particular view to promoting international trade" (UN General Assembly Sixth Committee 1965). Together these events converged to produce a fourth IO that would populate the increasingly dense ecology of international lawmaking and open up prospects of intense competition among lawmaking bodies.

The emergence of UNCTAD signaled a sea-change in UN politics and, more generally, in the political and economic interactions among all nations. The architects of the UN consciously sought to remedy deficiencies in the economic policies of the League of Nations by vesting the UN with authority over economic issues of global proportion, including issues of trade, finance and development. But by the time proposals for the UN's International Trade Organization had been finalized, governments' interests cooled. The US Congress declined to ratify the ITO charter in 1950, leaving international trade governed by the General Agreement on Tariffs and Trade (GATT), although the GATT initially had been conceived of as merely a temporary agreement pending implementation of the ITO (Hudec 1975). The failure

[21] Both conventions were UNIDROIT product. One, entitled a Convention Relating to a Uniform Law on the International Sale of Goods, governed the substance of these contracts and was first completed by an UNIDROIT working group in 1935 (Honnold 1965). The second, entitled a Convention relating to a Uniform law on the Formation of Contracts for the International Sale of Goods, addressed issues associated with the formation of these contracts. Also an UNIDROIT product, it had been drafted after WWII (id.).

to create a permanent alternative entity meant that the GATT took on unintended authority. The UN's promises of global representation began to look hollow. Developing countries quickly grew disillusioned with GATT, and looked to the UN for redress of their views, proposing in 1964 an international conference to promote economic growth, trade and development.

It was hoped that a UN body's focus on trade would create conditions for increasing the export earnings of developing countries and improve North-South relations. In its first session, UNCTAD produced a report identifying general principles to govern international trade relations, recommending trade preferences for developing countries, and establishing UNCTAD on a permanent basis. In a parallel move, developing nations joined together as a Group of 77, which involved both the creation of a political force and the articulation of a new economic order.

Debate within UNCTAD's first sessions had been centered on the *politics* of a perceived economic disequilibrium between the Global North and South, but it also raised the specter of divergent and conflicting *laws* as an obstacle to trade and, thus, economic development. The importance of international private lawmaking regained attention. UNCTAD reframed the issue in terms of the need for international private lawmaking as a route to economic development. Articulation of the connections between law, trade and development was path breaking, but questions regarding a locus for the codification of international private law remained deeply contested.

As a result, UNCTAD's role in the international lawmaking ecology played a part in the negotiations over its formation as a permanent UN entity. In its constitutive Statute, UNCTAD's competence to draft international conventions was left unclear, however. Although the General Assembly Resolution establishing UNCTAD refers to the new Conference's authority "to initiate action" for the "negotiation and adoption of multilateral legal instruments in the field of trade" (GA Resolution 1995, Art. II, para. 2(e)), this language more closely resembles proposals intended to limit suggestions that the Conference should itself draft international conventions.[22]

[22] The first Conference, in which UNCTAD's existence had been negotiated, expressly considered whether the new Conference ought to hold this sort of authority. Delegates from developing nations proposed that the Conference should be empowered "to negotiate legal instruments or multilateral agreements concerning international trade," while Western delegates were only prepared to authorize it to "study the legal bases for multilateral trade relations" and then make recommendations to ECOSOC regarding later action (Cordovez 1967). Neither of these proposals was, in the end, adopted word for word (Block-Lieb and Halliday, Ch.8 In Draft).

If no UN affiliated entity held authority over the formulation of international legislation on the substance of private law, and yet a case could be made that trade and law were inextricably intertwined, so much so, that if international trade were to expand, then legal "obstacles" to trade and development should be removed and, by implication, legal means to stimulate trade should be expanded, then the importance of the making of this international private law would increase significantly. Nonetheless, the locus for carrying out this new mission remained in the hands of IOs with their roots outside the United Nations – that is, with UNIDROIT and the Hague Conference on Private International Law. Indeed, resolution of a diplomatic conference to consider a draft convention on international sales law in 1964 might have appeared to some as a vote of confidence in The Hague and Rome as the proper places for such negotiation, although the uniformity claimed by that convention was premised, tenuously, on signatures from only eight national representatives, all from Continental Europe.

To quell a potential jurisdictional battle, Hungary proposed the creation of a new UN entity focused exclusively on the production of international trade law. As initially conceived, this proposal emphasized a need to reform not only the substantive laws relating to international trade, but also the private international laws coordinating discordant substantive laws, and specifically a need to unify, coordinate and clarify both types of legislation. Hungary's proposal, thus, competed directly with both the Hague Conference and UNIDROIT. Since the founding proponents of UNCITRAL needed to persuade the UN General Assembly that these pre-existing IOs had not already occupied this trade law "space," advocates sought to differentiate the new commission through a combination of arguments.

At its initial debate, several Sixth Committee[23] delegates engaged in boundary-defining maneuvers to argue that a new UN commission should offer both a concentration of focus and a broadening of interests: its mission would concentrate on that subset of private law relevant to trade, and specifically to the removal of legal obstacles to trade and development; and it would represent a broader range of national interests than traditionally had been considered by earlier organizations (Block-Lieb and Halliday, Chs. 1 and 2 In Draft). UNIDROIT and the Hague Conference, they asserted, had in the past concentrated on Continental European concerns. While more than

[23] The Committee of the UN General Assembly devoted to legal issues.

forty countries were members of UNIDROIT in 1964, including India, Iran, Pakistan and Brazil, the perception that UNIDROIT and the Hague Conference were Euro-centric was prevalent and accurate. And at the moment of decolonization and the heightened political profile of developing countries, the participation of the developing countries in the governing council of either existing body was minimal. Moreover, neither of the anchors of the postwar political orders, the USSR or the United States, were members of either UNIDROIT or the Hague Conference at the time.

UNCITRAL, it was proposed, would not only be more broadly representative of nations than the current lawmaking IOs, but its range of work would be narrower. Where the programs of work of UNIDROIT and the Hague Conference ventured far beyond trade, sometimes overlapping in their work and failing to coordinate very effectively, UNCITRAL would focus on trade alone, said Hungary, and would attend specifically to the structural reforms within developing countries that were necessary to stimulate trade. Despite the protestations of UNCITRAL's sponsors that it "had no intention of encroaching" on the activities of existing international organizations, representatives from UNIDROIT and the Hague Conference appeared at a second Sixth Committee debate on the topic of UNCITRAL's emergence (UNGA Sixth Committee 1966:11–16) to argue for various limitations on the scope of activity of the new commission (id.).

Other delegates retorted that the record of the Hague Conference was venerable but it could point only to a handful of conventions that had entered into force. Moreover, the United States was especially wary of conventions, given its federal structure and authority its states held over many areas of private law. The United States preferred working through model laws (Dubinsky 2005), a format many Europeans feared would not lead to uniformity.

In late 1966, the General Assembly sought to resolve the boundary disputes which its new entity had provoked by proposing that UNCITRAL would have the authority to formulate international trade law, but the extant lawmaking IOs, such as UNIDROIT and the Hague Conference, would continue to exist and would themselves observe the work of UNCITRAL and contribute to it (UN General Assembly Resolution 1966). The need for UNCITRAL was, thus, not explained substantively in terms of the distinct issues on which it was expected to format international instruments. Nor was UNCITRAL formed to fill a void in the jurisdiction of these organizations. UNCITRAL's reason for being was substantially justified on the grounds of its inclusiveness and its legitimacy. As a UN entity its legitimation warrants[24] would rest on the representation of all nations – or at least all UN members.

From the outset, the members of UNCITRAL's Commission were chosen to reflect a balance among all the world's geographic areas, legal families and levels of economic development. Moreover, UNCITRAL quickly developed a practice of allowing any member of the General Assembly to observe at UNCITRAL commission or working group sessions.[25]

UNCITRAL added other legitimation warrants that would enable it to compete favorably with the academic-dominated UNIDROIT and Hague Conference. On the one hand, it did not require, like the others, that delegates hold technical expertise in a subject matter (academic or otherwise). Each member state had the discretion to populate its delegation with any combination of civil servants, diplomats, academic experts, professionals or even industry representatives. UNICTRAL was to be led, not by a small governing council of academics, but instead by its governing Commission, populated by delegations from every member-state. On the other hand, quite early in its development UNCITRAL created a category of observer-delegations that gave its Secretariat the flexibility to invite international professional associations, international financial institutions, international NGOs – indeed, any international organization that had a demonstrable interest and expertise in a work product.[26]

Not inconsequentially, UNCITRAL also gave the United States a chance to push the reset button on conventions that had been drafted without its involvement. Although the United States consciously sat out earlier diplomatic negotiations under the auspices of UNIDROIT and the Hague Conference, it now sought a prominent place at a newly set table, a place where North and South, West and East would get a second bite at the several apples on the menu.

To a degree the settlement that emerged among the Hague Conference, UNIDROIT and UNCITRAL involved a new *segmentation* of the lawmaking social space. UNCITRAL's area of competence was

24 On the legitimation warrants and deficits of lawmaking IOs more generally, see Halliday 2007.

25 Our research indicates that observer states' participation in these meetings is indistinguishable from that of member states (Block-Lieb and Halliday, Ch. 4 In Draft).

26 In what may have been a gesture of comity, UNCTAD, UNIDROIT and the Hague Conference were given the status of permanent observers, with guarantees of entry to all commission and working group sessions.

limited to laws creating an obstacle to international trade and development. At the same time, UNCITRAL differentiated itself from the Hague Conference and UNIDROIT in terms of a *division of their labors*. As relates to the Hague Conference, UNCITRAL relied on the same division of labor as UNIDROIT previously had: the Hague Conference would focus on the procedural topics that formed the core of a "conventional" private international law convention (i.e., jurisdiction, applicable law and enforcement of judgments) and UNCITRAL would focus, mostly at least, on issues of substantive law. In contradistinction to UNIDROIT, UNCITRAL covered an ostensibly narrower range of issues but also a broader range of legal technologies and formal strategies in that UNCITRAL was expressly authorized by the General Assembly to formulate soft laws that both UNIDROIT and the Hague Conference had failed to produce. Specifically, the General Assembly's Resolution permitted UNICTRAL to promulgate not just conventions but also model laws, model legal provisions and model contract provisions. In addition, it directed the new Commission to promote "the codification and wider acceptance of international trade terms, provisions, customs and practices" (id., para. 8(c)).

UNCITRAL's emergence, thus, involved a renewed recognition of the presence of politics in trade lawmaking. UNICTRAL's creation in the wake of the G-77 suggests this politicization. Its structure as an inter-governmental organization in which state delegations draft international instruments under the observation and with the assistance of experts who are not directly engaged in decision-making confirms this move.

More than simply reinsert politics into the process, UNCITRAL's organization was structured to reconceive of the problem at stake. Harmonization of private law was sought as a means for removing obstacles to global trade and development, rather than as a goal in itself. This meant also that UNCITRAL focused more on the substance of law than the procedures attendant to its enforcement. Rather than eliminate the possibility that procedural public international law might impede trade, this focus on substance established hierarchies of issue areas whose resolution was more or less likely to remove impediments to global commerce. This was not a return to the substantive silos that had existed in the nineteenth century, but it was nonetheless a rejection of an insistence on the intellectually pure claim that all private law should be unified. UNCITRAL's emergence spelled not only a return to politics but also an embrace of pragmatism.

An interlude

While the Hague Conference, UNIDROIT and UNCITRAL were all created for the purpose of the unification of private law, and while over time their institutional structures have ostensibly come to resemble one another, their survival stories differ. Each organization adopted a contrasting pattern of adaptation to the political and economic crises after 1989. The adaptations in their practices (methods of work) and products (formal strategies) reflect in part the inertia endowed at their founding moments, as the terms on which each emerged as IOs continue to cast long shadows (Stinchcombe 2001).

In the twenty years after its founding, UNCITRAL enjoyed early successes in the field of international trade lawmaking on topics that ranged from the international sale of goods, international payments, international transport, and international arbitration and conciliation (Block-Lieb & Halliday 2006). It promulgated its Arbitration Rules in 1976, the Hamburg Rules in 1978 and the UN Convention on Contracts for the International Sale of Goods in 1980. The convention on the sale of goods and model law on arbitration were widely adopted.[27] These early successes quickly lent the new commission legitimacy among a broad range of countries.

Underlying its diversifying efforts was a more fundamental shift. As Table 11.4 demonstrates, UNCITRAL also began to diversify the forms of its products, combining the conventional production of treaties or conventions with rules, model laws and recommendations (Block-Lieb & Halliday 2007a and 2007b). The UN General Assembly Resolution creating UNCITRAL had directed it to focus on the "unification and harmonization" of "international trade law." While this text leaves interpretive room for the invention of legal technologies to supplement an international convention, the founding language does not suggest that soft law alternatives should be preferred over conventions; nor does it explain UNCITRAL's changing practices over time. And yet beginning as early as the 1980s, UNCITRAL's soft law instruments outnumbered its draft conventions.

This adaptation is best understood in light of the political influences exerted on UNICTRAL. UNCITRAL's embeddedness within the UN exposed it more extensively and directly to geopolitical shifts, not least

[27] The UN Convention on Contracts for the International Sale of Goods (CISG) enjoys wide adherence – eighty-three countries have acceded to its terms, including the United States, Brazil, China and Japan. Its Model Law on Commercial Arbitration has been implemented in sixty-seven countries.

TABLE 11.4 UNCITRAL's formal technologies, by decade

	1970s	1980s	1990s	2000s	2010s	Total
Conventions	××	××	××	×××		9
Rules	×	××			×	3
Recommendations		××		×	×	4
Model law provisions		×		×		2
Model laws		×	×××××	××	×	9
Legal guides		×	×			2
Notes			×			1
Legislative guides				×××	××	5
Practice guides				×		1
Unspecified reports				×	××	3
Total	3	9	9	12	7	

the General Assembly's request in 1979 that UNCITRAL contribute to the clarion call for a New International Economic Order.[28] On this front, UNCITRAL supplemented its record in developing the Hamburg Rules by producing work concerned with issues of procurement and infrastructure development. As it expanded across issue areas – from international sales and transport, to procurement, e-commerce and assignments of international receivables – distinct levels of involvement and reference to distinct audiences aided this expansion.

Since "unification" through multilateral treaties seemed too cumbersome and challenging, UNCITRAL began in the 1980s to reconstruct its organizational mission as broadly involving the "harmonization and modernization" of international trade law, an expansive characterization that effectively gave it carte blanche to take up any substantive topic at all which might be subsumed until the banner of "modernization" (Block-Lieb & Halliday 2007a; Halliday, Block-Lieb & Carruthers 2010). Once it had completed work on issue areas initially designated by its governing Commission as potential obstacles to trade (i.e., sales, transport, payments, arbitration), UNCITRAL turned to its mission of "modernization" to justify reaching into other areas of private law (at first, procurement and e-commerce; later, insolvency

[28] UN General Assembly Resolution, http://daccess-dds-ny.un.org/doc/RESOLUTION/GEN/NR0/377/77/IMG/NR037777.pdf?OpenElement.

TABLE 11.5 UNIDROIT's formal technologies, by decade

	1950s + 1960s	1970s	1980s	1990s	2000s	2010s	TOTAL
Conventions	×××	××	×××	×	×××	××	14
Principles				×	×××	××	6
Guides				×	×		2
Model law and model legal provisions					××	×	3
Model contract clauses						×	1
Total	3	2	3	3	9	6	

TABLE 11.6 Hague Conference on PIL: formal technologies, by decade

1900s	1910s	1920s	1930s	1940s	1950s	1960s	1970s	1980s	1990s	2000s	2010s
×××× ××	0	0	×	0	×××× ××××	×××× ×	×××× ×××× ××××	×××× ×	××	×××× ×	–

and secured transactions). UNCITRAL's widening range of substantive interests extended beyond conventional descriptions of "trade law."

UNIDROIT pressed forward in the 1960s through 1980s to bring to completion conventions whose preparatory work had begun in the 1930s and 1940s. Consistent with past practices, it focused exclusively on unification through multilateral treaties clustered on issues of commercial law (Table 11.5). In 1964, UNIDROIT promulgated two private law conventions on the international sale of goods; in the 1970s and early 1980s it promulgated several conventions on topics mostly related to contracts other than contracts for the sale of goods; in the late 1980s, it drafted an additional three conventions, mostly on topics of commercial finance.

Through the 1950s and 1980s, the Hague Conference similarly focused exclusively on the production of conventions (Table 11.6). These were the most productive years for the Hague Conference, with more than thirty conventions promulgated during this period.[29] These private international law conventions were sometimes focused on procedural aspects of specific disputes, mostly concerning some aspect of

[29] Even today, the Hague Conference produces only conventions on topics of private international law, not model laws, not legislative guides, not broad statements of principle (Table 11.6). By contrast, UNIDROIT would eventually include softer technologies within their lexicon of international lawmaking, but not until the final decade of the twentieth century and not as its predominate formal strategy. See Tables 11.3 and 11.5.

family law (i.e., marriage and divorce, wills and succession, the treatment of children and child support) but also disputes involving commercial transactions (i.e., international sales, corporate domicile, commercial and civil disputes, intermediated securities).

In the twenty-five years after UNCITRAL's emergence, interactions between UNCITRAL and the Hague Conference on Private International Law maintained a long-held division of labor: the Hague Conference worked exclusively on conventions to coordinate procedural aspects of a wide range of private disputes; UNCITRAL instead deliberated on the substance of issues of private law.[30]

The division of labor and segmentation of issues that distinguished the work of UNCITRAL and UNIDROIT started to become less settled by 1990, however. At the point of UNCITRAL's creation, the substance of their focuses had been segmented between issues of private law creating obstacles to global trade (over which UNCITRAL claimed jurisdiction) and all other issues of private law (UNIDROIT's domain). But UNCITRAL began to encroach on this dividing line as early as the mid 1970s with its work to develop a New International Economic Order – issues of procurement and infrastructure development pushed on the notion of what constituted "trade law" and so on what differentiated the work of UNICTRAL and UNIDROIT. Although UNIDROIT had not worked on these particular private law issues, UNCITRAL's reconception of its mission as involving the "modernization" of private law held the potential to undermine traditional limits on its jurisdictional reach.

At the same time, UNIDROIT began to narrow its range of topical interests so that it worked mostly on issues of commercial and financial law. UNIDROIT's narrowing interests and UNCITRAL's widening interests might still have been distinguishable on the grounds of a division of labor. But UNIDROIT's formal strategies also began to change during this period. Up until 1990 or so, UNIDROIT had worked exclusively on multilateral conventions, while during the same period UNCITRAL had begun to work increasingly on a range of soft law technologies. This clear division of labor would begin to get muddied by

30 UNCITRAL did, from its inception, work on international arbitration and conciliation, beginning with its Arbitration Rules in 1978. Work on this topic continues to date. And although arbitration might be viewed as involving procedural and not substantive issues of private law, the Hague Conference has not worked on enforcement of arbitral awards or other aspects of arbitration.

1994, when UNIDROIT first promulgated its *Principles on Commercial Contracts*.

With the unsettling of the relative roles and responsibilities of UNCITRAL and UNIDROIT, the possibility of reconfiguration and conflict within the ecology of international lawmaking organizations reemerged.

THE QUEST FOR ECONOMIC SALIENCE

As command economies failed to survive the fall of the Berlin Wall and as fledgling liberal economies were threatened by financial crises in Latin America, Russia and South-East Asia in the mid and later 1990s, the segmentation and division of labor that had marked boundaries among the Hague Conference on Private International Law, UNIDROIT and UNCITRAL shifted and began to resettle. The complexity of these intersecting political, economic and financial crises substantially increased demand for commercial and financial laws, which in turn induced the private lawmaking IOs to refocus their areas of expertise and divisions of labor.

Beginning in the 1980s, UNCITRAL had opened its mission to allow a broad expansion of its substantive boundaries and had begun to diversify its technologies in ways that were conducive to rapid responses to the shocks that would occur in its political, economic and legal contexts over the next twenty years. With a diversified and flexible range of legal technologies that could be deployed in pursuit of any modernizing goal, UNCITRAL was poised to react to the deconstruction and reconstruction of states and economies that would follow the collapse of the command economies in Central and Eastern Europe, and financial crises in South-East Asia and elsewhere.

Privatization of former command economies required structural reform in numerous areas of law – contract and property, insolvency and secured transactions, competition, corporate governance and so on. The demand for new law was met by a range of lawmakers – the European Union, the European Bank for Reconstruction and Development (EBRD), the Organization for Economic Cooperation and Development (OECD), even USAID dug into private law reform initiatives in Central and Eastern Europe. Although its focus was ostensibly global not regional, UNCITRAL worked on some projects in the 1990s, such as its Model Law on Procurement of Goods, Construction and Services, which had a direct relationship to the reconstruction of Eastern Europe.

To meet this step up in demand, UNCITRAL's overall lawmaking productivity increased (as measured by the number of texts produced per year), with the bulk of this increased productivity attributable to technologies other than conventions (Table 11.4). Although UNCITRAL had promulgated nearly as many soft-law products as hard-law conventions during the first twenty-five years of existence, after 1990 UNCITRAL's production of soft-law technologies overtook its work on conventions.[31]

UNCITRAL more than increased its workload; it also shifted its substantive focus. Its work on a Model Law on Cross-Border Insolvency was for the most part directed outside Europe (since a European Union Regulation on the same topic had largely been drafted), but UNCITRAL's Legislative Guides on Insolvency and Secured Transactions Laws were partly directed at domestic implementation within Europe and partly at implementation by emerging and developing economies that had been torn apart by the Asian Financial Crisis in the late 1990s. All of this work involved the harmonization or modernization of private law, but increasingly during this period, UNICTRAL's projects were more focused on international finance than international sales or shipments of goods (Block-Lieb & Halliday 2007a). As such, UNCITRAL's work moved beyond simply removing obstacles to trade and looked, as well, to assist in enabling countries to lay new legal foundations after the fall of the Berlin Wall.

This shift in focus continued as UNCITRAL's interests in economic rebuilding took on a new dimension in the late 1990s. As financial and capital markets in South-East Asia stumbled, creating economic backlash in Russia and even briefly in the United States, the IMF and World Bank rushed to provide emergency financial assistance but conditioned these loans on agreement to significant structural reforms across a broad range of private laws – insolvency, corporate governance, securities, bank regulation and other financial laws were targeted, in particular (Halliday & Carruthers 2009; Block-Lieb & Halliday 2015). But murmurings of the illegitimacy of the IMF and World Bank's policies of conditionality undermined institutionalization of these new

[31] Between 1968 and 1993, UNCITRAL produced four conventions and eight other technologies (model laws, recommendations and explanatory texts). After 1993, UNCITRAL produced five conventions and twenty-five other technologies (see Table 11.4).

structural reforms. To stanch such criticisms, the G-22 was formed in 1998 to enable central bankers and finance ministers from the twenty-two largest economies, including all of the Asian Tigers struck low by the financial crisis, to design the general parameters of a new financial architecture to prevent future systemic failure. In its report, the G-22 identified IOs, IFIs, transnational regulatory networks (TRNs) and private transnational organizations (PTOs) that were the likely sources of assistance. Despite the private law core of this project, neither UNCITRAL nor UNIDROIT were featured as prospective sources of lawmaking for the new international architecture (id.).

UNCITRAL nonetheless took matters into its own hands. Its mission in the "modernization" of commercial and financial law allowed UNCITRAL to style itself as an international standard setter focused on prevention of financial crises following the bank and corporate failures in Malaysia, Korea and Indonesia. Its earlier work on a model law to coordinate cross-border insolvency practices lent it the necessary experience and expertise to claim broad authority to articulate standards for corporate insolvency laws. Insolvency law reform had featured prominently in the G-22's report and in the recipes for restructuring that the international financial institutions had pressed on the crisis states of East Asia. Despite prior lawmaking exercises by the EBRD, Asian Development Bank (ADB), IMF and World Bank, UNCITRAL argued that it alone had the legitimacy and capacity to concentrate worldwide expertise and interests on this particular element of the G-22's vast and complex financial architecture.

That this project involved an expansion beyond UNICTRAL's previous trade lawmaking projects did not deter either the breadth or depth of the initiative. Ultimately, UNICTRAL's Insolvency Working Group spent five years drafting a Legislative Guide on Insolvency Law that offered states a fully defined set of legal standards and a complete set of institutions, ranging from mediation bodies to private professions, for entire corporate bankruptcy systems (Halliday & Carruthers, Ch. 9 [with Block-Lieb] 2009).

With only a slight lag, UNCITRAL took up a second call for action by the G-22 and embarked on an ambitious effort to produce a set of legal standards for the securing of finance, a project, it was thought, which would release credit to stimulate economic growth. Its Secured Transactions Working Group also spent five years drafting a Legislative Guide on Secured Transactions, as well as three years in drafting a supplement on the treatment of intellectual property collateral, and another three years on a Technical Legislative Guide on the Implementation of a Security Rights Registry.

UNCITRAL's expansion of its focus on "trade law" to include insolvency law reform went unchallenged by either the Hague Conference or UNIDROIT. UNIDROIT objected vociferously to UNCITRAL's work on secured transactions law reform, however. Unlike UNCITRAL, UNIDROIT had produced little during the 1990s, and certainly nothing directed at assisting in the rebuilding of new legal foundations for Eastern Europe or preventing the global or regional financial crises. It had produced a draft convention on stolen art objects, which it had been at work on for many years in partnership with UNESCO. It also published a set of principles on international commercial contracts and a guide to international franchise agreements during the 1990s. Much of this decade was also spent by UNIDROIT in preparatory work that would eventually lead to the Cape Town Convention on security rights in mobile equipment, and related protocols on aircraft, space assets and railway rolling stock.

When UNCITRAL created its working group on secured transactions law, UNIDROIT quite rightly noted the overlap with its own work in progress on international security interests. UNIDROIT had produced earlier conventions on international commercial leasing and factoring (see Table 11.5). Its focus on secured transactions in mobile equipment was a natural extension of those topics, or so UNIDROIT asserted. UNCITRAL had flirted with the topic of secured transactions law reform in the early 1980s, but publicly concluded after a period of study that there was too much dissensus in secured transactions laws for production of a model law on the topic to bear fruit. After that jettisoning of the topic, UNIDROIT worked on producing draft conventions on specialized issues related to secured transactions law, as did UNCITRAL with its 2000 draft convention on the assignment of international receivables.

When UNCITRAL established a secured transactions working group claiming broad authority to draft a model law or legislative guide on security rights in a broad range of personal property collateral, UNIDROIT felt that UNCITRAL was encroaching on its substantive territory. The two IOs previously had divided the international private lawmaking ecology into "trade law" and "all other private law" segments. Expansion of the definition of "trade law" was less threatening a move; but outright overlapping areas of interest spelled a different level of competition. UNIDROIT's objections were subsequently smoothed over with meetings among the governing secretariats of UNIDROIT, UNICTRAL and Hague Conference, and by drafting a meta-text to provide a clearer roadmap of each IOs territorial claims, at least as relates to lawmaking on secured transactions and their registry (Block-Lieb & Halliday, Ch. 8 In Draft).

UNCITRAL's disruption of the segmentation of the substantive issues divided between it and UNIDROIT was met by UNIDROIT's disruption of the division of labor that had distinguished the two IOs through much of the twentieth century. Until 1994, UNIDROIT had produced only draft conventions (Table 11.5). The multilateral treaties negotiated by UNIDROIT in the 1950s through 1980s covered a range of private law topics – transportation, international sales law, wills, agency contracts, factoring and leasing. Beginning in the mid 1990s, however, UNIDROIT began to discover the possibilities of drafting "soft laws" on various issues of private law. It published its *Principles on Commercial Contracts* in 1994, and its *Guide to International Master Franchise Arrangements* in 1998.[32] In 2002, UNIDROIT followed up on its Franchise Guide by promulgating a Model Franchise Disclosure Law. In 2004, partnering with the American Law Institute, UNIDROIT promulgated Principles of Transnational Civil Procedure; in 2008, a Model Law on Leasing; and in 2011, Model Legislative Provisions on State Ownership of Discovered Cultural Objects. With this spate of soft-lawmaking, UNIDROIT muddied an important division of labor between it and UNICTRAL.

After the Global Financial Crisis, UNIDROIT continued to expand its substantive reach, both by working on several protocols to the Cape Town Convention on railway rolling stock, space assets, and agricultural, and mining equipment and by working in an entirely new issue area – financial contracts. Thus, in 2009, it promulgated its draft Convention on Substantive Rules for Intermediated Securities and, in 2013, released its Principles on Netting of Financial Instruments.

With the mobile equipment protocols, UNIDROIT solidified and expanded on its "Cape Town brand." It also deepened its jurisdiction over secured transactions, more generally, and at a time when UNCITRAL was expanding its earlier Legislative Guide on Secured Transactions to include a supplement on intellectual property collateral, adding a Practice Guide on implementing a system for registering security

[32] Both the Principles (1994; 2004; 2010) and Guide (1998; 2007) have been revised and republished by UNIDROIT.

rights consistent with recommendations in the Guide, and "hardening" the Legislative Guide and Practice Guide by working on a draft Model Law on Secured Transactions.

With its draft Convention on Intermediated Securities, UNIDROIT pushed up against work that the Hague Conference on Private International Law had promulgated on the same topic. In 2006, the Hague Conference had finished its Convention on the Law Applicable to Certain Rights in Respect to Securities Held With an Intermediary, but consistent with past work out of The Hague this convention was limited to purely procedural issues regarding conflicts of law. UNIDROIT saw need for substantive regulation on the same topic, and consistent with past divisions of labor between it and the Hague Conference put out their Convention on *Substantive* Rules for Intermediated Securities.

With its Netting Principles, UNIDROIT did more than begin work on a new issue area. It acted in response to the political and economic events at the epicenter of the current Crisis. Many attribute the failure of Lehman Brothers and near failure of AIG and other systemically important financial institutions to the financial burdens implicit in the regulatory treatment of capital market transactions, such as derivatives, credit swap agreements and the like. The Netting Principles begin harmonization of these exemptions on a global basis. Although historically UNIDROIT had not reacted to geopolitical imperatives, with this project it did not wait for UNCITRAL to take up a proposal first initiated by the G-20 or Financial Stability Board.

The Netting Principles also transformed UNIDROIT's usual rhetorical practices and working methods. While historically UNIDROIT nearly exclusively worked on draft conventions, this work on financial instruments took the form of "principles." UNIDROIT's Netting Principles were written by a combination of regulatory, industry and academic experts and directed toward a legislative or regulatory audience. Unlike other Principles drafted by UNIDROIT, the governing council convened a Committee of Government Experts to vet them. While its Contracts Principles were written by academics for courts and practitioners, this inter-governmental involvement in the drafting of the Netting Principles allowed UNIDROIT to describe the Netting Principles as a legislative product drafted as much for consumption by national legislatures as courts or practitioners.

Thus, after nearly ninety years producing uniform rules on private laws for global markets through draft conventions, UNIDROIT very latterly has begun to alter its practices and product.[33] In addition to the political economy of the current Crisis, UNIDROIT likely was influenced by ecological factors. UNIDROIT's actions seem to have been motivated by scanning the work of other IOs engaged in norm and lawmaking projects. The G-20's embrace and expansion of the G-22's financial architecture project has lengthened the already long list of IOs involved in drafting global financial and commercial legal norms – the Financial Stability Board has been formalized as an entity charged with coordinating many IOs, transnational regulatory networks and private transnational organizations[34] – Bank for International Settlements (BIS), Organization for Economic Cooperation and Development (OECD), the Organization for International Securities Commissioners (IOSCO), FinCoNet (a TRN of those engaged in financial regulation) and others. Many of these projects have been framed either as small first steps or mere frameworks for future harmonizing work: high-level principles, key objectives, guidances, but not conventions (Block-Lieb & Halliday 2015). Perhaps tutored by the many new entrants to this lawmaking ecology, UNIDROIT also has learned to talk in terms of soft-law legal technologies.

The deliberate effort by UNIDROIT to escape the fetters of its founding has led to a convergence with UNCITRAL in the production of a range of international technologies centered on commercial and financial laws,[35] and to a slow transition away from the production of conventions and toward model laws, principles and other softer international legal technologies.[36] That convergence threatens conflict and thereby a re-appraisal of the negotiated interdependencies among all the IOs in the private lawmaking ecology and the most resource-full actors – states and non-state actors – on which the ecology relies. Crowding in the political ecology of international trade, commercial and financial lawmaking has prompted these international lawmaking bodies to negotiate intensely with each other to obtain or preserve a

33 Perhaps, ironically, its swift reaction to the current Financial Crisis may have been facilitated by UNIDROIT's governance structure. Its small size and epistemic insularity positioned UNIDROIT to change practices that were longstanding but not dictated by its constitutive statute.

34 For discussion of the emerging authority of PTOs, see Biersteker and Hall 2002.

35 UNIDROIT's private law work focused on non-commercial transactions has not evaporated completely, but this work has been limited to the production of a convention on Convention on Stolen or Illegally Exported Cultural Objects, which has been widely ratified across the world.

36 Although unlike UNICTRAL, the number of soft-law instruments formulated by UNIDROIT still does not exceed the conventions it has submitted to diplomatic conferences for ratification.

place for each in the lawmaking ecology (for discussion of these meta-bargains, see Block-Lieb and Halliday, Ch. 8 In Draft).

Boundary work therefore has re-emerged in efforts of potentially competitive IOs to co-exist in a lawmaking ecology for trade law in general and commercial and financial contracts in particular. UNCITRAL and UNIDROIT have tacitly negotiated a division of labor with the Hague Conference, to which both IOs delegated most matters of procedure; where procedure could not be avoided within UNCITRAL or UNIDROIT products, expert advice was sought from the Hague Conference.[37] Similarly, UNCITRAL and UNIDROIT engaged in segmentation of the lawmaking space, such that UNCITRAL deferred to UNIDROIT on questions of commercial finance involving mobile equipment (aircraft, space assets, railway rolling stock and the like), but retained authority over the designing of national secured transaction regimes more generally (UNCITRAL, Hague Conference and UNIDROIT 2011).

Nonetheless the division of labor between drafters of international conventions and drafters of these and other softer international instruments has blurred, mostly in relationship to the boundaries between UNCITRAL and UNIDROIT. While UNCITRAL attempted also to differentiate itself from both UNIDROIT and the Hague Conference through its use of a wider array of legal technologies to reach issues, its most powerful allies deemed fundamental to developing the new global financial architecture, UNIDROIT changed course to rely increasingly on soft-law technologies. As UNIDROIT has reinvented itself, the bounds of the lawmaking ecology itself have been widened. Other incidental lawmaking actors such as the IMF and World Bank have periodically asserted their lawmaking capacities. As a result, the institutional space has become partially unsettled, as demand, and so, the opportunities, for international lawmaking have expanded.

CONCLUSION

It is a presumption of economic sociology that markets do not spring fully formed out of atomistic aggregations of commercial relationships,

[37] UNCITRAL also worked out divisions of labor with the IMF and World Bank on mutually supportive roles on questions of insolvency and creditor rights, but not without some considerable political struggle with the Bank (Block-Lieb & Halliday 2012).

whether local or international. Indeed, whatever vaunted achievements are proposed for a *lex mercatoria*, in fact the massive expansion of global trade in its late nineteenth century and subsequent twentieth century manifestations have been enabled and constrained by the development of international laws and legal instruments governing private transactions. These laws, while they may emerge locally and from national lawmaking institutions, over the past century were spasmodically and later systematically shaped by international lawmaking bodies purporting to provide commercial law for the world. The shape of domestic and international commercial transactions increasingly has been hewed to contours set by international institutions and their increasingly diversified arrays of legal technologies embracing increasingly expansive areas of commercial life.

We have argued that these international institutions can most productively be understood in terms of an international lawmaking ecology, where the attributes of international lawmaking organizations, their resources, and above all their relations with each other come to define and concretize what types of transnational legal norms govern what types of international and national commercial transactions.

The international lawmaking ecology, we have shown, emerged over many decades, beginning with ad hoc conferences, then repeating conferences, then standing organizations emerging and encountering each other most directly after WWII. As each new IO entered the terrain of lawmaking they had to engage in a politics of legitimation and boundary-work, whether to preserve jurisdictions over which they had already staked claims or to enter jurisdictions as newcomers. This dynamic evolving set of competitive and cooperative processes produced more or less longstanding settlements that are familiar in other empirical sites to which ecology theory has been applied: relationships of full authority, of subordination, of division of labor and segmentation of the social space that is inhabited by lawmaking bodies.

From the point of view of *economic* sociology, therefore, the legal construction of global markets arises in substantial part out of an interorganizational set of ecological dynamics where IOs expand their lawmaking aspirations and invent new lawmaking technologies in response to organizational imperatives to enter and sustain themselves in a lawmaking ecology demand.

From the vantage point of the sociology of *law* this ecological analysis demonstrates that both the form and content of laws that constitute markets are heavily inflected not only by processes substantially indigenous to law, but also by an interplay of IO politics where law, if not simply a by-product of politics, nonetheless owes much of its form and content to ecological processes unfolding over the *longue durée*.

References

Abbott, Andrew. 1988. *The System of Professions: An Essay on the Division of Expert Labor*. Chicago: University of Chicago Press.

Abbott, Kenneth W., Jessica F. Green and Robert O. Keohane. August 2013. "Organizational Ecologies and Organizational Strategies in Global Politics." Discussion Paper 2013–57. Cambridge, Mass: Harvard Project on Climate Agreements, available online at http://belfercenter.ksg.harvard.edu/files/dp57_abbott-green-keohane.pdf.

Alter, Karen, and Sophie Meunier. 2009 (March). "The Politics of Regime Complexity." *Perspectives on Politics* 7 (1): 13–24.

American Bar Association, "Report of the Special Committee on a League of Nations" (1919).

Baty, J. 1914. *Polarized Law: Three Lectures on Conflicts of Law*. London: Stevens & Haynes.

Biersteker, Thomas J., and Rodney Bruce Hall. 2002. "Private Authority as Global Governance." In *The Emergence of Private Authority in Global Governance* (Rodney Bruce Hall and Thomas J. Biersteker, eds.). Cambridge: Cambridge University Press.

Block-Lieb, Susan. 2015. "Turn-Around: Reflections on the Present Day Influence of Negotiations on International Bankruptcy at the Fifth Session of the Hague Conference on Private International Law in 1925." *Brooklyn J. Corp., Comm. & Fin. L.* 9: 1–19.

Block-Lieb, Susan, and Terence Halliday. December 2006. "Legitimation and Global Lawmaking." Fordham Law Legal Studies Research Paper No. 952492, available online at http://ssrn.com/abstract=952492.

Block-Lieb, Susan and Terence Halliday. 2007a. "Incrementalisms and Global Lawmaking." *Brooklyn J. Int'l L.* 32: 851–903.

Block-Lieb, Susan and Terence Halliday. 2007b. "Harmonization and Modernization in UNCITRAL's Legislative Guide on Insolvency Law." Tex. Int'l L. J. 42: 475–514.

Block-Lieb, Susan, and Terence Halliday. August 23, 2011. "Social Ecology, Recursivity and Temporality: Towards a Sociology of Global Law-Making," paper read at the Annual Meeting of the American Sociological Association, Las Vegas.

Block-Lieb, Susan, and Terence Halliday. May 6–7, 2011. "Political Ecologies in Global Norm-Making for International Trade Law," paper read at Regional Colloquium on Globalization and Law, University of Chicago Law School.

Block-Lieb, Susan, and Terence Halliday. 2012. "Global Duelists: The Recursive Politics of the Text in International Trade Law." In *Socio-Legal Approaches to International Economic Law: Test, Context, Subtext* (Amanda Perry-Kessaris, ed.). London: Routlege Publications.

Block-Lieb, Susan, and Terence Halliday. 2015. "The Macropolitics and Microeconomics of Global Financial Crises: Bankruptcy as a Point of Reference." Forthcoming in *Sovereign Insolvency: Possible Legal Solutions* (Jasna Garasic and Nadia Bodiroga-Vukobrat, eds.). Springer Press.

Block-Lieb, Susan, and Terence Halliday. (In Draft). *Global Legislators: The Crafting of Trade Law for the World.*

Cordovez, Diego. 1967. "The Making of UNCTAD: Institutional Background and Legislative History. *Journal of Int'l Law* 1(3): 243–328.

Covenant of the League of Nations. 1919.

Coyle, John F. 2011. "Rethinking the Commercial Law Treaty." *Georgia Law Review* 45: 343–407.

Demogue, René. 1927. *L'Unification Internationale du Droit Privé.*

Dubinksy, Paul R. 2005. "Human Rights Law Meets Private Law Harmonization: The Coming Conflict." *Yale J. Int'l L.* 30: 211–317.

Farnsworth, Allen. 1962. "Formation of International Sales Contracts: Three Attempts at Unification." *U. Pa. L. Rev.* 110: 305–329.

Gutteridge, Harold Cooke. 1951. *The Codification of Private International Law: Seventeenth Lecture on the David Murray Foundation at the University of Glasgow on May 11, 1950.* New York City: Jackson, Son and Co.

Halliday, Terence. 2007. "Legitimacy, Technology and Leverage: The Building Blocks of Insolvency Architecture in the Decade Past and the Decade Ahead." *Brooklyn J. Int'l L.* 32: 1081–1102.

Halliday, Terence, Susan Block-Lieb, and Bruce Carruthers. 2010. "Rhetorical Legitimation: Global Scripts as Strategic Devices on International Organizations." *Socio-Economic Review* 8: 77–112.

Halliday, Terence, and Bruce Carruthers. 2009. *Bankrupt: Lawmaking and Systemic Financial Crisis.* Palo Alto: Stanford University Press.

Halliday, Terence, and Gregory Shaffer. 2015. *Transnational Legal Orders.* New York: Cambridge University Press.

Halliday, Terence, Josh Pacewicz, and Susan Block-Lieb. 2013. "Who Governs? Delegations in Global Trade Lawmaking." *Gov. & Reg.* 7: 279–298.

Higgins, A. Pearce. 1909. *The Hague Peace Conferences and Other International Conferences Concerning the Laws and Usages of War: Texts of Conventions with Commentaries.* Cambridge: Cambridge University Press.

Honnold, John. 1965. "The Uniform Law for the International Sale of Goods: The Hague Convention of 1964." *Law and Contemporary Problems* 30: 326–352.

Honnold, John. 1959. "A Uniform Law for International Sales." *U. Pa. L. Rev.* 107: 299–330

Hudec, Robert E. 1975. *The GATT Legal System and World Trade Diplomacy*. New York, Washington, London: Praeger.

Janis, Mark Weston. 2010. *America and the Law of Nations: 1776–1939*. Oxford: Oxford University Press.

Kennedy, David. 1987. "The Move to Institutions." *Cardozo Law Review* 8: 841–988.

Kennedy, David. 2006. "One, Two, Three, Many Legal Orders: Legal Pluralism and the Cosmopolitan Dream." Speech delivered at the International Law Association, available online at www.law.harvard.edu/faculty/dkennedy/speeches/LegalOrders.pdf

Koskenniemi, Martti. 2002. "Fragmentation of International Law: Postmodern Anxieties." *Leiden Journal of International Law* 15: 552–79.

League of Nations. 1920. "Report of the International Finance Conference (Brussels, Belgium)," available online at http://archive.org/stream/reportofinternat00interich#page/236/mode/2up.

League of Nations. 1920. Advisory Committee of Jurists; Permanent Court of International Justice. Documents presented to the committee relating to existing plans for the establishment of a permanent court of international justice.

League of Nations. 1921. Permanent Court of International Justice: Documents concerning the action taken by the Council for the League of Nations under Art. 14 of the covenant, and the adoption by the Assembly of the Statute of the Permanent Court.

League of Nations. December 1922. Economics and Financial Section, International Brussels Finance Conference of 1920 – The Recommendations and Their Application: A Review After Two Years.

League of Nations, Economic Committee. July 1923. "Unification of Laws Relating to Bills of Exchange and Promissory Notes": General Report and Individual Reports submitted by Prof. D. Josephus Jitta (Netherlands), Sir Mackenzie D. Chalmers (Great Britain), Prof. Dr. Franz Klein (Austria), and Prof. Ch. Lyon Caen (France).

League of Nations. 1924. Official Journal, Special Supplement No. 23, Records of the Assembly (Geneva).

League of Nations. January 1926. Official Journal, 7th Year, No. 1 (Geneva).

League of Nations. Feb. 17, 1930. Preparatory Documents: Drafts Prepared by the League of Nations Experts and Observations by Governments for the International Conference for the Unification of the Law on Bills of Exchange, Promissory Notes and Cheques, Official Doc. No. C.234.M.83.

League of Nations. May 13–June 7, 1930. Records of the International Conference for the Unification of Law on Bills of Exchange, Promissory Notes and Cheques, First Session, Official Doc. No. C.360.M.151.

League of Nations. February 23–March 19, 1931. Records of the International Conference for the Unification of Law on Bills of Exchange, Promissory Notes and Cheques, Second Session, Official Doc. No. C.294.M.137.

Mallard, Grégoire. 2014. *Fallout: Nuclear Diplomacy in an Age of Global Fracture*. Chicago: University of Chicago Press.

Moore, John Bassett. 1937. "Fifty Years of International Law." *Harv. L. Rev.* 50: 395–448.

Nadelmann, Kurt H. 1954. "Ignored State Interests: The Federal Government and International Efforts to Unify Rule of Private Law." *U. Pa. L. Rev.* 102: 323–366.

Nadelmann, Kurt H. 1964. "The US and Plans for a Uniform (World) Law on International Sales of Goods." *U. Pa. L. Rev.* 112: 697–709.

Northedge, Frederick. 1986. *The League of Nations: Its Life and Times – 1920–1946*. Leicester University Press.

Nussbaum, Arthur. 1943. *Principles of Private International Law*. Oxford: Oxford Univ. Press.

Pauly, Louis W. Dec. 1996. "The League of Nations and the Foreshadowing of the International Monetary Fund," Princeton University. Essays in International Finance No. 201.

Peters, Lena. 2012. *International Institute for the Unification of Private Law* (UNIDROIT). Walters Kluwer.

Rajagopal, Balakrishnan. 2003. *International Law from Below: Development, Social Movements and Third World Resistance*. New York: Cambridge University Press.

Shaffer, Gregory, and Mark Pollack. 2010. "Hard vs. Soft Law: Alternatives, Complements and Antagonists in International Governance." *Minnesota Law Review* 94: 706–797.

Stinchcombe, Arthur. 2001. *When Formality Works: Authority and Abstraction in Law and Organizations*. Chicago: University of Chicago Press.

Sturley, Michael F. 1991. "The History of COGSA and The Hague Rules." *Journal of Maritime Law and Commerce* 22: 1–57.

UNCITRAL, Hague Conference and UNIDROIT. 2012. Texts on Security Interests: Comparison and Analysis of Major Features of International Instruments Relating to Secured Transactions, available online at www.uncitral.org/pdf/english/texts/security/UNCITRAL-HccH-Unidroit-e.pdf.

UNIDROIT, International Institute for the Unification of Private Law. 1930. Rapport sur activité de l'Institute International de Rome Pour L'Unification du Droit Privé Pendant l'annee 1930.

UNIDROIT, International Institute for the Unification of Private Law. 1931. Rapport sur activité de l'Institute International de Rome Pour L'Unification du Droit Privé Pendant l'annee 1931.

UNIDROIT, International Institute for the Unification of Private Law. 1932. Rapport sur activité de l'Institute International de Rome Pour L'Unification du Droit Privé Pendant l'annee 1932.

UNIDROIT, International Institute for the Unification of Private Law. 1933. Rapport sur activité de l'Institute International de Rome Pour L'Unification du Droit Privé Pendant l'annee 1933.

UNIDROIT, International Institute for the Unification of Private Law. 1934–35. Rapport sur activité de l'Institute International de Rome Pour L'Unification du Droit Privé Pendant l'annee 1934–35.

UNIDROIT, International Institute for the Unification of Private Law. 1935–36. Rapport sur activité de l'Institute International de Rome Pour L'Unification du Droit Privé Pendant l'annee 1935–36.

UNIDROIT, International Institute for the Unification of Private Law. 1936–37. Rapport sur activité de l'Institute International de Rome Pour L'Unification du Droit Privé Pendant l'annee 1936–37.

UNIDROIT, International Institute for the Unification of Private Law. 1937–39. Rapport sur activité de l'Institute International de Rome Pour L'Unification du Droit Privé Pendant l'annee 1937–38 and 1938–39.

UNIDROIT, International Institute for the Unification of Private Law. 1941–44. Rapport sur activité de l'Institute International de Rome Pour L'Unification du Droit Privé Pendant l'annee 1941–44.

UNIDROIT, International Institute for the Unification of Private Law. 1945–46. Rapport sur activité de l'Institute International de Rome Pour L'Unification du Droit Privé Pendant l'annee 1945–46.

UNIDROIT, International Institute for the Unification of Private Law. 1950. Rapport sur activité de l'Institute International de Rome Pour L'Unification du Droit Privé Pendant l'annee 1950.

UNIDROIT, International Institute for the Unification of Private Law. 1951. Rapport sur activité de l'Institute International de Rome Pour L'Unification du Droit Privé Pendant l'annee 1951.

UNIDROIT, International Institute for the Unification of Private Law. 1952. Rapport sur activité de l'Institute International de Rome Pour L'Unification du Droit Privé Pendant l'annee 1952.

UNIDROIT, International Institute for the Unification of Private Law. 1953. Rapport sur activité de l'Institute International de Rome Pour L'Unification du Droit Privé Pendant l'annee 1953.

UNIDROIT, International Institute for the Unification of Private Law. 1954. Rapport sur activité de l'Institute International de Rome Pour L'Unification du Droit Privé Pendant l'annee 1954.

UNIDROIT, International Institute for the Unification of Private Law. 1955. Rapport sur activité de l'Institute International de Rome Pour L'Unification du Droit Privé Pendant l'annee 1955.

UNIDROIT, International Institute for the Unification of Private Law. 1956. Rapport sur activité de l'Institute International de Rome Pour L'Unification du Droit Privé Pendant l'annee 1956.

UNIDROIT, International Institute for the Unification of Private Law. 1964. Rapport sur activité de l'Institute International de Rome Pour L'Unification du Droit Privé Pendant l'annee 1964.

UNIDROIT, Statute, available online at www.unidroit.org/about-unidroit/institutional-documents/statute.

United Nations. April, 29, 1947. Documents on the Development and Codification of International Law, Part I, Historical Survey of Development of International Law and Its Codification by International Conferences, UN Doc. No. A/Ac.10/5.

UN General Assembly Resolution. 1966. U.N. Doc. No. A/95933; A/C.6/L.571, L.572, L.579 and Add.1 and 2.

UN General Assembly. December, 9, 1965. Sixth Committee. 894th Meeting, UN Doc. No. A/C.6/SR.894.

UN General Assembly. December 2, 1966. Sixth Committee, 946th Meeting, UN Doc. No. A/C.6/SR.946.

Van Loon, Hans. 2007. "The Hague Conference on Private International Law." *Hague Justice Journal*, 2: 3–12.

Voskuil, C.C.A. 1993. "Preface, The Influence of the Hague Conference on Private International Law:" Selected Essays to Celebrate the 100th Anniversary of the Hague Conference on Private International Law (Martinus Nijhod Publishers 1993), reprinted in [XL] Netherlands Int'l L. Rev. XI, at XIX.

Yannioupolos, A.N. 1965. "The Unification of Private Maritime Law by International Conventions." *Journal of Law and Contemporary Problems* 30: 370–399.

INDEX

CAMBRIDGE STUDIES IN LAW AND SOCIETY

Books in the Series

Diversity in Practice:
Race, Gender, and Class in Legal and Professional Careers
Edited by Spencer Headworth and Robert Nelson

Diseases of the Will
Mariana Valverde

The Politics of Truth and Reconciliation in South Africa:
Legitimizing the Post-Apartheid State
Richard A. Wilson

Modernism and the Grounds of Law
Peter Fitzpatrick

Unemployment and Government:
Genealogies of the Social
William Walters

Autonomy and Ethnicity:
Negotiating Competing Claims in Multi-Ethnic States
Yash Ghai

Constituting Democracy:
Law, Globalism and South Africa's Political Reconstruction
Heinz Klug

The Ritual of Rights in Japan:
Law, Society, and Health Policy
Eric A. Feldman

The Invention of the Passport:
Surveillance, Citizenship and the State
John Torpey

Governing Morals:
A Social History of Moral Regulation
Alan Hunt

The Colonies of Law:
Colonialism, Zionism and Law in Early Mandate Palestine
Ronen Shamir

Law and Nature
David Delaney

Social Citizenship and Workfare in the United States and Western Europe:
The Paradox of Inclusion
Joel F. Handler

Law, Anthropology and the Constitution of the Social:
Making Persons and Things
Edited by Alain Pottage and Martha Mundy

Judicial Review and Bureaucratic Impact:
International and Interdisciplinary Perspectives
Edited by Marc Hertogh and Simon Halliday

Immigrants at the Margins:
Law, Race, and Exclusion in Southern Europe
Kitty Calavita

Lawyers and Regulation:
The Politics of the Administrative Process
Patrick Schmidt

Law and Globalization from Below:
Toward a Cosmopolitan Legality
Edited by Boaventura de Sousa Santos and Cesar A. Rodriguez-Garavito

Public Accountability:
Designs, Dilemmas and Experiences
Edited by Michael W. Dowdle

Law, Violence and Sovereignty among West Bank Palestinians
Tobias Kelly

Legal Reform and Administrative Detention Powers in China
Sarah Biddulph

The Practice of Human Rights:
Tracking Law Between the Global and the Local
Edited by Mark Goodale and Sally Engle Merry

Judges Beyond Politics in Democracy and Dictatorship:
Lessons from Chile
Lisa Hilbink

Paths to International Justice:
Social and Legal Perspectives
Edited by Marie-Bénédicte Dembour and Tobias Kelly

Law and Society in Vietnam:
The Transition from Socialism in Comparative Perspective
Mark Sidel

Constitutionalizing Economic Globalization:
Investment Rules and Democracy's Promise
David Schneiderman

The New World Trade Organization Knowledge Agreements:
2nd Edition
Christopher Arup

Justice and Reconciliation in Post-Apartheid South Africa
Edited by François du Bois and Antje du Bois-Pedain

Militarization and Violence against Women in Conflict Zones in the Middle East:
A Palestinian Case-Study
Nadera Shalhoub-Kevorkian

Child Pornography and Sexual Grooming:
Legal and Societal Responses
Suzanne Ost

Darfur and the Crime of Genocide
John Hagan and Wenona Rymond-Richmond

Fictions of Justice:
The International Criminal Court and the Challenge of Legal Pluralism in Sub-Saharan Africa
Kamari Maxine Clarke

Conducting Law and Society Research:
Reflections on Methods and Practices
Simon Halliday and Patrick Schmidt

Planted Flags:
Trees, Land, and Law in Israel/Palestine
Irus Braverman

Culture under Cross-Examination:
International Justice and the Special Court for Sierra Leone
Tim Kelsall

Cultures of Legality:
Judicialization and Political Activism in Latin America
Javier Couso, Alexandra Huneeus, Rachel Sieder

Courting Democracy in Bosnia and Herzegovina:
The Hague Tribunal's Impact in a Postwar State
Lara J. Nettelfield

The Gacaca Courts and Post-Genocide Justice and Reconciliation in Rwanda:
Justice without Lawyers
Phil Clark

Law, Society, and History:
Themes in the Legal Sociology and Legal History of Lawrence M. Friedman
Robert W. Gordon and Morton J. Horwitz

After Abu Ghraib:
Exploring Human Rights in America and the Middle East
Shadi Mokhtari

Adjudication in Religious Family Laws:
Cultural Accommodation: Legal Pluralism, and Gender Equality in India
Gopika Solanki

Water On Tap:
Rights and Regulation in the Transnational Governance of Urban Water Services
Bronwen Morgan

Elements of Moral Cognition:
Rawls' Linguistic Analogy and the Cognitive Science of Moral and Legal Judgment
John Mikhail

A Sociology of Constitutions:
Constitutions and State Legitimacy in Historical-Sociological Perspective
Chris Thornhill

Mitigation and Aggravation at Sentencing
Edited by Julian Roberts

Institutional Inequality and the Mobilization of the Family and Medical Leave Act:
Rights on Leave
Catherine R. Albiston

Authoritarian Rule of Law:
Legislation, Discourse and Legitimacy in Singapore
Jothie Rajah

Law and Development and the Global Discourses of Legal Transfers
Edited by John Gillespie and Pip Nicholson

Law against the State:
Ethnographic Forays into Law's Transformations
Edited by Julia Eckert, Brian Donahoe, Christian Strümpell and Zerrin Özlem Biner

Transnational Legal Process and State Change
Edited by Gregory C. Shaffer

Legal Mobilization under Authoritarianism:
The Case of Post-Colonial Hong Kong
Edited by Waikeung Tam

Complementarity in the Line of Fire:
The Catalysing Effect of the International Criminal Court in Uganda and Sudan
Sarah M. H. Nouwen

Political and Legal Transformations of an Indonesian Polity:
The Nagari from Colonisation to Decentralisation
Franz von Benda-Beckmann and Keebet von Benda-Beckmann

Pakistan's Experience with Formal Law:
An Alien Justice
Osama Siddique

Human Rights under State-Enforced Religious Family Laws in Israel, Egypt, and India
Yüksel Sezgin

Why Prison?
Edited by David Scott

Law's Fragile State:
Colonial, Authoritarian, and Humanitarian Legacies in Sudan
Mark Fathi Massoud

Rights for Others:
The Slow Home-Coming of Human Rights in the Netherlands
Barbara Oomen

European States and their Muslim Citizens:
The Impact of Institutions on Perceptions and Boundaries
Edited by John R. Bowen, Christophe Bertossi, Jan Willem Duyvendak and Mona Lena Krook

Religion, Law and Society
Russell Sandberg

The Experiences of Face Veil Wearers in Europe and the Law
Edited by Eva Brems

The Contentious History of the International Bill of Human Rights
Christopher N. J. Roberts

Transnational Legal Orders
Edited by Terence C. Halliday and Gregory Shaffer

Lost in China?, Law, Culture and Society in Post-1997 Hong Kong
Carol A. G. Jones

Security Theology, Surveillance and the Politics of Fear
Nadera Shalhoub-Kevorkian

Opposing the Rule of Law:
How Myanmar's Courts Make Law and Order
Nick Cheesman

The Ironies of Colonial Governance:
Law, Custom and Justice in Colonial India
James Jaffe

The Clinic and the Court:
Law, Medicine and Anthropology
Edited by Tobias Kelly, Ian Harper and Akshay Khanna

A World of Indicators:
The Making of Government Knowledge Through Quantification
Edited by Richard Rottenburg, Sally E. Merry, Sung-Joon Park and Johanna Mugler

Contesting Immigration Policy in Court:
Legal Activism and its Radiating Effects in the United States and France
Leila Kawar

The Quiet Power of Indicators:
Measuring Governance, Corruption, and Rule of Law
Edited by Sally Engle Merry, Kevin Davis, and Benedict Kingsbury

Investing in Authoritarian Rule:
Punishment and Patronage in Rwanda's Gacaca Courts for Genocide Crimes
Anuradha Chakravarty

Iraq and the Crimes of Aggressive War:
The Legal Cynicism of Criminal Militarism
John Hagan, Joshua Kaiser, and Anna Hanson

For EU product safety concerns, contact us at Calle de José Abascal, 56–1°,
28003 Madrid, Spain or eugpsr@cambridge.org.

www.ingramcontent.com/pod-product-compliance
Lightning Source LLC
LaVergne TN
LVHW011531200926
848484LV00001B/227

* 9 7 8 1 1 0 7 1 3 0 9 1 3 *